TED BUNDY

SIX DAYS IN ASPEN

The 1977 Manhunt for Ted Bundy

© 2024 by Ric Conrad

All rights reserved. Without limiting the rights under copyright reserved above, no part of this publication may be reproduced, stored in, or introduced into a retrieval system, or transmitted in any form, or by any means, (electronic, mechanical, photocopying, recording, or otherwise) without the written permission of the publisher.

First Edition, December 18, 2024

Copy Editing by Sheri Conrad
Jacket design by Mark Myers and Ric Conrad
Jacket artwork created by Microsoft Designer AI, coupled with a frontal mugshot of Ted Bundy provided by the King County Archives.
Book design, art direction, typography, and layout by Mark Myers, Sheri Conrad, and Ric Conrad

Conrad, Richard J, - 1967-
Six Days in Aspen/Ric Conrad.

Ted Bundy—True Crime

Identifiers:
ISBN: 978-0-9887339-6-1 (Hardcover)
ISBN: 978-0-9887339-7-8 (Paperback)
ISBN: 978-0-9887339-8-5 (E-Book)

I. Title: Six Days in Aspen. True Crime.

Kahuna Books, LLC

KAHUNA

BOOKS

Published by Kahuna Books
Springfield, Oregon

Printed in the United States of America

"In this high-country fastness, we are used to a certain natural menace and uncertainty, to blizzards in June, sudden rains, drastic drops in temperature. We have learned that people are vulnerable to avalanches, freezes, lost footings, deep and dangerous water. We accept occasional automotive violence, fists to the jaw, street corner threats, but Bundy on the run was unique in our experience."

—The Aspen Times

DEDICATION

This book is dedicated to the men and women who participated in the manhunt for Ted Bundy in June 1977. There are many others, as yet unnamed, but they are never forgotten.

9NEWS (DENVER)
Lloyd Coleman
Edward "Ward" Lucas

ASPEN SECURITY PATROL
Paul "Stormy" Mohn

ASPEN VOLUNTEER FIRE DEPARTMENT
Cliff Little
Fire Chief Dick Miller

ASPEN MOUNTAIN RESCUE
Fred Braun
Dave Stapleton, Sr.

ASPEN-PITKIN COUNTY COMBINED COMMUNICATIONS CENTER
Nancy Baxter (Supervisor)
Carolyn Hougland (Asst. Supervisor)
Ann Ireland
Valarie Matthews
JoAnne Rando
Lynne Unger
Jean Zimmerman

ASPEN POLICE DEPARTMENT

Officer Michael Barnett
Officer Robert Bennewate
Officer Frank Burkeen
Detective Michael Chandler
Officer John Drake
Sergeant Bill Dreuding
Officer Kathy Earl
Officer George Fridell
Detective Sgt. Dave Garms
Officer John Goodwin
Bill Grikis (Animal Control)
James Hanas (Animal Control)
Sergeant Darrel Horan
Police Chief Art Hougland
Detective Ed Killam
Sergeant Dick Kreuser
Officer Nancy Lyle
Detective Rex McGuire
Mark Minter (Crime Prevention)
Anne Oakes (Detective Secretary)
Officer Terry Quirk
Officer Hugh Roberts
Officer Ann Thoreson
Officer John Burke Wood
Officer Chet Zajac

BASALT POLICE DEPARTMENT
Officer Jim Stryker
Police Chief Bill Thompson

CITY OF ASPEN/ADMINISTRATION
Civil Defense Director Betty Erickson
Aspen City Clerk Kathryn Hauter
City Manager, Philip "Mick" Mahoney
Aspen City Attorney Dorothy Nuttal

COLORADO BUREAU OF INVESTIGATION
Agent Leo G. Konkel

COLORADO STATE HIGHWAY PATROL
Trooper Bruce Berry
Trooper Del Cesko
Trooper Chancy Clark
Sgt. David Lacefield
Trooper Jim Loyd
Trooper Dan Ogan
Lt. Emile Wood

DISTRICT ATTORNEY'S OFFICE
3rd JUDICIAL DISTRICT, SALT LAKE COUNTY, UTAH
Deputy District Attorney David E. Yocum
Judge Floyd H. Gowans

DISTRICT ATTORNEY'S OFFICE
4th JUDICIAL DISTRICT, EL PASO COUNTY, COLORADO
District Attorney Robert Russel

DISTRICT ATTORNEY'S OFFICE
9th JUDICIAL DISTRICT, PITKIN COUNTY, COLORADO
District Attorney Milton Blakey
Deputy District Attorney Barry Bryant
District Attorney's Investigator Mike Fisher
District Attorney Frank Tucker

EAGLE COUNTY SHERIFF'S DEPARTMENT
Deputy Danny Williams

FEDERAL BUREAU OF INVESTIGATION
Special Agent Clark F. Brown
Special Agent Clifton D. Browning, Jr.
Special Agent Ramon M. Child
Special Agent Melvon C. Jensen
Special Agent Dave Yates

GARFIELD COUNTY SHERIFF'S DEPARTMENT
Sheriff Ed Hogue

Undersheriff Bob Hart
Al Maggard (Spokesman)
Deputy John Martin
Lucy Moreno

HICKORY HOUSE
Billy Stone
Phyllis Stone

HOLIDAY INN
Dick Bradley

KSNO RADIO STATION
Jeanette Darnauer

KSPN RADIO STATION
Todd Cipolla
Dave Danforth
Lee Duncan
Dave Judy
Deb Caulfield
Gailen Prague
Diane Tegmeyer
Ed Thorne

PITKIN COUNTY ADMINISTRATION
Shirley Dills (Court Clerk)
Nina Johnston (County Commissioner)

PITKIN COUNTY AIR RESCUE GROUP
Betty Pfister

PITKIN COUNTY SHERIFF'S DEPARTMENT

Casey Armstrong (Secretary)
Deputy Bob Braudis
Deputy Joe Collins
Colleen Curtis (Secretary)
Sergeant Don Davis
Marcia DeCamp (Secretary)
Deputy Floyd "Gene" Flatt
Deputy Lorrie Francis
Sergeant Ernie Hamblin
Deputy Maureen Higgins
Deputy Carol Kempfert
Sheriff Dick Kienast
Sergeant Rick Kralicek
Deputy Bill McCrocklin
Undersheriff Ben Meyers
Deputy Peter Murphy
Deputy Leon Murray
Deputy Clay Owen
Deputy Greg Quinlan
Sergeant Larry Spiers
Marta Steinmetz (Civil Deputy)
Deputy Lance Weber
Deputy David Westerlund
Deputy Gary White
Whitney Wulff (Secretary)

PITKIN COUNTY SHERIFF'S RESERVE
Fred Crowley
Captain Richard "Dick" Wall

SALT LAKE CITY COUNTY SHERIFF'S DEPARTMENT
Sheriff Delmar L. Larson

SARDY FIELD
Doug McCoy
Ken Roper

**UNITED STATES DISTRICT COURT
UTAH CENTRAL DIVISION**
U.S. Magistrate, Daniel A. Alsup
Asst. State's Attorney, James W. McConkie II

WALNUT HOUSE
Rick Newton

WRIGHT COMMUNICATIONS
David Wright

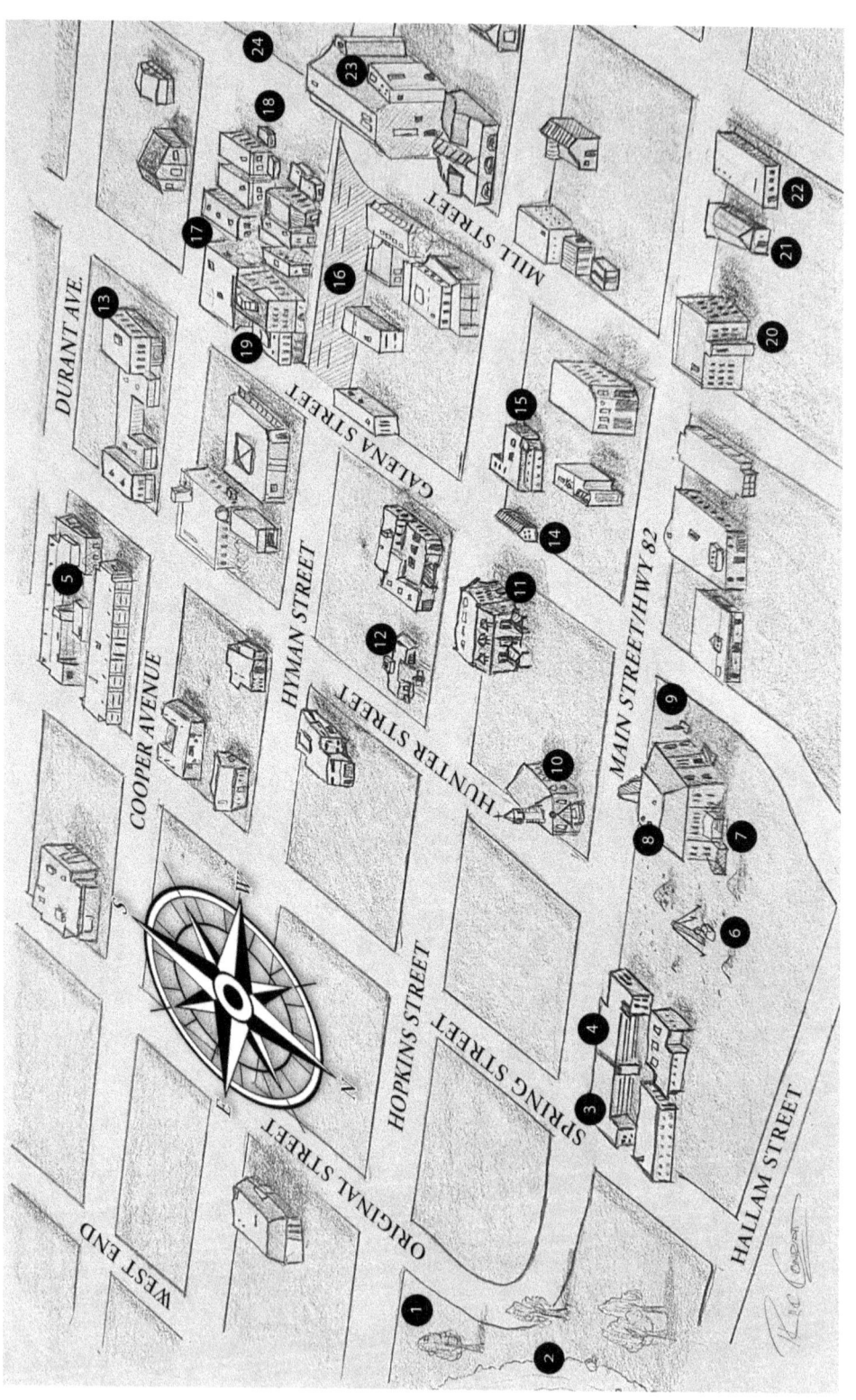

10   Ric Conrad

ASPEN

1.) Herron Park.
2.) Roaring Fork River.
3.) Freddie's Main Street Café.
4.) Concept 600 Building.
5.) Aspen Square.
6.) The Brickyard.
7.) Prisoner Exercise Yard.
8.) County Courthouse/Sheriff's Office.
9.) Civil War Statue.
10.) St. Mary's Catholic Church.
11.) City Hall/Aspen PD/Dispatch.
12.) Fast Eddie's Hats.
13.) Crossroads Drugstore.
14.) Little Cliff's Bakery.
15.) Aspen Fire Station.
16.) Aspen Pedestrian Mall.
17.) Red Onion.
18.) Village Pantry.
19.) Walnut House Films.
20.) Jerome Hotel.
21.) The Aspen Times/KSNO Radio.
22.) Carl's Pharmacy.
23.) Wheeler Opera House/The Pub.
24.) Wagner Park.
25.) Neale Street Bridge.
26.) Little Nell Lift.
27.) Explore Booksellers.
28.) Aspen Middle School.
29.) Aspen Elementary School.
30.) Aspen Mountain.
31.) Hickory House.

Six Days in Aspen

TABLE OF CONTENTS

1. Jackal on the Run 14
2. Dragnet 41
3. The Posse 75
4. The Black Bishop 95
5. Manhunters 119
6. Devil's Hour 146
7. Amos 167
8. The Dogs of War 194
9. Crestahaus 206
10. Cemetery Lane 224
Appendix A. The Caddy Stop 244
Appendix B. Roadblocks 259
Appendix C. Photo Illustrations 264
Acknowledgments 267
Bibliography 269
End Notes 280

TUESDAY

JUNE 7, 1977

CHAPTER 1
JACKAL ON THE RUN

Nancy Baxter pulled into the lot at Aspen City Hall, kicked down the stand on her motorcycle, removed her helmet, and pocketed the keys. She always parked the bike, her pride and joy, under one end of a covered walkway on the north side of the building. After all, Aspen has a nine-month snow season. Sighing, she wished she could ride up into the mountains and enjoy the fresh spring air. It looked like it would be a wonderful sunny day, so she promised herself a long ride at the end of her shift.[1]

Tucking her helmet under one arm, she noticed that Unit 101, the police chief's Saab, was already parked in its usual spot. The chief routinely parked here, as the south side of the building was reserved for patrol cars.[2]

Stepping through the rear entrance, Baxter was dreading this day. Tuesdays are court days. The handful of sheriff's deputies who patrol the county during the other six days of the week escort prisoners to court on Tuesdays. Nothing of any real significance happens when the deputies are all stuck at the courthouse.

Nancy had been hired when she was twenty-four and had worked her way up the ranks. Now, three years later, she was the supervisor of the dispatch center, which served the Aspen Police Department, housed within city hall, and the Pitkin County Sheriff's Department, a block north in the Pitkin County Courthouse. She was leading a team of six dispatchers.

She was buzzed through the locked door and made her way to the rear portico of the building. Her assistant supervisor, Carolyn, was there to greet her. Baxter wasn't surprised because Carolyn was married to Acting Chief Art Hougland, and the couple often carpooled.

"How did we get put on duty this morning?" Baxter asked sarcastically, an unlit cigarette resting between her lips. She smiled as both women knew she was the one who created the monthly schedule. Nancy preferred the night shift when most of the action occurred, and the big-wigs had already gone home for the night.[3]

Hunting for her lighter, she shook her head, knowing their shift was bound to be boring. Locating the lighter, she lit the cigarette, inhaled deeply, and exhaled a cloud of smoke. She was down to two packs a day. Keeping an eye on the clock, the two eventually stubbed out their cigarettes and headed back inside. Baxter slumped in her chair while Hougland set about brewing a large pot of coffee. It was time to get to work.[4]

While not fielding incoming calls on the switchboard, there were plenty of office duties to perform. An IBM typewriter was used to transcribe tapes and incident reports. The reports were kept in the records division for one year before being stored in the attic. Carolyn had taken the lead on handling the aging records. All old documents and files were being updated to microfilm.[5]

"Why don't you go upstairs and work on the microfilm project," Baxter suggested. Her friend nodded and headed up the stairs as Nancy rifled through the latest pile of transcripts.[6]

Tuesdays could be so monotonous.

◆

The state health department had decided that the jail cells in the Aspen courthouse basement lacked natural light and suffered from poor ventilation. New standards mandated that prisoners could be held in one of the five aging cells for no more than thirty days at a stretch. As a result, *residents* of Aspen's Pitkin County Jail were transferred to Garfield County Jail in Glenwood Springs, forty miles away. On court days, deputies from Aspen had to make that long drive in the morning, pick up their prisoners, and transport them back to the courthouse.[7]

Sergeant Rick Kralicek was just getting his day started, but Deputy Pete Murphy had worked the graveyard shift and only had this escort duty to perform before he could head home to catch some sleep. The two had performed multiple escort missions within the last two months.

When their vehicle was safe inside the garage of the Garfield County Jail, the deputies emerged and locked their weapons in a gun box before entering the cellblock. This was regular protocol, ensuring that prisoners could not obtain a weapon.[8]

The duo walked down the narrow cellblock and entered their prisoner's cell. They were greeted by a fairly handsome, thirty-year-old man clad in a gaudy striped cardigan. The man had worn this to court on several occasions. Usually, he had a mop of disheveled hair and a scraggly beard. Today, he was clean-shaven with a nice new haircut, making him look more like an off-duty ski instructor than a man accused of murder.[9]

Kralicek commenced a pat-down, searching for weapons. Having found none, the sergeant cuffed the prisoner's hands in front of him and led him down the corridor.

The prisoner seemed comfortable with the deputies, having become familiar with them during his transports. He was usually polite and personable. He could be witty and articulate, and his blue eyes seemed the epitome of the word *mischievous*. The lawmen knew that nice, charming even, was not the same as innocent.[10]

Sergeant Kralicek, soft-spoken, and Deputy Murphy, more outgoing, led their prisoner to the secured parking area where their white Ford Bronco was parked. Since the vehicle wasn't equipped with a partition screen, they assisted the inmate into the front passenger seat and affixed a chain onto his ankle restraint. One end of the chain was secured around part of the seat before affixing it to the second ankle bracelet. His seatbelt was then secured, and the door was closed.

Once their prisoner was properly secured, the deputies retrieved their revolvers. The transfer of custody occurred without incident. Kralicek radioed Nancy Baxter back in Aspen, noting the time of the prisoner transfer, the reading of the vehicle's mileage meter, and the prisoner's gender.[11]

Deputy Murphy dropped a cardboard box, heavily laden with the prisoner's law books and documents, onto the back seat. He pushed the box to the middle of the seat and climbed in beside it. The younger deputy sat stone-faced with his eyes obscured behind gold-framed sunglasses. He had six years of law enforcement experience but still had the youthful good looks of a college frat boy.[12]

Manning the wheel, Sergeant Kralicek had a thinning hairline, impressive sideburns, and full lips, partially obscured by a bushy horseshoe mustache. He eyed the passenger through aviator glasses as he turned onto the highway.

As Glenwood Springs began receding in the rear-view mirror, the inmate suddenly twisted around, locking eyes with Murphy. For no apparent reason, he started rubbing his shackled hands together. Without saying a word, Murphy calmly put his hand on his holster and unsnapped the leather strap, making an unmistakable *popping* sound. The prisoner stopped his antics, turned around, and behaved himself as the mileposts began to pass.[13]

Deputies were taking no chances with this guy. He'd been convicted of aggravated kidnapping of an eighteen-year-old in the state of Utah. Then, he'd been indicted for the murder of a woman near Aspen and had been extradited to Colorado. Now, he was preparing to stand trial for that homicide. Unknown to most of the folks in the valley, this prisoner was the prime suspect in the disappearances or deaths of eighteen young women throughout Washington, Oregon, Utah, and Colorado.[14]

When the district attorney's investigator first brought the prisoner to the valley, he warned authorities how dangerous this man was, so four deputies had been assigned to escort him at all times. Over the months, however, that security detail had dwindled to two.[15]

They passed through Carbondale, El Jebel, and Basalt. Around here, a free man could enjoy trout fishing, hiking, or water skiing. The scenery they were passing through was far better than the cold brick walls of the Utah State Penitentiary.[16]

Once they reached their destination and extracted their prisoner from his chains in the Bronco, Sergeant Kralicek gripped the man's left arm. He guided him up the sidewalk toward the rear entrance of the courthouse. Deputy Murphy followed a few feet behind, carrying the defendant's box of papers.[17]

A photographer saw the trio approaching and raised his camera to capture their arrival. The photos would be file material only, potentially usable during the upcoming trial, which was set for November 14, a mere five months away. Hearing the shutter, Ted Bundy flashed a smile.[18]

Entering from the northern end of the courthouse brings you directly into the basement level, the home of the sheriff's department and its five meager prison cells. Kralicek and Murphy placed their weapons in a gun locker when they entered the building. The handcuffs were removed from their prisoner's wrists, and he was instructed to carry his box of legal materials himself as they headed upstairs.[19]

Two floors up, Deputy Dave Westerlund stood near the staircase, just outside the courtroom. He was keeping an eye on a prisoner he had escorted from the basement cells, a young man who was scheduled for an 8:45 appearance before the judge. That proceeding would surely be brief, as Bundy was scheduled to appear before the judge fifteen minutes later. At the moment, this prisoner and his attorney were on a bench in the corridor having a private conversation. Westerlund was close enough to keep an eye on the kid yet far enough away that he could not hear him whispering with his lawyer.[20]

Kralicek and Murphy ascended the stairs with Bundy sandwiched between them. Westerlund watched as the trio passed him and entered the courtroom. Kralicek led his prisoner to a large table that would serve attorneys for both the defense and the prosecution.[21]

At this time of year, the nights are cold in the mountains, but once the day is in full swing, you can exchange jackets for summer clothing. The courthouse's second floor was already heating up as the Colorado sun beamed through the southern windows. The old courthouse did not have the luxury of a good air-conditioning system.

Bundy set his box of papers on the counselor's table and walked back toward the double entry doors, the only public access into the courtroom. Entering the corridor again, he turned left and went through another door. This brought him into the court clerk's office. Kralicek shadowed the man.[22]

After nearly five months of interacting with Bundy, Kralicek had noted the man's demeanor fluctuated drastically. The sergeant followed as the defendant made his way to the clerk's office and then back to the counselor's table three times in a row.[23]

In March, the defendant had petitioned the court to serve as his own attorney, citing his Sixth Amendment rights and stating he fully intended to prepare his defense, following the rules governing the conduct of criminal prosecutions in the state. He acknowledged that he would use the assistance of legal advisors. The matter had been debated for weeks, but in the end, the judge had to concede that the defendant was composed, intelligent, and—from all appearances—competent. The motion was granted, and the court-appointed lawyers would merely serve as advisory counsel.[24]

Serving as his own attorney, Bundy was permitted to move about the courthouse without handcuffs, leg shackles, or even a waist chain.[25]

On the western side of the second floor lies the courtroom. At the northern end sits the judge's bench, the counsel's table, and the jury box. The middle section has rows of benches for spectators, while the rear of the room holds the law library. The door to the corridor is just to the right of the spectator benches.[26]

Sergeant Kralicek walked over to Deputy Westerlund in the corridor. The defendant made a fourth trip into the clerk's office. Again, Kralicek dutifully followed behind but stayed at the entrance to the office. When it became evident that Bundy's case was ready to proceed, Kralicek directed his subordinate to take the other prisoner to the basement.

"Should I put him into coveralls?" Westerlund asked.[27]

"No," the sergeant replied. "Just pat him down good and put him in the cell block. Return as soon as you can." The sergeant was hoping to go downstairs for a while.

By the time Westerlund returned, court was already in session. Kralicek was sitting in the second row, near the door. The sergeant motioned for the two men to switch places. Once he was in the hallway, Kralicek sent Deputy Murphy home for some much-needed sleep.[28]

One of the legal advisors began his two principal arguments. First, he wanted to bar the press from pretrial evidentiary hearings. Secondly, should his client be found guilty on all charges, he wanted to exclude the death penalty, noting that there were no guidelines as to when a jury should impose such a sentence.[29]

When Kralicek returned to the courtroom, he sat next to Westerlund. The two whispered back and forth.

"I have to go downstairs to the office for a few minutes," Kralicek concluded, excusing himself once again.[30]

On another bench, a woman leaned in close to her friend and whispered in her ear.

"It's a little warm for that outfit, don't you think?" The women were questioning Bundy's fashion choices: a heavy cardigan, a turtleneck, and cords on a sunny day in a stuffy courtroom.[31]

As the defense arguments gradually unfolded and the sun continued to rise, Kralicek slipped back into the courtroom to speak briefly with Westerlund. Despite the sheriff's policy that Bundy was required to have a minimum of two guards, Kralicek departed the courtroom a third time, leaving Westerlund to look after the defendant.[32]

Six Days in Aspen   19

When the public defenders finished their arguments, his honor called for a recess.

"I'll hear from the prosecution when court reconvenes," said the judge.

The volume in the courtroom grew as people took the opportunity to stretch and chat after being quiet for over an hour. This volume decreased as everyone began filing out of the room and down the stairs.[33]

Bundy alone remained in the room. Slowly pacing, he wiped the sweat from his upper lip. He removed his sweater and dropped it on the counselor's table. The defendant exited the courtroom doors and entered the clerk's office, resting his hands on the counter. Westerlund stood watch from the doorway.[34]

"What can we do for you?" the clerk inquired.[35]

"Hi," Bundy smiled. "Has the judge filed that written order yet? The one I asked about the other day?" He was referring to one of his multiple requests, attempting to improve his jail conditions.

"No," she replied. "Not yet. I'll check on it."

Bundy nodded slowly and turned. He walked out into the hallway where his attorney was having a smoke. Deputy Westerlund watched as the defendant turned around and returned to the clerk's service counter.

"That order," Bundy mumbled. "Has the judge signed that order yet?"

The clerk gave a questioning look as she shook her head slowly. *Is he ill?* He had just asked her that same question.

"Would you mail this for me?" He pulled some crumpled-up envelopes from his back pocket. The clerk declined with a shake of her head yet again. *He knows that's against policy.*

The defendant walked out into the corridor, nearly colliding with the broad-shouldered Westerlund. Bundy apologized for the near-miss and reentered the courtroom. The deputy took a step back into the corridor. From here, he could allow the obsessive bouncing between the two rooms but still block any flight attempt toward the staircase down the hall.[36]

Westerlund watched as Bundy rifled through some papers at the counselors' table, then return to the corridor yet again, peering into the clerk's office before walking up to the deputy.

"I need to get some copies made," he stated.

Westerlund didn't bother to respond.[37]

A reporter entered the courtroom to retrieve her purse, catching a glimpse of the defendant as he stepped into the law library. Others were also beginning to trickle back into the courtroom as well, claiming their seats in anticipation of the pending proceedings.[38]

Westerlund lit a cigarette. He could overhear an interesting conversation happening on the nearby staircase and turned to see who was involved in the discussion. When he looked back to the courtroom, Bundy was out of his field of sight. This was not alarming. There was nowhere for the defendant to go.[39]

As the courtroom continued filling with spectators, another reporter entered the room. He looked back at Westerlund. Using a combination of facial expression and body language, he appeared to be asking for Bundy's location. In response, the deputy poked his head into the room.[40]

"I think he's in there," he said, pointing to a door near the front of the courtroom.[41]

"I hope so," the reporter replied.[42]

◆

Strolling down Main Street, on the south side of the courthouse, a man looked up at the judicial building and the statue of Lady Justice, high above the double doors at the front entrance. Unlike most such statues of Justice, he noticed that this one was not wearing her blindfold.[43]

Movement from the far left of the building suddenly caught the pedestrian's eye as papers drifted out of an open window. Shockingly, a man emerged, seating himself on the stone window ledge. He swung his legs out and pushed off! He jumped to the ground, landing hard. The window sits one-and-a-half stories above the lawn, so the force propelled the jumper forward onto the palms of his hands. The jumper rose quickly and ran eastward—right past the witness. Confused by what he had just seen, the pedestrian entered the courthouse, intent on asking questions.[44]

◆

Up on the second floor, Deputy Westerlund's attention returned to the stairs, hearing some attorneys ascending the wooden steps. The deputy walked to the courtroom's double doors while these men entered. The court stenographer approached him.[45]

"Where's Bundy?" he inquired. In response, Westerlund once again motioned toward the door at the front of the room. The stenographer, following this line of reasoning, walked to the door, opened it, and peered inside. Confused, he returned to Westerlund's side and whispered, "He's not there."[46]

The deputy turned to look down the corridor and called out to defense attorney Charles Leidner, who was sitting in a chair, calmly smoking a cigarette.[47]

"Do you know where Bundy is?"[48]

"Yeah...not really my turn to watch him," the lawyer replied sarcastically.

On the basement floor, three of the sheriff's secretaries were hard at work. One of them, a brunette with a fresh perm, was startled when a man suddenly walked up to her.[49]

"Is it normal to jump out of a second-story window here?" he asked.[50]

"No," she replied with a concerned look. "It's not."[51]

Sergeant Kralicek, standing close enough to overhear this odd question, cursed loudly and sprinted up the stairs. Bursting into the court clerk's office, he startled the judge and the clerk.[52]

"Is Bundy in here?" The sergeant interrupted.[53]

"No," replied the puzzled clerk.

"He's gone!" the sergeant bellowed as he shot out of the office.

Westerlund made his way to the rear of the courtroom. The law library, with its sea of beige reference books, was separated from the rest of the room by a five-foot-high partition. Frantically checking the aisles between each of the bookcases, the deputy's heart sank as he realized the horrible truth. A breeze blew through an open window.[54]

"Somebody went out the window!" he yelled.[55]

"Christ, almighty!" came a voice from somewhere down the corridor. "Bundy's gone!"[56]

Someone in the courtroom announced, "Bundy's escaped!" There was an awkward moment of silence followed by a buzz of conversation, oddly intermingled with laughter.[57]

Defense Attorney Jim Dumas was stunned. His colleague, Charles Leidner, caught his attention from the doorway and raised an eyebrow.

Leidner's mind was racing. *There are only two roads out of Aspen*, he thought. *How is he going to get out of here? Does he know where he's going?* He ground his cigarette in the nearby ashtray until the last of the smoke was stubbed out.[58]

◆

Down the street, Nancy was trying to stay focused on her typing. She found herself distracted by Sergeant Horan, who was using a small tool to dig inside the bowl of his pipe. He smoked tobacco called Mac Barons Latakia, and the aroma permeated the air. Nancy watched as Horan tamped it down on the edge of the counter.[59]

A garbled transmission came over the radio, and Nancy's attention was redirected.[60]

"10-9," she said into the radio, requesting a repeat of the transmission. "I couldn't understand you."[61]

"Bundy escaped!" Deputy Westerlund repeated excitedly.

Baxter and Sergeant Horan locked eyes.

"What?" the sergeant exclaimed.

"Oh, fuck!" Nancy shouted. "Bundy escaped!"

Chief Hougland was coming down the stairs, accompanied by the city manager.

"Art!" Nancy called out. "We've got a problem. Bundy escaped!" She reached for the dispatch radio.[62]

"All units, Aspen," she said. "Be advised that we have just received word that Ted Bundy has escaped from the Pitkin County Courthouse. Please standby for further information." She knew her announcement would be heard by the volunteer fire chief, officers, and deputies.[63]

Upstairs, Michael Chandler, a plainclothes detective and the head of the crime prevention team, heard Deputy Westerlund's frantic announcement coming from the bank of radios near his desk. Chandler knew how dangerous Bundy was and needed to alert his community.

The 6'5" detective bounded down the stairs. Nearing the counter, which led to dispatch, he yelled out, "I'm going over to KSNO Radio!"[64]

◆

Gary White, a plainclothes investigator, raced out to the front lawn of the courthouse with another deputy fast on his heels. As the two spilled out onto Main Street, they paused, awkwardly looking up and down the street. White felt his chest tighten. Like his companion, he was confused. He could feel his heart pounding, the adrenaline coursing through his veins. He didn't know where he should go from here. More deputies came flooding out of the building, scanning the streets for any sign of the fugitive. They began hollering back and forth as a plan began to form. Then, they scattered in all directions.[65]

Knowing the man could disappear into any number of stores and shops within town, White ran south along Galena Street, gun in hand. He passed city hall on his left, a bakery on the right, and headed toward the downtown shopping district. He wondered if he should inspect the local shops, but there were simply too many doors and alleys. The confusion and uncertainty felt paralyzing, even as he moved down the street, passing storefront after storefront. In a flash of clarity, he felt certain the fugitive would want to get out of the city limits as soon as possible. He continued south toward Aspen Mountain and the edge of town.[66]

◆

As Detective Chandler sprinted past Hotel Jerome on Main Street, he could hear details of Bundy's escape over his radio. He dashed inside the building emblazoned with the sign, *The Aspen Times*. It was the same building where KSNO Radio Station made its broadcasts. Staff at the station had no idea why the detective was there, but they knew who he was and didn't stop him as he stormed into the announcing booth.

"I need to get on the air right now," he said plainly. "Get up from your seat."[67]

"Fine," the DJ replied, knowing full well Chandler was a detective.

"Alexander Bundy has just leaped from the second-floor window of the courthouse," Chandler said into the microphone, "and is now on the run." Alexander Mundy was a character in the popular TV show *It Takes a Thief*. Brushing aside the mild embarrassment at his faux pas, the detective pressed on without hesitation. "The suspect is six-feet-one-inch tall, 150 pounds, with ear length, wavy brown hair. He is wearing a brown turtleneck, beige corduroy slacks, and brown loafers."[68]

◆

Doubting that anyone could have jumped from the upstairs window, a secretary walked out of the courthouse to determine for herself if this was a possibility. Spotting papers on the grass near a lilac bush, she dashed over to see if they were of importance. One of the pages was marked with a near-perfect shoe impression. Picking up the sheet, she noticed deep heel prints in the turf.[69]

◆

Word of the escape was spreading like wildfire. Reports of possible sightings began to flood into dispatch. Construction workers, who claimed to have seen Bundy's jump, stated he had turned right, ran around the western corner of the building, and headed north. This was in direct conflict with what the initial witness had reported.[70]

One witness said he'd been in the alley behind Freddie's Main Street Café, just two blocks east of the courthouse. He saw a man running full speed right past him. Another witness reported the man passing a condominium complex on the east side of town.[71]

As they came into dispatch, Nancy pieced together the preliminary witness reports and could now retrace Bundy's escape route. From the front lawn of the courthouse, he had headed east and scaled a six-foot-high fence. This would have provided him access to an alley hidden from the view of motorists on Main Street. He ran past the Concept 600 Building and behind Freddie's Café. If he had continued heading east, he would have passed the bus stop and crossed the Roaring Fork River near a trailer park. He could be hiding in Herron Park. Best to send some officers down to investigate.[72]

"All units, Aspen," came Baxter's voice over the police scanner. "Be on the lookout for Ted Bundy, a white male suspect who may be headed, on foot, east on Main Street or north behind the courthouse. Suspect last seen wearing tan pants, a turtleneck, has dark hair, and is approximately six feet tall, 175 pounds."[73]

Chief Hougland bailed out the front door of city hall. Turning right, he ran north along Galena Street, past the construction workers, and arrived at the front entrance of the courthouse. Hearing their fugitive was most likely headed toward the park, the chief joined the pursuit through a parking lot dubbed The Brickyard, a staging area for a project on the Aspen Mall. As the men maneuvered their way through the lot, they looked like they were competing through an obstacle course. Ducking under the wires of a gin pole derrick, racing around hills of dirt, and hurdling over stacks of bricks, they did their best to maintain an easterly course. Finally, they regained their bearings and ran down the alley behind Freddie's Café.[74]

◆

At the courthouse, Deputy Westerlund had raced down two flights of stairs to retrieve his revolver from a gun locker. He had holstered the weapon and took off in pursuit down Main Street's sidewalk. Over his radio, the deputy heard there was a possible sighting east of the bus stop. If this was true, Westerlund could not catch up on foot, so he returned to the courthouse to get in his patrol car.[75]

◆

Chief Hougland and several officers descended into Herron Park, a small recreation area that wouldn't take long to search.

A kindergarten teacher was hosting an end-of-the-school-year picnic here for her class. The children were running around excitedly, all under the watchful eye of their teacher. She was surprised to see officers appearing through the woods, weapons drawn. A group of her students reported

SHERIFF DICK KIENAST

seeing a man crossing the water at the trailer park. The teacher gathered the children, herding them back toward the school.[76]

Searching the foliage along the banks of the river, Art Hougland made a misstep. Unable to recover his balance, the chief fell into the water. Struggling to return to his feet, he realized his gun and radio were soaked. This was a problem, as the police department only had four or five spare hand-held radios.[77]

◆

On East Hopkins, an apartment manager received a call from an officer she was dating.

"Lockup," he said. "Stay inside." He told her an escaped convict had been seen running through her neighborhood.[78]

Her roommate helped barricade the front door by tying a rope from the doorknob to a nearby railing. They pushed their couch up against the back door and grabbed two baseball bats. They almost couldn't breathe when a knock came at the front door.[79]

"Stay home," came a muffled voice. Peering out through the curtains, the young women could see a couple of officers running through the complex.[80]

◆

Though he was off duty, Deputy Gene Flatt heard the announcement of the escape over the radio. The twenty-four-year-old felt a wave of emotion, an uncomfortable combination of discouragement and embarrassment. Knowing full well what the fugitive was capable of doing, he realized that Aspen was a target-rich environment for such a killer. Flatt's protective instincts kicked in. Bundy had an affinity for attractive women with long hair. *Where would these women be*, the deputy wondered while running his fingers down his horseshoe mustache. *They're in danger.*

Near the base of Smuggler Mountain and less than a mile from Herron Park, there was an old roadbed for a narrow-gauge railroad. The tracks had been removed ages ago, but the gravel trail had become a popular place for locals to jog. On several occasions, during authorized exercise breaks behind the courthouse, Bundy had asked deputies questions concerning Smuggler Mountain, the historic mining area northeast of town. Why had he been so interested in the peak?[81]

That's where I'll go, Flatt decided.

Climbing into his baby-blue Chevy pickup, he set out for his self-assigned destination without checking in with the sheriff's office. He was

Six Days in Aspen

merely protecting his community with the first thought that came to mind. The deputy grabbed his gun and badge and slammed down the accelerator. He remembered the words he had so often heard in the 2nd Armored Cavalry Regiment—*failure is not an option.*[82]

◆

The news photographer was running down Galena Street, knowing he had something valuable in his possession. He burst into Walnut House Films, a block south of city hall, and handed over a roll of film to be developed. He had taken photographs of Bundy entering the courthouse earlier in the morning. Surely, these images were now considered Kodak gold.[83]

The camera store owner took the film roll into the back of his shop. The chemicals were already mixed in his darkroom, but it would take at least an hour before he could provide the photographer with what he needed. In total darkness, the film was loaded into a lightproof developer tank.[84]

◆

Detective Sergeant Dave Garms was handsome, with a strong jaw and impressive physique, but his shaggy hair hadn't seen a barber in months. His mustache, however, was well-maintained. In his denim jeans and matching jacket, he didn't look like the second-highest-ranking member of the Aspen PD. The only member of the force who outranked him was Art Hougland. The chief had extensive administrative skills, but he didn't have any law enforcement experience. While Garms found Hougland to be a likable guy, the chief was not the man the officers turned to for tactical police strategy. It was Garms who provided that leadership.[85]

A few months earlier, the prior police chief had departed, leaving a vacancy in the department. Garms let it be known that he would seek the position. The city manager, however, appointed his administrative colleague, Art Hougland. Garms was the longest-serving member of the force and had served under three superiors. His experience could not be denied. To the officers, he was considered the principal decision-maker in the field.[86]

His priority now was to determine who was on duty and where those officers were presently located. Armed with this knowledge, he would work with Nancy Baxter to have personnel assigned to specific tasks.[87]

Garms knew roadblocks were necessary, but he also believed Bundy was too smart to sit in a vehicle and attempt to pass through a security checkpoint unnoticed. With the knowledge that these roadblocks were being created, Garms wanted to move on. He had other fish to fry. His prime objective was Bundy himself. The detective wanted in on the hunt.[88]

◆

Nancy began spinning a web, dispatching several police officers to block traffic at a section of the highway in Aspen's east end, adjacent to Crestahaus Lodge. A heavy snowpack had been plowed in late May, opening Highway 82 up to Independence Pass. Soon after Memorial Day, however, a landslide occurred. Drivers could now only make it a third of the way up the pass. Still, there had been at least two sightings of Bundy heading east, and Crestahaus Lodge was ideally situated for a roadblock, preventing anyone from exiting the city in an easterly direction.[89]

To quickly halt traffic heading westbound on the highway, Baxter dispatched another officer to create a checkpoint at Castle Creek Bridge on the western side of town.

A friend of Nancy's, who had jogged over from the courthouse, entered city hall and didn't even wait to enter the dispatch office. She raced up to the counter, bent her head down, and spoke to Nancy through the small cashier slot. She said some boys from town were grabbing their guns and headed toward the bridge. It took a second, but Baxter soon deciphered what her friend was trying to communicate. She was talking about Maroon Creek, not Castle Creek. Hearing that Bundy had escaped, some of the fellas from town had grabbed shotguns from the gun racks of their trucks, revolvers from their glove compartments, and were en route to Maroon Creek Bridge. Aspenites were fulfilling a need, and this made Baxter smile.[90]

Maroon Creek Bridge sits about a mile west of Castle Creek Bridge. With low sides and damaged guard rails, the extremely narrow span did nothing to alleviate Baxter's fear of heights. Once, her motorbike had seized up in the middle of that bridge, and a small delivery truck had barely missed running into her. As always, that momentary flashback caused a little shudder. She could have been pitched off the span, but she had no time to think about that right now. If residents were grabbing their guns and congregating at the bridge, it would put another plug into the downvalley traffic. This slender span was a perfect bottleneck that just might ensnare a jackal on the run.[91]

Carolyn, covering the mouthpiece of her phone, passed along information as she was receiving it. A couple of guys from Wildlife-Fish and

Game would join the lone officer who had been dispatched to Castle Creek Bridge. Their shirts and patches somewhat resembled law enforcement. They had a mixed bag out west at the bridges, but what a great response from the community.

"Call the city shop," Baxter told Carolyn as new ideas began to formulate. "Have them advise their personnel in trucks or out in the field to keep an eye out for Bundy, but do *not* have them apprehend him if he's sighted. The water department, road department, building department—let's get on it! Anyone who carries a radio can monitor the police band, but advise everyone to keep the transmissions to a minimum."

Next, Nancy directed a patrol unit to head to Slaughterhouse Bridge on the northwestern outskirts of town. Also on the call list was the tower out at Sardy Field, the local airport. She wanted eyes on every passenger departing the resort town via the airfield.

Nancy and Carolyn reached for their phones. It was time to call the off-duty deputies as additional manpower was needed.[92]

◆

In Sheriff Kienast's office at the courthouse, a secretary approached him while holding Bundy's cardigan sweater. It had been left on the attorney's table. Kienast smiled.

"Sergeant Davis!" he called out, wanting one of his sergeants to request tracking dogs from nearby counties.[93]

◆

Deputy Gene Flatt brought his pickup truck to a halt in Smuggler Park, near the base of Smuggler Mountain. He slammed the door of his rig and began scrambling uphill through the sagebrush. He didn't need to climb as high as the mine shaft, but just shy of it, where the old railroad bed used to be.[94]

As the deputy reached the trail, he saw no one to his right. Looking back to his left, however, he spied a female jogger heading west at a pretty good clip. He had just missed her. Flatt called out, but she ignored him. She appeared quite athletic and was already placing distance between herself and the lawman. *I can't leave her up here with Bundy running around.* He attached his walkie-talkie to his belt beside his holster. Fishing his badge out of his pocket and gripping it tightly in the palm of his hand, he started sprinting after the woman.

He ran uphill as fast as he could, pursuing a citizen he desperately wanted to protect. Within a minute, he was already reassessing the situation. Gene considered himself physically fit. He was young and had been discharged from the Army in the last twelve months. Still, he was barely gaining on the woman.

"Stop!" Flatt called out.[95]

The female jogger refused to turn around, but it was evident she had heard him. Her pace increased, and the deputy watched in horror as she flew uphill like a gazelle. Her rhythmic movements were fascinating. Gene had clearly underestimated her abilities.[96]

His ego gifted Flatt with another burst of energy. Running at full speed, with every ounce of strength at his command, he soon concluded that he could never catch this woman.

"Stop!" he cried out, more desperate than before. "I'm a deputy sheriff!"

Miraculously, the woman stopped. She didn't turn her entire body; she merely turned her head to see who was behind her. She didn't even appear to be breathing heavily as she raised a hand to shield her eyes from the glare of the sun.

"What do you want!" she screamed.

"Look, lady," Gene replied, gasping for air. "Ted Bundy has escaped." He held up his badge to demonstrate that he was a legitimate deputy. "You need to go home. Go to your house and lock your doors."

The woman paused for a moment. The man behind her wasn't dressed like a deputy, and that badge could be just about anything from this distance, but she saw the gun in his holster. Without replying, she just turned downhill and began bounding cross-country, transforming from a gazelle to a mountain goat.

Flatt watched with his mouth agape. The jogger seemed to know which rocks were firm and which were unstable. One wrong move in those tennis shoes, and she'd surely break an ankle. He watched as she dropped a good fifty yards or more below his position in the blink of an eye. Then, she turned and ran through the dry grass back to a black BMW parked right next to Flatt's pickup.

Knowing he'd accomplished something, the deputy permitted himself a little break. There was a significant oxygen debt to repay. His lungs screamed. He shook his head, marveling at the athleticism he'd just witnessed.

That woman could have run circles around Ted.[97]

◆

Two officers assigned to the northwest end of town slowed their Saab near the intersection of Red Butte Drive and Cemetery Lane. They parked off the side of the road, near a set of mailboxes and a little split rail fence. Popping the trunk, they retrieved their shotguns and trotted out to the middle of the Slaughterhouse Bridge.[98]

The very center of the span marked a jurisdictional boundary. Here, you could keep one foot within city limits while placing the other on county terrain. On a typical Tuesday, jurisdiction was a boundary line that was firmly maintained. This was no ordinary Tuesday.[99]

The officers scanned the waters of the river, swiftly flowing below the bridge. By placing this checkpoint at this junction, they could stop anyone coming up Cemetery Lane or Red Butte Drive, attempting to gain access to McClain Flats Road.[100]

"Aspen," one of the officers radioed into dispatch. "1-16 and 1-18 are 10-23, 10-53."[101]

"10-4," Nancy replied.

◆

About four miles past Slaughterhouse Bridge, the W/J Ranch can be found with its small clusters of kit-built cedar log homes. One of these rentals housed Deputy Bob Braudis and his four roommates.[102]

After finishing the graveyard shift, the deputy played racquetball at the athletic club, driven home, and caught about ninety minutes of sleep before his telephone began ringing. He knew it could only be bringing him bad news.

"Bob!" Nancy was yelling into the phone, knowing she would have to rouse Braudis from slumber. "Get your gun and get into the office. Bundy jumped out the courtroom window." It took a second for Braudis to shake the cobwebs from his head and understand the implications of what the dispatcher had just said. "You gotta get back in your car and get in here. All hell is breaking loose."[103]

The deputy jumped up and slipped on a pair of corduroy pants and a blue and white striped rugby shirt.

Braudis knew Bundy. The deputy had transported him several times during the defendant's required trips between Glenwood Springs and Aspen. He'd enjoyed some long conversations with the convicted kidnapper during these journeys. When they'd first met, however, the six-foot-six, 250-pound lawman set the boundaries for how their relationship would unfold. As they were climbing the stairs of the courthouse for the first time, the deputy had his powerful hand wrapped tightly around one of his prisoner's biceps.

"Theodore," Braudis had said, pulling the man even closer to his side. "The judge doesn't allow sidearms in his courtroom. The courthouse was built in 1890, and it's not secure. Ergo, if you get more than three feet away from me...I'll rip your head off."[104]

Braudis laced up his hiking boots, grabbed his Colt Python pistol, and headed out to his beat-up, four-door Buick Estate Wagon.

◆

Cars were backed up solid on Main Street, clogging all the side roads and alleys leading to shops and businesses. The Castle Creek Bridge checkpoint had been created to do just this—immediately stop traffic. It had succeeded. Trunks, cargo spaces, truck beds, and even barrels were being searched, anything that could conceivably conceal a man. Drivers were scrutinized. No one was above suspicion. Vehicles were being searched under the assumption that Bundy might be holding the driver hostage, or he might be back at the driver's house, holding a family captive while he sent a spouse out for supplies. Did anyone seem more nervous than they should be?[105]

The first few roadblocks had done their best to stop Bundy from heading east or west along the highway. Now that some time had passed and he hadn't been captured, checkpoints were being created at other designated locations. Sheriff Kienast, Detective Sergeant Garms, and Nancy Baxter had to be realistic. The web would have to expand to points more distant from town. With the Slaughterhouse Bridge and Maroon Creek Bridge checkpoints in place, the Castle Creek Roadblock was disbanded so the officers could be used elsewhere.

Baxter used the direct line to Sheriff Kienast, asking if he could work with authorities in Garfield County. Maybe they could spare some deputies. Perhaps they could man a roadblock at the Catherine Store, a heavily used turnoff to Carbondale. The store is past Snowmass, Basalt, and El Jebel, a full twenty-seven miles from Aspen, in a neighboring county.[106]

The Catherine Store, a cinder-block curio shop, had shelves loaded with antiques, blankets, animal pelts, day-old bread, and glass cases featuring Native American arrowheads. Vintage photos, skeleton keys, and stuffed gophers were available near the candy counter and a lone cashier. After purchasing a candy bar, or arguably the coldest beer in the valley, customers could walk outside, where a small assortment of chainsaw-carved wooden bears could be found. On prominent display, outside the front door—a life-sized white pine cigar store Indian. In leather leggings and a brightly colored headdress, the recognizable landmark draws attention past the gas pumps.[107]

With its siren blaring, a Garfield County sheriff's sedan screeched to a halt in the middle of the highway in front of the store. Two deputies emerged, flagging down motorists that were coming down from Aspen. Near this site, it was said that you could throw a softball, and it could soar through three different counties before it was caught: Pitkin, Eagle, and Garfield County. Deputies from the latter jurisdiction had answered Sheriff Kienast's call and happened to have two deputies on patrol not far from the proposed checkpoint. The Catherine Store Roadblock was now erected, and a handful of curious bystanders began congregating in a pasture behind a low, barbed wire and split rail fence meant to keep the cows and horses away from the road.[108]

♦

In addition to a request for help from the Garfield County Sheriff's Department, the Colorado State Highway Patrol, seventy-three miles north in the town of Eagle, was also alerted. Kienast was seeking any assistance the CSP could provide. State Trooper Jim Loyd grabbed his radio, stating he understood and would be assisting shortly.[109]

Conveniently, Loyd was in his patrol car heading east on Highway 82 between Catherine Store and Aspen. He and his wife lived in a small cottage on the outskirts of Basalt, as they couldn't afford the steep prices in Aspen. Still, the trooper enjoyed patrolling his assigned sections of the highway and county roads surrounding the mountain resort community. The young couple was thrilled to live near one of the premier skiing destinations in the country.

The trooper thought it was strange when some people in town started taking a liking to Ted Bundy. Loyd couldn't claim to know the defendant, but he had certainly run into him in the hallways of the courthouse. Loyd spent a lot of time at the courthouse and was well-familiar with its construction and layout. *Ted jumped from the second floor?*[110]

About fifteen miles downvalley from Aspen, the trooper spotted the sign for the Conoco gas station at the intersection of Old Snowmass Creek Road.

Inside the convenience store, a man was at the counter, paying for his gas. While the attendant was making change, they heard strange sounds emanating from outside. There was a car horn, something that sounded like tires squealing, and raised voices.

The customer exited the store through a double-glass door configuration, a vestibule that served as a buffer to keep cold air outside. This was a good place to kick snow off one's boots in the winter and check the mail, as a wall of four-inch mailboxes lined one side of the entryway.[111]

Now outside, the customer checked his car, which was parked at one of the two gas pumps. In addition to the gas station and the convenience store, there was an auto repair shop.[112]

Out in the intersection in front of the store, a Pitkin County sheriff's sedan had stopped in the middle of the road, and deputies were already halting westbound traffic. From the west, a white Plymouth Fury approached with its red gumball light flashing on top of the car. There was another screech of tires when Colorado State Trooper Loyd brought his Fury to a stop in the middle of the highway, helping to obstruct the traffic flow. The trooper grabbed his radio and—as call sign 372—radioed dispatch in Eagle that he would be assisting at the Old Snowmass Conoco Roadblock. It was an ideal location to halt vehicles heading down the valley and everything running north to south along Old Snowmass Road.[113]

As the only trooper on the scene, Jim Loyd stood out from the other lawmen. At six feet tall and 180 pounds, he was dressed from head to toe in a polyester blend uniform. His khaki pants had a black stripe running down the sides, and his blue uniform shirt matched the color of his service cap. The deputies near him appeared comfortable in their short-sleeved shirts, but Loyd was already miserably hot in his ensemble.[114]

Loyd was right-handed but wore a left-hand draw holster on the side of his hip. In it, he carried a .357 Magnum Colt Python with a four-inch barrel. He popped the trunk of his car to retrieve his shotgun.[115]

◆

At city hall, Nancy took a moment to indulge in a personal call. She dialed a friend who worked as a housemaid up and down the valley, and her sole means of transportation was hitchhiking. When Baxter's friend finally answered the call, Nancy realized that the young woman looked like one of the girls the fugitive was suspected of killing in Washington State.

"Sandy, don't hitchhike today," the dispatcher whispered into the phone. "Bundy escaped."[116]

Nancy was hanging up her phone when Carolyn signaled her to pick up another line.

"Line 3," Carolyn whispered. Nancy nodded and punched the illuminated button.[117]

"This is Nancy. How can I help you?"

"I'm out in Mountain Valley, and I was in my backyard," a woman was spilling out her story, loud and fast. "I may have seen that guy that's on the loose!"

"Whoa, calm down, ma'am," Nancy said, hearing the frantic woman's voice on the other end of the line. "Tell me what's going on."

The distraught woman took a deep breath and proceeded with her story.

"I was just sitting in my backyard, and this man peered over my fence. I got a real good look at him," she said. "I believe it's Bundy."

"Okay, ma'am. I'm sending an officer to your place right away. Please stay on the line with Carolyn here while I work on this." Nancy handed the receiver to Carolyn and grabbed a radio.

"X-1, Aspen," Nancy said with her eyes closed, hoping Detective Sergeant Dave Garms was near the area.

"X-1, go ahead," his voice cracked over the airwaves.

"We have a report of a possible sighting in Mountain Valley. Could you have one of your units 10-25 the residence to speak with a woman who says the suspect may have just been in her backyard? Break." She provided the detective with the address.

"10-4," Garms replied. "X-1 is 10-76, ETA three minutes."

"10-4, X-1, 1104."

Nancy set the radio aside and grabbed the telephone from Carolyn.

"I have an officer en route, ma'am. Please remain on the line until he arrives, and let us know if you see anything else."

As they waited, Carolyn mentioned the possibility that Bundy could take this frightened woman as a hostage. Nancy thought about it for a second and realized that Detective Chandler was at the Crestahaus Roadblock, not far from the woman's house. Both he and Garms were trained in hostage negotiations.

Let's hope it doesn't get that far.

Nancy's heart was pounding. Had Bundy gotten past the officers at the Crestahaus and was even now, creeping around the Mountain Valley district? That was Nancy's neighborhood. She knew she hadn't locked the front door to her apartment this morning. She never locked it and wasn't even sure that she owned a key to the place. She didn't know anybody who took their keys out of their cars. Folks generally left them either in the ignition, on the floor, or in the ashtray.[118]

Ironically, someone now reported that they were missing items from a car that was parked in the alley behind First National Bank. Men's clothing was among the items that may have been stolen.

"X-1, Aspen," Baxter radioed Garms. "The suspect may be wearing a blue and white striped rugby shirt and tan pants." Garms acknowledged receipt of the message and asked her if she could contact the radio stations to get a revised description of the suspect out to the public.[119]

When Garms arrived at the woman's residence, he showed her a photo of the fugitive.

"That's him!" she declared. "That's the man!" And then, back-peddling a bit, she added, "Well, there's an eighty-percent chance that's the man."

That was good enough for Garms. He ordered a house-to-house search of the Mountain Valley neighborhood, stressing to his officers the importance of checking all of the outbuildings. He also directed that the searches be conducted swiftly, as he knew Bundy's trail was growing colder with every passing minute.[120]

Baxter and her roommate rented the middle-floor apartment in a large three-story house near the witness. Her landlord, a deaf woman, lived with her husband and son on the third floor of the residence. The sound of the toddler's pounding feet above her could be maddening to Nancy at times, but it went completely unnoticed by the mother.

Baxter realized the mom couldn't hear the radio broadcasts and, if her husband was at work, would have no idea a fugitive was on the loose. If she was home alone with their son, they were vulnerable. Nancy's biggest fear was that Bundy would grab a hostage. He could easily sneak up on the deaf woman while she was gardening and seize that little boy. Nancy grabbed the radio and dispatched a deputy to the woman's residence.[121]

The switchboard lit up with another call from the same neighborhood.[122]

"Aspen Police," Nancy said. "Can I help you?"[123]

"I think he's on my porch!" a woman screeched at Nancy.

"Who?" Baxter replied.

"That guy from the radio is on my front porch. He has a gun, and he's pounding on my door! I can see him through the window."

"What does he look like?" Nancy inquired.

"Oh, he's a giant. He's got on a blue and white striped rugby shirt and has dark hair. I *know* it's Bundy! He—"

"Wait a minute," Baxter cut her off, "Where do you live?"

"66 East Lupine Drive, in Mountain Valley."

"Oh, my God," Nancy exclaimed. "Hold on just a minute."

Baxter picked up a radio.

"6-2, Aspen," she said, calling Deputy Braudis. "What is your 10-20?"[124]

"66 East Lupine Drive," Braudis replied, wondering if there had been a break in the case.

"Well, the lady that lives there says Ted Bundy is outside her door. He's in a blue and white rugby shirt."

Braudis lowered his head to inspect his attire. Corduroy slacks and the very rugby shirt the woman had described.

"That's me," the deputy chuckled.

"You need to take off your shirt."

"What?" Bob replied, completely baffled by Baxter's request.

"You need to take off your shirt. Are you at Nancy Dick's house?"

"Yes."

"Please take off your shirt."

In the dispatch center, Baxter resumed her conversation with the woman on the phone.

"Is the guy taking off his shirt?" Nancy asked.

"Yeah," the woman replied, a bit perplexed.

"Okay, that's Bob Braudis. He's one of our deputies," Baxter assured the woman that she was safe and advised her to lock up her home. Then, she addressed the deputy on the radio again.

"Get your ass back to the office. And...put on a uniform."[125]

◆

At the 9News station in downtown Denver, Ward Lucas was walking out of a meeting when he noticed a small gathering around the radio on the other side of the room. Not unusual. Lucas tossed his beige camel hair blazer over the back of his chair, loosened his striped tie, and took a seat at his desk.

"Ted Bundy has escaped," the radio crackled.

Lucas whirled around in his chair.

"Did he say, Bundy?" he called out to the crowd. Without waiting for an answer, he made his way across the room and muscled his way into the group. A friend advised him they were listening to Radio Station KSPN, broadcasting from the basement of the Hotel Jerome in Aspen.[126]

"Bundy was last seen wearing a brown turtleneck sweater and tan corduroys. He's described as 5'11" with brown, wavy, ear-length hair. The sheriff says he is dangerous and you should not try and apprehend him. If you spot Bundy, call the sheriff's department immediately."[127]

The DJ then played the next song for his listeners. It was "Me and Bobby McGee," and Janis Joplin's lyrics were soon heard throughout the office—*Freedom's just another word for nothing else to lose*.[128]

Lucas had been working for the Denver station for less than a year. Three years earlier, he had been working at KJR Radio in Seattle, Washington. There, he had been ideally situated to report on a series of mysterious disappearances. Beautiful college girls from the University District, Olympia, Ellensburg, and Burien had simply vanished in the night—one in February, the next in March, then April, May, and June. There were no clues, no leads to follow.

Members of the press quietly referred to the cases as the calendar-girls mystery. At some point, Lucas began numbering the young women on the air— "Girl Number Four, Girl Number Five." The reporter felt a little guilty when other journalists in the region started doing the same.[129]

In July 1974, things changed. This time, two young women disappeared from a lake on the same afternoon. They had been sunning themselves one moment, then they'd walked away with a stranger the next, all within full view of thousands of people.

Ward Lucas had lived just a couple of miles down the road from the lake. A police officer notified him of the double abduction, and, as a journalist, he was soon covering the story. Five witnesses described seeing a handsome man, with his left arm in a sling, attempting to pick up on pretty young women. He was asking if they could help him load a sailboat onto his car. Witnesses who saw him leading one of the women away from the beach overheard him introducing himself as *Ted*.

Skeletal remains of the missing girls were later discovered amid the heavily wooded foothills of the Cascade Mountains. A suspect emerged. It was a law student named Theodore Robert Bundy.

Now, confronted with the news that Bundy had escaped in Colorado, Lucas marched right into the office of the Denver news director—Ron Scott. The two men were polar opposites. Lucas, six feet tall and thin, was known for his boldness. Scott was shorter, a little rotund, and fairly conservative. Lucas attempted to explain the situation: the homicides in

Washington, similar murders in Colorado, and the kidnapping conviction in Utah. Everything pointed to the escaped convict. Lucas was seeking authorization to fly to Aspen to cover the manhunt.

"No dice," Scott said dismissively. "It's not a 9News story. I'm not going to spend the money for it."[130]

"Ron," Lucas replied in his deep, baritone voice. "I was in Seattle when these things were happening. This is a *big* deal."

"Well, it's *not* a big deal for Denver because we don't even broadcast in Aspen. No...you're not going."

Lucas insisted that it was a big story that other stations would pick up. It would go national. It was worthy of being reported. Getting nowhere with his arguments and unwilling to be fired over the matter, Lucas stormed out of the office and returned to his desk. The reporter slumped in his chair, unable to think about anything else.

A killer was out there, somewhere. Lucas wanted to keep his job, but Ted Bundy—on the loose—was not in the public's interest. The reporter made a decision based on emotions but knew he could live with whatever consequences came from his pending actions. He had been taking flying lessons at the Arapahoe County Airport, so he picked up the phone and dialed his flight instructor. As Lucas seized his blazer, the twenty-eight-year-old, Emmy award-winning investigative journalist asked one question of his friend.

"How much to fly me and a cameraman to Sardy Field?"[131]

CHAPTER 2
DRAGNET

Gary Haynes could tell there was some trouble ahead. He downshifted his Jeep CJ-7 while crossing the plate girder spans of Maroon Creek Bridge. Coming to a stop, he was confronted by two armed men. Haynes recognized a roadblock when he saw one, but this checkpoint was manned by civilians rather than officers. Revolvers, rifles, shotguns—anything that could expel pellets or a bullet was present. He inquired as to the nature of the stop.[132]

"We're looking for an escapee," came the response. "We need to check for passengers." Haynes had no issue with volunteers, but these fellas were *scary-looking*, and he would have been more comfortable seeing fewer bandoliers and more police badges.[133]

The men added that they'd been directed to stop all cars headed out of town. Haynes bit his tongue, holding back the urge to point out that he was actually headed *into* town. He merely waited in silence while the men searched his vehicle. It didn't take long to inspect a two-door, open-body Jeep, but he used that time to survey his surroundings. He was stopped on a 600-foot-long trestle bridge, ninety feet above the babbling waters of Maroon Creek, which were flowing through a deep ravine. The sheer slopes of the gorge walls acted as silent sentinels, guarding access to the resort community. For a roadblock, this was ideally situated; it was a textbook example of a military choke point.

Once he was cleared, he drove the last two miles of his 750-mile journey to Aspen. The wind was in his hair, and he had high hopes for a new chapter in his life. He was serving as a juvenile officer in Missouri's 5th Judicial District, assigned to the St. Joseph Police Department.

During a significant drug investigation, one of his friends had been an undercover officer, resulting in multiple arrests of what could only be described as some *very bad characters*. Haynes and two other officers concluded that, for safety reasons, a geographical move of a significant distance would be prudent. Agreeing with this assessment, their employer told them about job openings in the Roaring Fork Valley of Colorado.[134]

Haynes was pursuing a deputy position with the Pitkin County Sheriff's Department, so here he was, ready for his job interview. Parking his Jeep on North Galena Street, he glanced at his watch. It was 11:40 in the morning. For a man arriving for an interview, he wasn't nervous. Besides, with an escaped felon loose on the streets, he was doubtful that the sheriff would have time for their scheduled meeting.

Although Haynes, twenty-three, already had a bachelor's degree in criminal justice and had attended the police academy in Missouri, he knew he'd have to repeat the latter job requirement within a year if he was hired by Dick Kienast. Spending six or seven weeks at the academy in Golden would be a small price to pay for landing a coveted position in one of the nation's premier resort towns.[135]

Haynes crossed the street to approach the courthouse's western flank. He knew he was to report to the basement offices of the two-story brick structure. He walked down a short flight of rough stone steps to the sheriff's department.[136]

Once inside, it didn't escape his attention that this small town was knee-deep in crisis mode. Secretaries were cradling the handsets of their telephones between their collarbones and their jaws; their hands were busy flipping through Rolodexes and reams of handwritten notes. One woman had spun around too many times, causing her coiled phone cord to wrap awkwardly around her neck and shoulders. Somebody was asking about dogs. Someone else was calling Sardy Field, while another appeared to be asking one caller after another to *hold, please*. The five clear plastic line buttons near the base of the faceplate were all flashing in discord. Plenty of folks were calling in. Important conversations seemed to occupy every nook and hallway. Somewhere, amid this cacophony of energy and sound, he heard the name of the fugitive.

Who's Ted Bundy? Haynes wondered.

After checking in, the job applicant was directed to Kienast's office in the northeast corner of the basement.[137]

The sheriff was wearing a sweater vest and glasses. He never wore a uniform, never carried a gun, and rarely displayed his badge. He didn't have to identify himself to the members of his community. They knew him well. The sheriff was studying a map of Colorado on his office wall when Haynes darkened his doorway.

"Bad time," the sheriff remarked to his guest, stating the obvious.[138]

"Yeah...I'm getting that," Haynes replied. Even though the Missourian was a smoker, he marveled at the sheer number of unfiltered Camel cigarette butts in the sheriff's ashtray. Kienast smoked two packs a day.[139]

◆

Over at the Walnut House Films office, the shop owner was hard at work. Armed with the negative image that had been taken of Bundy, he began the process of making a usable print in his darkroom. Once the negatives were dry, he switched on his amber safelight and carefully placed the negative into a device that projected the image onto a piece of enlarging paper. The enlarger lamp was turned on, exposing the paper to the projected image. Fifteen seconds later, the paper was placed into a developer tray. He watched quietly. The positive image gradually appeared in the liquid—the turtleneck, the corduroy slacks, and the variegated sweater—Ted Bundy in black and white.[140]

◆

Deputy Bob Braudis trotted up the stone stairs to the front entrance of the courthouse. He needed to get rid of his rugby shirt and replace it with a uniform. He headed upstairs and peeked into the courtroom. Off to the side, someone had ensured that the fugitive's box of legal paperwork was sealed, waiting for his return.[141]

Heading downstairs in search of a more appropriate shirt, Bob thought about how there had been warning signs even while ol' Ted was still in their custody.

Braudis had enjoyed working the day shift, living up to the road warrior's unofficial motto: *look good, drive fast, and save lives!* All of the first-year rookies, however, had to rotate through jail duty: transferring prisoners to the courthouse, guarding defendants while court was in session, and returning them to the Garfield County Jail.[142]

The deputy had found Bundy to be quite charming, even during their lengthy prisoner transfers. Bundy had even asked Braudis for a favor.

"Could you spare any topographical maps of the mountains surrounding Aspen?"

The deputy didn't reply but offered a crooked grin. Braudis then glanced at his rear-view mirror. The image reflected in the cracked mirror was Ted, the merry prankster, who continued the conversation.

"Any chance you could go to the library," Bundy said, suppressing a smile, "and get me a copy of Harry Houdini's biography?"

"You know," Braudis had said, knowing the prisoner was a flight risk, "The First Amendment says you have the right to a free press, but no way am I going to give you Houdini's life story to take to your cell, and maps on how to get outta here. No way."[143]

Bundy had merely laughed.

For the past few weeks, Braudis had been working the graveyard shift. Since there wasn't a lot of action occurring in the dead of night, he had spent his time studying the documentation concerning Ted Bundy, even reading a psychological assessment written by Dr. Al Carlisle of the Utah State Prison. Braudis had come to a prophetic conclusion concerning their prisoner. *If he has the incentive to escape, he will.*[144]

◆

The photographer ran north on Galena Street toward the courthouse. Tucked under his arm were the prints developed in the darkroom at Walnut House. He had black and white photographs that showed exactly what Bundy looked like that very morning. There could be no better description of the fugitive than a current picture.[145]

The photographer rushed the prints to the sheriff's office. The courthouse was the only place in town that had a large copy machine. There, on the second floor of the building, flyers would be created utilizing the prints the journalist was handing over to the sheriff's office.[146]

Beside the Xerox machine, a court clerk glanced out a window. She could see a group of volunteers assembling on the lawn behind the courthouse. It was a scene right out of an old western; men were arriving bearing shotguns and old M1 carbines. These weapons were standard ranch rifles used to control the coyote and bobcat populations. If they were good enough to be used for hunting varmints, they were good enough for a manhunt.

"The Keystone Cops ride again," she whispered.[147]

Weeks earlier, the clerk had been standing in this same place when she realized that Bundy could jump out this window. She mentioned this scenario to the chief investigator in the district attorney's office. The investigator had pressed for details and learned that Bundy regularly made photocopies in this hallway. Bundy always insisted on making his copies himself. The hallway could get pretty warm, so the window was frequently left open. The clerk realized that the defendant, unencumbered by chains or cuffs, could leap out the window. The investigator, believing the theory to be plausible, had passed along the information to the sheriff's department. Again, escape had been predicted. Bundy had just merely chosen a different window for his escape.[148]

◆

Just after noon, Deputy Braudis was appropriately attired and back in his Buick, heading south through town. Something caught his attention as he rolled to a stop at the corner of Galena and Cooper. Crossroads Drugstore was on the ground floor of the Independence Hotel, and it happened to be one of the few places in town where you could legally purchase a gun. There were dozens of women standing in a line that extended out the front door. They were there to buy firearms.[149]

Braudis called it in.[150]

◆

At city hall, the chief of police asked the city attorney if banning the sale of guns and ammunition throughout Pitkin County was even legal.

"Just close the gun stores," the attorney said. "I'll find some justification."[151]

"Aspen to Glenwood, sixty minutes," Nancy was on the phone, reporting a lengthy laundry list of driving times. "Aspen to Carbondale, forty-five. And thirty minutes each for Aspen to Basalt, Snowmass Village, Woody Creek, or Aspen Village." There was no true interstate highway, no multi-lane byway that could help speed motorists to their destinations. Highway 82 was just a two-lane paved road, now choked with various barriers to progress. "No problem. Thank you for calling."

"East Sopris," Carolyn said, reaching for her ringing telephone. She was reminding her supervisor that they still had one major strand in their spider web to create.

"Aspen Dispatch. This is Carolyn. How can I help you?"

"We need more people," Nancy whispered in response.

"I see," Carolyn said to the caller. "Please hold." She turned to Nancy with a look of disbelief. "The Lord works in mysterious ways. Line two."

Nancy punched the blinking button at the base of her phone.

Six Days in Aspen

"Aspen Dispatch," she said. "This is Nancy. How can I help you?"[152]

It was a reserve deputy. He had been at the shooting range near Basalt when he heard the news. He was presently on Highway 82, near Wingo Junction and the Lazy Glen Trailer Park, wondering if he should come in. Baxter paused and then gave Carolyn a thumbs up. She began describing a perfect spot for the man to stand post. It was halfway between a roadblock at West Sopris and the Old Snowmass Conoco. There was a particular intersection that had a small bluff on the righthand side of the road. If he could back his rig in and just tuck it behind the bluff, no one could see him, but he'd be able to see for miles. The deputy interrupted Baxter before she could finish describing the spot.

"I know *exactly* where you mean," he remarked. "I'll head there immediately." He hung up, anxious to contribute to the team.[153]

Nancy just smiled. The reserve deputy had his dog, a radio, and a weapon in his truck. She calculated how long it would take him to get to the little side road on East Sopris Creek Road. She knew the sheriff would appreciate an extra set of eyes in that huge valley. Only a handful of people drove out that way during the off-season. This reserve deputy would be able to spy the dust trail of a getaway car from quite a distance.

"Perfect timing," she said to Carolyn. "Let's have a celebratory smoke." Nancy felt confident that their web was in place. Working with the sheriff and Detective Sergeant Garms, they had managed to shut off any possibility of someone getting past law enforcement in a car without some type of encounter. She reached for her pack of cigarettes.[154]

♦

The house-to-house search in the Mountain Valley neighborhood was still in progress. The task was being hindered because anxious seniors were hesitant to open their doors to people who didn't look like cops. Officers in Aspen had been allowed to forgo traditional police uniforms in favor of denim jackets and Levi's.[155]

When Dave Garms received a stack of flyers with a black and white photo of the fugitive, he drove back to the house of the woman who had seen a man peering over her fence. Confronted with the photograph, a snapshot taken only hours earlier, the witness shook her head and stated it was *not* the man she saw. The house-to-house search was terminated, and those officers began to be reallocated.[156]

♦

Northwest of the airport, Deputy Carol Kempfert stepped out of her station wagon. At least two other coworkers were already on the scene, and, thankfully, things were running smoothly out here. Earlier, when she had shown up at the sheriff's office looking for an assignment, she had encountered an environment that could only be described as pure pandemonium. Looking for one of the sergeants in the crowd, she bumped into Deputy Murphy. An awkward silence prevailed for a moment as Murphy had been one of the deputies who had transported Bundy from Glenwood Springs to Aspen only a few hours earlier.[157]

"I should have listened to you," Murphy whispered. "All the way back up here...he was rubbing his hands."[158]

Even before heading to the Garfield County Jail this morning, Kempfert had offered some advice to her coworker.

"If Bundy's hands are calm," she began, "he's pretty calm. If he's clenching them, he's planning something. When he's rubbing them, like he's putting lotion on them—*watch it*. He's up to something."

Kempfert searched for words of encouragement. Finding none, she watched Pete walk away and disappear around a corner. Bundy had been rubbing his hands, betraying the fact that he thought he was getting away with something.[159]

Reflecting on that uneasy encounter, Kempfert slipped a half-empty pack of Marlboros into her shirt pocket and reached for her radio.[160]

"Aspen, 7-2," she called in to dispatch.[161]

"Go ahead, 7-2," Nancy replied over the airwaves.[162]

"I'm 10-23, Brush Creek and 82."

"10-4, 7-2."

Nancy was pleased, knowing what Carol brought to the intersection—her memory. When Bundy was first transferred from the Aspen Jail to Glenwood Springs, it was Kempfert who manned the wheel. She had worked with Dave Westerlund that day, and the two deputies had placed Bundy in the requisite belly chains, handcuffs, and leg irons. The prisoner had ridden in the shotgun seat right next to Carol. She could recognize the fugitive on sight and wouldn't even need one of the flyers that were being delivered to nearly every roadblock.[163]

◆

Charles Leidner, one of Bundy's lawyers, had returned to Glenwood Springs and was walking toward his office. What a morning. On top of all the chaos in Aspen, he had been stopped at the Castle Creek Roadblock and was asked to exit his vehicle while it was searched. Farther down the road, the attorney found himself stopped at the Old Snowmass Conoco Roadblock. As before, he was asked to exit the vehicle while the trunk was popped, and a proper search of its interior was made. He was stopped a third time at the Catherine Store and, by now, had grown weary of the multitude of barriers between him and his desk. As soon as he walked into his office, he was flagged down by his secretary.[164]

"There's a guy in the jail," she said. "He was just arrested. He wants to talk to you."[165]

Leidner walked over to the county jail where two men were behind bars, charged with possession. The attorney asked how he could be of service.[166]

The tall, muscular man had been driving from Vegas to Detroit with his buddy. They spent last night at his sister's house in Carbondale. This morning, they found themselves sitting in their dark blue sedan, bumper-to-bumper, at the Catherine Store Roadblock. When deputies approached their vehicle, the lawmen noticed an aroma. The driver and his passenger were asked to exit the vehicle, and the trunk was popped. Deputies discovered 500 lbs. of marijuana. The two men were booked, and the weed was logged into evidence.

The muscular man leaned against the bars, closer to the attorney.[167]

"What was the name of the fugitive you guys were looking for at the roadblock?" he asked.

"Ted Bundy," Leidner replied.

"Ted Bundy," the prisoner noted and then repeated the name as if ensuring he could commit it to memory. "I sure hope you catch him because *I'd* like to talk to him myself."[168]

♦

At the Arapahoe County Airport, southeast of Denver, investigative reporter Ward Lucas donned a pair of sunglasses. He hadn't had the chance to change his clothes or call home to notify his wife that he was flying to Aspen despite his boss's denial of the assignment. An avid fan of aviation, Lucas had been taking flying lessons and already had sixty-five hours of flight time under his belt. Still, that was not enough to qualify him to fly over the Rocky Mountains.[169]

Walking across the tarmac by his side was Lloyd Coleman, one of only two cameramen who were willing to work with Lucas because of his reputation for covering controversial and dangerous topics on live TV.

They had started by exposing blatantly racist bouncers in Denver's busy nightclub scene. When that story proved to be popular with viewers, they moved on to more daring reporting.

Rattled by Ward's exposé-style of investigative reporting, the station's principal cameraman had warned others about shooting in the field with Lucas.

"Don't work with Ward," the man had advised. "He's going to get you in trouble."[170]

Coleman, however, handled the assignments without a hitch. Tall, thin, and clean-shaven, he had been a pilot with the Royal Canadian Air Force and was thrilled to fly out of Denver with Ward on this adventure. Coleman hugged his video camera as he boarded a Mooney single-engine airplane.

Lucas had no experience flying such an aircraft. He had typically flown Cessna 152s and, on a solitary occasion, a Cessna 150, a more complicated aircraft. He found his seat, buckled the belt, and considered his decision to disobey his boss. To reinforce his resolve and once again receive confirmation that he was doing the right thing, he recalled his days of reporting in Washington State.

The parents of the missing girls would call the KJR newsroom, wanting to speak to him. Lucas didn't want Colorado families to undergo the anguish he had witnessed with the Washington families.

The plane turned and began its journey down the runway. Thunderstorms had been predicted for the high mountain passes. The nose of the aircraft was somewhat heavy, so the pilot manipulated the yoke. Gaining sufficient speed to climb, the aircraft was soon airborne and banking west toward the highest mountain range in the nation. It was going to be a rough ride.

◆

Only two deputies physically intimidated Ted Bundy—Sergeant Davis and Deputy Braudis. At 6'5" and 225 pounds, Don Davis had ten years of law enforcement experience, and though he smoked like a chimney, he worked out regularly. It was not uncommon during meetings for Davis to suddenly drop to the floor and commence a series of push-ups, all while the meeting around him continued. He was an intimidating presence when he wanted to be, but deep down, he was a kind person. The sergeant would be genuinely interested in how you were doing, but if you wanted to get aggressive, he was more than happy to accommodate.[171]

Being physically able to handle the rigors of law enforcement can carry an individual far up the ranks, but Don Davis had much more to offer. He served as director of operations. If the sheriff was the head of the organization, then Davis was surely the legs. Even though the sheriff was legally and morally in charge of the entire manhunt, he was smart enough to take advice from his sergeant. The sheriff and undersheriff may take turns before the cameras and reporters, but behind the scenes, it was Don Davis making the primary decisions on behalf of the sheriff's department.[172]

Davis received bad news. His request for tracking dogs had met with a snag. Aspen Airways, not understanding the significance of the request, refused to have the dogs board the aircraft in Denver. Their policy clearly stated that all canines had to be secured within individual pet crates. As the flight from Denver to Aspen took off, the tracking dogs remained on the tarmac.[173]

♦

Officer Kathy Earl was riding shotgun in a patrol car while another officer manned the wheel.

"Refresh my memory," the driver asked, one hand on the wheel, one hand holding a Styrofoam cup of coffee. "How long have you been with us?"

"A whopping three weeks now," she replied, causing both officers to smile, given the fact that a manhunt was underway.

"Yeah, he said. "I noticed you're not armed."

Since Kathy hadn't attended the academy yet, she was not permitted to carry a firearm. She had been told she could direct traffic, handle non-injury car accidents, and help with liaison work; she just wasn't a fully-fledged officer until she graduated.

"They had me carrying a ticket book and chalking car tires," she chuckled as she glanced down at a stack of *fugitive flyers* in her lap. She held one up, to show to her fellow officer. "After he jumped, I was walking down the street, hearing all this commotion over the radio. I could tell that a lot of people were upset over something. I kept listening, thinking... *what's a Bundy?*"[174]

Piping hot coffee nearly shot out of the driver's nostrils as he laughed at the anecdote.

The Saab took a right onto Cemetery Lane. It wasn't long until Kathy spotted a line of cars, the result of the Slaughterhouse Bridge Roadblock. She looked down at the flyers in her lap. There was a black-and-white picture of the fugitive, an ordinary man in a cardigan. Whomever this joker was, she reasoned, her colleagues seemed genuinely concerned about getting him back into custody.[175]

The officers stepped out of their vehicle wearing the standard police uniforms of blue jeans and blue short-sleeved shirts with yellow aspen leaf patches on the upper arms. ASPEN POLICE was embroidered across each leaf. Even she knew, with her blonde hair and slim figure, she looked like she had stepped out of an episode of "Charlie's Angels."[176]

She and her partner delivered the flyers and took over the roadblock duties. All officers knew that this critical intersection was used by anyone attempting to head toward Woody Creek. Earl would lean into the car windows and inspect the occupants. As she went about her duties, she was given details about the fugitive who was set to go on trial for murder. She recognized the name of that poor nurse from Michigan, the one who had been murdered and left in a snowbank on the side of a road.

◆

At city hall, Nancy's mind was working overtime. Someone walking down the hall mentioned Caryn Campbell, and this name snapped the dispatcher out of her train of thought. She pictured an intersection just south of the airport along Highway 82. It was the turn onto Owl Creek Road, the very gravel-strewn road where Caryn Campbell's killer had discarded her body. Nancy had taken the call the day Caryn's body had been found in the snow.[177]

By turning at that intersection, one could gain access to the parking lot behind the Buttermilk Ski Area. By continuing up Owl Creek Road, one could wind their way up to Snowmass Village. But, adjacent to the Buttermilk parking lot, there was a smaller roadway called West Buttermilk Road. This splintered farther on into a multitude of subsidiary roads. Was Nancy missing anything? *No.* She believed she had that section of terrain covered by the roadblocks at Brush Creek Road and the Prince of Peace Chapel.[178]

◆

The private, single-engine airplane transporting Ward Lucas and his cameraman from Denver to Aspen experienced a sudden, turbulent elevation loss. The ground topography was breaking up the flow of the wind, creating powerful gusts that changed rapidly. This got the passenger's attention. Coleman appeared particularly nervous.[179]

"Could I take the controls for a few minutes?" Lucas asked. The pilot, who was Ward's flight instructor, wisely shook his head.[180]

Looking out the windows, Lucas and Coleman received terrifying glimpses of passing terrain. They were flying between mountains, with sheer canyon walls rising on opposing sides. There were clouds nearly everywhere. The pilot, fully rated to use instruments, was flying and navigating without them.[181]

Lucas stole a glance at the altimeter. They were just under 12,000'. Of the 100 highest summits in the Rocky Mountains, sixty-two exceed 13,000'. As they hit more turbulence, Lucas felt his stomach lurch—like a teen on a roller coaster.

◆

Colorado State Trooper Jim Loyd had moved from the Conoco Roadblock to the intersection of Highway 82 and Watson Divide Road. A two-door car was slowing down and approaching his position. *What the hell kind of car is that?* He raised his left hand, signaling the driver to stop. The silhouette of a lone male driver was visible. Loyd, holding his shotgun in the port arms position, cautiously approached the driver's side door. A shaggy-haired man behind the wheel rolled down his window.

The trooper looked the man over and knew he didn't have to ask for identification. The driver was handsome, with an athletic build, a ready smile, and a helmet of blonde hair that was the envy of every regional news broadcaster. Loyd recognized him as a former senior detective of the Aspen PD. These days, this man served as the police chief for the town of Vail.[182]

"Please step out of the car," Trooper Loyd said. "I need to check the trunk."[183]

The smile on Chief Wall's face slowly dissipated, and he declined the trooper's directive.

"We've got a problem here," Loyd said.

"Well," Chief Wall remarked, "I'm not going to let you in the trunk."

Loyd paused. What earthly reason would cause a law enforcement officer to disobey a legal directive? Was there something back there? Was it Bundy?

"Sir," Loyd said calmly yet firmly. "I realize who you are, but I am going to arrest you if you do not allow me to do my job."

As the chief of police, Wall knew that Loyd could legally have him arrested. He knew there was a fugitive on the run and was certainly familiar with standard operating procedures at checkpoints.

The trooper was desperately trying to read the driver's face. What was he hiding back there?

Is this a test?

"Well," Loyd finally said to the chief. "I'm calling for a tow truck, and we're going to tow your car." He radioed dispatch, adding, "Driver is by himself. He's not going to allow me to view the trunk of his car, and I will have him in custody here shortly." This transmission was overheard by a sergeant who was driving his patrol car on Highway 82.

"Jim?" the sergeant's voice was heard over the radio. "Hold on a second. Who...*who* did you say you are about to arrest?"

"Gary Wall," Loyd replied. "Chief of Police, Vail, Colorado."[184]

"Um, Jim. Can you stand by for just a little bit? Cause we're about fifteen minutes away."

Oddly enough, the chief stood near his car without incident while Loyd searched other vehicles and permitted them to pass. As promised, a lieutenant and a sergeant pulled up in a patrol car. They emerged, and the looks on their faces said it all: confusion mixed with slight irritation.

After Loyd explained the situation, the lieutenant stepped closer to Chief Wall, who was holding his car keys in his right hand. The lieutenant was from the town of Eagle, had dealings in Vail on an almost weekly basis, and personally knew the chief. Still, he couldn't decipher the man's intent.

"Trooper Loyd here," the lieutenant addressed Wall, "is, by rights, able to do what we're about to do. Give me your keys or open your trunk. You know me."[185]

"No," Wall replied. "I'm not going to let you guys get in the trunk of my car."

Lieutenant Wood took a step closer and spoke much slower, locking eyes with Wall.

"Give me the keys to your trunk. That way, we won't have to arrest you and take you to jail."

Nothing.

The lieutenant grabbed the keys out of the chief's hands and walked to the back of the car. Wall offered no protest. The key was inserted and turned, and the trunk was opened.

Empty.

Lieutenant Wood closed the trunk, walked over to the chief, and handed him his keys.

"You're more than welcome to leave," he remarked.[186]

As Wall drove away, the sergeant and lieutenant seemed somewhat amused. Trooper Loyd, however, was unabashedly baffled. How much time had the chief wasted? It wasn't a typical lazy Tuesday, where maybe the incident could be passed off as a joke. A convicted kidnapper was on the loose. A man who was wanted for questioning in nearly twenty mysterious disappearances and homicides might be hiding in one of these cars. Why on earth did this bizarre encounter have to occur?

The lieutenant told Loyd to let it go and focus on the task at hand. All three troopers got to work inspecting the long line of cars that Chief Wall had contributed to creating.

♦

The idea that the fugitive might have had assistance during his escape gained traction when an employee of the Garfield County Jail talked to the press. She said Bundy hadn't carried any cash with him when he departed Glenwood Springs this morning.[187]

Then, there was the Daniel Kellum situation. Kellum, twenty-four, had been sentenced to a year in county jail for possession of stolen property. He and Bundy got along well, but the mystery began four days ago. Kellum had simply failed to report back to jail after a work-release job. Could he be an accomplice? Could Kellum have stolen a car, waited for Bundy, and then whisked him out of town before roadblocks could be erected? It was certainly an uncomfortable possibility.[188]

Authorities were rifling through the contents of Bundy's jail cell. There were loose papers, books, calendars, and a Filofax planner. A deputy thumbed through pages of this planner and stopped at the handwritten entry marked May 23.

"FBI," the entry read. "Now, what's a nice FBI agent like you doing snooping in a book like this? Best regards. Never again, Ted."[189]

♦

Nancy, the miracle worker in the dispatch center, was getting frustrated with Deputy Braudis. He spoke too slowly, and it was maddening to her. Ten different people could use the same radio frequency within a single minute. Streamlined communication was essential, and systems like ten-code greatly assisted all concerned. When Braudis took thirty to forty seconds to relay a message, he was hindering communications from other parties on the sheriff's dedicated frequency. *Spit it out, 6-2!* Baxter wanted to yell, referring to the deputy's number.[190]

Nancy realized she was walking along the razor's edge. She was ordering a lot of people around, sometimes without consulting with the chief of police or the sheriff. Baxter had been fired seven or eight times by the previous chief. Usually, after twenty-four hours, that man had calmed down and come to his senses. Nobody was willing to do what Baxter could do. She was continually rehired. She was barking orders so quickly today that her job might be in jeopardy once again. She was using her experience and her training. People were simply taking her directions. Her plan to seal up the exits out of town was working, but her nerves were getting a bit frayed.[191]

Nancy turned, breaking out into laughter when she saw Carolyn Hougland looking back at her cross-eyed. Carolyn was running on black coffee and Pall Malls. *Thank God for Carolyn, and God help us if Bundy gets out of town!*

Jean Zimmerman walked into dispatch to take over for Carolyn. Knowing that schools would be evacuated, Carolyn was planning to head home to be with her son and three stepdaughters.

Before leaving, Carolyn entertained Jean with some of the day's highlights.

"Over at the Aspen Inn," she began, "someone listing their name as T. F. Bundy rented a room. Management said it was a couple that had been there for several days. They checked out yesterday."

"Couldn't have been him," Jean nearly whispered, completely intrigued.

"No," Nancy interjected, "but Ted's got a younger brother. We're going to need to figure out how old that kid is and where he's been for the past twenty-four hours."[192]

"We got another call," Carolyn continued, "saying a *T. Bundy* rented a car in town earlier this morning. Don had Lorrie check it out, but it was just a regular guy—nothing to do with Ted. That raised a good point, though. We've got folks going through the records of all the local car rental agencies." Authorities didn't feel that anyone assisting the escapee would use Bundy's name, nor would the fugitive himself, but such a scenario had to be checked out.[193]

"Um...there was a pilot for Aspen Airways that called us from Denver. He'd flown a plane from Sardy Field to Stapleton this morning and thought he'd accidentally carried an extra passenger. He checked the flight manifest and, *boom*, sure enough, there had been an unidentified passenger aboard. He's back at Sardy now, so we sent one of the boys out there with a picture of Ted. Nope. Don't know who his mystery guest was, but it wasn't Bundy."[194]

"I tried to get Aspen Mountain Rescue," Nancy added.

"They wouldn't be able to help in an official capacity," Jean noted.

"I know," Nancy nodded. "They said they were not in the habit of trying to locate someone who wasn't interested in being found." Jean agreed and leaned forward, intent on hearing the tale her supervisor was spinning. "But one of the rescue guys—"

"Doc!" Carolyn called out over her shoulder. She was referring to a local dentist.

"Right," Nancy said. "He was at his office and heard over the radio that Bundy had escaped. He got really worried about his wife, so he called her and told her to lock the windows and doors. He just got home and saw that his wife had followed his direction, but…" Her voice trailed off for dramatic effect.

"She left her key *in* the lock on the front door?" Jean asked.

"Dangling out of the doorknob," Carolyn said, unable to contain her laughter.[195]

"Tell her about the ice cream," Nancy said while answering an incoming call.

"I didn't catch which parlor," Carolyn chuckled, "but there's a sign up at an ice cream parlor offering the Bundy Sundae. There's no cup, no toppings, and no ice cream. There's *nothing there*, just like Bundy's jail cell."[196]

Again, a round of laughter.

Nancy, still on the phone, cupped the handset and whispered to her friends.

"Ted's probably sittin' down at Hotel Jerome or the Cooper Street Pier, nursing a few cocktails while this zoo is unfoldin' around him."

After Carolyn left, Jean dove right into a mental exercise with her supervisor. It was one designed to help bring Jean up to speed on the current logistics of the manhunt and to help determine if Baxter had missed anything. Jean bombarded her friend with street names—avenues of escape—and Baxter was to reply with where Bundy would be stopped.

"East, out of town," Zimmerman intoned, "headed for Independence Pass?"[197]

"Crestahaus Roadblock," Baxter replied without missing a beat.

"Westbound on Gibson Avenue?"

DETECTIVE SERGEANT DAVE GARMS

"North Mill Street Bridge Roadblock."

"Meadowood Drive?"

"Prince of Peace Roadblock." The exercise would occasionally be interrupted by an incoming telephone call or radio request, but the ladies kept the game going for quite some time, confident it might reveal some small hole in the spider web that Bundy might be able to exploit.

◆

Around 2:00 p.m., the little Mooney aircraft that had carried journalist Ward Lucas and his cameraman over the Rockies touched down at the airport in Aspen. Due to the incredibly turbulent flight, both men were thrilled to depart the aircraft.[198]

Lucas telephoned his wife and filled her in on his plans. Getting behind the wheel of a rental car, he knew where to head first—police headquarters, surely a hub of activity.

◆

Three women wrapped up a meeting in city hall. Marta Steinmetz was working as a civil deputy for Sheriff Kienast. Betty Pfister was a highly respected pilot who had been contacting agencies to see about increasing the number of helicopters available for the manhunt. Betty Erickson, the city's civil defense director, had been trained for emergency operations and natural disasters. Ted Bundy fell somewhere in between. It was Erickson's training in emergency evacuation that was now in sudden demand.[199]

Throughout town, children of all ages would need to be safely transported from their schools to their residences. *How do we make that happen?* Multiple means of transportation and custody transfers would need to occur in waves. A message from the police, directing parents who could pick up their kids at school to do so, had already been aired over the radio. Housewives hurried down to the schools to pick up their young ones. Other folks, stuck at work and unable to retrieve their children, grew upset and made frantic phone calls to the school, the police, and even the radio station.[200]

In addition to the radio address, the parent-teacher association phone tree began to sprout. School administrators were directed to call ten predesignated households. The waterfall of communication that followed caused other parents to head for the schools. The only folks in town who possessed a pager were first responders and a select group of health providers at the hospital. Still, the PTA phone tree was proving successful.[201]

Based upon the plan devised by Erickson, Pfister, and Steinmetz, authorities from the schools were directed to call their bus drivers in early. Due to Bundy's escape, all students whose parents had to remain at work must be taken home via the buses. In this unusual environment, with a convicted kidnapper on the loose, an additional adult would be aboard each bus and serve as an escort—from bus door to front door. As an additional safety measure, the driver was not permitted to leave the vehicle.[202]

The plan was to send the older children home first, students primarily from Aspen High School. Following this wave, students from Aspen Middle School and Aspen Country Day School would be escorted home. Elementary schools would come next.[203]

Specialty schools were also folded into the city's plan. A few miles east of the Crestahaus Roadblock, along the road up toward Independence Pass, was the Wildwood School. This nontraditional preschool consisted of earth-covered domes filled with future artists and songwriters. The valley's oldest youth non-profit organization, the Aspen Valley Ski Club, had to be contacted as well. This alternative school, for students who desired a strong background in ski racing, was on the far western border of town.[204]

Eleven-year-old Heidi Braudis waited patiently outside Aspen Middle School for her mother to pick her up. She had enjoyed her day so far, having spent it with half of her fellow sixth graders on a field trip. Their bus had returned only a half-hour ago, but the kids were not permitted to reenter the school. Things seemed a little chaotic. Heidi learned a prisoner had escaped and law enforcement was involved in a manhunt. Her dad, Deputy Bob Braudis, was surely involved in the search efforts. *Cool!*

Heidi had skipped a grade, so even though she and her older sister were in the sixth grade, Heidi was a year younger than her sibling. Her sister had already left the school aboard a bus that would take her to their mom's house in Smuggler Grove, near the city limits on the eastern edge of town. Heidi had missed that bus and was now waiting for her mom as patiently as she could.

Although her dad was considered a new deputy, the sheriff's department was already becoming like a family to the Braudis girls. Heidi's mom and dad were divorced, but Sheriff Kienast ensured the girls were always welcome down at the courthouse. He was like a kind and funny uncle, filled with hilarious stories. It was a tight-knit group whose family crest was a shiny badge.

She heard a siren in the distance. She turned her head in the direction of all the commotion. A manhunt? Crazy.

Heidi normally took the bus, so it seemed strange to be returning home in a car. She felt bad for the members of the sheriff's office. Even the preteen understood that this could impact someone's job or, at the very least, make the department appear inept.[205]

◆

When Ward Lucas and his cameraman arrived at city hall, they were disappointed. A solitary officer was walking around outside the dispatch office. Everyone else was out assisting in the manhunt.

They walked down the street to the courthouse, and once there, Lucas approached a nearby deputy.

"Excuse me. Can you show me where Bundy jumped?" the reporter asked.

The lawman led them to the southwestern corner of the building.

"That's the window," he remarked. The deputy didn't have much information to offer other than the prints in the grass. There was something about the law library, lawyers arguing over the death penalty, and the leap itself. The reporters would simply have to do their best with what scant information they possessed.[206]

Lucas thanked the deputy for his time while Coleman readied his CP 16 video camera. The scene opened with an establishing shot of the courthouse window. Doing his best to fill in the blanks in the gripping narrative, Ward began reporting.

"Bundy jumped out of this second-story window at the front of the Pitkin County Courthouse this morning. He was scheduled for a court appearance and had been locked into the law library by sheriff's deputies while attorneys were arguing a motion to strike the death penalty."[207]

Coleman panned to the left, expanding the range of visibility. In a few hours, this footage would appear on television screens throughout Colorado and Utah.

"Witnesses say he left in a hurry. However, no one saw him open the window. And, he escaped—clean, in an unknown direction."

Ward Lucas wasn't the only journalist on the front lawn of the courthouse. One of the sheriff's secretaries was being interviewed near the base of the stone stairs leading up to the front door. She acknowledged that the department had been aware the defendant had been a flight risk and that a deputy was present when the escape occurred.[208]

Not long after Bundy had been incarcerated in the Utah State Prison, guards discovered a forged driver's license, road maps, and notes on airline schedules in his possession. Whatever escape plans he had been working on in the Beehive State were blocked, and he had been transferred to maximum security as a result.[209]

When pressed for the name of the deputy in charge of Bundy this morning, the secretary declined to provide that information. When asked how the fugitive managed to flee, she stated that this particular information would be released by the sheriff.

"Bundy is very dangerous," she added, "extraordinarily dangerous. Nobody should approach him."

The sheriff and undersheriff appeared behind her, and the reporter had the opportunity to ask two of the town's top officials for an update.

"This is an extremely dangerous man we're dealing with," Ben Meyers noted quietly. "Very dangerous." He added that Bundy was being hunted by sixty officers, deputies, and volunteers from six counties, and more personnel were due to arrive in the morning. The topic of potential hostages came up, and Dick Kienast nodded his head, recognizing this was a scenario he had considered.[210]

"Any man desperate enough to jump twenty-five feet," he remarked, "and risk broken legs and ankles is dangerous."[211]

"How could this have happened?" the reporter asked.

"I really don't know what happened this morning in terms of the guard," Kienast said. "Basically, as I understand it, the defendant was in the courtroom, and the guard was at the door. The last time he looked, the defendant was there. The next time he looked, he was gone." Kienast snickered, clearly uncomfortable.[212]

"So, he didn't keep him in sight at all times?" the reporter inquired.

"Apparently not."

"Will he be disciplined for that?"

"I assume so."

Sheriff Kienast had known Bundy was a flight risk and had repeatedly requested that his prisoner be shackled in the courtroom. Fortunately, this was public knowledge. On the other hand, he was the sheriff, legally and morally responsible for the escape. The community spotlight had never shined so brightly on him before.

◆

Normally, the sound of a descending chopper—its rotor blades slapping the thin air of the high country—indicated a medical emergency. Today, however, witnesses marveled at how low these aircraft were flying, continually buzzing over town like aggressive honey bees.[213]

Deputy Braudis was aboard one of these choppers, a pair of binoculars in his hands. As he stuck his head out the window, the high winds ripped his expensive Vuarnet sunglasses right off his face. He turned to the pilot in mild embarrassment. Both men smiled.[214]

The thunder of the helicopter filled the air as it ascended the valley. A broad, arching turn, and then, it shook its way back down.

◆

Sergeant Horan was parked at Sardy Field, waiting for the plane with the tracking dogs to arrive. A deputy was in a separate vehicle parked directly behind him. Both agencies had provided drivers to transport the dog handlers and their specialized canines to the courthouse.

Rocky Mountain Airways was transporting the dogs since an initial airline had not allowed them onboard. This time, to avoid rejection, the canines were listed on the manifest as guide dogs for the blind. They all loaded aboard a nineteen-passenger de Havilland Twin Otter STOL. No kennels required.[215]

Soon, Sergeant Horan was watching the excited German shepherds leaping into the back seat of his Ford. He was grateful he wasn't driving a Saab. Introductions were exchanged between the sergeant and the dog handlers, officers from the Denver Police Department. Horan couldn't help but notice his guests were wearing big city uniforms and shiny shoes. Where were their hiking boots? Were these men prepared for the altitude and the terrain?[216]

The search dogs were finally delivered to the courthouse lawn four-and-a-half hours after the prisoner had escaped. Five were from the state capital, while the sixth had been discovered in Cherry Hills Village. The handlers had their animals on tight leashes.[217]

One of the men speaking with these handlers was Larry Spiers. He had been with the Jefferson County Sheriff's Department earlier in his career and recognized some of the officers from Denver. Kienast's predecessor required his deputies to wear cowboy hats and western shirts with pearl buttons as uniforms. Larry continued to adhere to this dress code, tipping his white Stetson as a sign of respect to the ladies who passed by the courthouse steps.

After Kienast's predecessor resigned from his position last August, Undersheriff Ben Meyers became the acting sheriff. Spiers had risen in the ranks to become a shift commander and got along well with Meyers, personally and professionally. Then, Dick Kienast had been elected. The two men had respect for one another but disagreed on the fundamental question of what it meant to be a law enforcement officer. Spiers resigned from his position and took a job as an electrical contractor at Highlands Bowl. Half a year after he'd handed in his notice, Larry was being called in to assist in the manhunt.[218]

Spiers had sworn an oath when he was commissioned as a deputy under the previous administration. That oath had been reaffirmed under Kienast, so it was not required now since Dick was still serving as sheriff. Ben Meyers had handed Larry his old badge and identification card, and that was that. Larry Spiers was back in the department. Now, with his revolver in his holster, he waited for an assignment.[219]

Deputy Gary White, carrying a Remington pump-action shotgun, ambled over toward the southwestern corner of the courthouse. He lingered beside a Civil War statue. White could see the location where Bundy had so forcibly landed. There were heel marks in the grass, an inch-and-a-half deep. From here, Gary observed the dog handlers discussing search patterns near a low iron fence on the front lawn. The deputy was soon joined by Sergeant Don Davis.[220]

White had been hunting and trapping for years and considered himself adept at reading various signs. He knew a fresh trail was better for tracking and discovering what you were looking for. He had never worked with search dogs before, but he had employed drug-sniffing dogs. Still, White knew the fugitive had been gone for a while and that the signs were getting older and fainter with every passing minute. *The longer we screw around here,* he was thinking, *where we know Bundy isn't, the higher probability we have of getting other scents mixed in with his.*[221]

Bundy had left his sweater behind in the courtroom. That garment was now torn into several pieces and handed to different dog handlers in small plastic bags. The officers permitted the canines to catch the scent.

Let's get going, White was thinking.[222]

Unlike in the movies, where the search dogs shoot off howling and tugging profusely at their leashes, the canines merely accepted the assignment and set to work. One explored the heel prints in the grass. *There it is!* He caught the fugitive's trail. The hunt was on.[223]

The dogs tracked Bundy's scent eastward, following the course that a couple of witnesses had reported seeing, along Main Street, to the alley behind the restaurant, and amid the trees of Herron Park.

Deputy White, Sergeant Davis, and two other deputies were following the dogs at a distance. They didn't want to disrupt the process. White felt in his gut that too many people were pinning their hopes on these canines.²²⁴

At the Neale Street Bridge, spanning the babbling river, the dogs suddenly lost the trail. Did Bundy enter a car at this point? A couple of the handlers even led their hounds across the water to the opposing bank.²²⁵

Nothing.

◆

Ward Lucas and his cameraman had made their preliminary taping from the courthouse and were wondering what to do next. Lucas decided to interview random people on the street.

"What do you think of the escape?" he asked multiple citizens. They didn't seem to be encountering anyone panicked or even remotely concerned. Flagging down cars, Ward asked the occupants what they knew of the manhunt. Many of the people he was interacting with hadn't even heard of the escape.

"Man," Lucas sighed in frustration, "they don't know who they have running loose around here."

Back when he was considered a cub reporter in Washington, Lucas had earned a pretty good relationship with law enforcement officers. He didn't carry a camera and only used an audiotape recorder to put folks at ease. He accompanied vice cops and homicide investigators out to grisly scenes that never seemed to lose their impact on him.²²⁶

Late one night, the reporter found himself sitting in a car with undercover officers outside a house in Seattle. Officers were interested in the '68 tan Volkswagen Beetle parked outside. Lucas wasn't sure whom they were monitoring, but Lynda Ann Healey—the first confirmed murder victim—had lived only a mile away. The reporter later learned he had been part of a stake-out, tasked with monitoring a suspect named Theodore Robert Bundy.²²⁷

◆

Deputy Maureen Higgins and her partner were working the roadblock at West Sopris Creek. One would converse with the driver while the other would monitor the situation, ready to contact dispatch should any emergency present itself. There was a radio in the patrol car, but each deputy carried a portable unit attached to their service belt. A coiled cord was attached to this radio, and the microphone was clipped to the breast pocket of their shirt. Higgins could hear progress reports on the manhunt over the airwaves.[228]

Most of the vehicle traffic Higgins was encountering were people she was familiar with, but not everyone was in a car. Some folks trotted by on horseback. Everyone was curious as to why the deputies were set up at the crossroads.[229]

The irony of being assigned to this particular rural setting had not been lost on her. She had been roused from slumber after working the night shift and was told to report back to the courthouse for an assignment. She had rolled out of bed, scooped up her bell-bottom jeans, and buttoned up her forest green shirt, slightly wrinkled from her previous shift. At least her badge and nametag were still pinned in place.[230]

In the driveway, she had climbed into her fiancé's Bronco. It was always unlocked, as was her home in Basalt. Her deep red hair blew in the breeze as she pulled onto the highway. It usually took thirty minutes to get to the courthouse from her home. Today, it had taken forty-five as she had been detained at more than one roadblock. After passing through all those barriers, she had been directed to man a post only miles from her front door.[231]

◆

The five o'clock news hour brought word of the escape to other states.

"Good evening," a news anchor began, "Convicted Utah kidnapper Theodore Bundy has escaped—*escaped*—from an Aspen, Colorado courtroom and remains, at this hour, the subject of a manhunt."[232]

A reporter who had been covering the Utah kidnapping case since the beginning had been dispatched to interview the chief detective for Salt Lake County. The reporter asked him what it was like to have Bundy back on the streets.

"Well, I'm concerned," the hard-nosed detective replied. "Concerned that this individual had been on the street. We'll, of course, take all necessary precautions with our witnesses who testified against him in our case here. And, of course, we'll assist any way we can with Colorado, to see that he's apprehended."[233]

"Are you worried that he might hurt somebody else?" the reporter inquired.

"Well, there's always this possibility."

Another reporter asked if Carol DaRonch, the woman Bundy had been convicted of kidnapping, would receive a protective detail.

"I'm not going to start such protection," the detective replied, "unless I know Bundy has left the Aspen area and is headed back here."[234]

◆

As the sun started dropping in the west, the rain started coming down. Searchers soon grew wet, weary, and worrisome. Morale seemed to be taking a hit, not just because of the damp conditions but what this meant for the search dogs.

"The rain washed it away," one of the handlers said regarding Bundy's scent. "Them dogs haven't got anything to sniff now."[235]

◆

A local ranch hand got wind that a posse had formed somewhere near the mouth of East Maroon Creek. If true, those posse members were on private property without permission. He decided he'd better investigate and drove toward the site. He'd barely heard of Ted Bundy until today. *This is one hell of a dangerous man.*

Now, as the rancher approached his destination, he found a roaring bonfire surrounded by men in boots, hats, and heavy wool, spitting tobacco and chugging cans of beer. Surveying the situation, he noted that both alcohol and high-powered rifles were present, and that could be a bad mix.

"You're on private property," the rancher announced.[236]

The silence that followed was broken by the crackling of the tree sap exploding in the fire. The assembled men looked at him like he'd lost his mind.

"We've been deputized," someone claimed. "We're gonna catch Ted Bundy tonight, and you'd best not interfere."

The rancher had adequately registered his complaint, but he offered up a final bit of advice.

"If you built a bigger fire, ol' Ted might be drawn to the flames like a killer moth."[237]

◆

The Holiday Inn and The Hickory House had offered to provide meals and beverages to the law enforcement agencies involved in the manhunt. There were hot meals in impressive portions, with a heavy emphasis on slow-cooked meats. Every available thermos had been gathered and tossed in the back of a car. The Hickory House would soon have them filled with piping-hot black coffee.

Betty and Marta had volunteered to deliver the food, drinks, and supplies to the various personnel in the field. They would start at the eastern roadblocks and work their way in a westward direction. The ladies would have to periodically return to the restaurants for the next supply run. What they didn't know was the precise locations of the roadblocks. Jean, at dispatch, was putting the finishing touches on a handwritten list of every checkpoint in and around Aspen. Officers and deputies were instructed to be patient as food was on the way.

The sheriff decided that roadblocks would be retained throughout the night. Roving patrols would be implemented on various hiking trails.[238]

The food and beverage deliveries took longer than expected, but Marta's yellow '67 Kaiser Jeepster Commando had no problems reaching the checkpoints, even on the steepest and muddiest of roads. Betty sat in the passenger seat, observing the steady rain in the headlights and listening to the music emanating from the cassette deck, co-mingled with the whine of the windshield wipers.[239]

They kept their eyes peeled for any movement along the highway. Was anyone broken down on the side of the road? Were there any spectral shadows sticking their thumbs out into the glare of the headlights, requesting a ride? Not that the ladies wanted to encounter Bundy in the darkness, but Betty was prepared if they did. Her gun was tucked into the right side of her vinyl upholstered seat. She had a spare revolver as well.

"You don't get to be my age without old friends," she laughed, referring to her firearms.

Right at ten o'clock, they heard Nancy's voice on the radio, going through the roster for the 2200-hour time checks.

"All units, Aspen, time check," she began. "6-2?"

"10-4," Deputy Braudis replied over the airways.

"6-6?"

"10-4," came Deputy Higgins.

Before the stroke of every hour and at the half-hours during the graveyard shifts, it was protocol to announce a time check. The dispatcher would call for all officers on duty. Everyone in the field had to be accounted for. This required check always started with the lowest number, which, at the sheriff's office, would be 6-0.

"X-1?" said Nancy, beginning the x-series, indicating Aspen PD detectives. And then, in one of the clearest displays that a manhunt was truly underway, the top of the pyramid was prodded for a reply.

"S-1?" Nancy inquired.

"10-4," Sheriff Kienast replied. Having the top dog in the field at this time of night confirmed the scale of the operation.

"All units accounted for, twenty-two hundred hours, KWV594," Nancy stated after going through the entire roll.[240]

Once the airwaves were officially cleared, Betty picked up her radio.

"Aspen, it's Betty. We are pulling up to the Old Snowmass Conoco Roadblock."

Deputies recognized Marta's bizarre-looking Jeepster and waved her over. Their hunger pangs led them to a logical conclusion. They left one man in the intersection to man the post while the other officers ate voraciously. In just a few minutes, they rotated positions.

There were only two more roadblocks to visit before the women could return to city hall. They headed south on Old Snowmass Creek Road for two miles before taking a right turn onto East Sopris Creek Road.

◆

At dispatch, Nancy was also required to check in with her counterpart in Eagle County—every hour on the hour. She switched radio consoles and hopped on the Colorado State Highway Patrol channel. Every law enforcement officer in the region had to be accounted for.

"Aspen, 1-18," came a man's voice on the radio. "I am also 10-8."[241]

Nancy understood that an officer had been out on a traffic stop and had forgotten to check back in with her as 10-8 when he cleared. If an officer was conducting a car stop, the officer or deputy had to check in with dispatch at least every three minutes. This was to ensure things were running smoothly. If the officer failed to check in, a request for a response was conducted. If this did not produce the desired result, dispatch would send reinforcements to the officer's last known location. A fugitive was on the loose, cold and desperate. Any car stop was cause for caution and adherence to policy. Nancy was looking forward to having Marta and Betty back. Coffee and cigarettes never sounded so good.

◆

Out on East Sopris Creek Road, the ladies in question ran into a problem. Marta and Betty were parked in the middle of the road, where the pavement intersected with a little dirt road that headed uphill. The windshield wipers and the idling engine were the only sounds. Marta had silenced the cassette tape. This was Nancy's final section of the spider web, the final plug that would prevent Ted Bundy from escaping the valley in a car. Off to the right was a tall bluff dotted with sagebrush and scrub pine. There was supposed to be a pickup truck hidden there. Where were the reserve deputy and his dog? The ladies looked around. Nothing, only dark and rain-drenched bushes.

"Where is he?" Betty said, looking at the directions Jean had provided her. Marta killed the engine and grabbed a flashlight. Illuminating the paper, she verified that they were at the correct spot. A reserve deputy was supposed to have backed up behind that bluff, with the front of his rig facing the road. No one approaching the scene from either direction could have seen his truck tucked in position.

The rain pelted the white vinyl top of the Jeepster.

"Something's wrong."[242]

◆

Officer Hugh Roberts entered city hall, dressed for a cold night on yet another graveyard shift. Unlike a handful of his coworkers, Roberts took the cold seriously. One night, the temperature plummeted to negative 39 degrees. He and other officers had been instructed *not* to shut off their patrol cars so that their vehicles would remain operational if needed. They were even issued duplicate keys so they could leave their cars parked with the engines running but securely locked. That had been a brutally cold night. Ever since, Roberts grew a beard in fall and maintained it until summer arrived, merely to ensure his face stayed warm.[243]

"Guess what happened?" a colleague across the room yelled to him as he entered the building. "Bundy escaped!"[244]

Roberts nodded. He had already been called in as soon as the escape occurred. His experience with weapons had been needed. After the troops were armed and deployed, Detective Sergeant Garms had cut him loose.

Crime within the town wouldn't cease just because a manhunt was underway. If anything, petty crime could rise, as folks knew the eyes of law enforcement were focused elsewhere. Officer Roberts and others were needed on the graveyard shift simply to handle the standard calls that came into the police department.

◆

Marta continued driving slowly along the long, straight stretch of East Sopris Creek Road. If they just kept going, they'd end up in the old township of Emma, now no more than a broken-down brick storefront façade and a few dilapidated farmhouses. There was nothing to see out here except clumps of sagebrush along the edge of the road. As they headed northbound, around a slight curve in the road, a man suddenly stepped into their path. Marta slammed on the brakes, sliding slightly in the mud. The armed man was walking toward them. He had recognized the unique Jeepster and had correctly guessed that refreshments were in order. Betty rolled down the passenger side window.

"Hello, ladies!" the reserve deputy called out as he sidled up to the car. He was wearing a broad Cheshire grin. "You sure are a sight for sore eyes. Not much happening back here. Was hoping the moon would be out, but looks like that ain't gonna happen tonight."[245]

Marta put it together. This was the missing reserve deputy. *What the hell is he doing here? This isn't even an intersection.* His rig was parked in someone's driveway. The dark gray silhouette of a private residence was visible through the rain.

The reservist kept talking, something about having no idea that when he volunteered his services, he'd still be manning his post at so late an hour. He graciously accepted their food and warmed his hands around the large thermos they handed him. He touched the brim of his hat, climbed into his truck, and offered one final wave goodbye.

No one mentioned that he had parked in the wrong location. Had he made a mistake? Or had Jean simply written down the wrong directions? They certainly didn't want to announce anything over the airwaves. There was only one more stop to make before they could return to dispatch to solve this mystery.[246]

◆

Over on the east end of town, Deputy Gene Flatt was waved through the Crestahaus Roadblock. With his windshield wipers working overtime, he continued driving eastbound on Highway 82 at a moderate pace. A couple of Eagle County Sheriff's deputies were waiting for him three miles down the road, and he didn't want to spook anyone with itchy trigger fingers.

Gene slowed down as he approached the turnoff to an unnamed dirt road that led to Difficult Campground. Here, deputies would be able to spy anyone coming up the road from quite a distance away without being visible themselves. It would allow deputies plenty of time to walk out onto the road, stand in the center of the two-lane highway, and flag down vehicles with their flashlights. There was no way to skirt this roadblock as the northern side of the road was bordered by large boulders and stately pine trees packed tightly into steep hillsides.[247]

Sheriff Kienast inherited Deputy Flatt from his predecessor, and the young man seemed far more conservative than the liberal lawmen Kienast wanted on his payroll. In marked contrast to the new breed of left-leaning road warriors, Gene was one of the *good ol' boys* from America's Heartland. He was known for pulling over motorists, even if they exhibited only the slightest hint of impairment in their driving.[248]

Still, Gene seemed to get along just fine with his fellow high-altitude deputies. He was an ex-Army serviceman, and his wife was a schoolteacher in nearby Basalt. Together, they served as caretakers for a home in the exclusive Starwood neighborhood. They lived across the street from superstar John Denver, and they were always willing to host friends at their home. Gene was appreciated for being a country boy, always eager to increase his skills. Plus, he always seemed able to take a joke at his own expense.[249]

Once Gene was in place, he notified Nancy, who then released the officers at the Crestahaus Roadblock from their duties. Their checkpoint was no longer needed, and the resources there could now be allocated elsewhere.[250]

The fugitive was out there, somewhere, amid peaks that stretched over 11,000 feet into the sky. The rain had been steady, and Bundy was surely soaked.

Deputy Flatt deliberately had his headlights off. Two Eagle County deputies were in another car just a few yards away. Gene manually clicked the windshield wipers on now and then. He didn't need them on all the time, and the constant movement across his field of vision could get monotonous, if not downright hypnotic. Sipping coffee from a Styrofoam cup, he settled in for an uneventful night.

Whump!

It was a loud, earthy sound that was hard to place.

Whump!

Whatever it was, it shook the car. He increased the wiper speed and switched on his headlights. There, right in front of his car, were two massive boulders that had dislodged from the steep hillside. He heard a car door close, followed by a rapping on his window. He rolled the window down.

"I don't know where the next one's going to hit," the Eagle County deputy chuckled.[251]

Gene was not amused. These weren't rocks. They looked just like the colossal-sized boulders seen in Saturday morning cartoons featuring

Wile E. Coyote.

"Aw...shit," he said. "Why do I get myself into these situations?"

◆

Close to midnight, Marta and Betty walked into dispatch, carrying trash bags filled with empty Styrofoam cups. There were plenty of brightly-colored Tupperware containers and thermoses as well. These would need to be washed before making the next meal run.

As they unloaded everything in the back of the office, Betty reached for the phone on the records desk to call folks over at The Hickory House. Their cook had stayed late to prepare meals for the guys up on Red Mountain, as well as for search teams that were scheduled to gather first thing in the morning. She still had to call a friend at the Holiday Inn as well, to give him a headcount before he left work. Who knew how long this manhunt would last?

Marta slowly unzipped her purple down coat, approaching Nancy in a way that betrayed the fact that she was the bearer of bad news. Both Jean and Nancy could read her body language and braced for whatever was to come next.

"That one reserve deputy with the dog?" Marta said while she unfolded the piece of paper she'd been given hours earlier.[252]

"Yeah?" Nancy replied slowly.

"Left at Old Snowmass Conoco," Marta began reading directions from the paper.

"Yes?"

"Up Snowmass Creek Road to the tri-intersection by Windstar Ranch. Right onto East Sopris Creek Road."

"Yes, yes," Nancy urged her to get to the point.

"Pass by Rose Spur Road on your left. Keep going about three football field lengths, and you should see his truck on your right, up against the knoll."

"Marta?" she repeated, this time in a raised voice, almost pleading.

"He wasn't there, Nancy."

Baxter could feel a knot in the pit of her stomach. "No. Please, God. No."

"How bad is it?" Marta asked.

Nancy turned to the console, intent on asking for the lone deputy's 10-20—his location.

"No need," Marta said. "We found him. He's just on a straightaway on

East Sopris, south of Maureen's position."

"Don't tell me that," Nancy said, slumping back into her chair and staring at a wall as if calculating something important.

"How bad is it?" Marta repeated.

It was as if Nancy hadn't even heard the question. She was sick—outright nauseous—and felt like running outside to scream up at the night sky. She remembered everything. That reservist had interrupted her when she was trying to provide him with directions to the intersection. She could hear his voice. *I know exactly where you mean. I'll head there immediately.*

"Fuck!" she shouted. "Do you realize what this means?" Closing her eyes, Nancy mentally retraced those back roads in rapid succession. Prince Creek Road, Highway 133, East Sopris Creek—that entire expanse of forested hills interlaced with fire roads.

"We might have let Bundy slip through our web. Sometime in these last..." She looked up at the clock on the wall. "Shit! Eleven hours? For over eleven hours, there's been an open 200 to 400 square miles of wilderness?"

Jean quietly nodded, agreeing with her supervisor's assessment.

"Well, what do we do?" Marta whispered. This seemed to snap Nancy out of her cocoon of guilt.

"Damn," she said. "I should have verified that idiot was in position. Jean...we've got the shift change in a few minutes. Pick one of the fresh deputies coming on and talk to him privately. Have him go out to wherever the reservist and his dog are and send them home for the night *with* our profound thanks. Have our deputy wait for a while, then have him go out to the *real* intersection and post up for the night."

"On it," Jean replied.

"I'll notify the sheriff," Baxter sighed. *This is awful*, she thought. *Why did I ever assume he knew where I meant? God, help us.*

WEDNESDAY

JUNE 8, 1977

CHAPTER 3
THE POSSE

The rain-soaked streets of Aspen were dark except for the reflection of the streetlights glittering across the asphalt. It was the dead of night, but Officer Hugh Roberts, a regular at The Bagel Nosh, was already looking forward to the end of his shift. That's where all the *good-looking chicks* liked to grab a quick breakfast. He approached a roadblock and rolled down his window when he saw two officers illuminated by his headlights.

"How are ya' doing?" he called out. "Anything going on?"[253]

"No," they moaned. They looked drenched and miserable despite their hooded jackets. Roberts was glad to be in his warm patrol car.

◆

On the other side of town, Officer Terry Quirk was battling exhaustion. He, too, was in a warm and dry Saab, only a few hours away from the end of his shift. After it was confirmed that a prisoner had successfully bolted and disappeared, city officers like Terry had been called back to work to help rectify the predicament. He'd searched for this elusive troublemaker all day along the trails bordering the river. Then, he had to go straight to his swing shift. He was now running on coffee fumes as he passed under the streetlights.

He couldn't help but compare his search efforts with those he had heard over the radio. That Mountain Valley neighborhood seemed *so hot* for a while. It was interesting just listening to the message traffic as the house-to-house search progressed.

Alone, he had combed through the trees and patches of ninebark shrubs. He loved hiking and had spent a lot of time in the backcountry, so the footpaths beside the river were an enjoyable enough assignment. The trails he had investigated were within walking distance of his home. While hiking the perimeter of Hallam Lake, where he had taken a break at the water's edge, he watched as a swarm of acrobatic swallows nabbed flying insects on the wing. The officer had spent hours searching wetlands, his surroundings a far cry from his years in Detroit.[254]

Based upon the scant information he had received at headquarters, he guessed that the fugitive would avoid the streets and head for the hills instead. He was aware of the jurisdictional issues, but if the sheriff could grant legal status to posse members, couldn't the same be said for city officers? Everyone had been too busy to ask these questions. The officer happily searched for the renegade on trails that were outside of his jurisdiction.

Quirk may have only been in town for seven months, but he had been a federal agent before he arrived in Colorado. He served as a criminal investigator in Michigan and received weapons training in Washington, D.C. He was offered a position with the DEA, but they wanted him to work undercover on the streets of New York City. *No, thank you.* President Nixon had frozen all federal transfers, and Terry found himself in a quandary. Stick with the feds or go local? He had been told that the resort communities in Colorado could be a little wild and crazy. Drug trafficking was on the rise, and cocaine was emerging as a controversial problem. These reservations aside, he and his wife packed their bags for Aspen.[255]

Folks in town kept their distance, suspecting the DEA might be paying Quirk under the table to spy on their idyllic little town. He felt like a lone wolf, trying to earn his spurs in the valley.

He hadn't paid much attention when Bundy had been extradited from Utah. The scruffy young man seemed to attract too many Salt Lake City reporters. For Terry, the fugitive was just another pseudo-celebrity prisoner.

We'll get him.[256]

◆

Nancy Baxter just sat at her desk in the dispatch office, tapping her pencil. She felt responsible for the confusion over the East Sopris Creek Roadblock. Had Bundy slipped through? If he had hitched a ride, he could be in Utah by now.

Bing!

An egg timer went off, snapping the dispatcher out of her latest fixation. She habitually set the timer on thirty-minute intervals throughout the graveyard shift so she wouldn't forget to do the half-hour time checks. Glancing at the clock, she saw that it was 2:30 in the morning.

Jean Zimmerman leaned forward, seized the timer, and burst out laughing. All the numbers on the dial were missing.

"What, on earth, happened to this?" she asked.[257]

Baxter had sprayed a strong detergent on the timer. When she wiped it down, she discovered that all of the identifying numbers had been erased. No bother. It was easy to determine where the thirty-minute position was, and the timer appeared to be working just fine.

The regular shifts for dispatchers were eight in the morning until four in the afternoon, four until midnight, and midnight until eight the following morning. There were normally two dispatchers on the first two stints, but there was only one lone dispatcher during the graveyard shift. That schedule had been thrown out the window as soon as Bundy had jumped out of one. Nancy was still the principal point of contact with the sheriffs in nearby counties. She continued scribbling in her logbook where each lawman was, crucial decisions that were made, and transmissions of importance.[258]

There was only one small space heater in the office, and there was a constant draft running through the room. Nancy wore long johns under her jeans and a white turtleneck under her uniform shirt, but even these precautions weren't enough to keep her warm.[259]

Folks in town listened to police scanners as a cheap form of entertainment. As a result, everyone had to be careful what they said over the airwaves. Dispatchers used the Ten-code system, the language used to communicate issues over the radio without alarming the public. 10-7 translated to out of service, 10-3 directed an officer to cease transmission, while 10-6 indicated one was busy but—standby.[260]

When Nancy completed the half-hour time check, she stood to stretch her legs, lit a cigarette, and inhaled deeply. Then, lost in thought, she let it hang down from her fingers. It felt good to stand.

If I were Bundy, she thought, *I'd sleep during the day and follow the river downstream toward Glenwood Springs. How fast could I run? How desperate would I be?* Nancy stared at a blank spot on the wall.

The lone space heater in the room just didn't seem to be cutting the chill. She shivered. *Caryn Campbell had been cold, dying in the icy mountain air—all alone.* Those incoming calls were burned into Nancy's memory. The first—the report of her disappearance. A month later—the discovery of her body in the snow. *In reality, Caryn hadn't been alone - her killer had been there.*

Nancy hadn't taken another drag on her forgotten cigarette, and the ash had continued to collect and smolder at its tip. Eventually, the long gray column of burnt tobacco fell, getting carried away in the draft flowing through the room.[261]

Across the room, Jean was working on indexing police reports. She'd pull the contact cards for any individual or location indicated in the report and add a CR#, date, and type of incident to each of the cards. Some establishments, like The Pub, had card after card clipped together due to a multitude of bar brawls over the years, while other individuals may have just a single entry. If an officer called in for any *priors* when a subject was detained, the dispatcher could quickly inform the officer about the subject's legal history.

Nancy returned to her typewriter, putting her headphones on but covering only her left ear. She began listening and transcribing an officer's recorded statement. She kept her right ear uncovered so she could still hear incoming transmissions on the radio.[262]

There was a huge reel-to-reel audio tape recording machine behind her, stretching from floor to ceiling. Gigantic magnetic tapes, thirty in a case, were stored in a cabinet nearby. Two reel-to-reel systems were operating simultaneously. If Nancy didn't understand a radio message, she could stop the upper reel and play it back, listening to the transmission again. The lower reels kept recording without interruption. Every call that came into the police station, the sheriff's office, the fire department, and all the radios were recorded and stored.[263]

JoAnne Rando was buzzed through the door. She had been called in to help pick up some of the slack. Bundy's escape had unnerved her more so than her fellow dispatchers. JoAnne couldn't quite say why.

"The bars in town are closing," she announced. They all knew what this meant: drunk drivers, fistfights in parking lots, and domestic disputes. These occurrences would certainly pull officers away when they should be focused on the manhunt.[264]

A man was buzzed into the office, armed with coils of telephone wire and years of experience. He'd been called in to make any upgrades he could—on the fly.

"Sorry I'm so late," he said.²⁶⁵

"Late?" Nancy kidded. "I was just going to thank you for coming in at all. Do you ever sleep, Dave? I'm just so grateful you came. It's been quite a day, and you're a welcome sight for sore eyes." He blushed and bent to install another line.

Nancy had worked with Dave before, drafting a grant proposal to upgrade the county's communication systems. Of principal concern were the various blind spots throughout the valley. Once a deputy was dispatched up into certain outlying valleys, like Maroon Creek or Castle Creek, radio transmissions could cut out. If that happened, a deputy was truly on their own, with no method of calling for backup. Months earlier, Carolyn Hougland, who was deathly afraid of heights, surprised herself by joining Dave on a helicopter ride. They flew over Red Mountain, scanning for locations to set up poles for repeater sites. These locations were chosen, but as of yet, these poles hadn't been erected.²⁶⁶

◆

Around three in the morning, Officer Chet Zajac was still rattling locked doors and peering into windows of vacation homes and rentals in the Red Mountain area. The rookie had a Remington Model 870 shotgun slung across his shoulders, so the weapon laid across his chest, bandolero style. If needed, he could just grab it, point, and pull the trigger. The shotgun was a new accessory presented to him yesterday by the department's firearms expert, Officer Roberts. Zajac didn't give much thought to the .38 in the pocket of his duster. The department-issued gun would barely *take out a squirrel*. He preferred the shotgun, even if he were to engage the fugitive at close quarters.²⁶⁷

At the moment, his eighteen-inch flashlight was his most useful tool. Long and narrow, it could be used as a baton if needed. He held the flashlight up to a dark window of a vacation home. He cupped his free hand and held it up to the glass, slowly sweeping the beam across the room. There was a twin bed, two nightstands with lamps, a dresser, and a chair. Nothing seemed out of place.

He had no issues with his assignment, but the steady rain was taking its toll on him. Mercifully, his feet were warm and dry. His duster was performing admirably, but the pantlegs of his jeans were soaked from scrambling through the brush. He had to do this to reach the various floors of these mountain homes.

Dispatch had assured him that someone was heading his way to feed all the officers on Red Mountain. That was good, as he was famished. Reaching the walkout basement level, he peered through more windows and checked behind a stack of firewood.

With the current residence inspection complete, Chet huddled down in a nook next to the garage for a few minutes. This had become his routine in the rain. He'd inspect a home, find a small spot out of the elements, and pull out his pen to check off the house on a real estate map. Then, he reported his progress to dispatch before moving on to the next house.

In contrast to Officer Terry Quirk, who had a beefy law enforcement resume and had been on Aspen's payroll for seven months, Officer Chet Zajac had no prior experience and had only been on the job for seven weeks. As a new officer, he was working four nights a week, which included weekends.

As a rookie, Chet's first thought when he was called in to join the manhunt was—*I'm gonna get whatever shit job they're going to give me.* This hunch had made him snicker. He knew he wouldn't be manning a desk in any tactical command center.

He usually wore a parka during the graveyard shift, but he figured he'd need something more substantial to guard against the wind and rain. He had stopped at a small thrift store before reporting to headquarters. There, he had purchased an authentic Western duster. Next, he drove over to Fast Eddie's, one of the most popular retail stores in town. It would be an insult to state it was merely a cowboy clothing store for the rich and famous. Here, Zajac purchased an 8X beaver fur blend cowboy hat. It was dark blue, which seemed appropriate for an officer of the law. A cowboy hat, a full-length duster, a gun on his hip, *and* a mustache—it was as if Doc Holliday had returned to Colorado.[268]

Seeing the headlights of a car approaching, he was pleased when he heard the tires crossing the uneven terrain of the gravel driveway. It was Marta and her legendary Jeepster. She stopped and opened her car door and umbrella in rapid succession. As the rain pelted her unfolding canopy, she trotted forward, cradling something in her arms.

"Hey," she called out to him. "How're ya' doing?" She was carrying a small cardboard box with a couple of sandwiches wrapped in wax paper. Chet was overjoyed when she also magically produced a soda can from her coat pocket. He hadn't even brought a stick of gum and was famished.[269]

At twenty-three, the tall, young man had caught the eye of some of the dispatchers. He lived in a trailer eighteen miles downvalley from Aspen. He had owned a karate school and had just graduated with a degree in criminal justice. Enjoying a healthy lifestyle, he declined Marta's offer of a cigarette.

"I stopped smoking when I was twelve," he laughed.

Marta had food to deliver to the other officers in the area.

Yesterday, six grown men had traveled to this area in one small Saab. The first two men climbed into the driver and passenger seats. The implausibly large collection of four remaining officers jammed themselves into the back seat, the barrels of their shotguns scraping unpleasantly on the windows until someone thought to roll them down.

As far as assignments go, this wasn't too bad. Searching properties in one of the region's most exclusive neighborhoods? Red Mountain homes were perched, some precariously, atop the highest knoll in Pitkin Green. With stunning, expansive views an everyday occurrence here, price tags on these residences continued to climb. From those spacious wooden decks, the owners could see from Independence Pass in the east to Mount Sopris in the west. Majestic Aspen Mountain was just across the narrow valley. Alpine paradise. At least, it was until the moisture-laden clouds decided to unleash their rain.

"You okay?" Marta repeated.

"Yeah, coach," Zajac replied with a wry grin. "Put me back in the game."

◆

Officer Hugh Roberts had parked his Saab and was now patrolling the streets of Aspen on foot. This was a pattern the officers on the graveyard shift would follow: drive around for a while, make your presence known, stash the car, and begin walking from bar to bar. Establishments were all closed now, but it was a good way to catch hippies smoking reefer or drunks fumbling with their car keys outside their trucks.[270]

Roberts walked quietly through the dark streets, wondering if Bundy had truly committed the heinous crimes that investigators claimed he had. *What would motivate such a man?* He mulled these thoughts over in his head but could only come up with one conclusion. Bundy had to be completely stark-raving mad, yet somehow be *passing* successfully amid his community. The officer had heard about the conditions of the bodies that had been discovered. *How could someone do that to a fellow human being...and* *then merely discard them like an empty paper cup?*²⁷¹

◆

The alarm clock at Deputy Gary White's house roused him from his slumber. Running a hand through his hair, Gary sighed deeply. Sleep had eluded him until two in the morning. Lighting a Winston, and after taking two deep drags, he walked over to the fridge and grabbed a bottle of Pepsi. *How long will it take to get down to the courthouse?* A posse was scheduled to form in an hour, and Gary wanted to be there early.²⁷²

He had never wanted to be a law enforcement officer. Four years ago, he was earning hefty paychecks by transporting dangerous chemicals across the Southwest. He would load sulfuric acid in El Paso, Texas, pass through Las Cruces, New Mexico, and deliver it to the copper mines back in the hills at Monarch, Arizona. At a truck stop in Las Cruces one day, he bumped into two friends, detectives in a local police department. While they were catching up, one of them mentioned that the next class for their police academy would be starting in three weeks and recommended that White apply. Gary could barely contain his laughter when he heard the suggestion.

"No, thanks," he finally managed to say. "I'm not really interested in doing that."²⁷³

Throughout that weekend, White made several more runs. He would crack up every time he thought of himself in uniform, keeping the city streets safe and secure. Each time, though, he noticed he was laughing less and less. *Why not me? It would mean a pay cut, to be sure, but it sounds interesting and challenging. I used to ride bulls for a living. Surely this would be easier.*

Before he knew it, he was enrolled in the academy. Classes were traditionally fifteen weeks, but there was a desperate need for officers, so the curriculum was compressed. Working fifteen hours a day, every day for seven weeks, he walked out the door wearing a badge. His superiors stuck a gun in his hand, sat him in a car on the graveyard shift, and said, "Go get 'em, kid!"²⁷⁴

That night, he prayed the radio would remain silent. He'd be answering scores of calls in the years that followed, from petty disturbances to fugitives on the run.

◆

Deputy Gene Flatt wanted to be a deputy from the time he was a small boy and lived his whole life, from childhood through his teens, with

NANCY BAXTER

that one goal in mind. After high school, he joined the Army and served a tour with the 2nd Armored Cavalry Regiment, providing border security along the Iron Curtain. It was the proudest day of Gene's life when he was hired by the Pitkin County Sheriff's Department. He was twenty-three.[275]

Freshly deputized, Flatt didn't know what to make of the first sheriff he worked under. One morning, Sheriff Whitmire demanded that all his deputies assemble in one room, whether they had worked the graveyard shift or not. He was angry, ranting and raving for two hours.

"You know!" he shouted. "I could fire every one of you sons of bitches right now. I can do it, and it will be legal, and not a damn thing you could do about it." As a veteran, Gene was no stranger to ass-chewings, but this really freaked him out. He'd been used to guaranteed military paychecks for years. His first civilian employer was now threatening his job. *Oh, Lord. I just got hired, and I'm gonna get fired.* Fortunately for Gene and his colleagues, no one got the axe that day.[276]

Sheriff Whitmire left office in early August of 1976. Dick Kienast ran for the position and won. Gene was surprised by the leadership style of his new sheriff. Right away, Kienast said, "Don't sweat the small stuff," which put the deputy at ease. Within three months, the sheriff had cleared out a considerable number of deputies that he felt were outdated or overbearing. He didn't want heavy-handed law enforcement but, instead, public servants who happened to carry badges.[277]

It seemed that the new sheriff was providing a kinder, friendlier work atmosphere for those who worked for him. Now, some folks in town were wondering if Dick Kienast had been too soft, and perhaps this had contributed to the recent escape.[278]

◆

Just before daybreak, officers were congregating behind the courthouse in what was called the lower lot. At one end was a small yard surrounded by a chain-link fence. Prisoners were brought here once a day to spend an hour in the fresh air. Behind this, there was a large, undeveloped tract of earth that sloped downhill toward the river. Along this steep grade were substantial piles of sand, silt, and clay that had recently been placed there by dump trucks. City workers would be using the dirt to fill in sections of uneven ground.[279]

Near sunrise, there were only twenty officers in this lot, but soon, volunteers began arriving in large numbers: forty, seventy, and then, the crowd swelled to 150. There were plenty of men eager to protect their families and their community, drinking coffee out of paper cups. Cowboy hats, shotguns, and more than one set of bandoliers were visible. Folks had heard stories of previous manhunts from their fathers and grandfathers. It was now their turn to be part of a real-life western posse, with the full blessing and legal authority of the sheriff.[280]

Nancy had walked down to the courthouse, running an official errand. She watched as the mountain posse formed. Trucks hauling horse trailers were pulling in, one after another. She flinched as a rancher dropped a rear ramp like a Higgins boat hitting Omaha Beach. There was a deafening thud that Nancy felt through the soles of her shoes. "Goodness!" she exclaimed as she stopped to watch the cowboy unload two large mares.

The horses tromped down the ramp, clouds of vapor flowing from their nostrils as they exhaled and snorted in the cool mountain air. Ranchers throughout the valley were volunteering their time and their animals. Six tracking dogs were already tugging on their leashes, ready to work.[281]

"Oh my God," Nancy said. "So many people coming out of the woodwork." She bit her lip as she saw Sergeant Darrel Horan walking her way.[282]

"Morning," he said, nodding at her.

Nancy returned the greeting. She leaned in close, took a deep breath, and told him that there had been a gap in the checkpoints. Bracing herself, she waited for his reaction.

"It's okay," he said, seeing that she was tormented by the mistake. "There's no way Bundy could have made it that far on foot during that timeframe."

Nancy shoved her hands into her coat pockets. She couldn't help but wonder if the fugitive had an accomplice. Desperately hoping he had injured a knee in that incredible jump, she recalled the credible witness sighting of the fugitive running full speed down an alley. *No, there's nothing wrong with Bundy's legs.*

The Aspen Airport manager, an avid horseman with connections up and down the valley, had sent out a call for reinforcements. Many experienced ranchers were here in response to his call for assistance. The involvement of these men was greatly appreciated, especially since Garfield County Search & Rescue was busy fishing out a truck that was stuck in the river near Glenwood Springs.[283]

Although Aspen Mountain Rescue was not officially responding to the manhunt, several of its members volunteered to join the posse. They knew the terrain very well and were happy to help their community.[284]

Volunteers mingled with members of the Pitkin County Sheriff's Office, their reserves, the fire department, the city police, and even the state patrol. Sunburns and five-o-clock shadows marked the men who had volunteered their time to the manhunt the day before. The mood among the posse members was positive.[285]

The Silver King was a hot topic of conversation. It was a sprawling, middle-class apartment complex at the foot of Red Mountain that many of the officers and deputies called home. There were some vacant rooms, and the doors could be jimmied with a simple credit card. Everyone knew this. There were plenty of places for a fugitive to lay low.[286]

High-ranking members of the Aspen PD debated over which destination their quarry had in mind. Independence Pass? Not a chance. It wasn't just the steep terrain. A man on foot, making his way up toward Twin Lakes, would be exposed for significant portions of his journey. Helicopters were out, and neighboring agencies were on the lookout for the man. The river? Yes, the river was safer, and it afforded more methods of concealment. If there were no accomplices and no vehicle, Ted would most likely be following the river.

The sheriff's reserves were included in the posse, and they would answer to Undersheriff Ben Meyers, a husky man whose brown hair partially hid his eyes behind square glasses. A man of few words, he spoke privately with the captain of the reserves.

The captain was a member of the Snowmass Ski Patrol. This volunteer, who routinely looked for lost souls in need of rescue, was now being tasked to search for a man who didn't want to be found. The officer stepped forward to speak to the crowd.[287]

"First," the captain began, "let me say that unless you are licensed to carry a gun, we want you unarmed."

"I ain't afraid of him," came a voice from the crowd. "I can take care of myself."[288]

"Check each house," the officer continued, ignoring the comment, "particularly if they appear to be vacant or open. If occupied, knock on the door and ask those inside if they would like you to check their house. Don't try anything on your own. Get in touch with the officer nearest you."[289]

"What about the FBI?" a reporter called out.

"I've spoken with the feds," Meyers replied curtly. "If ol' Bundy remains on the run after sundown, they'll issue a federal warrant for his arrest."[290]

It was announced that deputies would be required to work sixteen-hour shifts. Schools were closed for the day, and the recommended buddy system remained in effect. The ban on the sale of guns and ammunition also remained.[291]

When the captain completed his instructions to the posse, the reporters turned their attention to a secretary from the sheriff's department.

"We've had no new leads," she confessed. "Nothing at all to indicate where he might be. We do believe he's still in the area." When reporters implied that the sheriff was to blame for the botched security measures, she noted, "Courtroom security has always been a matter between the district attorney and the judge. We were not allowed to have him in handcuffs once he was in the courtroom. We always have considered him a security risk. Never, *ever*, has there been a specific warning, or even an indication, that Bundy would have tried to escape. Had there been, we certainly would have taken extra precautions."[292]

A journalist leaned in. "What about Sergeant Kralicek and Deputy Westerlund? They were directly charged with the defendant's custody."

"We believe," the secretary sighed, "that would be futile. Those persons have been searching harder and longer than anyone else."

"If he had access to the library here," one of the volunteers nearby remarked, "and I think he did, he had access to maps. With maps, a man can go twenty miles a day."[293]

Behind the courthouse, Detective Sergeant Garms reigned in a group of volunteers that had been assigned to him, twenty men in all. At least half of these had numbered Nordic racing vests over their shirts or jackets. The detective approved of the bibs, as they'd be visible at great distances, and this would cut down on the chances of searchers being accidentally shot.[294]

Garms and three other officers all took a knee while the rest stood so the group could all see a large map spread out on the ground.[295]

Most of the officers were garbed in the *Hershey uniform*: light blue shirts, denim jackets, and traditional jeans. Former Chief of Police Marty Hershey had promoted the idea of dressing more casually, and this trend remained after he left the department.[296]

Groups reviewed their assigned search sectors for the morning, making sure that teams didn't accidentally cover the same terrain. Seeing a somewhat cavalier attitude on the part of several of the men, Garms reminded them of the seriousness of the operation. They were after a very dangerous character.[297]

♦

Officer Kathy Earl was walking south along Mill Street. She was on her way to the police station a bit early, but she wanted to grab her gear and begin her shift writing parking tickets. She worked a steady Monday through Friday, and though she didn't have an assigned quota, Earl knew how many times a day she could make her rounds and how much revenue she could generate. The sheriff's office and city police were racking up overtime hours due to the manhunt. Someone had to pay for those extra hours.[298]

Officer Earl knew she fit the offender's type, but she wasn't worried. If Bundy were still in town, he would be trying to avoid officers, and Earl's distinctive uniform was easily identifiable from a block away. Unlike other women in town, Earl had a radio which, at the first inkling of trouble, she could use to call in her *big brothers* from the city police.

Even during her off-duty hours, she wasn't overly concerned for her safety. At the base of Red Mountain stood a Victorian home that housed the Ticor Title Company. If the young couple cleaned the interior spaces each weekend, could they live in the house's attic? The owner readily agreed. Earl was either in the company of her boyfriend or hidden away in the garret of the century-old residence, safe and sound.

She suddenly had to suppress a smile. Behind the courthouse, she saw the sheriff's posse. Deputy Gary White looked as if he had stepped out of a painting by Frederic Remington or Herbert Dunton. Boots, blue jeans, and a colorful—almost garish—long-sleeved shirt. In one hand was a rolled-up piece of paper. In his other, a shotgun. There was a shoulder belt that wound from his right shoulder, down and around his left hip, the bandolier containing a dozen cartridges. Above his bushy mustache, White's eyes were hidden behind a pair of sunglasses. On his head was a weathered yet respectable felt bush hat. He was smiling, more than happy to hunt down a dangerous criminal.[299]

Officer Earl watched as men on horseback fanned out from the courthouse. She was a self-proclaimed beach girl from Southern California and had never seen a mounted posse before. She watched as the horses trotted down the street. It all seemed surreal. *Wow! A real-life sheriff's posse in the American West.*[300]

◆

Officer Terry Quirk walked out of the city council chambers on the second floor of city hall. He considered the meeting he had just attended to be a waste of time. It had been led by a couple of the sergeants, but they seemed to be in a hurry to get outside and join in on the action.[301]

Terry wasn't overly excited about another day on the job. After his graveyard shift had ended, he had only managed a couple of hours of sleep. Resources for the manhunt were needed, and he felt like an exhausted cog in the greater machine.[302]

When he emerged outside, he looked longingly at Little Cliff's across the street. There was no time to stop in for a donut. The roads were quieter than usual, and he wondered if some folks were hidden at home. Terry knew people were frightened.[303]

Soon, he was standing near his car at a trailhead near the Slaughterhouse Bridge. The plan was to search the Rio Grande Trail on foot and, upon reaching its terminus at Puppy Smith Street, radio dispatch. They would ensure an officer picked him up and returned him to his vehicle. He would then proceed to another trail, and the cycle would continue.

Quirk started walking eastbound along the trail, tracing the banks of the Roaring Fork River. Off to his right, the water was babbling by at the bottom of a fifty-foot hillside. Contrary to the usual noise and chatter on the city streets, he was now exploring the peaceful valley floor, surrounded by the whir of broad-tailed hummingbirds.

He wondered how far a man could get wearing a pair of brown loafers. Several of his fellow officers thought Bundy had been wearing his Utah state penitentiary-issued boots when he jumped. No one could say for sure what kind of shoes the fugitive had been wearing. Ironically, the photo taken of Bundy entering the courthouse failed to show his footwear.[304]

The path ahead wound its way through the cottonwood trees. *Could Bundy be hiding behind one? Was he crouching behind some sagebrush?*

◆

As the sun continued to climb, Sergeant Darrel Horan was noticeably bareheaded among a sea of cowboy hats. He knew the hats fell off too easily when you were wrestling with a drunk or chasing someone down an alley. He had already lost an expensive silver Stetson. Accompanied by two other officers, Horan would scout the Rio Grande Trail above the crystal-clear waters on the far side of the footbridge.

For the most part, large groups were heading up Smuggler Mountain. There was a lot of peat bog up there and a host of old mining cabins—plenty of places to hide. Still, Horan didn't believe Bundy would head that way unless he knew the area well or was with someone who did. Word had spread that the fugitive had asked deputies a lot of questions concerning the mountain during exercise periods behind the courthouse. There was a government trail that ran across the top of the mountain, extending over to Independence Pass and then down Deadman's Ridgeline. The sergeant knew Bundy was not dressed for such a journey, but everyone had believed twenty-three feet was too high for a prisoner to jump.

Anything was possible.[305]

♦

At the corner of Monarch and Hyman stood the Crystal Palace, a two-story, red brick building that was the town's famous dinner theater. On the second floor, above the cigar mural featuring a large owl, employees stopped working when they heard a commotion outside. Like a mob of Meerkats emerging from their burrows, they popped their heads out the window. Below, a police car slowly took the turn onto Monarch Street. An external speaker mounted to the roof of the vehicle was blaring an announcement—*Bundy was on the loose.*[306]

♦

Deputy Bob Braudis, carrying one of the flyers, was going door to door on the eastern side of town. This is where most of the Bundy sightings had taken place. He knocked on yet another door and greeted a young barefoot lady in cut-off shorts and a halter top.[307]

"Have you seen this man?" Braudis asked her.[308]

"Hey," she replied with interest, taking the flyer to get a closer look. "He's good-looking. I'd go home with him," she smiled, clearly admiring the man in the photo. The deputy shook his head, yanked the flyer, and continued to the next house. *Doesn't she know? Ted's a viper in the grass.*

♦

Nancy darted into the sheriff's office, astounded at the sheer number of ringing telephones. One of the secretaries sighed heavily as the phone in front of her rang just as she ended her previous call.[309]

"Yes," she explained to the caller on the other end of the line. "We are still looking for him."[310]

Another secretary was nearby, jotting notes on a yellow notepad, her phone balanced precariously between her shoulder and her face.[311]

"Where did you see him?" she inquired. When she came to the end of this conversation, she turned her attention to a man who was waiting at the reception counter.

"I hear you need volunteers," he said.

"Fill this out," she handed him a piece of paper as she sized him up. He looked to be 6'4" and in his twenties. He could take care of himself and probably had more stamina than most of the men outside. "I think they'll want you up on Red Mountain."

According to the scent dogs, Bundy ran east and down toward Herron Park, where the river courses through town. At least two reliable eyewitnesses placed him heading east as well. When standing at the water's edge, he had three options. A right turn would lead back to town and the highway, where one can head east to Independence Pass. A second option would have him fording the river and continuing to head east. If he had taken a left, however, and headed north, he would have proceeded up a hill toward Smuggler Trailer Park. This third option would have him winding his way through a minefield of old mobile homes before reaching Smuggler Mountain, where he could hide in dense brush or any number of old mining claims. If he continued hiking up the valley several miles, he could escape from the region.[312]

The second area designated for a thorough search was Red Mountain. This wasn't a well-developed region, but the houses up there were mansions or vacation homes, residences that were only used during holiday vacations. Over fifty people were beating the bushes, searching for the man who had so quickly galvanized the resort community. Red Mountain was being explored by horseback, by four-wheel-drive vehicles, and on foot with tracking dogs. Overhead, helicopters were searching from the air.[313]

◆

At the Garfield County Jail, guards entered Bundy's abandoned cell. The fugitive had been on the lam for nearly twenty-four hours. His things had already been searched, but that was to determine if there were any clues to where he was headed. Recognizing now that he might have successfully escaped, they entered his cell to remove all of his legal materials. There were transcripts, books, an index card collection, and office supplies. All were seized and sealed for what everyone hoped would be a short time. Once the man had been apprehended, such materials could be returned to him.[314]

Garfield County deputies placed traces on all of Bundy's female pen pals. The names of the women who had corresponded with him were placed on a list, and the investigation began. Where are these women now? Are any of them present in the valley?[315]

Information concerning a city employee, who noticed how much clothing Bundy had worn at his hearing, had leaked to the press. This appeared to indicate that the prisoner had known he was going to attempt an escape and dressed accordingly. Deputies were indeed investigating the matter. The real question was, had he received any help?[316]

There were four ways the prisoner could have communicated with a potential accomplice. The first was via the telephone. Since he was serving as his own attorney, Bundy had been awarded the privilege of using one of the county's credit cards to make private calls. Judge Lohr had not only authorized its use but determined that such communications could not be monitored. Deputies were already scanning the official logbooks, trying to determine how many times they had escorted the man down to the privacy of the sheriff's office. How many calls had he made there? To whom?

One of Bundy's frequent telephone contacts was a private investigation firm in Denver. Ted was permitted to hire an investigator—at taxpayers' expense—to examine the homicide case. Other calls were to California numbers. Investigators determined these were legitimate as well. Bundy was communicating with a forensics laboratory, attempting to refute the FBI's report concerning the hair fibers that had been discovered in his Volkswagen. The defendant had even gone so far as to demand hair samples from all his friends who had ever ridden in his bug. He wanted those samples compared against the state's evidence. It seemed that most of the man's calls were directly connected with the preparation of his defense. Two collect calls gave deputies some hope. They were to Washington State, where Bundy had plenty of family and friends. When traced, however, both calls led to a well-known reporter for The Seattle Times—another dead end.[317]

A second method, to enlist the assistance of an accomplice, was via the US Postal Service. Where was Bundy's mail? Who had he been corresponding with, besides his female admirers? Had he initiated the correspondence?

A third method was visitation. Who visited him while he was in Colorado? A few college girls had come to leave the prisoner cigarettes and candy, but they were never permitted to speak with the man. An employee at the jail did some digging and discovered that in the eight weeks that Bundy had been housed at the Garfield County Jail, his only visitors had been members of the media.[318]

The fourth method was to simply have a fellow prisoner deliver a message to the outside world. A spokesman for the Garfield County Sheriff's Department acknowledged that they were seeking the whereabouts of one of Bundy's former cellmates. Last week, that prisoner had simply walked away from a work-release program in Glenwood Springs. Could that man have assisted in his friend's escape?

Seriously, there was not one, but two fugitives on the run?[319]

◆

Women in Aspen, barred from purchasing handguns, had no problem voicing their displeasure with their local law enforcement agencies. Through reporters, the public learned Bundy was not just a convicted kidnapper accused of murder. He was under investigation for many unsolved homicides in multiple jurisdictions. Washington detectives were investigating him, hoping for a connection between the mysterious disappearances of eight young women. In Utah, Bundy was a murder suspect. Here, in Colorado, Investigator Mike Fisher and his colleagues were investigating the fugitive in the abductions and murders of not one but three women. Most of this information was not known to the residents of Aspen. Fear was now mixed with anger.[320]

Learning these details from the press, one woman reacted by saying, "The sheriff's office was patently naive, bordering on criminally stupid, to leave Bundy in the courtroom alone."[321]

"The whole thing distresses me," another woman added. "This man is dangerous enough for the police department to warn people to stay inside and lock their doors, but he wasn't dangerous enough for them to watch him while he was in the courtroom?"[322]

These concerns were not falling on deaf ears. District Attorney Frank Tucker voiced his criticism over the lack of security.[323]

"There's no excuse for what happened yesterday," he informed reporters outside his office in Glenwood Springs.[324]

Ted had been annoying Tucker for months. He had filed multiple pretrial motions. He had sought and received authorization to bring in a dietician to the jail in Aspen to review their menu. In both Aspen and Glenwood Springs, he had received authorized trips outside of his cell to see a barber, a physician, and a dentist. He asked the judge for an electric typewriter, a lamp, a chair, pens, pencils, and legal pads.

Tucker was convinced the prisoner was planning some type of escape and said so to the judge. The attorney even submitted a scrap of paper deputies had found in the jail, though not in Bundy's cell. It was a hand-drawn schematic of the various conduits, air ducts, and vents above and surrounding the cellblock. The judge still ruled that the defendant could use a typewriter, paper, pencils, and legal pads, but he denied the request for the chair and pens.[325]

"I told that sheriff over and over again," Tucker said angrily, "we had to have Bundy watched every minute. We kept tellin' him Bundy's an escape risk!" While the county sheriff's department, local police force, and outside agencies continued to engage in the manhunt, Tucker announced that he would now be filing escape charges against the fugitive.[326]

"We have invested a lot of time, money, and personal effort in this case," he sighed. "It is difficult to stand by and watch somebody blow the whole thing, in a split second, through inattention."[327]

CHAPTER 4
THE BLACK BISHOP

A helicopter, on loan from Grand Junction, banked right. Deputy Sergeant Larry Spiers was riding in the passenger seat. A department-issued 12-gauge shotgun lay across his lap, with the barrel pointing out the side of the aircraft. He was tasked with searching the remote cabins in the Castle Creek area, just south of town. Spiers pointed to his first destination, and the pilot landed in the nearest alpine meadow, bordered by a grove of aspen. The sergeant grabbed his trademark white Stetson and hopped out of the aircraft. When he was clear of the rotor downwash, he placed the hat on his head and held the shotgun at the ready.

He was in a unique position, and he knew it. Spiers was deputized, acting in an official capacity, but since he had resigned from his job six months earlier, he was no longer directly attached to the sheriff's department. As far as the chain of command was concerned, he reported directly to the undersheriff. There were many dead spaces in the valley where communication with dispatch was not possible. In many ways, the sergeant was on his own, searching for a man who desperately didn't want to be recaptured.[328]

Spiers had left the department before Bundy's legal journey from Utah to Colorado. The undersheriff had kept Spiers apprised of the progress in the case as the months unfolded. Still, the sergeant wished he had firsthand knowledge of the man he was hunting. *How resourceful was he? How cunning?*[329]

◆

Journalist Ward Lucas and his cameraman were on South Hunter Street, on the east side of St. Mary's Catholic Church. They had been busy taking B-roll footage of women walking down the street. As Coleman filmed these ladies approaching in their printed knits and wedges, Lucas would ask how they felt about the manhunt. Many women didn't seem to have any concern for their safety, even after the reporter let them in on some of the facts and accusations surrounding the homicide cases. Lucas didn't like what he was hearing.[330]

He noticed Mike Fisher, the chief investigator for the district attorney's office, approaching them on the sidewalk. There was no hurry as the man was hobbling on crutches. Lucas identified himself and asked if Fisher would consent to a filmed interview. The investigator declined the offer but agreed to make a few comments on the record.

"Bundy is a dangerous man," he said, "and folks in town just don't seem to realize it." He cast a few obscenities toward the sheriff's department. "I warned Dick Kienast repeatedly that Bundy has a penchant for planning escapes. The sheriff is criminally negligent for allowing him to escape." This was a pretty serious accusation for one senior lawman to make about another, so Lucas asked again if this was on the record. The investigator agreed that they could quote him.[331]

Fisher had every reason to be angry. He was the person responsible for getting Ted extradited to Aspen. He learned of the escape yesterday as he emerged from the bewildering haze of anesthesia following knee surgery. He had rubbed his pale blue eyes, looked down at his knee, and called for the doctor. The investigator demanded all the paperwork needed to be discharged as soon as possible. The hunt for Bundy was on, but the region's top investigator was forced to sit on the sidelines.[332]

Journalists were close by, interviewing locals about the buddy system in Aspen in light of the escape. The mayor even got caught in their crosshairs.

"No one in Aspen likes to go home alone anyway," one woman remarked. "The system seems to be working."[333]

"Oh, I'm certainly afraid to be on the streets," another woman remarked. "But, he's pretty good-looking. I might even help him out."[334]

"The bars were at least as full as normal," the mayor added. "Single women were walking around. There isn't a hell of a lot of fear in this town because everybody lives on the line." The mayor did his best to deflect pointed questions about how law enforcement had allowed Bundy to slip through their fingers. He did add that most Aspenites believed the fugitive had already left the area.

The city manager shook his head, knowing full well how difficult the terrain was surrounding their community.[335]

"It's rugged country up there," he noted. "Bundy, probably, is a scared man right now."[336]

◆

State law permitted officers and deputies to patrol the streets for up to a year before required attendance at a training facility. The smaller mountain towns were permitted to send their officers to the Colorado State Patrol Academy in the town of Golden. Two different programs operated side-by-side at this facility: one for the specific needs of the state troopers and one for deputies and officers.[337]

Deputy Leon Murray was in his fifth week of the six-week program when he heard of the chaos in his hometown. He dialed the direct line to the sheriff and got straight to the point.[338]

"Let me drop out of the academy and come back to help you guys," he said. Murray was volunteering to terminate his training program and drive 190 miles back to the office. "I know you're short-handed."[339]

"You can't drop out," Kienast replied without hesitation. "You gotta graduate, so stay down there in Golden." The sheriff was anxious to get off the phone as he had to meet with the county commissioners. More money would be needed to fund the manhunt. Helicopters don't come cheap.[340]

◆

Ward Lucas drove their rental car while his cameraman shot footage of the scenery as they explored the back roads outside of town. Ward kept his eye out for the fugitive, secretly hoping they might get lucky and run into him. It might just be a snipe hunt, but if they stumbled upon him, they could offer a ride, play dumb, and drive directly to the police station. Ward could ply the man with questions during the journey, yet another journalistic scoop in his career. From the rustic log cabins for rent in the Woody Creek area to the mansions of Red Mountain, the newsmen traveled over roads more suited for a Jeep than a rental car.[341]

◆

Bill Grikis, the cherub-faced supervisor of animal control, and his small team handled any animal injuries, nuisances, or random dangers to the community. Got an abandoned puppy? Discovered a porcupine wandering through your outdoor cocktail party? Perhaps a skunk crawled under your car. *Call Bill.* He often reeked of skunk but considered it a badge of honor.[342]

Thinking a dog catcher has no legal authority and committing a crime right in front of one had resulted in the arrest of more than one defiant young man. Such a belief soon came complete with free accommodations in the local jail. Bill and his team were sworn police officers, their Aspen PD badges clearly visible on their denim jackets.

He sat alone in his green pickup truck on Twining Flats Road. He had been asked to keep an eye out for Ted Bundy.

Bill's rig, which had the animal control insignia on the side doors, was equipped with a police radio. He had been monitoring the radio traffic all morning. He watched the cars that passed him, paying attention to their license plates. Any vehicle registered in the county had a ZG, a two-letter code prefix on its plate. Vehicles from Garfield County showed a WM prefix, while Eagle County residents displayed their YM identification. There weren't enough folks in any given town in the valley to use up more than the 9,999 digits each plate could have held. These prefixes provided officers with an easy way to identify whether passing motorists were locals or out-of-towners.[343]

A stray dog crossed the road right in front of Bill's truck. He opened his door and coaxed the canine toward him.

"Come here. Yes...that's a good boy." He scooped up the pup, and as he was carrying him back to his rig, the officer noticed that the little dog had an identification tag. He put the canine in a large wire cage in the back of his truck, climbed back into the cab, and grabbed his clipboard, which contained a list of practically every pet in the county.

Folks typically get their dogs licensed by one of the two veterinarians in town. Animal control received a copy of these forms, and Bill used the data to create a list of the registered pooches. There were about twenty dogs per page, and once he found a license number, he could see the contact information for the owner. This little guy, for instance, belonged to Claudine Longet, an actress who owned a home up on Red Mountain. Typically, stray dogs were brought to the only animal shelter in the county. Bill opted just to return this dog to its owner so he could get back to his assigned task, keeping an eye out for the fugitive.[344]

He turned the ignition and started driving toward his destination. Returning a nomadic pooch to one of the area's celebrities, Bill Grikis was living up to his self-proclaimed sobriquet—"Dog Catcher to the Stars."[345]

◆

Ward's drive in the country had taken him out to the airport, about four miles west of Aspen. This airport had been in operation for decades but had only begun to be modernized in recent years. Wanting the ability to have larger aircraft use the facilities, the runway had been widened to eighty feet, and twenty-nine acres had been set aside for expansion. Even before construction was completed last year, a spacious aircraft parking apron had been created. Before this, the airport consisted of a trailer sitting on this property, looking out at a much smaller airstrip.[346]

Sheriff Kienast was approaching one of his deputies, and Ward nudged his cameraman, wanting to capture the scene. Coleman raised his CP 16 video camera and started recording. Kienast was easily recognizable by his sweater vest and glasses. He had spotted the film crew but chose to ignore them as he spoke with Bill McCrocklin. The deputy rested the butt of his shotgun on his thigh. Deputy Bob Braudis and Undersheriff Ben Meyers were nearby, having a conversation of their own.[347]

The sheriff's department managed to obtain the services of a pilot and helicopter from Fort Carson, south of Colorado Springs. This Army chopper was equipped with a heat-detection camera, and experts said it was sensitive enough to detect a human's heat signature, even if he was hidden in the forest.[348]

Only a week earlier, Sheriff Kienast had completely restructured his organization. Traditionally, the undersheriff handled operations while one of the senior sergeants handled the staff. Mysteriously, Kienast removed the operations duties from his undersheriff and assumed those responsibilities himself.[349]

Before this restructuring, Meyers had been responsible for Bundy's custody. The undersheriff personally escorted his prisoner from the basement cellblock to the courthouse upstairs. In his absence, Meyers would assign two deputies to Bundy's security detail, and this system appeared to be working. To his recollection, Meyers had only left the defendant with one guard on a solitary occasion. It was during a court session, and Investigator Mike Fisher happened to be in the room. Although Kienast's recent reorganization could be seen as a demotion amid the ranks, Meyers could at least take comfort in the knowledge that he could not be held responsible for Bundy's escape, as he was no longer in the chain of command concerning operations.[350]

It was Deputy Braudis who would be boarding the helicopter to look for the fugitive from the air. The undersheriff handed him a high-powered rifle.

"Bob!" Meyers shouted as the rotor blades began to spin. "All we want is *your* story."

"What do you mean?" Braudis asked.

"I only want to hear *your* side of the story. If you get the S.O.B. in your crosshairs, kill him." There was a significant pause as the deputy processed what he had heard.

"Okay," he replied. He understood what Meyers wanted, but he wasn't comfortable with the directive. He turned and boarded the chopper.[351]

Deputy Braudis had only been on the job for three months, even though he had moved to Aspen with his wife and two daughters eight years earlier.[352]

As part of the interview process for the sheriff's department, Braudis had been instructed to drive to an office in Vail, another resort community 100 miles away. He did as he was told, smoking a joint during his road trip. When he arrived at the office in Vail, a man fastened a blood pressure cuff and pneumographs, explaining that he was about to ask some control questions. Braudis was prepped for a polygraph exam.

"Do you use drugs?" the examiner inquired, monitoring the device.[353]

"Yes," Braudis answered quietly, knowing marijuana was an illegal substance.

"When was the last time?" the examiner continued, making some notes. Braudis looked down at his wristwatch.

"About an hour ago, in Glenwood Canyon."

Hours later, back in Aspen, a stone-faced sheriff asked to speak privately with Braudis. Knowing he had blown his big opportunity, Bob sighed, following the sheriff into his office.

"Hey," Kienast began, clearing his throat. He was searching for the right words. "My polygraph guy said...he's never met anyone as honest as you. There was no deception in your polygraph." Their eyes locked, and Braudis could feel the sweat dampening his shirt. "I'm offering you a job."[354]

"Wow!" Bob was completely surprised. "I thought you were going to can me for smoking weed on the way over."

"Well," Kienast leaned forward, finally cracking a smile. "Let's *talk* about that." The two men erupted in laughter.[355]

Braudis was a merry prankster and a man not easily intimidated. Having researched Ted, he tried to see if he could squeeze some information out of him during one of their road trips.

"You're famous for putting a sling on your arm," Braudis said, "asking some girl to help you load your kayak, or your surfboard, on your car... and they're never seen again." Bundy hadn't taken the bait. As the mileposts continued to pass, Braudis learned not to ask direct questions or even discuss the criminal allegations surrounding the man. Still, change the subject to the beauty of the Cascade Mountains or the pros and cons of the legal system, and Bundy would entertain you for miles.[356]

◆

There had been a lot of Bundy sightings in the previous twenty-four hours, and officers were tracking down leads in town while deputies pursued shadows in the country. Reported sightings came from Denver to the east, Fort Collins to the north, San Francisco out west, and as far away as Brooklyn. Everybody had an eye out for the runaway. The last confirmed sighting was along the riverbank west of Herron Park yesterday morning, only minutes after the escape.[357]

Detective Michael Chandler was cruising down Main Street in an unmarked patrol car. The crime prevention program he had developed was ranked number one in the nation by the National Crime Preventionist Organization. As a result of this work, he was known throughout the valley. This now worked in his favor as he was checking in with the owners of lodging facilities in town, asking if there were any single men matching Bundy's description staying in their hotels.

For decades, Detective Chandler's dad had been beaming into living rooms across Colorado right around supper time. He brought his viewers their weather forecast in a traditional, downhome manner on Channel 7 out of Denver. When young Michael was growing up, he found himself living in a fishbowl, with the entire community staring at his family whenever they went out in public. Michael couldn't stand being stared at, pointed at, or talked about.[358]

Ironically, by college, he found himself pursuing a degree in journalism. After graduating from the University of Colorado, he couldn't find a position at any of the local television stations despite his father's connections. Michael was married, and the couple already had a baby. Mouths had to be fed, and bills had to be paid, so he worked for the Forest Service in the summer, a ski company during the winter, and starved during the off-season.

"What are you doing?" he was once asked in reference to his career.[359]

"Starving," Chandler jokingly replied.

"Why don't you become a cop?"

"Are you insane?" Growing up, Chandler never had a good relationship with the police. As the son of a celebrity, every state trooper seemed to place a target on his back. Desperate men make desperate decisions, and working for the police meant year-round employment with benefits. Putting the needs of his family first, he found himself knocking on the door of city hall.

Michael was hired on the spot. This occurred so fast that he wondered if the chief just wanted to brag that he had hired Warren Chandler's son. Maybe being the grandson of a chief justice of the Colorado State Supreme Court had some influence on his quick employment. There was that.

Soon, Michael Chandler was on the firing range at the academy in Golden. He became a patrolman for the Aspen PD and worked his way up to patrolman first class, patrol sergeant, and eventually, detective.

He was keenly aware of the competition between the city's police department and the sheriff's office. The adversarial relationship between the two agencies meant scant information was emerging from the courthouse. Yesterday's operations mainly fell under the jurisdiction of the sheriff. The car rental companies, the issues out at the airport, helicopter operations, and the search efforts out of town were all overseen by deputies. What information had been gleaned from those operations? Where was the information sharing? Chandler was somewhat forgiving of Sheriff Kienast holding his cards close to his chest because that type of competition also extended into the upper ranks of the police department.

Everyone in town knew, going on four years now, that there was a complicated and strained relationship between Detective Chandler and Detective Sergeant Garms. Michael understood that their somewhat immature relationship was based on impressively sized egos, and he recognized that their ongoing competition was counterproductive to their roles as law enforcement officers.[360]

The issue started in the spring of 1972. Garms had simply walked into town looking like a drifter, down on his luck and in need of some cash.

For eight months, he cultivated friendships, purchased marijuana, and eventually sold it up and down the valley. Selling weed led to a handful of cocaine transactions, earning him more friends in town. By the morning of November 10, if you asked anyone in Aspen who Dave Garms was, you'd receive the same reply—a dope-dealing, beaded-necklace-wearing hippie. That evening, everything changed.

Garms, accompanied by members of the Aspen PD as well as federal drug agents, announced to his "friends" that he had been working undercover for law enforcement all along. By dawn the following morning, fifteen of the town's residents were behind bars, baffled as to how this outsider had managed to pull it off.[361]

As luck would have it, Michael Chandler's first week on the force was the same week Garms and the chief of police sprung their trap on these unsuspecting folks. Big cities were used to the concept of undercover officers, but this had never happened before in Aspen. Chandler was at the jail that night, charged with guarding the stunned citizens. He glanced at their paperwork and discovered that many of these people were merely recreational users of marijuana. Michael was horrified that this was one of his first jobs as a police officer. He and Garms did not view the sting operation through the same lens. Garms saw a win for law enforcement, while Chandler only witnessed betrayal. From that week on, the two were usually at loggerheads over any given subject, policy, or case.[362]

Chandler eventually volunteered to take Garms up North Maroon Peak to focus on what they had in common rather than dwell on their differences. After hours of hard work ascending steep snow ramps and navigating through rock bands, the duo stood just shy of the summit—exhausted. Chandler noticed that Garms had a childish, almost impish, look on his face.

"Go ahead," Chandler said, extending another olive branch. He could see that the other man wanted to be able to tell others that he had been the first to reach the top.[363]

Detective Chandler wasn't having any luck finding signs of Bundy at the local motels, but he was dutifully going down his list and knew this was the type of pressure that would keep the fugitive out of doors and, thus, more vulnerable to the elements.

From what the detective was hearing, the convict was already achieving some type of folk hero status in the community, and this did not sit well with him. The irony of the situation was not lost on residents. On one hand, they had an accused killer running loose. On the other hand, books like *Papillion* and *The Count of Monte Cristo* became bestsellers simply because their authors were able to tap into our natural desires to root for anyone on the lam. Anyone. Yes, doors and windows that were never locked were suddenly being bolted, but the collective imagination of the populace was on fire. There seemed to be a natural desire to support the fugitive. Rules didn't seem to apply to this man.

◆

Local merchants employed a little dark humor to loosen one's wallet. Wanted posters, tacked up in a local watering hole, were for sale. The poster listed the notorious fugitive as "Aspen's foremost jumper and cross-country specialist." Down at the Hotel Jerome, an impromptu, alcohol-infused fundraising effort was underway. A well-oiled patron at the bar thought it would be a good idea to install a brass plaque on the front lawn of the courthouse, precisely where the fugitive's heel prints in the grass remained.[364]

"Ted Bundy leapt here!" the inebriated man suggested.[365]

Over the radio, listeners were treated to *The Ted Bundy Request Hour*, with selections such as "Movin' On, I'm Walkin'," and "That Ain't No Way to Treat a Lady."[366]

T-shirts were now available at The Shirt Off Your Back store. "Bundy's Free!" one proclaimed. "You Can Bet Your Aspen on It!" Women were spotted wearing shirts emblazoned with the words, "Theodore Bundy is a One Night Stand." Another garment had a slightly more veiled message, "Bundy's in Booth D." This was a humorous nod to a recent report in Newsweek magazine, which claimed a tourist who wanted cocaine only had to ask for "Booth D" in town. This came as news to many of the residents as there were seventy restaurants in Aspen, none of which contained such a booth.[367]

In the restaurants, three dollars could bring you a "Bundy Burger." Remove the top half of the bun, and you'll notice that the meat has escaped. The "Bundy Cocktail" made an appearance—rum, tequila, and two Mexican jumping beans. Speaking of *jumping*, after Bundy made his now legendary leap, he sprinted past Freddie's Restaurant, where a witness spotted him. A joke began circulating through town. *On his way by, Bundy ordered a ham-on-rye-on the fly!* Actual sales of the sandwich skyrocketed. One young man in town owned a dog named Bundy. The owner brought his canine companion down to the police station and attempted to turn him in—to face justice.[368]

Rumor had it that one of the hotels in Snowmass was holding a Ted

Bundy look-alike contest. First prize, so the tale goes, was a year in the Pitkin County Jail, with an option to escape after one week.[369]

A hitchhiker was spotted along Highway 82. Wearing jeans, an old pea coat, gloves, and a fedora, he was hoping to catch a ride over the Rockies. Standing in the snow, he carried a hand-written sign that read, "I am *not* Bundy."[370]

Meanwhile, the names of Bundy's alleged victims seemed as obscure as his present whereabouts. Despite the murders he was accused of perpetrating, his desperate bid for freedom was now good for a laugh. The dark humor appeared to pervade the valley.

◆

In 1880, the Stapleton family settled in the valley, homesteading where Sardy Field now sits. Ninety-seven years later, their great-grandson was walking down the hall in the courthouse en route to the sheriff's office. Dave Stapleton was a member of Aspen Mountain Rescue, and he felt confident that this was why the sheriff had called him in for a meeting. There was a frenetic pace of activity in the basement as Stapleton entered Kienast's office.

"Okay, David," the sheriff began, "you're with mountain rescue, and you know the cabins around here. Let's put you with a deputy."[371]

The sheriff wasn't enlisting the assistance of Aspen Mountain Rescue in a formal capacity. Kienast wanted Dave—just Dave—and for a very specific purpose. Stapleton had helped to build a series of high-altitude cabins that climbers and skiing enthusiasts could use during the winter months. They dotted the remote mountains south of town, stretching down to Crested Butte. Dave knew where the closest access roads were and how to approach each cabin as quietly as possible. The sheriff wanted to provide Dave with an armed deputy, not only for protection but to ensure the legality of his presence should there be a confrontation with the fugitive. The local businessman couldn't help but notice that Kienast was already headed for the door. It appeared the *mission* wasn't open for debate.[372]

◆

As a journalist who had reported on the missing person cases in Washington, Ward Lucas found himself being interrogated by fellow reporters outside the courthouse. Ward brought them up to speed on the fugitive: his state campaign work with Republicans, his time as the vice-chairman of the Seattle Crime Prevention Advisory Commission, and his recent

WARD LUCAS

stint as a law student in Utah. Bundy had even chased after and apprehended a purse snatcher. Ward explained that Ted could be outspoken and gregarious and seemed to be on track for a career in the public eye. The big question, though, was what sinister acts was Ted committing… when no one was looking?[373]

Ward speculated about Bundy's decision not to fight extradition to Colorado while he was serving time in Utah. As a law student, Bundy would have known that Mike Fisher's case against him was circumstantial. A gas receipt, placing Ted within forty miles of the Wildwood Inn on the day that Caryn Campbell went missing, was the strongest piece of evidence. Any competent lawyer, however, could raise the issue of reasonable doubt. Bundy stood a fair chance of winning his case here in Aspen. If so, he'd return to the Utah State Penitentiary to serve out the remaining years of his sentence in the kidnapping case. Why bother agreeing to come to Colorado? Ward believed he knew the answer.[374]

In the Utah prison, Ted was subject to maximum security measures. If he were transferred to Pitkin County, however, he'd be housed in a modest jail, whose aging cells had been securing prisoners for eighty-seven years. Surely, it would be easier to escape from Aspen's quaint little facility than the high prison walls in Utah. Bundy hadn't fought extradition to have the opportunity to clear his name in the Campbell homicide; he simply desired an easier cage from which to escape. Again, it was only speculation, but worth consideration.[375]

◆

Dave Stapleton was riding shotgun in a deputy's four-wheel-drive Bronco. They were eleven miles up Castle Creek Road, passing the ghost town of Ashcroft. Although he grew up with guns and owned several rifles, Dave hadn't brought a weapon with him. His deputy, who served as a bodyguard and escort, was armed. Still, they were hunting a dangerous man. Dave had a wife and five children at home, and he intended to return to them.[376]

He looked to his left, past the deputy, and glimpsed the remains of the historic silver mining town. Aging cabins huddled in a cluster amid an alpine meadow bordered by aspen trees. The deserted, dilapidated structures included a post office, a couple of saloons, and a hotel. A long-sought rail link to Crested Butte never came to fruition, and the mines themselves turned out to be shallow deposits. This town simply vanished.[377]

"Anyone checking these structures for Bundy?" Dave inquired.

"No clue," the deputy replied.

Eventually, the pair saw a grove of conifers. Some were upright, while others were weeping. They parked the Bronco and made their way through the trees, treading lightly. The deputy couldn't see anything ahead, but Dave knew they were getting closer to the Lindley Hut. At the foot of Star Peak, nestled in this grove at 10,440', the hut was easy to miss if you didn't know it was concealed within the grove. The fourteen-year-old structure was named for a man who had perished in a plane crash.[378]

Dave pointed out the front door to the deputy, who pulled his service weapon. There was no lock on the door. The cabin was officially open to mountaineers and alpine skiers from Thanksgiving through the end of May. The fugitive had been on the run long enough to manage to reach this destination. They approached cautiously.[379]

The deputy pushed the door open slowly, doing his best to remain silent. He entered, and Dave followed close behind. The hut was nicknamed The Icebox due to its concrete floor and walls and an appalling lack of insulation. As ski enthusiasts would say, "If it's ten degrees below zero outside the hut, it will still be ten degrees below zero inside." One man searched the main floor. The other checked the loft, large enough to comfortably sleep fourteen. Nothing.[380]

There were five more cabins to check.[381]

◆

Chief Hougland was stopped outside city hall by a reporter. Hougland confirmed that he and his officers were working around the clock.

"Everyone has orders not to make any contact," he began, referring to civilian members of the posse.[382]

"How about leads?" the reporter asked. "Do you have any good ones yet?"

"Not really. We're just exploring the possibilities that we might have as far as... any reports we get. We make sure we follow up on every one of them."

◆

The dog handlers were hiking through a region near Smuggler Mountain. The area was strewn with abandoned cabins, decrepit sheds, and discarded railroad ties. The German Shepherds were panting, their long muzzles and black noses darting from side to side as the search party advanced over the uneven terrain.

Deputy Gary White stayed behind the handlers. Although he was wearing sunglasses, he pulled down the brim of what he referred to as his "doper-hat," a felt bush hat he had worn during multiple undercover operations in the Southwest. With his experience combating heroin coming out of Juarez, Mexico, he was no stranger to difficult assignments. He wasn't surprised that the fugitive was still on the loose.

The deputy was convinced that a domino effect of bad decisions had played a role in the successful escape. During the winter, before Bundy's transfer to Glenwood Springs, Gary had interacted with the prisoner on many occasions in the county jail. Bundy had submitted court documents arguing for more exercise outside. White couldn't refute this argument. There was only a small fenced-in area behind the courthouse for prisoners to gain some physical exercise. The deputy began to see a trend in Bundy's slew of legal arguments and delays.

The prisoner demanded more nutritious food. Gary was not pleased with this request at all. Prisoners in the Pitkin County Jail received their meals from the local Holiday Inn. Law-abiding citizens paid their hard-earned money to receive the same food Ted Bundy was being handed behind bars. How was the prisoner being denied anything? The judge ruled in his favor, however, so authorities had to start obtaining prisoner meals from the hospital. Next, Ted expressed a keen interest in mining and asked for topographical maps of the region.

White had personally observed Bundy measuring out his cell, followed by incessant pacing, day after day. The deputy finally asked the inmate why he paced so much. Bundy said he wanted to ensure he walked at least five miles a day. Gary had chuckled and said something about the man not having anything better to do.

Hindsight, as a community, was now uncomfortably sharp and distinct. The prisoner had been a master manipulator.

We've given this guy every tool he needs for a successful escape, Deputy White was thinking as he continued to check the sheds and piles of abandoned lumber.[383]

◆

Dave Stapleton and his bodyguard were approaching the Tagert Hut from the safety of the forest. This would hopefully hide their presence from anyone peering out the expansive front windows.

"Okay," Dave whispered. "Now…we can go *here*," he pointed to the wooded area, "because we can stay in the heavy timber. Bundy can hear us

Six Days in Aspen

coming, but he can't see us. Or, we can go up *this* way, from the back." He tilted his head to indicate the other direction.[384]

This structure was a traditional A-frame cabin in the Elk Mountains, and it had seen seventeen winters come and go since its doors were first opened. Trails to the various mountain huts were not marked, so if the fugitive were inside, it would mean he had stumbled across the cabin. There was only one entrance, and that was through the front door. The deputy cautiously opened it now, weapon drawn.[385]

As before, Dave followed behind the deputy, thinking, *what else can I do to make sure I don't take a shot to the head?* He was nervous as they checked every nook and cranny inside the structure. This cabin could accommodate seven comfortably. Dave scrutinized the familiar interior. Bundy wasn't here, but was there any sign that he had been? The stacked firewood appeared in order, and Dave held his hand out to the wood-burning stove. Cold.[386]

◆

Nancy and her fellow dispatchers were not police officers. They wore uniforms simply because they had received too many complaints. Visitors who came to their departmental window preferred to deal with uniformed personnel rather than "just an office girl."[387]

Baxter was at her best in stressful situations. She informed prospective applicants that they must prioritize calls that came into the station.

"If we don't take care of an illegally parked car as fast as a fire," she noted, "people should be understanding. All it takes are nerves of steel and the ability to think faster than a speeding bullet."[388]

Each dispatcher had to maintain an image of where everyone was on a three-dimensional map in their brain. They had to know which deputies were manning each roadblock and which police officers were driving around in four-wheel-drive vehicles as opposed to standard patrol cars. It was also crucial that dispatchers knew the voices, speech patterns, and mannerisms of all the law enforcement officers in the region. If a criminal got possession of a radio and successfully impersonated an officer, confusion and chaos could follow. Knowledge of the local geography was important: Woody Creek, Smuggler Mountain, Redstone, West Village, Red Mountain, and Pitkin Green. Access roads, location of radio towers, culverts—the list seemed endless. One thing was sure. Copious amounts of alcohol would need to be distributed and consumed when this whole affair was concluded.[389]

◆

In the late afternoon, with the understanding that the rain had washed away any scent of Aspen's newest folk hero, the dogs were dismissed. Volunteer searchers were also thanked for their time and sent home for the day. They were asked to rendezvous at the courthouse in the morning and continue with the efforts. Morale seemed low.[390]

There were no new leads. The helicopter, with its modern heat-detection camera, had been flying over the Woody Creek and Red Mountain region all day without yielding results. The pilot had landed periodically so Deputy Braudis could explore abandoned cabins in the mountains surrounding town.[391]

◆

Dave Stapleton and his deputy were exploring the Markley Hut, another mountain cabin. This one was located at the base of Green Mountain. The thirteen-year-old structure was faring well, but, like its brethren huts, it was empty. No sign of a disturbance had been found.[392]

Most Aspenites had heard of these mountain huts south of town. Several had even enjoyed their overnight accommodations. Few knew, however, just how many other such structures were in the region. Thirty years ago, various Forest Service cabins and sheepherder shelters had been constructed in the Maroon Bells-Snowmass Wilderness. Some diehard skiers in the valley were familiar with some of these sites, but Stapleton knew them all. He could take you from door to door without a map or a compass. There were also scores of vacation rentals and summer residences tucked into these backwoods. There were too many places to hide, and dusk was coming fast.[393]

◆

Georgia Hanson was watching the escape coverage on GrassRoots TV, a local non-profit media network. It just didn't seem likely to her that Ted could be as diabolical as the media was making him out to be. She was somewhat skeptical about all the charges being filed against him. Her husband, sitting beside her, seemed unconcerned that a fugitive was on the run in their area.

There was a knock at the front door.

Mrs. Hanson bolted out of her recliner. She studied the image of Bundy on the television screen while Mr. Hanson ran into another room to load his shotgun. Inexplicably, Mrs. Hanson stepped forward, opened the door just a few inches, and peered out. A bearded stranger greeted her.

Stealing another glance at the television screen, she saw a file photo of Bundy, who happened to have a beard.

"I'm from the water department," the stranger said. He was performing repairs to the water tank that was in the cemetery adjacent to the residence. "Just wondering if I could use your phone?"

Mrs. Hanson could feel her heart beating in her chest as she opened the door. A helicopter swept right over the roof of the house, with maybe twenty feet of clearance. Her initial belief in Bundy's potential innocence vanished as swiftly as the chopper. She didn't take her eyes off the stranger the entire time he was on the phone.

"Thank you," the man said when the errand was finished. As he exited the house, the Hansons could hear the helicopter departing for other parts of town.[394]

Mr. Hanson reappeared, brandishing his shotgun. He'd been aiming it at the mirror in the other room, practicing wounding the fugitive in the leg. You know...*as a precaution.*

◆

Eleven-year-old Heidi Braudis had put the first steps of a ruse in motion. Her friend wanted to run away from home, so they hatched a plan. The girls would meet outside on Park Circle. Heidi and her sister were not grounded, but their mom had forbidden them to have friends over for sleepovers for the next few weeks. The girls had been staying up late at night, jabbering about the cliques in school, boys, and any other preteen topic that came to mind. Invariably, the laughter grew too loud, much to their mom's displeasure. Temporarily banned from having company overnight, Heidi told her mother she was leaving to spend the night at her friend's house. The Braudis girls had not been forbidden to have sleepovers elsewhere.

As she walked through the living room, the television was on, and KUTV Newswatch 2, out of Salt Lake City, was broadcasting the evening news. Anchor Sandy Gilmore, with his perfectly coiffed haircut, appeared calmer than he had last night.

"Good evening," Gilmore began, "Convicted kidnapper Theodore Bundy is still on the run after yesterday's escape in Aspen, Colorado. Bundy escaped during a hearing in his murder trial at the county courthouse. That escape has prompted one of the largest manhunts the area has ever known."[395]

Heidi slid open the screen door. She didn't have a backpack or major food supplies. As she departed her mom's little log-sided house, she knew she'd have to appear as if she was simply equipped for an overnighter. Soon, the girls successfully rendezvoused outside.[396]

The runaways headed north.

◆

Though residents of Aspen did not have access to 9NEWS, Denver residents tuned in to their evening broadcast. "Ever since yesterday morning," Ward Lucas's voice was heard over the B-roll footage of the manhunt, "when suspected killer, Ted Bundy, jumped from a second-story window in the Pitkin County Courthouse, the news releases have talked about the thorough house-to-house searches being conducted throughout Aspen. But the news releases are mostly fiction, despite some surveillance along the roads and occasional air surveillance from a police helicopter, most of Aspen remains unsearched. Meanwhile, life in Aspen goes on as usual. Single, unescorted women walk the streets, presumably unconcerned. They apparently don't know, or don't care, that Ted Bundy is a chief suspect in the murders of at least eighteen, possibly thirty, young women in four states. Each of those women disappeared without a trace, frequently from well-traveled areas just like downtown Aspen. The only trace of many of those women was the pile of skulls, no other bones, just skulls, found on the side of a deserted mountain slope in Washington State."[397]

◆

Deputy Sergeant Larry Spiers leaned to his left as the helicopter he was riding in banked sharply to the right. He gripped his shotgun and nodded to the pilot. All day, the two men had worked together but with minimal conversation. Remote cabins in the Castle Creek area had been explored one at a time, but by necessity, in random order. Even if Spiers cleared a structure one moment, there was nothing to say Bundy couldn't enter it after the sergeant had left the scene.

Spiers, craving a Pall Mall, shook his head when he thought about the judge. His honor's decision not to have the fugitive shackled in court was, in the sergeant's opinion, a major contributing factor to the escape. There was just no way around it.

Spiers and the pilot agreed that they had time to check out one of the nearby mountain passes before dusk.[398]

◆

The pair of pre-teen runaways were walking north along Midland Avenue on the eastern outskirts of town. Heidi, the mastermind of the scheme, was feeling confident. A helicopter buzzed overhead, and she wondered if her dad, Deputy Bob Braudis, was aboard the aircraft.

Once the paved portion of their journey gave way to a narrowing gravel road, the girls discussed their limited supplies. Then, the road turned into a full-fledged Jeep trail, which wound its way through the low sagebrush.

They slowly ascended the southern slopes of Smuggler Mountain. The girls had no trouble staying on course. Small mounds of grass edged the road that led up to the old mine tailings. Most folks stopped where a pull-out had been created as a turnaround for vehicles. From here, the girls could see the entire region, from Independence Pass all the way down the valley toward snow-topped Sopris Mountain. Walking just a little farther up the trail brought them to their destination.[399]

The Smuggler Mine, the oldest operating silver mine in the district, looms over the northeastern edge of Aspen. In its heyday, the site provided one-fifth of the world's silver output. The elaborate tunnel system leads 1,200 feet into the mountain and even extends to portions underneath the town. Many of those old tunnels are now flooded. In 1894, a 2,340-pound silver behemoth had been discovered, but it proved too large to bring up to the light of day. Miners were forced to break it up into three pieces.[400]

The girls had no interest in exploring the subterranean labyrinth below. They wanted to camp out under the stars, looking over the town. They rested for an hour and then set about gathering firewood.

♦

Deputy Gary White stood in the exercise yard behind the courthouse. The sun had set, and he fought off a shiver in the darkness. He removed his glasses and drew the bill of his hat farther down. He'd been working since sunrise, and he felt it. Mentally, he was still trying to get into Bundy's mind and figure out where he was heading.

Gary had stood here many times, leaning against this chain-link fence, keeping watch as Bundy enjoyed his daily dose of freedom. Ted was always so courteous and easy-going with the deputy. For a while, Gary pondered Bundy's guilt or innocence. When he learned that Mike Fisher had a gas receipt that placed Bundy in Glenwood Springs on the day Caryn Campbell was abducted, the deputy's view of the prisoner shifted. As the months progressed, Gary came to know more about the complex man who regularly did push-ups in the exercise yard. In the deputy's mind, the prisoner was a master manipulator with a profound ability to compartmentalize his life. For Gary, there was no longer any doubt that Ted Bundy was a living, breathing monster.

Deputy White was struggling with the contradictions of his job. As a law enforcement officer, he was required to presume innocence until a defendant was proven guilty. Perhaps the lawman was trying to alleviate some guilt for believing Bundy was a murderer, but one day, White mentioned to the man that there was a box in the basement containing a checkerboard, magazines, a handful of books, and a few puzzles.

"Thanks," Bundy had said, "but chess is my game, not checkers. Do you play?"[401]

"I do," Gary replied, though he hadn't played a game in several years. He had participated in a few round-robin tournaments back in the day and felt he had a pretty good game. The optimum word there was—*had*. Was he still any good?

A week after that conversation, White happened to pull a shift in the jail, a welcome break from his duties along the county roads. He got to thinking about the box of amusements he had mentioned to Bundy. He found it and rummaged through its contents. He fished out the chessboard. It was cardboard and folded down the middle. There was a paper sack as well, filled with a handful of red and black checkers, one die, and a handful of pencils. There were also thirty of the thirty-two pieces necessary to play a game of chess. They were cheap, plastic pieces. A white pawn and one black bishop were missing.

Bundy was supposed to be so intelligent and calculating; it would be interesting to play against him. The deputy hesitated. He would be embarrassed if anyone discovered he played chess with a killer. Curiosity got the better of him.[402]

He brought the goods to Bundy's cell. The prisoner didn't seem to be looking at Gary but rather *through* him. The lawmen believed that everything Ted did was calculating; he was looking for an advantage or an angle with everything he asked for, did, or said.[403]

"Would you be interested in a game of chess?" Gary finally asked.[404]

The prisoner took a step forward, his left eye now fully illuminated and framed by one of the square holes in the door.

"Yes," Bundy replied in a low, raspy voice.

The lawman laid out the ground rules. The game would need to be played as if they were long-distance friends, competing via correspondence or over the phone. Bundy would set up the game in his cell, and whenever White happened to be nearby, he'd make a move. The deputy occasionally pulled a shift in the jail, but he also had to report back to the courthouse after every shift. He could walk back to the jail just to make a move. It would be a significantly protracted game, to be sure, but the prisoner looked intrigued.

"I don't see why that wouldn't work," Bundy remarked.

The deputy gave his opponent his choice of color. Gary wasn't surprised when the man chose black. As the cell door was created out of steel plates, about a quarter-inch thick, with three-inch squares cut into them in a grid pattern, White had to fish out his keys. He unlocked the opening in the door used to serve the prisoner meals and handed Bundy the folded chessboard and the bag. Ted got down on all fours and set up the board in the front corner of his cell. He soon realized that there were a couple of missing pieces. Gary suggested they use one black checker piece and one red to replace the missing pawn and bishop.

The men began their game. The deputy moved first, then gripped the brim of his hat, a quiet way of taking his leave while also signaling that he'd return when he could. Over the following week, move after move was made, and both opponents appeared to be enjoying the game.

One day, the prisoner acted a little edgy. He wore a hangdog expression, saying he had accidentally bumped the board and sent the pieces flying. Since he had been unable to return them to their previous positions, they would need to start over.

Teasing him, Gary blamed his opponent for knocking it over because he had been losing.

Bundy was indignant, scoffing at the accusation. The deputy was surprised because he was sure the tone of his voice and his body language had conveyed the message that he was only poking fun at his opponent's expense.

The board was reset, and the men began again. As before, this game progressed slowly, but it did last considerably longer than the first.[405]

Now, in the dark exercise yard, White felt like he and Bundy were playing another game of chess. The fugitive was on the run. What would his next move be? If Gary was merely a white pawn in law enforcement, surely Theodore Bundy was now the missing black bishop.

◆

Aspen was settling into their second night with a dangerous fugitive on the loose. On the east end of town, residents who peeked through their curtains spied a beautiful night sky, aglow with brilliant stars stretching over the horizon. But, on the lower slopes of Smuggler Mountain, what was that?

Fire!

Calls came in to dispatch; there was a fire up near the old mine. Down at The Pub, in the basement of the Wheeler Opera House, folks began hearing a strange beeping sound. It was multiple pagers announcing that something was up. The bar was a favorite hangout for fire department volunteers. Several men bolted from their tables, heading for the exit. Adrenalin was sobering them up quickly as they bounded up the stairs. They began sprinting for the station. Luckily for everyone, a baker who worked the night shifts right next door to the fire station was always sober. He was the designated driver for the fire engine.[406]

Up at the Smuggler Mine, Heidi and her friend were enjoying their bonfire. They knew nights in Aspen could get cold, but they were feeling fine and toasty now, proud that they were able to build such an impressive fire on their journey to freedom. Then, they heard the unmistakable sound of a siren and soon spotted the red lights of the fire engine coming up the road. A white spotlight, mounted atop the engine, was illuminating the dark hillside.

Heidi knew they were in trouble. The fire wasn't in any danger of spreading. The girls had constructed their bonfire in the middle of an extensive rockpile. When the firefighters arrived, they simply extinguished the blaze, scolded the girls for causing such a fuss, and directed them to go home. Heidi couldn't believe her luck. It didn't look like authorities would call her dad—a deputy—or her mom, who would be furious. The volunteers didn't even offer to drive the girls down the hill. Instead, they just told the children to leave.

Fifteen minutes later, Heidi and her friend were back in their neighborhood, still facing their original problem. One wanted to run away while the other was volunteering to assist in this endeavor. Had that dream been extinguished along with the flames? It was cold, and they were hungry, but not enough to return home. Wait...over there. Now, *there* are some overnight accommodations. In the dark, the girls climbed over a small decorative fence and into someone's front yard. Near one side of the lot was a sizeable doghouse. It would be their Holiday Inn for the night.[407]

THURSDAY

JUNE 9, 1977

CHAPTER 5
MANHUNTERS

Stupid Saabs. They were underpowered and not very stable at high speeds. Officer Hugh Roberts would have preferred a traditional police car. He was not in the best of moods as he, again, patrolled the streets of Aspen on the graveyard shift. The friction between Dave Garms and Michael Chandler was known to all, but few knew of the tension between Officer Roberts and Terry Quirk.

Roberts had served in Vietnam and returned to the States with shrapnel in his foot. The chief of police in Laramie, a former Marine, hired veterans because he could count on their work ethic and discipline. Roberts proudly served under the man for two years before he moved on to Aspen. A few years later, Veterans Affairs informed him that he needed another surgery on his foot. Once this was done, he healed quickly and was soon back on the force.

Officer Quirk felt that the injury had rendered Roberts incapable of performing his duties and, therefore, he had committed outright fraud by applying for work at the police department. Quirk got up into Roberts' face, demanding that he resign his position or face a fraud charge. Roberts explained that the chief was fully aware of his injury, and he had been walking the police beat for two different cities for over five years now. How was he unable to perform his duties? Now, the damned chief assigned them both to the night shift this month.[408]

Roberts wasn't the only officer on the Aspen PD payroll who had suffered a foot injury while serving his country. Sergeant Dick Kreuser had been an MP gate guard, assigned to his post alongside a member of the Army of the Republic of Vietnam. This mirror-guard duty served a practical purpose—increased security—but was also symbolic; we were their allies, after all. The young Vietnamese soldier had been armed with an M-1 carbine, which he carried slung over his shoulder, its muzzle pointed toward the ground. There was a magazine in the weapon, and the chamber was charged. During one of their pacing maneuvers, the man fiddled with the trigger, and the carbine fired. The bullet went through Kreuser's boot, his foot, and down into the pavement.[409]

◆

If anyone felt that Roberts or Kreuser's foot injuries were a problem, they'd surely take issue with one of Dick Kienast's new hires. Deputy Bill McCrocklin, thirty, had something wrong with the clotting mechanism in his body. The sheriff was aware of the man's condition but hired him anyway. Not long after arriving in the valley, the deputy suffered a minor accident that forced him to seek medical attention at Aspen Valley Hospital. There, he received a transfusion and was put on observation for nearly a week. He had been placed on Heparin to keep his blood from clotting.

During a visit to the hospital to check on her new, soft-spoken friend, Nancy Baxter had challenged Bill to a game of cards. At some point, the patient's IV drip line suddenly disengaged, and Nancy watched in horror as blood spurted all over the wall. Screaming for the nurse, she tried to remain calm, but Bill's rugged face had already turned too pale. Fortunately, the nurse who responded got things under control in no time. Bill struggled to look normal again, obviously a bit smitten with his pretty, new caretaker.

Bill knew he was living on borrowed time, but that wasn't going to keep a good man down.[410]

◆

Shortly after Kienast was elected, the liberal sheriff floated the idea that deputies should forgo carrying guns because the weapons were too dangerous and seemed to run contrary to the concept of a peace officer. The guns, he proposed, could be left behind, locked up at the courthouse. Officer Hugh Roberts couldn't believe what he was hearing. "What if we're responding to a burglary in progress?" he had asked. "Should we arrive at the bank and announce to the criminals—please wait a few minutes. We need to go back to the department to get our guns." Suffice it to say, the revolvers remained in their holsters.[411]

Deputy Carol Kempfert had problems with Kienast from the moment he assumed his new position. She learned her employer was into something that could only be described as "wellness."

Kienast brought a professional in to teach his deputies how to be *well* and live in the moment. Carol thought the New Age hipster, who summoned everyone to the courtroom, was surely a hired clown. His garish clothing and demeanor made Carol think, *if this guy is an example of being well, I want to be sick.* Wary, most of the deputies kept plenty of distance between themselves and the spiritual guide. The lights in the courtroom were dimmed, and the wellness instructor flipped the switch on his film projector. Over the rhythmic clattering of the film sprockets, the guru began to drone on and on about detoxification, human potential, and alternative medicine. As he spoke, the deputies were subjected to grainy footage of clouds rolling by, couples running barefoot through the grass, and sunflowers bending in the morning breeze.

What-the-hell? Carol thought. Nearly every deputy, Kempfert included, broke out their Marlboros and Lucky Strikes, filling the courtroom with smoke until the end of the required spectacle. Carol wasn't sure if the sheriff would survive the next election.[412]

Deputy Kempfert would be back at the Brush Creek Roadblock today, inspecting cars and trucks. She was confident that Bundy had already made it out of town and was probably already out of the valley. In all likelihood, he was still in Colorado. Perhaps they'd find him at a bus station or hitchhiking along Highway 70.

◆

Out at the Difficult Campground Roadblock, Deputy Gene Flatt paced beside his patrol car, his hands in his jacket pockets to help keep him warm. He'd become friendly with the Eagle County deputies who had been assigned to the same checkpoint. The men asked Flatt if he had any prior dealings with the fugitive. He had.

In addition to guarding Bundy in the exercise yard, escorting him from the jail in the basement up to the courtroom and back, and bringing him his meals, Gene Flatt had served on the Bundy transportation detail on at least two occasions.

A month or so ago, Gene was at the courthouse, and he was told the sheriff wanted to see him. Ever one to believe his job was in jeopardy,

Gene assumed the worst. *What the fuck did I do?* While passing through the bullpen, he found himself walking beside Deputy Greg Quinlan. Both men realized they were heading toward the same destination.

"What the hell you doin' here?" Gene whispered.[413]

There was no time for a response as they were ushered into Dick Kienast's office. The door was quietly closed behind them by Sergeant Don Davis, who was evidently going to remain for whatever ass-chewing was forthcoming. Davis sat on one corner of the desk while the sheriff remained in his chair, quiet and seemingly deep in thought. Davis began explaining the situation.

A jailhouse snitch had let authorities know that Bundy and another prisoner were planning an escape. Ted had completed a preliminary hearing and was due to return to the Garfield County Jail. Another prisoner, a man on trial for rape, was also finished with his day's legal requirements and would be headed downvalley with Bundy. During the journey, these two prisoners planned to feign an argument and start fighting. This would distract one deputy, and—it was hoped—they could grab his pistol. They planned to kill him and then the driver. Both bodies were to be thrown over an embankment. They would then make their escape in the unmarked police car.

Flatt was fascinated with the tale until it sank in as to why they'd been summoned.

"Rock, paper, scissors?" the other deputy chuckled.

Gene recognized that Bundy never knew in advance which deputies were going to be assigned to transport him to and from the courthouse. Would it be the broad-shouldered Bob Braudis today? Or, worse, Don Davis himself? Bundy must have beamed with anticipation when the young Midwestern lawman popped back into the jail to retrieve him. As for Gene, he had to suppress a smile. Deputies on duty in the jail had chained the two prisoners up so well that they resembled a Harry Houdini publicity stunt.

A half-hour later, they were headed westbound on Highway 82. For some of these regular transport assignments, deputies used a large, yellow, unmarked Ford. It had a white vinyl top and civilian license plates. Anybody not familiar with the department's vehicular assets had no idea what dangerous cargo was chained up inside. Gene had taken the wheel while Quinlan was in the back, sitting with Bundy and his companion. The journey appeared to be unfolding without incident, and the deputies were thinking that the ambush wasn't going to happen.

As if on cue, Bundy started yelling at his fellow prisoner. The argument began, just as planned, but when it came to fighting—the men were merely struggling against their chains. Their *fight* amounted to nothing more than two grown men wiggling profusely amid an impressive, heated quarrel.

Quinlan got one prisoner in a chokehold just as Gene veered over to the side of the road and slammed on his brakes, throwing the men against the back of the bench seat. The outburst came to a sudden halt. Gene unbuckled his seat belt and turned around, facing his prisoners. Drawing his Magnum, he waved it at them.

"We know what you're doing," Gene barked. "Cut the fucking shit. It ain't going to work, okay? If you keep it up, I'm going to be obliged to shoot you both." The deputy was bluffing. He knew that if he fired that weapon in the confines of the car, he'd injure his eardrums. The men settled down like two disgruntled brothers.[414]

◆

Young Heidi Braudis and her girlfriend were roused from their fitful night's sleep inside a doghouse. They were cold and carefully crawled out of their self-imposed retreat. Soon, their bodies began to register hunger. The scant provisions they had smuggled out of their homes were not going to take the edge off of their desire for good, warm food. Reality struck. Though the girls had planned a successful escape, they hadn't paid enough attention to what they should be doing once they were free. They decided, reluctantly, to return to their homes and face the music.

When Heidi walked through the front door of her house, she was surprised that no one was angry. In fact, no one had missed her. How was it possible that her friend's mom hadn't called the house? Heidi sneaked over to the phone and realized that Duke, the family's German Shepherd, had knocked the receiver off the hook sometime during the night. No one could call into the house. As she gently replaced the receiver onto its cradle, Heidi knew the current tranquility was only temporary. There'd be hell to pay once the girls' escapades were officially unearthed.[415]

◆

Deputy Flatt was pleased that Eagle County had responded, providing a couple of brothers-in-arms to help man the Difficult Campground Roadblock. These fellow deputies had to make quite a journey merely to reach their assigned post, and Gene was certainly grateful for their assistance.[416]

All three were at the end of their shift, but the Eagle County boys wanted one more tale from their newfound friend. Gene said he had another transport story, but it wasn't nearly as exciting as the other. He was pressed to tell the story anyway, so he relented.

There wasn't a set policy on where a prisoner needed to sit within a patrol car. As there was no steel cage separating the front seat from the back, Sergeant Kralicek and others wanted Bundy chained up front, right next to the driver, where they could keep a better eye on him. This would also mean the secondary lawman could ride in the back and continually monitor the prisoner the entire time. Gene preferred prisoners to ride in the back seat, and that's where Bundy was on this particular journey: on the passenger side. They were in the yellow, unmarked Ford, just outside of Glenwood Springs, bound for a day at court in Aspen. Gene had been driving, and a fellow deputy was riding shotgun.

Keeping watch on his side mirror, Gene realized that a car had been pacing them ever since departing the Garfield County Jail. The deputy stayed in the slow lane while the mystery car was in the fast lane, matching their speed. Gene wasn't voicing his thoughts, but he was wondering if the other driver was a family member of one of Bundy's victims, out for revenge.

"Hey, watch out!" Bundy called out from the back seat. He, too, had noticed the odd vehicle in the fast lane, a car that had been pacing them for far too long to be a coincidence.[417]

Gene cocked the rearview mirror to get a better view of his prisoner. Bundy looked shaken. Perhaps he had come to the same conclusion that a father or older brother of one of his victims had traveled down from the Pacific Northwest to exact some form of vigilante justice. Bundy whipped his head around, watching to see what the other car would do. The more nervous he got, the more his chains rattled.

The deputy maintained his speed. Eventually, the mystery car accelerated. Gene alternated his view from the road to his side mirror. He heard a rustling of chains from the back seat, but the lawman kept his attention on the other car, ready for anything. As the vehicle passed, Gene looked at the other driver directly, but that man didn't even glance in Gene's direction. The deputy kept his eye on the other car until he felt they were out of danger. Once he felt it was safe to do so, Gene stole a glance in his rearview mirror. Bundy was gone. The deputy impulsively turned to investigate the empty back seat. The normally cocky and charismatic prisoner was crumpled down in the footwell, a look of fear in his eyes.

"What's wrong, Bundy?" Gene asked playfully. Ted clearly didn't like to be the one hunted.[418]

◆

Deputy Maureen Higgins noted the differing opinions she encountered as locals passed through the West Sopris Creek Roadblock. Those who thought Bundy was an incredible threat to the community brought food and drinks to Maureen and her partner as a way to show their appreciation. Some felt that, by fleeing from justice, Bundy was guilty of the charges against him because an innocent man doesn't run. Others questioned his guilt, believing such a good-looking young man couldn't possibly be a prolific killer.

Maureen was surprised at how many of the deputies competed over key positions in the manhunt. Several of the men, wanting to be *the* deputy who captured the fugitive, competed for high-profile assignments—helicopter reconnaissance, assisting with the hounds, and residential inspections. It would indeed be worth a host of accolades, a boost to one's career, and it wouldn't hurt their reputation with the ladies. Higgins had no assignment preferences and was merely content to be doing her job.[419]

There were extended periods where no truck, tractor, car, or bicycle was in sight. She and her partner still had to maintain position, entertained by the dry grass rustling in the valley breeze, the sound of bleating sheep, and the occasional racket of a downy woodpecker.

From her standpoint, even if Bundy was not a killer, he had broken the law simply by leaping out of that window. She had no interest in trying to point the finger of blame. Bundy had escaped, period. It was now their responsibility to apprehend him. She wasn't about to toss her proverbial hat in the ring to try and land a position as a team leader on one of the various search parties. She knew the importance of the roadblocks and had no issue standing her post, no matter how remote that post might seem.

Truth be told, she thought Bundy was long gone. The man was no fool. Several of her colleagues believed the same, but they needed to demonstrate that law enforcement was not assuming the fugitive had escaped the valley.

Maureen had grown tired of the relentless teasing, interspersed with insults, heaped upon the women who stuck around and graduated from the academy. The prevailing attitude toward female deputies appeared to be... *Keep them out of the way*. She felt women in law enforcement were disliked by most of the old-school deputies, and they were barely tolerated by Kienast's new breed of road warriors.[420]

The sheriff had instituted a policy that no female deputies could serve as security escorts for Bundy. Higgins and Deputy Lorrie Francis had tended to other prisoners—so, why not this one? Their male superiors were convinced this convicted kidnapper could use his charms on these women, and these "gals" would forget to perform their duties properly, or so the reasoning went. In addition, her superiors thought she resembled the man's preferred victims, and they wanted her to keep her distance.

Maureen was quick to point out that none of the female deputies had abandoned Ted Bundy Tuesday morning. Men had earned that distinction. In Maureen's mind, everyone was so concentrated on keeping the defendant away from female deputies that the actual mission—the physical security of the prisoner—had failed.[421]

Deputy Higgins doubted Bundy was even capable of murder. Still, she was a deputy. She enforced the law and was annoyed that anyone would even hint that she could be swayed from performing her duties.

Maureen's call sign was "6-6," and she was continually teased about her soft, feminine voice. She was efficient, capable, and as big and strong as any of the wiry guys wearing a badge in town. She believed this disturbed some of them to the extent that they went out of their way to say things that made her appear weak. She also wasn't out doing drugs or boozing it up, despite its apparent sanctioning by at least one member of the committee who had interviewed and hired her.[422]

She did her best to ignore the men's patronizing behavior. She was no stranger to this type of work atmosphere. A few years ago, she had climbed telephone poles for Mountain Bell, which turned heads a lot more than her current position. She had been a Molybdenum miner, for Pete's sake. No one was going to force her to quit her job, not that her position in the department was in jeopardy. As the manhunt entered its third day, not everyone could say the same.[423]

Higgins liked the sheriff but did not respect him as a leader. She felt he willingly overlooked what was clearly a drug problem in the valley. It was her hope, however, that Kienast was availing himself of the experience and wisdom of Sergeant Don Davis. Higgins respected Davis, top to bottom.[424]

♦

Under Colorado law, the sheriff was required to have a chief deputy, called an undersheriff. Ben Meyers, forty-six, was the former chief of police in Grand Junction. He was forced to leave that position over a year ago due to political differences with two members of the city council. One of these men was Meyers' forerunner as the police chief, and according to Meyers, every change he tried to implement was taken as an insult by his predecessor.[425]

The local newspaper, The Daily Sentinel, appeared to be against him as well. On this front, however, Meyers acknowledged he never got off on the right foot with its principal reporters. He wished he had better public relations skills but was proud of the work he had done in Mesa County.

Last May, Meyers was hired to serve as undersheriff for Pitkin County. In his initial meeting with his new subordinates, Meyers acknowledged he had a controversial time in Grand Junction but that he was working on getting his law enforcement career back on track.

"I told my sergeants and lieutenants," he remarked to Aspen reporters, "that whatever they've done in the past is dead and gone. The only thing that counts with me is what happens from here on in. I just hope the community will have the same attitude toward me and the department. I don't ask everyone to like me, but I want you to respect me. I want to prove what I can do."[426]

Meyers had been true to his word. He had already worked with the sheriff and the city council reorganizing and expanding the department. Residents were surprised when Meyers was able to prove that it took 4.8 deputies simply to ensure that one patrol car remained on the streets, twenty-four hours a day, 365 days a year. He continually worked with county commissioners, successfully noting that the department was understaffed. Meyers was credited with helping raise the number of deputies and sergeants from eleven to twenty-one, all within his first year.[427]

He wanted to focus on preventing property crimes such as auto theft, burglary, and larceny. Small-time drug use by the townspeople was not a concern unless it led to the very property crimes he was hoping to prevent. His reputation among the townspeople was beginning to improve, just as he found himself the unwittingly subject of a legal spotlight.

On April 4, Meyers had attended one of Bundy's pretrial hearings in the courtroom. He watched as Elizabeth Harter took the stand. The state's key witness, who had flown in from California, was ready to provide her crucial identification. She had been at the Wildwood Inn on the evening Caryn Campbell disappeared, and she had seen a strange man near the elevator. Authorities had shown her a stack of mug shots a year after Caryn's murder. Harter had pulled Bundy's picture out, identifying him as the man she had seen by the elevator.

The undersheriff watched, waiting for the moment when Harter would finger the defendant. What was out of the ordinary was that Harter was now explaining that she had seen two men on the evening of the disappearance. The prosecutor proceeded cautiously.

"Do you see anyone in the courtroom that looks like either of these men?" he asked.[428]

"Could I have one of them stand up?" Harter asked.

"Certainly."

"The man in the first row," she said. "Stand up."

Ben Meyers felt the spotlight on him. Harter had looked right past Bundy at the counselor's table. She was staring directly at *him*—the undersheriff. She was now pointing at him.[429]

"Referring to the man in the blue pants, in the blue jacket?" the prosecutor asked, visibly uncomfortable with this sudden, unforeseen turn of events.

"Uh-huh," she nodded. "In the blue jacket."

Meyers stood, nervous and upset. He was middle-aged, slightly paunchy, with a receding hairline and brown eyes. Bundy was thirty, fit, with a full head of wiry brown hair and blue eyes. How on earth could the witness be so off?

At the counselor's table, it was everything the defendant could do to suppress his laughter.[430]

◆

In marked contrast to Maureen Higgins' view of her male-dominated department, Officer Kathy Earl thoroughly enjoyed working with the *boys* of the Aspen PD. They were great guys, big brothers, who consistently showed her respect. They seemed to be a very cohesive group. Other than her supervisor, Kathy was the only female officer in the department. She knew she'd receive some comments about her skirts later this summer, but that would be nothing compared to the vulgar jokes and teasing the fellas were already giving one another. She never claimed to be a feminist and wasn't out to prove anything to anyone. She simply found her job to be interesting, and her male colleagues seemed to pick up on this. Kathy certainly gave the impression that she was going to stick around. She felt like she was part of the group, focused on the common goal of finding their fugitive. There were a lot of strong women in Aspen.[431]

◆

Betty Pfister heard the helicopters as they flew up and down the valley. She had taken point, working with aviation companies in the surrounding counties to enlist the services of various choppers and their pilots. Her work with Marta and Betty on Tuesday led to an orderly and safe evacuation of all the school children. She was a woman who was used to difficult assignments.

When she was a freshman in college, she disobeyed her dad and paid a dollar for a ride on an airplane. She was immediately hooked on the thrill she received, soaring above the fairgrounds. She entered a negotiation with her father. If he would pay for her to take flying lessons, she would stay in college.

With the arrival of the Second World War, Betty found herself answering her nation's call for women who held a pilot's license. Assigned to non-combat flights, she was thrilled to be at the controls of a B-17 or B-24. Shuttling aircraft wasn't her only responsibility. After the damaged aircraft had been repaired, it was her job to act as a test pilot and ensure everything was now in working order.[432]

After the war, Betty ended up flying cattle to Central and South America, once losing a bull on the tarmac at Miami Airport. She eventually purchased a plane and began competing in air races. She twice won the International Air Race in the early 1950s.

It was around that time she went skiing in Aspen, noticing a particular man waiting in the lift line. A sign was hanging around his neck. "If you think I'm handsome," it read, "I'm available." Betty eventually married that man.[433]

She then dedicated herself to aviation-related issues in her new community, planning and overseeing the construction of the heliport at Aspen Valley Hospital, the first such heliport in the state. Betty had also organized the Pitkin County Air Rescue, coordinating missions out of her living room whenever there was a downed aircraft or lost skiers in the mountains. She'd lobbied outside the doors to the Federal Aviation Administration, demonstrations that led to the construction of the control tower at Sardy Field.

Now, she was coordinating the air operations during the most extensive manhunt the valley had ever seen.

Nope. Ted Bundy wasn't going to slow Betty Pfister down.[434]

◆

Paul "Stormy" Mohn ran Aspen Security Patrol, one of the two security companies in town. He oversaw security for many of the mansions along Red Mountain Road. Word was getting out across the nation; Ted Bundy was loose in Aspen. Homeowners from California and Texas were calling Mohn, all wanting extra security coverage on their vacant secondary homes.[435]

Mohn stood at the window from which Bundy had made his escape. He looked down twenty-three feet to the ground. He leaned his arms on the windowsill and just peered down at the grass; it was so far away. *This Bundy character was a desperate man.*[436]

◆

Dave Stapleton had heard that the escape had put the fear of Christ into the whole community.

"Man," he said to the deputy escorting him. "I have a wife and five kids at home, and here I am, driving around in a 4-wheel drive in the mountains with a sheriff's deputy, looking for a guy who's killed people?"[437]

"Nervous?" his companion asked.

"Oh, hell yeah. Absolutely. Scares the bejeebees out of me to tell you the truth."

The duo got out of the vehicle and cautiously approached the Banard Hut, doing what they could to silence their boots as they navigated around piles of snow.[438]

The deputy pulled his revolver.

The two men slowly opened the door to the ten-year-old hut, some seven miles south of the summit of Aspen Mountain. It was dark inside, but they entered, checking the main floor as well as the loft. Just like the cabins they had inspected yesterday, the Barnard Hut was empty. Only when he stepped back outside did Dave realize that you can't really train for a manhunt. It just has to be something to be experienced.[439]

"Not my average week," he said, thankful to be heading back to the safety of the vehicle.

◆

Deputy White maneuvered the Ford Bronco up the winding Frying Pan Road north of town. His chosen destination had been determined after some major brainstorming. The manhunt had entered its third day, and multiple members in the sheriff's department felt Bundy had already skipped town. If the fugitive had an accomplice with access to a vehicle, or if he had stolen a car within the first twenty minutes of the escape, he could be sipping margaritas in Barstow by now. Gary disagreed.

He felt that the fugitive was still around but outside the city limits. The deputy could feel it in his gut. He eventually slowed the Bronco, coming to a complete stop right in the middle of the road. He opened the door and breathed in the mountain air. The temperatures hovered in the low fifties this morning.

Stepping out of the vehicle, he could see Sloane Peak to the south and knew he was just a couple miles east of Ruedi Reservoir. If Bundy headed toward the reservoir and continued east, he could skirt the small towns of Meredith and Norrie, towns that had no roadblocks or significant police presence. Past that, the roads turned to dirt, and eventually, he could be on the streets of Leadville. Bundy may be physically fit, but he wasn't a mountain man, so he'd most likely steal a car in a small town. Then, he could head to Denver in no time, and from there, he could go virtually anywhere.[440]

Scanning the vast amount of mountain terrain, Gary was only too aware of the small size of the police and sheriff's departments. *We need more men.*[441]

He retrieved his shotgun and deliberately left his door open. Any vehicle approaching from the east would surely see the insignia of the Pitkin County Sheriff's Office and recognize that the Bronco belonged to law enforcement.

He'd been one of four deputies hired from New Mexico during the previous year. White had been investigating everything from thefts to homicide cases. He worked well either in the group setting or as an individual. He wouldn't be working alone this morning.

The passenger door of his Bronco opened, and a high school student stepped out into the morning sun. It was White's younger brother, Greg, who happened to be in town visiting for the summer. Gary had come up with a novel idea. Rather than leave the teen home alone, why not deputize him, so to speak?

Greg wore one of his big brother's uniform shirts, complete with a badge on the left breast pocket. He rolled his sleeves up to his elbows and adjusted his ball cap. He was tall for his age, lanky, and clean-shaven. He was nervous but excited.

OFFICER KATHY EARL

Looking west, the brothers spied a vehicle approaching from the town of Basalt. The deputy walked around to the side of the Bronco and handed his brother the shotgun, reminding him to adhere to the procedures they had already discussed in detail. The teen had been advised to stay near the rig, keep the weapon always pointed at the ground, and observe quietly while Gary interacted with the drivers. Neither brother would display a cavalier attitude. The young man understood that the good guys were understaffed and in a serious situation. He nodded just as the car was approaching.[442]

Greg stood still, brandishing the shotgun.

Gary spoke with the driver, asking if she had seen any strangers in the area. He requested to search the trunk and, after doing so, sent the motorist on her way with a respectful nod.

Gary turned around to face his brother. *All clear. One down, how many more to go?* With the bravery his kid brother was displaying, perhaps he'd earn a sheriff's department hat and a fishing excursion at the reservoir. Young Gregory beamed. He was posing as an armed deputy looking for the elusive Ted Bundy. Gary White was doing what he could.[443]

◆

Officer Chet Zajac was spending his third straight day searching the exteriors of the luxury homes in an affluent neighborhood north of town. He had just finished checking off another house on his real estate map and decided to sit down for a break. He was tired. The lack of sleep was affecting his ability to concentrate and focus. Classic symptoms of sleep deprivation. His bed... how long had it been since he'd been there?

When he had been hired seven weeks ago, another officer had pulled him aside.

"No sense in living up in Aspen where it's so danged expensive," said the other officer. "Come downvalley. My buddy's got an old trailer he's trying to rent, which is right across the field from me. We can be neighbors." When Zajac learned what his monthly pay would be as a rookie, he agreed to take a look at the trailer, a stone's throw from a rough-cut sawmill.[444]

Zajac wondered if Bundy would need to be back behind bars before officers could get a good night's sleep again. He figured the fugitive was still in the valley since the terrain surrounding the town was brutal, just brutal. It would not have been difficult for him to reach the mountain road that wound its way up into this affluent region of town. Inside these dark and locked-up houses were full wardrobes, wine cellars, food, supplies, and maybe even weapons. Zajac wasn't sure if Bundy had access to this type of information before his escape. The fugitive could break into one of these residences, rest, live off their supplies, and lay low until the roadblocks came down.

He's here, all right. Maybe even in the house I just checked.

◆

Atop the service counter in the reception area of the sheriff's office, there was a stack of pamphlets titled "What to Do Before the Burglar Comes." The sheriff grabbed a felt-tipped pen and altered one of the pamphlets. It now read, "What to Do Before Bundy Comes." On a more serious note, the sheriff knew that his search sector was no longer the town of Aspen. He had tried to be orderly and look in every location that seemed logical, but he was now faced with a new search sector—a thousand square miles of forest.[445]

There was the side the sheriff showed to the public, and then there was his private side. Publicly, he held a press conference and seemed more confident in front of the cameras than he did on Tuesday. When asked whether he felt folks in town should still feel threatened by the fugitive, Kienast replied, "As a citizen of Aspen, I am no more concerned for my health and welfare than I was four days ago."[446]

When he went into his office for a moment of privacy, however, the sheriff picked up the phone, dialing the number to the Colorado Bureau of Investigation in Montrose. Reaching Agent Leo Konkel, Kienast formally requested assistance. Could the CBI conduct an independent investigation into how Bundy managed to escape? The sheriff didn't want to conduct his own investigation, as it would lack any authenticity or objectivity from the viewpoint of county residents.[447]

"If you have any ideas on how we can catch this bastard," the sheriff chuckled. "Well...if you can catch him, that'd be fine. But really, your job up here would be to find out what happened."[448]

Konkel suppressed a smile, understanding full well that Kienast was hoping to gain the assistance of the CBI in the manhunt itself. He informed the sheriff that he'd be at the courthouse as soon as possible.

◆

In a recurring feature called "What Do You Think?" in the local paper, reporters asked residents what they thought of Bundy's escape. The responses exemplified the town's divided reaction.

"I'm a little worried," one woman admitted. "It's scary. It makes me nervous. I'll be home with my door locked tonight."[449]

"I can't believe it," said another. "I'm not afraid. I think he'll be found."

"I thought it was sort of funny myself," a radio DJ added, "but it wasn't funny to the people involved."

"I think it's typical of the casual attitude in Aspen in general," another said, "which once again seems to have filtered over into the Pitkin County Sheriff's Department. In this case, it particularly distresses me since Bundy's known to be dangerous, and his escape endangers the lives of women in town."

Criticism of the sheriff's office was a hot topic in the cafes and shops in town. Some argued the merits of permitting Bundy to conduct business in the courtroom without restraints. The defendant was not only legally presumed innocent until proven guilty, but he was also serving as an attorney in his own case. Lawyers, wearing shackles in open court, would be hard-pressed to find unbiased, open-minded jurors willing to listen to their case. During Bundy's multiple months as a *guest* of Colorado law enforcement agencies, he had never provided them with reason to doubt his sincerity in defending himself and clearing his name.[450]

The sheriff's supporters pointed to the fact that Kienast had even testified before the judge, requesting restraints on Bundy the moment he arrived in his jurisdiction. Judge Lohr had only granted the sheriff's request for Bundy to appear in handcuffs on his first court day.[451]

Kienast's supporters added that the potential for Bundy to flee was a recurring topic among reporters before the actual event. The fact that the defendant had been left alone in the courtroom was, they said, a common occurrence. One reporter had even nudged another with his elbow, asking which window he thought Bundy would select. The defendant wasn't beyond testing the judge's boundaries, requesting to be free of the handcuffs during transport from Glenwood Springs to Aspen. Such stories, freely exchanged before Bundy's jump, should have provided the sheriff with enough red flags to indicate that a *leap* was a distinct possibility.[452]

In the wake of Bundy's escape, Judge Lohr granted authorization for specific prisoners to be shackled in his courtroom. Armed guards would also be permitted before the judge. Times were changing in this carefree mountain town.[453]

◆

Around 3:30 p.m., at the Aspen Times Building on Main Street, the latest edition was hot off the press. Stacks of newspapers were bound with twine, and the distribution process began. Several people were on hand to gather stacks and transport them to various distribution boxes strategically placed around town. Enterprising kids purchased other stacks.[454]

An ambitious boy ran into the building and purchased two stacks at a discounted price. He then walked through town, hawking copies as he went. There were plenty of customers in the shopping district, city hall, and the drug stores. Customers in restaurants were always guaranteed sales, but if there was a true Mecca for paper sales this week, it was at the courthouse. The newspaper only cost twenty cents, but most officers and deputies paid extra, encouraging the young businessman.[455]

Deputy Gary White was gathering his thoughts on the front courthouse steps with a fresh bottle of Pepsi. He called out to the newsboy and handed the lad a dollar bill, no change required. Gary took a good look at the front-page headline of The Aspen Times, "Escaped Kidnapper Bundy Eludes Helicopter, Hounds, Manhunters." During the last two days, Gary had been hearing more about the crimes Bundy was accused of in Washington State, and his heart went out to the family members of the victims. This wasn't mere sympathy but the empathy that stemmed from personal trauma.[456]

Fifteen months ago, Gary was just about to head out on a double date when his phone rang. Figuring it was work-related, he felt obligated to answer. It was actually his mother. Deciphering what she was trying to say, Gary learned that his father had just died as a result of a stabbing. Jumping in his car, he made the five-hour journey to the small town of Gallup.

Few cars were on the desert highway after midnight. Gary did his best to process what his mother had said. His dad had been in his car in the parking lot of a shopping mall waiting to pick up his wife, Gary's stepmom. It was late, and when the woman opened the passenger side door to get in, she discovered her husband dead behind the wheel. An unknown assailant had savagely attacked him.

In the morning, Gary had introduced himself to the authorities investigating his father's homicide. Because he was a fellow police officer, Gary was permitted to learn specific facts of the case that ordinary family members would not have been privy to. Due to the blood evidence, it seemed as if the attack had started on the passenger side of the car. Mrs.

White, however, had discovered Joe in the driver's seat, slumped over the steering wheel.

Gary was permitted to attend his father's autopsy. It was highly unusual for a family member to receive this type of access or information. He appreciated all the cooperation he was receiving from authorities, but deep inside, he just wanted to know they were doing everything possible to solve the crime. From the autopsy, he learned that none of the twenty-seven stab wounds had been termed fatal, but there were so many injuries that the poor man simply bled to death. Gary stayed in town for a week, assisting in the investigation. In the months that followed, there were no arrests, no suspects, and very few clues.[457]

For Gary, safety mattered. Law and order mattered. These weren't catchphrases for him. He knew people in Aspen were scared, and rightly so. He stared at the full-length picture on the front page of the newspaper. It was Ted Bundy, being led into the courthouse Tuesday morning by Kralicek and Murphy. There was something peculiar about Bundy—those eyes.

◆

Only a few weeks before the escape, JoAnne Rando and Carolyn Hougland walked up to the courthouse to watch one of the preliminary hearings in the Caryn Campbell case. This particular hearing was closed to the public, but when the guard at the door recognized them, they were permitted to enter the courtroom.

Bundy was standing at the counselor's table, having just finished addressing the court. He had made some sort of joke which, apparently, entertained the judge. The defendant was grinning, amplifying the premature laugh lines at the outer corners of his eyes. He appeared as charming as ever, reveling in the spotlight. He turned, hearing the ladies entering the room. He looked right at JoAnne, and their eyes locked. Instantly, the atmosphere in the room changed. Like a chameleon, his bright blue eyes darkened. His dimples disappeared under his scruffy, full beard just as his smile vanished from his face. It was as if a switch had been flipped, and the room was now filled with an eerie, palpable tension.[458]

JoAnne felt as though the pace of the courtroom slowed drastically, unnaturally. Lawyers and deputies—even Carolyn—began to fade away. JoAnne noticed the sharpness of his nose, for some reason, below those dark eyes. Eyes that never wavered, never blinked.

She felt a disorienting spin and a tingling, numb feeling that began in her throat and quickly spread. The hair on the back of her neck bristled, and she froze in place. Her body seemed nearly foreign to her. She thought the greatest physical threat in these parts would be an encounter with wildlife on the outskirts of town. But here she was, face-to-face with a predator in the very building that symbolized civilization and safety.

Those eyes.

Carolyn was taken aback by the strange scene, instinctively reaching out to help her friend to a nearby bench. As JoAnne slowly recuperated, she was mortified. Had anyone else caught a glimpse of what she had just seen? That wasn't a man staring her down, but some malevolent creature. At that moment, JoAnne's perception of safety and danger was shattered, replaced by a chilling realization that evil could lurk anywhere, even in the most seemingly secure places.[459]

◆

Things in the dispatch office were finally starting to calm down and becoming, for lack of a better word, routine. One of the deputies had made a passing remark to a reporter. "Now, Washington State has two famous heroes—D.B. Cooper and Ted Bundy." There seemed to be no end to the macabre sense of humor in town. Nancy looked toward the front door and spied a familiar face.[460]

Marta walked through the door. She was a colorful character with a diminutive frame accentuated by her oversized square glasses. She worked for the sheriff as a process server and had an uncanny knack for tracking down folks who passed bad checks or men who were behind on their child support payments. It was a common occurrence in the valley for this gray-haired woman to suddenly pop out from behind a hedge and serve someone with court papers. She knew the whole valley like a bloodhound.[461]

She was a delightful mass of contradictions. She had a part-time job as a waitress at The Red Onion, Aspen's oldest restaurant. She could do a fair impression of Flo from the popular television sitcom *Alice*. "Well, kiss my grits!" In marked contrast to this blue-collar persona, she had a license to officiate at civil wedding ceremonies. She could spend an entire afternoon in heated discussions with deadbeat dads and then go home to unwind at her Bodhi Riwo meditation center off Conundrum Road. For seventeen years, Marta had been running the two-acre Buddhist retreat dedicated to promoting world peace and supporting the Dalai Lama. She was the only woman Nancy knew who could enter a conversation concerning increasing jail sentences and turn it into a serious discussion over

Tibetan teapots.⁴⁶²

For three days, she had been working with local restaurants to procure sandwiches and meals to feed searchers. Aspen didn't allow fast-food franchises within city limits. Marta was committed to bringing the night and morning crews steaming hot cups of caffeinated coffee.

She had just returned from making delivery rounds and needed something at city hall. As she passed the dispatch office, she saw Nancy wink at her from behind the counter. Marta put her palms together and gave a slight bow. Nancy beamed and returned the gesture.

◆

A Chevy Blazer pulled into the parking lot behind the courthouse. A man in his late thirties emerged and walked toward the building. He was in plain clothes, but as he moved, there was a glint off a badge visible on his belt. His brown hair was peppered with the first signs of grey, and there was a confidence in his stride as he stepped through the door leading into a corridor.

The man's career in law enforcement began at the Los Angeles Police Academy. He had been an officer with the Newport Beach Police Department for eleven years, rising in the ranks to detective sergeant in charge of the narcotics department. Entering Sheriff Kienast's office, the man stepped forward with an extended hand. Agent Leo Konkel, now employed by the Colorado Bureau of Investigation, introduced himself.

The sheriff had called in Agent Konkel to conduct an independent investigation into how the fugitive managed to escape. Konkel wanted to inspect the courtroom and the law library where the incident occurred. He was led upstairs by personnel only too happy to receive assistance from one of Colorado's most respected agencies. The Rocky Mountains were strewn with small-town police forces who, overall, could maintain law and order on a daily basis. When anything out of the ordinary occurred, however, and an experienced investigator was needed, an agent from the CBI was called in. The escape certainly fit the criteria.

Agent Konkel had been working for the CBI for two years, primarily in an undercover role on the Attorney General's Organized Crime Strike Force. He was one of only three agents whose jurisdiction covered the entire Western Slope. Konkel had already read the newspapers and scanned the FBI teletypes. As he ascended the stairs, the agent was thinking, *if I get an opportunity, I'm going to get something out of this rascal.* He really wanted to assist Mike Fisher in gleaning more information out of Ted about the homicide in Snowmass. They would have to find him first.[463]

Konkel entered the courtroom for a cursory examination of the scene. He'd return later with a tape measure to create a diagram of the room's layout, but for now, he simply wanted an understanding of the situation.

He observed that the courtroom was located on the western side of the building's second floor. The three sections of the room were quite clear. In the north were the judge's bench, the counselor's table, the witness stand, and the jury box. In the central section were the rows of benches for the public, and to the south, the law library. There were ten large windows in the courtroom: one on the north, six on the west, and three on the south. Now, counting the doors and windows, Konkel realized there were just too many possible methods of exiting the room.[464] Bundy simply couldn't resist the temptation.[465]

The agent wandered into the law library and carefully peered out the window from which Bundy had made the transition from prisoner to fugitive.

Okay-that's impressive.

◆

Garfield County deputies had spent a considerable amount of time tracking down the whereabouts of Bundy's female pen pals. If a woman had corresponded with him at any point during the year, she was placed on a list and investigated. Every name had been run down, and their locations were verified. All were nowhere near the Roaring Fork Valley during or just prior to Bundy's escape.[466]

Deputies from the Pitkin County Sheriff's Department had been pulling sixteen-hour shifts for two days. They were tired and hungry, and yet their bonds of friendship and camaraderie continued to grow. Kienast's ranks seemed to be new, enlightened peace officers. Police officers cracked jokes about the new regime at the courthouse, but the sheriff had the community's support.

Officer Roberts ignored the palpable tension between the police department and the sheriff's office. This was mainly felt and fed by senior members of both organizations. Hugh could get along with almost anyone who wore a badge. When working the graveyard, for instance, a mere radio call would bring the nearest deputy for a late-night cup of coffee. They joked with one another and teased each other, but it was all in good fun, reminding Hugh of his days in Vietnam with his fellow servicemen. *We're all on the same team here; there's no need for competition.*[467]

Perhaps the conflict between the two agencies arose due to how different the two departments were run. Chief Hougland was merely a temporary band-aid meant to keep the department running while a search for a more experienced individual could be undertaken. It essentially meant that men like Detective Sergeant Dave Garms were running the show.

The sheriff had assured his constituents that, even though he had a master's degree in theology from Notre Dame, he was no holy roller. He wanted his deputies to be comrades, not simply folks who punched a clock. He had his team go out on multi-day wilderness experiences: hiking, rafting, and climbing together. None of this had anything to do with police work, but it proved to be integral in uniting the department as a whole. Hard-nosed southwestern lawmen, former businessmen, and Peace Corps volunteers. It was a pretty eclectic group of people. Kienast helped them come together to prove to people that they could be effective as deputies yet still be sensitive to the community. You either got with the program or you didn't, and Kienast had been busy culling those who did not embrace his philosophy.[468]

◆

When agents of the Federal Bureau of Investigation learned that there was a fairly credible report that the fugitive had been spotted in Riverton, Wyoming, they were ready to jump into the manhunt. The sheriff was hesitant about this development. The agents advised Sheriff Kienast that Bundy was technically a prisoner of the state of Utah, and merely by escaping in Colorado, the fugitive had crossed state lines. The feds didn't need anyone's permission to enter the case.[469]

Federal agents contacted the Salt Lake County Sheriff's Department. Together, members of the two agencies shared what scant information they possessed. Authorities in Utah welcomed any assistance the bureau could provide. The Salt Lake City County Attorney's Office issued a federal warrant for Theodore Robert Bundy. The filing charged him with violation of Title 18, U.S. Code, Section 1073—unlawful flight to avoid confinement.[470]

Agents in the Salt Lake City FBI field office began sending teletypes to their counterparts in Denver and Seattle. In this initial all-points-bulletin, Bundy was described as a white male, born November 24, 1946, in Burlington, Vermont. The teletype concluded with, "In view of type of crime subject has been convicted of, he should be considered armed and dangerous—escape risk."[471]

◆

Dave Garms was one of several detectives dispatched to investigate multiple Bundy sightings. Not everyone was cooperative or even kind to Garms. Some still held a grudge over his trailblazing—if controversial—undercover work.

Following the historic drug bust, Garms wasn't at all surprised that his former friends in the marijuana and cocaine world were angry with him. He was, however, taken aback by the response he received from average residents. He thought he'd be hailed as a hero, but residents felt betrayed by "David," their dope-dealing hippie friend. This was a peaceful town, after all. Death threats, which arrived by telephone, took on a more credible tone after Garms' car was set on fire. When asked about the incident years later, he had a new perspective on the incident.[472]

"I've always wondered what it would be like to be an outlaw," he remarked. "Working undercover was the only way I could find out and still hold on to a two-way ticket. I mean, if I turned outlaw any other way, I'd lose any chance of being a cop again."[473]

Most men in this situation would have taken their pay raise and potential promotion and moved on. Not Garms. He liked this valley and was going to remain. Staying didn't come without repercussions, however. One night, he walked into a pub just to enjoy a night out and was met with a hostile reaction. Thirty-five inebriated patrons turned on him, and he was forced to flee. On top of that, he still flinched whenever a car backfired.

For over four-and-a-half years, Garms worked very hard in his new community. Slowly, residents began to warm up to him. Eventually, his friendships with the people he had arrested began to resume. One had even invited him to their wedding.[474]

Garms wasn't convinced that the man on the run had even left the county, let alone the state of Colorado. The fugitive was too smart to allow himself to pass through a roadblock. Garms figured the runaway would find a secluded spot on the outskirts of town and dig in. This would permit him easy access to the town for provisions. He could lay low and wait for the inevitable order to be given: the removal of roadblocks. Then, after stealing a car, the thief would simply drive away, vanishing in the dark. Bundy wasn't physically prepared to attempt a cross-country escape on foot. Convinced that the man was still in the valley, the detective didn't feel it had been necessary to call in the feds.[475]

Detective Michael Chandler was in complete agreement. Bundy was probably holed up somewhere, perhaps in one of the vacation homes, but certainly not in Wyoming. Besides, the bureau didn't like city cops, and the city cops didn't trust the feds.[476]

Four years earlier, Chandler was new to the force but was not yet a sworn police officer. The chief wanted more income for the department, so Chandler came up with a novel idea. Enter Aspen's first meter maid—Mr. Michael Chandler. Taking the job in stride, the young man did what he could to impress his new boss. He wrote, on average, over 100 parking tickets a shift. On multiple occasions, while Chandler was standing on the side of the road writing tickets, folks in passing cars threw garbage at him.

"We hate you, Garms!" they yelled.[477]

"I'm not Garms!" he hollered back, shaking his head. Then, he mumbled, "I had nothing to do with that." Chandler understood how people could mix the two of them up. Both had similar physiques, dark mustaches, and matching clothing. He made it his mission to get acquainted with his fellow citizens, confident that, with time, his true character would be revealed.

Sergeant Horan wasn't surprised that Bundy still eluded authorities. He figured the fugitive was hiding out somewhere and would, when the moment was right, steal a car. He welcomed the assistance of the FBI. He was especially pleased that the agents were locals from Glenwood Springs—Special Agents Dave Yates and Cliff Browning. These were men you could trust.

Yates seemed to be a true professional who was always willing to help a person out. Browning didn't come up to town too often, but he was a well-known figure among regional officers, and he had been an agent for fourteen years. Together, the agents had cracked multiple drug cases in the valley.[478]

Deputy Sergeant Larry Spiers gripped his shotgun tightly while riding in one of the helicopters high over Ruedi Reservoir. Like most of his colleagues, he didn't believe Bundy had crossed the state line. *He's here*, he thought. *He's here, somewhere*. Still, the sergeant knew Agents Browning and Yates and figured they would make great advisors. They would have access to additional resources if needed. The helicopter changed direction. Spiers kept his eyes on the lakeshore below.[479]

◆

Nancy felt fatigued from working in the dispatch office for three long days. She'd only gone home for a quick shower and to grab a clean pair of jeans. Changing her shirt, however, wasn't as easy. Levi Strauss & Company sponsored all the department uniforms for the Aspen PD. The department had collectively designed a two-toned shirt for all the dispatchers to wear. Add a pair of Levi's, and your uniform is complete. Nancy, like everyone else, had plenty of jeans, but clean shirts were now in high demand. No one had time to do laundry.[480]

Betty Erickson, who was rapidly becoming a Mother Teresa to the law enforcement officers throughout the valley, walked up to the front counter. She slid slices of hot pizza through the slot in the cashier's window. It was dinner time. Nancy was famished, and the pizza smelled divine.[481]

◆

Louise Bundy, the fugitive's mother, sat down with reporters from The Seattle Daily News in Tacoma, Washington. She had planned to visit her son in just a few weeks. That wouldn't be happening anytime soon, even if Ted was recaptured. The reporter asked what she thought about having a boy on the lam.

"A person can't spend the rest of his life running," she remarked quietly, avoiding the reporter's gaze. "If he could hear my words, the first thing I would say to Ted is that we love you. Then, I would plead with him to turn himself in—to give up. All too often, people shoot first and ask questions later. It happens in Seattle, in Tacoma, and it could happen in Colorado."[482]

When asked if she felt her son was innocent, she replied without hesitation. "We have no doubts, whatsoever. It's just impossible for him to be the kind of person who would murder. His friends have always maintained that Ted is innocent. They believed in him then, and they believe in him now."

When asked why she thought her son would mount such an audacious escape, she was sure it was "an unplanned, spur-of-the-moment decision." She pointed out that her son had written her letters, indicating that he was enduring intolerable conditions while incarcerated. He was feeling a sense of hopelessness, believing the general populace had already judged him guilty during the pretrial hearings. Louise stared at a place on the floor. She wasn't seeing the carpet per se, but some private scene that she alone was privy to—a place deep in the recesses of her mind.

"Ted is out of jail," she eventually managed to say. "But, he's not free. He's a hunted man…and that's not freedom."[483]

FRIDAY

JUNE 10, 1977

CHAPTER 6
DEVIL'S HOUR

As the "Devil's Hour" quickly approached, the graveyard shift officers patrolled the streets of the downtown sector. Aspen's daily street maintenance would begin around four in the morning, so towing would start about an hour beforehand. Those drivers who forgot to move their vehicles in time would be left wondering, *where the hell is my car?*[484]

Officer Quirk cruised the streets from north to south while Officer Roberts covered the streets from east to west. They stopped to shine their flashlights inside the handful of vehicles that were designated for towing. There had been no reports of stolen cars this week despite the surprising number of unlocked cars that still sat with keys in plain view. This didn't mean that the fugitive, wet and cold, hadn't found temporary sanctuary inside a vehicle.

Roberts viewed Quirk as full of piss and vinegar, ambitious, and aggressive, and there may have been some truth to that. They had had their good times and their bad times, but Quirk didn't feel animosity toward Roberts despite their differing views. Both men felt the other was somewhat of an outsider.

Officer Roberts' attention returned to the manhunt. How many people had been out looking for this clown? So many people. So many assets had been plucked from their usual duties to track down a dangerous convict.

Roberts was impressed with the leadership skills demonstrated by the senior members of the department, Detective Sergeant Dave Garms in particular. That man just seemed to have his finger on the pulse of the community, and he wasn't afraid to tell a superior if a course correction was needed.[485]

Now, if the department could just catch a break.

◆

Just before sunrise, Officer Bill Grikis—Dogcatcher to the Stars—rambled along Castle Creek Road in his green Ford truck. He was approaching Ashcroft, south of Aspen. Prairie dogs had completely overrun this little ghost town, and the nearby barn cats and coyotes weren't enough to keep the varmints in check. Ranchers had expressed concern that, with the apparent overpopulation, the plague could return. Though this theory sounded far-fetched, these concerns had been brought before the city council, and because the ghost town was popular with tourists, a strategy for confirming or disproving this concern had been set in motion.

Samples were needed, so a couple of weeks ago, Grikis found himself downwind from an obvious burrow in the deserted town. With the golden rays of the rising sun announcing the start of a new day, the critters began to poke their heads out of the earth. A bullet whizzed across the field and killed one on the periphery of the burrow. Bill reloaded his single-shot, bolt-action .22 rifle and aimed again and then again. He carefully bagged the carcasses and brought them to downtown Aspen.

The three carcasses were combed for fleas, and then the rodents and their parasites were analyzed. Sure enough, the bacterium related to the plague were present. City officials were alarmed. What could be done? The population of the prairie dogs had to be thinned. At first, strychnine was utilized, but the local ranchers didn't want too much used, and they were wary of even stronger measures. So, every morning for the past few weeks, Grikis made the drive out to Ashcroft. He'd position himself and shoot as many prairie dogs as he could in about an hour.[486]

When he had started this grisly chore, Bill collected as many as fifteen of the critters at a time and brought the carcasses back to be analyzed. The cycle continued, though, with fewer and fewer numbers being culled. He wasn't keeping a running tally, but as Bill stepped out of his truck and entered the remains of the old mining town, he figured he had bagged about 150 so far. He slung his rifle and walked toward today's job site.[487]

The prairie dogs weren't relegated just to Ashcroft, and they weren't the only animals that could carry the disease. If Bundy was merely hidden on the outskirts of town, maybe he would contract the bubonic plague. The residents of Aspen were already talking about the possibility. It would be a fitting punishment for a varmint like ol' Ted.[488]

◆

Officer Zajac shuffled his boots, back and forth, across the heavily worn rust-colored flooring leading past the dispatch office. He was bone-tired after three days scrambling through the wet, brushy hillsides, searching through elaborate vacation properties on Red Mountain.

"Zajac!" a sergeant called out. "You need to get your ass home and get some sleep. You look like shit!"

Like a zombie, the young officer froze, taking in the information and sending it through an endless cycle of logic filters. Had he heard that correctly? *Sleep?*

"All right," he finally managed to mumble. "Sounds good to me," he said to no one in particular as he made his way out the door.

The officer miraculously managed to drive to his trailer near Basalt. When he arrived, his primary goals were food, shower, and sleep, in that order. He stripped off his duster, hat, and the rest of his clothing and staggered over to the fridge. An ice-cold Coca-Cola would at least take the edge off his thirst. He popped the top off the bottle and, as he lumbered down the carpeted hallway, greedily guzzled the contents.

He slowly opened his eyes. He was so groggy that he felt like he was fighting his way out of drug-induced sleep. He didn't remember laying down to go to sleep. As his sight slowly began to come into focus, he couldn't figure out why he was looking into the bathroom. The left side of his face hurt, and he started spitting out carpet fibers. He finally realized that he was lying on the floor in his hallway. *What the fuck am I doing here?* He thought. *I must've passed out.*

He rose carefully and stepped into the bathroom, butt-naked. Squinting at the mirror, he noticed that the left side of his face had unmistakable rug burn, red and raw. He made his way to the phone and dialed a pal.[489]

"Mike," Zajac said. "I feel all right now, a little woozy, but this is what happened..." Chet relayed the bizarre set of circumstances, including the downing of the soda.

"Oh, yeah," his friend replied. "Your heart probably skipped a beat from being exhausted and slamming down a cold, wet thing, and...uh...you just passed out." There was a lengthy pause.

"Um...okay. Do I need to go to the hospital?"

"Probably not. You'll be just fine. Get some food, get some sleep, and we'll see you in a few hours." His friend was a paramedic, so Zajac figured he was going to live as he stumbled into his soft bed.

♦

Deputy Kempfert rolled down the window, and cool air rolled across her elbow and into the Bronco cab. Carol was riding shotgun after she and another deputy had been sent on a potential lead in Vail. Their journey had turned into a wild goose chase, and the deputies were irritated that their time had been wasted.[490]

Now, they found themselves in a painfully slow line of cars on Highway 82, near the base of the Buttermilk Ski Area. They were only advancing a car length at a time. *It'll clear up,* she thought. Turning her head, she spotted the Holiday Inn. She had been called out to this location a couple of months back over a disturbance in progress.

Gary White had also responded to the disturbance. White didn't particularly like to respond to crimes committed at the inn, as the establishment refused to press charges of any kind. Motel management typically wanted *badges* to settle the situation, then fade away into the night as quietly as possible. The last thing a motel needed was bad press.

The deputies proceeded to a room where a significant amount of shouting could be heard. Gary pounded on the door.

"Pitkin County sheriff's deputies!" he yelled. "Open the door!"

Someone from inside turned the knob and allowed the deputies to enter the cramped motel room. Gary encountered five men and white powder—*everywhere*. It was spilled on the floor, on the coffee table, the nightstand, the bed, the sink, the toilet seat, and lying around in open bags.

Three of the men in the room identified themselves as undercover DEA agents from Denver. Apparently, when the two drug dealers learned the identity of their potential cocaine customers, they panicked and tried to flush the drugs down the sink and the toilet. There had been a significant scuffle, which accounted for the scattering of the white powder.

This all made sense to Gary. The Holiday Inn was ideally situated for drug trafficking. Dealers could drive in from Denver, get a room, make their deals, and disappear back to the city like smoke in the wind without ever having to take any chances by going into town.

Aspen PD officers were predominantly anti-drug, and they had a small slice of legal jurisdiction that they patrolled quite diligently. Pitkin County, however, was a different story. Word was getting around the state that the new sheriff had a more liberal attitude when it came to drug enforcement. Sheriff Kienast disapproved of undercover agents working in his county, especially without alerting him in advance that a sting operation was underway.

"How can we work this out quietly?" an agent asked Gary. He didn't elaborate on what he meant. He didn't have to. This put Gary and Carol in an awkward position. They now stepped aside to discuss the matter privately.[491]

There were so many angles to the request which had just been made. The DEA should have notified Kienast that they were operating within his jurisdiction. They failed to do that and had been caught with their fingers in the cookie jar, so to speak. By all rights, the prisoners should be taken to jail at the courthouse, as the crime itself occurred in Pitkin County. What would happen then? They all knew of the sheriff's liberal views and figured the dealers could get off scot-free. Aspen was currently ranked as the fifth largest cocaine distribution point in the nation. The town seemed wide open. Conservative law enforcement officers like Carol and Gary preferred to see the dealers facing justice. They just couldn't be sure justice would be served in the valley.

They came to an agreement. The DEA agents would be responsible for cleaning up the coke, but then they could transport their prisoners to Denver. Carol would write the report of the incident but preserve the identities of the undercover agents.

Carol and Gary went their separate ways once they got back to the courthouse. As the one who volunteered to handle the documentation, Carol felt she had to be cautious and craft a carefully worded report. She believed the sheriff was too cozy with reporters and shared too much information. Her report omitted details as well as the names of the agents. She turned in her paperwork.

"No," the sheriff noted, handing it back to her. "This won't do. I want details...I want the names."[492]

Carol felt adamant that an undercover agent's identity should be protected so that the agent could continue working undercover. She couldn't prove it, but she was sure her employer would share the information with reporters if she divulged their identities and badge numbers.

"Uh...I didn't get the names," she lied. Kienast was putting her in an awkward position. She wrote another draft, essentially a repeat of the first one, but this time, she added more details concerning the events that transpired in the motel room. She turned it into Kienast and found a way to dodge off, out of his range.

Later in the afternoon, she found the sheriff speaking with reporters from The Aspen Times, showing them her report. Carol wasn't surprised and felt vindicated. Drug dealers are the bad guys and should be prosecuted. Undercover agents were the good guys, and their identities should be protected. To her, it was that simple. This was a crucial moment for her, as she realized that the cocaine problem in Aspen would not be handled in this manner.[493]

Her thoughts snapped back to Bundy, the current focus of local law enforcement. Kempfert was confident that the runaway had bolted out of town, and she wondered if he was getting frustrated during what was surely a difficult journey. She had seen the fugitive frustrated before.

Kempfert had been assigned, along with a male deputy, to take Bundy downstairs to the jail where he ate his lunch during the preliminary hearings. The defendant carried one box of legal paperwork, while Kempfert carried a second. When they approached the open cell, Bundy wanted both boxes carried inside. Carol perceived that something was not quite right.

"No," she said calmly. "Take what you need, but you're not taking the boxes in." Carol watched as the prisoner's entire appearance changed. The charming law student with stunning blue eyes evaporated, and a new man was in his place. His eyes—something about his eyes—they morphed. He took two steps toward Carol, all puffed up, and looked down at her with dark, livid eyes. At 5'6", the deputy stood her ground, refusing to back down. The deputy repeated her directive.

After an uncomfortable pause, the prisoner before her deflated and then retreated into his cell. Before this, their professional relationship had been just that, professional and businesslike. That day, she had a front-row seat, witnessing a man shift into quite a different creature and back again.[494]

◆

There seemed to be two sides to Deputy Gene Flatt as well. There was the laid-back, good ol' boy during the off-hours but a lawman with unbridled enthusiasm during business hours.

He was manning the West Sopris Creek Roadblock today, waiting for Deputy Maureen Higgins to join him at this rural checkpoint. He was bored, so he tossed small stones into the gurgling creek, which lends its name to the nearby road. Apart from the dirt and gravel intersection, the only other sign of civilization was a cluster of mailboxes. He saw a pony in a nearby field and it made him chuckle.

When Gene was just a newly minted deputy, fresh from the Midwest, he was patrolling along the Holland Hills Straightaway, admiring the lush pastures dotted with livestock. Suddenly, he spied several horses lying in a field. He pulled over and radioed in an emergency—possible livestock poisoning! Everybody and their brother's uncle responded to the scene when suddenly, up popped the horses. Like Lazarus, they began running around, rising from the dead. Where Gene came from, he had never seen horses lying down, and his friends in the valley never let him forget it.[495]

His kind, comical side ran contrary to the passion the deputy displayed when it came to arresting drunk drivers. Before Flatt arrived in the department, locals who drank and drove were taken care of rather than punished.

"Hand me the keys," deputies would say, opening the door to the patrol car. "Get in. You'll find them in the sheriff's office in the morning." Then, the drunk driver would be delivered home to sleep it off.[496]

When Gene arrived in the valley, he learned quickly that Aspen seemed addicted to cocaine. It just appeared to be everywhere. The department didn't have enough manpower to stem the tide of drugs coming through. "It would be like trying to pull the *Titanic* out of the ocean," he told friends. He then noticed the number of drunk driving incidents in and around town.[497]

The mountain resort community was seeing a rise in DUIs and accidents due to two key culprits. Tourists would fly in, drink heavily, and then hit unfamiliar roads at night. It couldn't all be blamed on tourists, however, as it was a well-known secret that bartenders in Aspen poured heavily for locals.[498]

While some displayed wisdom by sobering up with a late-night breakfast of blueberry pancakes and obscenely-sized omelets at The Village Pantry, others chose a riskier path, attempting to navigate treacherous roads immediately after their last drink.

The vibrant Aspen nightlife was a thrilling experience for tourists, who eagerly mingled with locals and emptied the bars, often their wallets, too. However, it was the individuals who miscalculated their alcohol intake that stirred a deep concern in Gene Flatt.[499]

The deputy, driven by a deep sense of duty, saw an opportunity and made a resolute decision. If he couldn't dismantle the mountain of cocaine flowing into town, he would take a stand against the drunk drivers. It wouldn't be a glamorous task, but one could not argue with the undeniable results.[500]

As Gene pulled a suspected drunk driver over, he'd conduct sobriety tests. After asking the driver for identification, he'd ask them to step out of the vehicle so Gene could observe the person closely. Had they staggered, swayed, or outright fallen out of the car? Was there any slurred speech? He'd shine his flashlight in their eyes. If someone were highly intoxicated, their eyes wouldn't work correctly, especially if he asked them to look sidelong at him. There was the Horizontal Gaze Nystagmus Test, where he'd move his finger around and ask the driver to follow it with just his eyes. There was the one-leg stand exam, the walk and turn, and the Romberg Test, which usually garnered results. Feet together, head back, eyes closed for thirty seconds—sometimes, it could be pretty comical. Then, Gene would take the driver's keys.[501]

"Watch these keys," he'd say, holding them up to the driver's beltline. "I'm going to drop these keys on your foot. All you have to do is move your foot before the keys get to it." If the driver was intoxicated, they never seemed to move their boot or shoe in time. The deputy typically performed this test three consecutive times. Deputies and officers had slightly varying tests they'd perform, but the city and county agencies had just entered a federally funded project to try and standardize field sobriety exams.[502]

Sometimes, Gene could arrest two drunks a night. When that was the case, it could take the entire graveyard shift just to process those two cases. Pitkin County Sheriff deputies, coupled with Aspen PD, were arresting as many as ten drunk drivers a week.[503]

The sentence could be anywhere from five to 365 days for a first-time offense. This seemed extreme compared to the local celebrity, Claudine Longet, who had been sentenced to only thirty days in the county jail for shooting her boyfriend. What would a murderer get if he was convicted of kidnapping and killing a young woman? Three months?[504]

A handful of deputies stayed clear of Gene Flatt, considering him a loose cannon, motivated by his quest for racking up the DUIs, which were earning him accolades. The Midwestern man seemed untouchable, though; he was providing a great source of revenue for the county's legal and judicial system while taking the focus away from the rise of drug use in the valley.

Gene celebrated his success quietly. Deaths due to drunk driving accidents in the region dropped in less than a year. Some folks were walking, breathing, and laughing, completely unaware that they were alive due to his efforts. That was something Gene could hang his hat on.

Deputy Higgins pulled up in her fiancées Bronco. She gave a comical salute to Gene as she started unloading supplies she had brought for the checkpoint. She wasn't expecting any trouble, but if the fugitive was ensnared in her checkpoint, she had plenty of protection. She could rely on today's partner, her flashlight-baton, her pepper spray, her revolver, and the shotgun in the back of her rig.

As the deputies waved for a vehicle to proceed, Gene repeated something he'd heard the sheriff say.

"Bundy's too clever to still be around," Kienast had said. "He's probably in Acapulco."[505]

◆

Deputy Gary White started his law enforcement career in New Mexico. He and a friend climbed into Gary's '74 Ford pickup one day and headed north to Wyoming for a job interview. Although they had made a pact not to drink during their cross-country journey, they had stocked a large cooler in the bed of the pick-up with beer and liquor in case of an emergency. Once they hit the Colorado state line, they began to surmise that having a lone Coors beer wasn't considered "drinking."[506]

Soon, the lone beer became a *few*, and they decided to take a detour to visit their ol' buddies in Aspen. Happy with this change of events, Gary searched the glove box and every nook and cranny in the truck's interior within reach. He found what he was searching for underneath the seat and fished it out. It was an 8-track cartridge of Neil Sedaka's greatest hits. He popped it into the dashboard player, and "Calendar Girl" blared through the speakers. Gary drummed on the dashboard with one hand while he steered with the other. The duo sang along with the international superstar, "I love, I love, I love my calendar girl!" Soon, armed with sailor's logic, they determined that they'd have one, only one, *real* drink.

Out of the cooler emerged 7-up and vodka for Gary, while his buddy settled on Jack Daniel's with just a dash of Coca-Cola. The more they drove, the more they drank, and the more they drank, the louder they sang. With the windows rolled down, they serenaded the coyotes and the prairie dogs, one hit song after another. At some point, they decided just to keep playing "Calendar Girl" over and over again as the mileposts disappeared behind them.

With his guardian angel working overtime, keeping the pickup truck from plummeting over the steep switchbacks of Independence Pass, Gary soon cruised into Aspen. Not sure where the sheriff's office was, Gary stopped his truck right in the middle of the road, completely unaware of any cars blocked behind him. He exited the vehicle, leaving the driver's side door wide open. Off to his right, he saw a building with businesses on the ground floor and what looked like apartments on the second. A man stood on a balcony, so Gary hollered up, asking for directions to the sheriff's department.

"Right next door!" the man called down through cupped hands. "In the courthouse. Just drive around the back and go in!"[507]

White pulled up as directed, belting out the song's chorus. "Yeah, yeah, my heart's in a whirl!"

With the confidence of an overabundance of alcohol, Gary burst through the rear door of the courthouse. Fortunately, his friend Sergeant Don Davis was present and immediately took note of Gary's condition. As Gary stopped to mime out a saxophone solo, Sergeant Davis quickly maneuvered his friend into a nearby office and closed the door behind them. Gary was told to go get some sleep, sober up, and come back to the office first thing in the morning.

With a hangover that could drop a moose, Gary dragged himself down to the courthouse the following morning. Though his eyes were a red latticework of capillaries and regret, he was introduced to the sheriff while Don Davis sang his friend's praises. Doing his best to maintain his balance, Gary stayed relatively silent and was surprised when he was offered a job. He accepted, and he returned to New Mexico to pack his bags. Within two weeks, a sober and reinvigorated Deputy White was patrolling the backroads of Pitkin County.[508]

◆

Leaving all shenanigans behind, at this moment, White and Davis were making their way toward a helicopter when they passed a third transplant from New Mexico. Gary had learned valuable lessons from this friend and Davis during their years combating heroin coming out of Juarez, Mexico. This trio had seen their share of difficult assignments.[509]

DEPUTY GENE FLATT

White did his best to suppress a smile as he passed his friend, known for being a little too generous with the mace when it came to breaking up scuffles. Police officers, civilians, grandmothers, you name it, they all got sprayed, and soon, tears were flowing amid a potent shower of aerosol.[510]

Davis and White boarded the chopper and were soon flying over the Castle Creek area south of Aspen. They were after a predator who knew how to hide in the shadows.

"Any chance he headed up and over Aspen Mountain?" Gary asked, using his headset.[511]

"Not the path of least resistance," Don shrugged. "Ted's not a mountain boy."

"I agree," Gary replied. "He's a city kid. He's not going to get too far too quick."

Then again, Gary knew Bundy. The fugitive had been exercising rigorously; he was desperate, and he was unable to resist his impulses. The deputy patted the pilot on the shoulder to gain his attention.

"Can we fly over Conundrum Creek?" he asked, while pointing at a map.

Unfortunately, three days had passed since the escape, and with each sunrise, the chances of recapture appeared to be dwindling. Gary wondered if Bundy was alone or if he was receiving outside assistance. Ted had his own ensemble of female admirers—pen pals who remained under suspicion. Also, he wasn't the only missing prisoner from Garfield County.

◆

About an hour's drive west of Denver, one of the community's two fugitives was finally taken into custody. After a week on the run, Daniel Kellum, the man who had disappeared from a work-release assignment, was apprehended near the Eisenhower Tunnel on Interstate 70. Ted's former cellmate offered no resistance during his arrest.

When he was brought in, FBI agents pounced on him in an attempt to extract information on Bundy's whereabouts.

"I'm telling you, fellas," the prisoner gestured with his manacled hands. "I had no part in Ted's escape."

"It's just a coincidence then that you escaped just before him?" an agent asked.

"That's all it is," Kellum confirmed.

"Okay, Dan," the agent leaned forward, trying a different tactic. "You know the man well. You probably know his capabilities. You're a sharp young man. Be my expert witness. Where do *you* think he is?"

Flattery worked, and the blond prisoner was more than happy to share his thoughts on the matter.

"Pitkin County, but...outside city limits," he rationalized.

"Can you be more specific?" a secondary agent asked.

"Well," Kellum thought for a moment. "Hunter Creek region would make a great escape route."

The site had already been searched with no trace of the fugitive, but agents knew Bundy could have waded through the winding creek on the thickly wooded hillside, throwing off the scent-tracking dogs.[512]

"In fact," Kellum was back on the defense. "I warned the sheriff that Ted might go, you know?" This was the second person to make such a claim, despite a declaration from the department that they had no prior knowledge indicating that Bundy was a flight risk.[513]

◆

At high noon, two young men were heading toward the Aspen Pedestrian Mall, each carrying a stack of pink papers. Two years earlier, these fellas had wondered what to do in a mountain town that didn't have a college, so they decided to invent one. Marc Demmon was soon dubbed "Dr. Slats Cabbage," president of their fictitious educational institute. Al Pendorf adopted the persona of "Fulton Begley III, Dean of Women and Equipment Manager."[514]

Out of thin air, these two had founded the Aspen State Teacher's College (ASTC) and even had a student store in a basement over on Mill Street. With its headquarters in Pendorf's print shop, the college—fueled only by imagination—took off. One only had to look around town to see proof of the school's existence. T-shirts, car decals, and even student IDs were on display. They printed handbooks, and one enterprising young man used his student ID to get a U-Rail pass in Europe. They even created a mascot, the ASTC "Broom," which came in handy for their undefeated football team. The boys published a game lineup with the likes of Michigan and Notre Dame. All games were to be home games, so when their opponents failed to show up for the event, they lost by forfeit—GO BROOMS![515]

Their monthly newsletter, the *Clean Sweep*, brought the most smiles in town. The bulletin managed to garner real-life advertising dollars while spoofing the entire concept of a college education. Within its pages, the professors (locals) provided course descriptions. These ranged from

"Advanced Texan 243," which described how to handle students from the Lone Star State, to "Auto Mechanics 202," which explained how one could start a '49 Jeep in the dead of winter.[516]

Dr. Slats Cabbage and Fulton Begley III were now handing out the June 1977 edition of their newsletter. This edition was printed on pink paper because that's what was most abundant at the print shop. "Bundy to Star in Movie," read the splashy headline, making readers smile before they could dive into the story. What would Slats Cabbage have to say about the valley's newest folk hero?

> Last Tuesday, Theodore Bundy made what he called a "giant leap" in his soon-to-be-established movie career. In an exclusive interview with Aspen State, Bundy stated on Monday, Paramount Pictures made him an offer that he couldn't refuse. Consequently, his quick departure from town on Tuesday morning, without even saying goodbye to many friends, was something that had to be done. Reportedly, Bundy will be starring in a Robert Altman film entitled, "Butch Cassidy and the Sunday Bundy," which will begin filming next week in an undisclosed location. Ted, as he is known on the set, is excited about the opportunity and is especially looking forward to his singing debut. In the film, he will sing both "By the Time I Get to Phoenix" and "I Love Paris in the Springtime."[517]

Where the cover photo should have been, only the words "Bundy unavailable for Photo" were present. Turning the page, readers glimpsed a notice under the heading of New Courses. "Escapism 234," it announced. "Jumping, running, and hiding will be the main focus of this course, which is highlighted by the lecture, *Successful Use of Legal Loophole Leaping*. Professor Bundy." If that wasn't enough, in the classified section, "Ride Wanted" was listed. "Law student desires ride anywhere. North, south, east, or west. Will share driving. Hope to leave soon. Call Bundy 925-5192."[518]

♦

As the deputy responsible for Bundy at the time the prisoner jumped, Deputy David Westerlund understood an interview with the Colorado Bureau of Investigation was inevitable. He sat, terribly uncomfortable, in front of Agent Leo Konkel and was asked for his version of the defendant's escape.[519]

"I don't know how in the world he got away from me," Westerlund began, clearly embarrassed. "I was watching the door all the time and…I *was* watching him. I never, ever thought that anybody would try to jump out of the window. That wasn't where I was focused. I tried to watch him. About the only way he could try to escape would be by coming through the door, and I knew I wouldn't let that happen."[520]

"I'm not here to reprimand you," Konkel stated. He was here to determine the circumstances that led to the prisoner's brazen departure through a courthouse window. "Tell me about any interactions you had with Bundy prior to his vanishing act."

"Well…I helped transport him from the courthouse to the Garfield County Jail."

"On one occasion?"

"Yes, just the once. That was the day he had to move from our jail to the one in Glenwood Springs."

"And how was he secured at that time?" Konkel asked, scribbling in a notebook.

"He was in leg shackles, had handcuffs, and a belly chain. Carol drove, and Bundy rode shotgun. I was in back, behind the driver."

"Okay. Any other interactions with him since January?"

"Served him a couple meals in the cellblock, but that's it. At no time had I been instructed to carry a firearm while in the courtroom or to have the defendant in cuffs or irons while court was in session."[521]

There was still no written policy concerning how to handle prisoners accused of major crimes inside the aging courthouse.[522]

◆

Ward Lucas and his cameraman turned in their rental car. For three days, they had driven the back roads of Aspen, hoping against hope that they'd bump into the fugitive and be hailed as heroes. Shoot…delivering an escaped convict back to jail? *That* would have been a journalistic scoop. Since a glorious capture seemed to elude them—and authorities—the investigative reporting team decided it was time to return home and report back to work at their Denver television station.[523]

Recalling the turbulence they encountered during their journey to Aspen, Coleman was adamant that they return to the capital via a commercial airline. Chuckling, Ward reached for his credit card once again.

◆

Jean was buzzed through the security door in dispatch.

"What's the scoop, I Dream of Jeannie?" Nancy teased.

"It's getting pretty strange out there," Jean replied, her eyes wide.

"How so?"

"Brunettes are getting nervous. They're changing their hair to blonde, red, or any color other than dark brown. Some have even chopped the length off—anything other than the Bundy-brunette look."[524]

Nancy held up a finger, a signal for Jean to hold her last thought as a transmission came in.

"10-23, the parking lot just east of Little Annie's," said an officer. "Quite a 10-10 underway. We're on it."

"A fight in progress?" Jean seemed surprised. Nancy's hand gestures indicated there was really nothing to the dust-up.

"Tourists," she plainly said.

"10-4," Nancy replied to the officers.

"Well," Jean sighed while sitting down in a chair. "I think I should cover for you for a minute. I think you need to go see Dave."

"Why?" Nancy asked, shuffling paperwork.

"He looks like he lost a fight with a badger."

Upstairs, Detective Sergeant Garms felt his eyes growing heavy, begging him for sleep. He'd been running full throttle for days now, and one day of searching had blurred into another. He sat down at his desk and laid his head down on his forearms. He fell asleep right there. Someone gently draped a blanket over him.[525]

It was Nancy.

Garms came off as a guarded man, rarely forthcoming with his thoughts. Nancy knew, however, that Dave was a brilliant, diligent detective. And, like scores of other women in the valley, Nancy hadn't failed to notice that Garms was *very good eye candy*, as the ladies in the department liked to say.[526]

◆

While the grueling game of hide-and-seek continued, bars and bistros were doing a bang-up business, selling Bundy Burgers and Bundy Cocktails. Ted's defiance of the law was already becoming the stuff of folklore. Anyone in the valley who'd had any interaction with the man was suddenly finding their fifteen minutes of fame. Bundy tales were the newest form of entertainment and sought-after commodities.

Marty Stouffer was a local resident and a respected wildlife documentary producer. He spent nearly a year in South Africa filming *Botswana, Where a River Dies*. He shot the wildlife sequences that were used in the *John Denver Rocky Mountain Christmas* special. He even worked with Robert Redford on *The Predators*. His promotion of nature conservation was a source of pride for the entire community.

Oddly enough, the producer had one of the best stories around, and he was a natural-born storyteller. Back in January, jury selection began for the Claudine Longet trial. The pending trial would determine if the death of Vladimir "Spider" Sabich would be ruled as a homicide or merely a tragic accident. Marty showed up at the county courthouse along with other prospective jurors who had received a summons.[527]

It was Judge Lohr who addressed the crowd, asking if anyone present had any reason why they felt they couldn't serve on a jury. Hands shot up throughout the room. Two lawyers were excused, one of whom happened to be handling the deceased's estate. Five people were discharged by providing documented hardships. The town's mayor was excused because he had already publicly stated that he believed the defendant was guilty as charged. Another man was dismissed because he had once asked Spider Sabich to judge a wet t-shirt contest. Marty had heard enough, so he raised his hand as well.[528]

"Look, your honor," he began. "My name starts with an S. I'm going to sit here all week, cluttering up the place with all these people. I knew Spider. I saw him with Claudine around town, and I saw them arguing on multiple occasions. I read the thing in the paper—what she wrote in her diary. I understand that's supposed to be inadmissible as evidence because it was an illegal search and seizure. But…based on the diary and based on me witnessing their arguments, I think she *shot* him, and I'm sure I won't be selected for the jury. Therefore, I would like to leave now and not be on this jury."[529]

"Well, Mr. Stouffer," Judge Lohr replied, not appreciating the young man's tone. "You can sit down and wait until I get to your name alphabetically. Whether it's Thursday or whenever it is, at that point in time, we will address those issues." And here it was, one of those moments in Marty's life where he felt he was justified in his logic, and the need to rebel just rose to the surface.

"Well, sir, you can kiss my ass. I'm leaving now," the filmmaker snapped as he defiantly walked out of the courtroom. Judge Lohr didn't raise any alarms, didn't call the bailiff, nor even raise an eyebrow. He merely wrote a note on a pad of paper.

Those who ended up serving on the jury found Claudine guilty of negligent homicide. This would have meant a maximum sentence of two years behind bars and a fine of $5,000 to $30,000. The judge sentenced her to only thirty days in the county jail. Community members were appalled when Lohr said the defendant could serve on weekends, two days at a time.[530]

A month or so after the trial, Marty received a summons in the mail. His presence was demanded at the courthouse to answer for his insubordination during jury selection.[531]

"Well, Mr. Stouffer?" the judge asked him. "What do you have to say?"[532]

"Well, sir, as I explained to you at the time, I believed that she was guilty. I believed that I saved us all a lot of time and trouble, and I declined to be on the jury."

"That's not good enough, and I'm giving you some time to think about it. And the next time I ask you a question, you'll know how to answer properly. I'm giving you twenty-four hours in the local jail for contempt of court." And with that, the judge's gavel came down with a *bang*, indicating that there would be no more discussion on the matter.

"If that bitch got off with thirty days," Marty remarked in disgust, "I should get five minutes."[533]

BANG! BANG! BANG!

The impact from the gavel, along with the look the judge shot the bailiff, resulted in Marty's quick escort out of the courtroom.

Reporting to the sheriff's office to begin the entrance procedures, he carried a cardboard box containing a clean t-shirt, a change of underwear, a handful of nature magazines, a notepad, and a pen. A deputy took all the items from Stouffer's pockets: keys, wallet, and his Swiss Army knife.

"I'm taking this," the deputy declared, plucking the pen out of the box. "You could use it as a weapon."[534]

"Nobody is going to get stabbed to death with an ink pen," Marty grinned. Being led deeper into the jail, he found himself being folded in with about half a dozen prisoners returning from a day's labor in the work-release program. There was no laughter and only sporadic conversation. The atmosphere was somber and relatively quiet until a deputy pulled the large handle, which unlocked the barred entry door to the jail. The scraping sound of the door was an assault upon the eardrums.

The group was ushered forward into a small holding cell. There was a table with chairs here, a solitary communal toilet, and a sink. The gate screeched again, closing behind them. The work-release prisoners proceeded into their predesignated units. Marty was directed to the last of five cells and was told he'd have the top bunk.

Lying on the bottom rack was a bearded man, silent as the grave, seemingly detached from reality. This man didn't even acknowledge the existence of his new cellmate. Marty recognized the prisoner and thought it best not to disturb him. Bundy clearly wanted to be alone with his thoughts.

The cellblock's newest arrival sat down on a small bench in the back of the room. He realized that if he wanted to, he could reach out and touch his cellmate's shoulder. When dinner was delivered, Marty ate quietly, noting that Bundy left his meal untouched.

Chewing slowly, Marty observed his roommate in silence. There was no radio, no television, and he wasn't interested in perusing his magazines. Bundy was more interesting. *Why hadn't he greeted me? What is he thinking about?* Marty studied the man's face and believed he was mentally cataloging something like he was doing homework in his head.

After he finished his meal, Marty no longer had an excuse to be within his cellmate's immediate proximity. He changed into his boxers and a clean T-shirt and climbed up into the upper bunk. A couple of guys in the adjacent cell were talking quietly. It seemed strange that, though the outer gate to the cellblock was closed and locked, all of the individual cell doors were still folded back in their open positions.

Marty laid back on his rack, staring straight up at the solitary light bulb in the ceiling. *Wonder when they'll turn that off?* He was confident that Ted Bundy had murdered that nurse abducted from the Wildwood Inn. How was he supposed to sleep in the room with a killer? He closed his eyes.

Brrring, brrring. Marty's eyes shot open. *Brrring, brrring.*

"Sheriff's office," he heard a deputy say down the hall at the processing desk. Soon, like a scene straight out of a prison movie, a deputy ran his baton along the bars near the entry door.

Brat-tat-tat-tat-tat-tat-tat!

The overhead light was burning holes through Marty's eyelids, and who knew if the lights would be turned off any time soon. The phone seemed to be ringing every five minutes, and he could hear the deputy's end of the conversations.[535]

He reached over and emptied the contents of his cardboard box. He tore a U-shaped section out and then placed the box over his head. His neck fit snugly into the torn-out portion. By doing this, he effectively created an artificial "night."

Brrring, brrring!

"Sheriff's office," a deputy said into the receiver. The sound was a bit muffled now, but it was still obnoxious.

Marty managed to retain his sense of humor. *Okay*, he thought. *I'm lying in jail, in my underwear, not really looking to make any new friends. I have a cardboard box over my head, and I'm sleeping above Ted Bundy, with a locked gate barring my only exit. What could possibly go wrong?*[536]

SATURDAY

JUNE 11, 1977

CHAPTER 7
AMOS

In the morning, Deputy Sergeant Spiers and FBI Agents Yates and Browning were studying potential leads in the case when a teletype machine sprang to life. The electro-mechanical typewriter began spitting out its information here in Aspen, but also the field offices in Atlanta, Newark, New York, Philadelphia, Salt Lake City, San Francisco, and Seattle.

"What do we got?" Yates asked. Browning perused through the message as the rapid white keys danced across the page.

"Apparently," he began. "Bundy's name at birth was Theodore Robert Cowell. Identity of his biological father is unknown, but we're being told to be on alert for the usage of the last name *Cowell*."

"Cowell, eh?"

"Looks like there's an updated description of Teddy. Okay...not good. His height, initially reported as six feet, is...being modified to 5'11'."[537]

"That's nothing."

"Yeah, but the weight," Browning squinted. "He's now being listed as weighing between 145 and 155 pounds."

"Whoa," Spiers turned around in his chair. That's about—"

"Thirty pounds lighter than initial estimates," Browning remarked, interrupting his colleague. "Okay, okay. Here we go. Blue eyes which are somewhat of an attractive feature—deep-set. Is known to wear glasses and dark glasses as disguise. Dark brown, normally wavy hair, parted on right

Six Days in Aspen

side. Currently collar length. Sideburns to ear lobe. Hair partly covers ear."

"This isn't helpful," Yates said. "We have *all* that from the reporter's photograph."

"Hair is very wiry," Browning continued reading, "and when washed, appears almost afro-like. Easily manageable and worn in various styles. Currently clean-shaven, however, has worn full beard and, in past, has used false mustaches and beards as disguise."

"Interesting," Spiers mumbled.

"Sallow prison pallor complexion. Slim build. Wiry. Muscular, athletic build. Wrinkles on forehead—"

"He's only thirty," Yates snorted.

"Prominent wrinkles extending down from nostrils. Thin nose. No noticeable scars or marks."

"They're describing a long-distance runner," Yates sighed.

"Let's hope not," Browning remarked while handing the teletype to Spiers.[538]

◆

For four straight days, Nancy had been practically living in the dispatch office. Today was day five of the manhunt, and the momentum had dropped drastically. The weekend had finally arrived. Nancy and her friend Ann had poured out their souls supporting the police chief and the sheriff in the search efforts.

There were other gals available to cover dispatch, so the two decided to conquer the mountain roads on their motorcycles this morning. Both were craving fresh air and sunshine, so they rode up the winding road that led to Ruedi Reservoir. Nancy loved the sense of freedom she felt as they crossed the railroad tracks near Holland Hills. They rode like crazy up the winding, narrow road beside the Frying Pan River, passing the prime fishing holes. The trees, the water, the big blue sky. This is what Nancy loved most.[539]

Her Honda 550 was her pride and joy. She had recently divorced a darn good man. Her ex-husband had wanted multiple children, whereas Nancy wanted multiple motorcycles. Their lives weren't on the same track. She genuinely encouraged her ex to find someone to spend the rest of his life with while she built a life for herself in Aspen. She just wasn't looking for another man to fill his spot at this point, but that didn't mean that she was opposed to men altogether.[540]

Fraternization was strongly discouraged at city hall and the courthouse, especially between dispatchers and cops. Nancy agreed with this policy, understanding that a dispatcher needed to be fair to all law enforcement officers.[541]

Deputy Bill McCrocklin had a charming smile and a scraggly beard. With his glasses on, he could look very studious. In uniform, his 6'6" frame was eye-catching.[542]

For nearly a year, Bill and Nancy both served on the county's emergency disaster council. The sheriff had formed this committee hoping to improve the scope and effectiveness of the county's haphazard ambulance and accident response services. Over simple dinners, Bill and Nancy had hashed out proposals they wanted to present to the council as the plan for the county progressed.[543]

Dinners eventually turned into overnight retreats at a little rented cabin nestled in the Castle Creek area. After working for hours, they'd step outside into the bracing air. Under the spectacular night sky, strewn with so many stars that seemed within arm's reach, they'd admire the deep silence of the snow-covered trees and mountains.

Grabbing their cross-country skis, they'd set out into the moonlit pasture, down little slopes, and through the aspen groves. Their nighttime forays were special and peaceful, save the whooshing of their skinny skis slipping across the dry, crystalline snow. Nancy erupted in laughter when Bill flew off the path between some trees and crashed headlong into a deep snowbank.

As they raced to the next grove, their shrieks of laughter pierced the cold, crisp night air. Those playful shrieks only intensified as they flew too fast on the downhills, speeding past tree stumps and occasionally catching air over a hummock. Then, they'd just chat as they struggled in a climb up to the next hillock.

Eventually, they'd end up at the upper pool of Conundrum Hot Springs, a well-kept secret where they could soak beneath the steam clouds that hovered over the pools of hot mineral water. Here, the couple would shed their clothing, edge into the spring through the fog, and slowly submerge into the warm thermal pool.

They'd discuss their failed relationships and their plans to steer clear of heartache and focus on the responsibilities of their positions. Invariably, their conversation would turn back to the grant proposal they were working on for the council.[544]

The dead areas greatly worried Nancy. She was always concerned for deputies when she had to dispatch them to remote regions of the county where their radio signals couldn't reach. What she wanted, what the department really needed, was for a repeater to be installed atop Red Mountain. This would not only improve standard transmissions but cover more of the dead areas. Bill agreed. Someday, something would happen, and they would need those systems in place.[545]

A month ago, Nancy had her twenty-seventh birthday. She invited everyone from the Aspen PD and the sheriff's office to celebrate with her at the Aspen Mine Company restaurant—eggs Benedict, White Russians, or whatever they wanted. Bill couldn't make it, though he promised to stop by her new apartment after a court appearance to drop off her birthday presents.[546]

At the party, Deputy Bob Braudis, wearing a cowboy hat and an equally large grin, approached Nancy. He wished her a happy birthday, and she chided him a little due to his gapped teeth, his towering height, and the fact that he seemed to talk slower than a developing Polaroid.

I mean, spit it out already, she thought.[547]

After the party, Bob followed her out to her little red convertible Volkswagen. The deputy reminded her of the county's new regulations regarding drinking and driving. Nancy had tackled a few White Russians. Bob said he'd make sure she made it through town and home safely. Nancy didn't argue the point as she simply wanted to get home and get a few hours of sleep before her birthday dinner later that night. The two cars slowly wound their way through town and up to her apartment in Mountain Valley.

Nancy parked at the base of her incredibly steep driveway, which had patches of ice. She did her best to dissuade Bob from following her up the slick incline, but the deputy said he should really use the bathroom before he drove home. She paused. He emphasized that he definitely needed a restroom break after drinks at her celebratory breakfast. She relented.

Once inside, Bob dropped his green and yellow uniform jacket on a chair. He tossed his 4X Stetson, and it landed on the dining room table. Bob started heading down a long hallway toward the bathroom. Nancy's roommate emerged from her bedroom and spied the lawman walking her way. Looking past him, she shot Nancy a look like, *What is up with you guys?*

At that moment, Nancy heard a car door slam, and she raced over to her window. Looking out, she saw Bill. He was carrying a couple of wrapped birthday presents, and he was doing his best not to slip and fall on the ice. She motioned for her roommate to keep Braudis occupied in the back of the house whenever he emerged from the bathroom.

She greeted Bill at the door with a friendly hug and a peck on the cheek. He shook the snow from his hat and tossed it on the table, oblivious to the fact that it had landed only a foot or two from Bob's cowboy hat.

"I can only stay a minute," Bill remarked. "I'm due back in court, but I'll catch up with you later to discuss dinner plans?"

She assured him that she'd be in better shape once she had a few hours of shuteye.[548]

Bill retrieved his hat, still failing to notice the nearby Stetson. Nancy suppressed a smile, thinking, *how can two deputies be in the same apartment at the same time and not even notice? Maybe Bill should go into a different line of work*, she chuckled. *He'd be worthless as a detective.*

She watched silently as he zipped up his jacket and made his way cautiously back down the driveway toward his rig. As he drove off, she turned and put her hands on her hips. *Now*, she sighed. *What am I going to do about his cohort?*

When Bob returned from the bathroom, he immediately began recounting a tale of one of his rough and tumble adventures. Nancy laughed on occasion, blowing cigarette smoke off to her side as Bob animatedly told his story.

Where does he get his energy?

Nancy enjoyed his company, but she was just exhausted. Her eyelids grew heavy, and she finally had to stand up and hand Bob his hat. All she wanted was a shower and some sleep.

"Please be careful," she mumbled. "Don't fall on the way down, and thanks for the escort, Bob." The deputy took the hint and grabbed his coat. They headed toward the door.[549]

Over the following weeks, Bob began showing up at her apartment armed with steaks and potatoes. He'd tell more stories as she whipped up a meal. Braudis just had a totally different demeanor than other men she knew. It didn't hurt that he was 6'6" tall. Nancy was a respectable 5'9" and enjoyed feeling petite around him.

Nancy was overjoyed to learn that Bob loved to read and was interested in sharing books. He wasn't joking, either. They were reading in bed one night, and she was shocked when he suddenly ripped an enormous paperback in half. It was the 1,243-page bestselling novel *Shogun* by James Clavell. He had already finished the first half, so he handed it to her, thinking she'd enjoy the story. Nancy's jaw dropped. She had been raised to respect all books, paperback or not.

As May was coming to an end, Bob finally convinced her to come over to his bachelor pad at the W/J Ranch. It was not what she was expecting. At work, Deputy Braudis wore the standard-issue pressed trousers and shirts. She was used to seeing him with clean clothes with sharp creases. Nancy was shocked when Bob greeted her at the door wearing wrinkled, yellow corduroy pants, a pink shirt under a green sweater, and hiking boots. She considered herself a casual gal, but she had never seen such garishness. Nancy also discovered that the divorced man lived with four other roommates. She had to wade through a sea of dirty dishes in the kitchen.

Bob was beginning to realize what a busy life Nancy led. She had a secondary job selling fine Native American jewelry and pottery at The Squash Blossom. She was taking a photography class in a little building behind Aspen High School. It seemed to Bob that Nancy didn't have much time for him. She couldn't be available at a moment's notice. She had wanted an independent and interesting life, and she was living it.[550]

Bill McCrocklin, on the other hand, was a no-pressure kind of guy, but he and Nancy routinely returned to the same conversation—funding for improvements to the emergency communication systems. They realized they'd make better friends than lovers. Besides, she was the only one who knew that Bill had a crush on one of the local nurses.[551]

He'll be fine.

Nancy and Bob planned to spend more time together in June. Now, with Bundy on the run since Tuesday, that time together failed to materialize.

Bill. Bob. Was there room for romance in this new life she had created for herself? She wanted to believe in Bob Braudis and believe there was a future together. Underneath, however, she knew it would probably only be a chapter in her ongoing novel. They had been dating for less than a month, and that was only known by a handful of select friends in this notoriously small town.

Nancy and Ann saw a little clearing up ahead, overlooking the reservoir, and they slowed their motorbikes enough to park safely off to the side of the road. Cutting the engines and peeling off their helmets, they both smiled. Not another human in sight. Just the birds, the insects, and the sparkling water below. The tall pines and green aspens were so much more appealing than the cramped four walls of the dispatch center.

They climbed atop a boulder, removed their shirts, laid back, and closed their eyes. Sunglasses, shorts, hiking boots, and blue sky. *Freedom.*

Once she was warmed by the sun, Nancy sat up, picked up her blue pack of Parliaments, pulled out a cigarette, and lit it. Just hanging out with a friend, away from all the stress at the office, was therapeutic for both. Nancy had brought a copy of Thursday's edition of The Aspen Times. The banner headline said it all: "Escaped Kidnapper Bundy Eludes Helicopter, Hounds, Manhunters." This was the first time she'd even had an opportunity to read the local paper.[552]

"Wait a minute," Nancy said. "He could be *here*. Ah, we're in deep shit."[553]

"That's okay," Ann said. Sitting upright, she pushed a piece of her long, dark hair from her face. Then, she patted her .357, which was snug in a holster secured to her leather belt. "I'm not afraid to dust the fucker, if he shows his face. You can count on that." She extended her arms and clasped her hands together, mimicking holding her gun. "Pow! Pow!" She then blew into the barrel of her invisible gun, Charlie's Angels style.[554]

"I'm glad," Nancy chuckled. "He would have to get *really* close if it was up to me." She humorously patted a borrowed, snub-nosed Derringer that was in a holster on her belt. "Wouldn't it be great," she added, "if Bundy popped up and, here we are...half-naked?"[555]

Ann leaned back against the warm boulder and closed her eyes.

Nancy stared out over the water. Bill, Bob, Bundy. She had the morning off, but her mind wouldn't stop. She began going through her mental map of the region, from east to west. *He should be there, trapped within the boundaries we've set for him.* Just as a child shakes their Etch A Sketch toy to erase their drawing, she wiped her brain clean to start the mapping process again.[556]

"Well, I might as well pack it up and head back into the office," she said, knowing that she wasn't going to free her mind from work.

◆

At 10:30 a.m., a telephone rang at the reception desk in the sheriff's office. Deputy Carol Kempfert picked up the line. The caller was reporting a break-in at a cabin. He was not the owner of the property, but he kept an eye on the place. The last time he'd checked on the property, everything appeared to be in order. That had been a week ago. This morning, he discovered a broken window and a note left behind to explain the damage. There was something about the note. It didn't match the situation. Carol took down the details, thinking this sounded like a burglary. Daily life and criminal activities didn't end just because a manhunt was underway.[557]

"I think we should go check this place out," Deputy Kempfert called out. The sheriff gave a nod, and Carol soon departed.[558]

◆

Deputy Gary White and Sergeant Don Davis were back in a helicopter, soaring up the slopes of the mountains and gliding above the valleys south of town. Like others, they had come to the manhunt Tuesday morning, bursting with enthusiasm. Though many volunteers' fascination and eagerness had slackened, it was White and Davis's job to continue the pursuit, even if it was beginning to look unpromising. Gary was tired, having only scant hours of sleep during the past few days. He was glad the feds had a close eye over the borders of Utah and Wyoming.

Gary and Don scanned the terrain below, tapping the pilot on the shoulder and pointing when they wanted to hover over a particular point of interest. As the chopper started heading downwind on a steep incline, the main rotor suddenly began vibrating, and the aircraft rapidly started losing altitude. The deputies exchanged looks of concern but knew they were helpless at the moment. Gary knew they weren't above the hovering ceiling for the aircraft but was at a loss to explain whatever aerodynamic condition they were experiencing.

He had no way of knowing that the helicopter had entered a Vortex ring state, where an upward airflow strikes the inner blade section of the main rotor. When this occurred, a secondary vortex—in addition to the standard wingtip vortices—materialized. The resulting turbulence, significant loss of rotor blade efficiency, and jerky drops in altitude were the inevitable results. Gary watched as the forested mountain slopes seemed to rush past the windows.[559]

Whup whup whup!

The aircraft spun downward, and he thought they'd strike the side of the mountain. He could tell the earth below was rising faster than their ability to escape.[560]

The passengers braced for impact.[561]

When the chopper smacked the ground, Gary felt pain radiating through his lower back. Grimacing, he looked outside. They had managed to land in a small clearing bordered by quaking aspens. The pilot had used his skills to prevent the worst outcome, but they still ended up experiencing a hard landing, a technical term that didn't give enough credit to how forceful the impact truly was.[562]

Next, there was a sudden temperature change. Following the lead of the pilot, White and Davis unbuckled, popped open the door, and slid out of their seats. As soon as Gary's boots hit the ground, pain shot through his hip and down the back of his thigh. He was all too familiar with this type of agony.

In mid-March, Gary had gone skiing for the first time. He had no issues during his initial runs down the slopes, and this gave rise to a certain level of confidence that might not have been justified.

What the hell, thought Gary. *I can do this. One more run.* So, he rode up the lift to make another go on the easiest slope at Buttermilk Ski Resort. Successfully unloading at the top of the lift, he turned and headed down the slope, making his turns and doing quite well. *A cowboy on skis, how bout' that?* His confidence grew, so he permitted himself to gain more speed. He was a man in his element. He began to go faster and then faster still. Then, there was that awful sensation in the pit of his stomach when he knew his speed was more than he could handle. Instead of looking where he was going, he looked down at his skis.

When Gary finally looked up, he spied a sizeable mogul dead ahead. It was too late to avoid, and Cowboy Gary launched off the ramp of hardened snow like an Olympic hopeful. Thoughts raced through his mind. He knew he was in full view of skiers riding the nearby chairlift. Beautiful snow bunnies in brightly colored snow gear, were watching to see if this daredevil would complete his acrobatic stunt with flair and finesse. Based on the curving arch of his flight trajectory, he knew he would be landing right underneath the lift. Praying to the patron saint of skiing aside, the deputy knew there would be no graceful landing, no manly deceleration on the outrun, followed by a triumphant fist pump to the crowd.

Gary fell from the sky in a beautiful explosion of snow, Lycra, and nylon. When he crashed, his goggles went one direction, his poles another, all while he double-ejected from his skis and sent them sliding downhill without him. Facedown in the snow, his arms outstretched, he slid to a halt. He snorted through his snow-crusted nostrils. Skiers on the lift above him erupted in hoots, whistles, and applause. He knew he'd broken his collarbone at the moment of impact, but when he was able to roll over to look up at the sky, he realized he had a dislocated shoulder as well.[563]

Needless to say, Gary was pulled from his regular patrol work on the county roads and—due to his injuries—was temporarily assigned to guard duty in the county jail. As luck would have it, Claudine Longet began serving her thirty-day negligent homicide sentence soon after this. With his broken clavicle and sore shoulder, Gary found himself entertaining the actress with the story of how he earned his sling.

Order and balance. These were important to Gary. Sure, he was impressed with her beauty. Even with her hair in pigtails and dressed in prison-issued coveralls, she was beautiful and charming. And, let's face facts, he was a sucker for her French accent. Claudine was a prisoner, though, doing time for fatally shooting her lover in the stomach. Gary had not only heard the testimony in court but had personally seen evidence that was not permitted to be aired in open court.

He observed her reading about 100 letters a day, even the hate mail. There were a lot of folks upset with her minimal prison sentence.

Her cell walls had been covered with graffiti, so she volunteered to paint over it. Free labor? That was fine. Andy Williams, her ex-husband, was permitted to see Claudine because he accompanied their children to visit their mother.

The sheriff permitted Mr. Williams to bring Claudine a stack of books, though jail policy was only one book at a time for each prisoner. She was working on a project concerning her adventures in Aspen, presumably including details of the murder of Spider Sabich. As such, she could be expecting as much as 1.25 million dollars for the book and movie rights. Since her children were present, even the sheriff looked the other way when it came to the posted visiting hours.[564]

One day, Mr. Williams walked in carrying a tray of melting ice cream cones. Gary's first thought was how short the celebrated singer was. He was only 5'7". Williams asked if he could bring dessert to his ex-wife. Also, there were extra cones in case any of the deputies wanted a treat. Gary couldn't wait too long to answer because the ice cream was melting. He doubted there was any contraband hidden inside, so he authorized the delivery, picked a chocolate cone for himself, and enjoyed a moment of pure indulgence.[565]

Now that Bundy was on the loose, Gary had removed his sling and was back to standard duties. His left shoulder was feeling better, but his clavicle was still sore. Due to the helicopter's *hard landing*, his lower back was shooting waves of pain down his leg, stealing his focus.

"You fellas, okay?" the pilot asked.

"Yep," Gary lied through clenched teeth. "I'm fine." He was not about to be taken out of the game for this. Surely, he'd feel better tomorrow. He declined to alert anyone of his condition. He should, and he knew it, but that would mean he'd be pulled from the manhunt, and he wasn't about to let that happen.

The pilot inspected the tail boom and then looked at the rotor.

Helluva way to spend my birthday, Gary mused.[566]

◆

Deputy Kempfert slowed her Bronco and came to a halt on the black-top road. Checking her surroundings to be sure that she was approaching the correct cabin on Castle Creek Road, she killed the engine. Exiting the rig, she removed her sunglasses and took a good look at the two-story cabin, which was not far off the main road. Quaking aspens nearly surrounded the structure, greeting her with a shimmer of dancing leaves in the bright mid-day sun. She could hear the high-pitched buzzing of bees as they visited a multitude of blue and white wildflowers. A scrub-jay announced his presence high in a tree, and a hummingbird whizzed past the deputy, making sure that Carol knew she had entered his territory. The vacation residence was tucked into this tranquil little glade.

The deputy strolled around the cabin. The windows were covered by three-quarter-inch plywood bolted to the window frame on the inside of the house. Upon closer inspection, one solitary window was only protected by a wire mesh screen. Carol could see that this screen had been put back into place over a shattered window. There, a handwritten note had been left to explain the damaged pane. *Tom*, it read, *Sorry, broke this when putting in plywood. Will have another put in immediately—Amos*. The caretaker, who had found this note, said the owner's name was not Tom, but rather Fritz Kaeser. The concerned custodian suspected the place had been burglarized and had called the sheriff's department.

Finding the door unlocked, Kempfert cautiously stepped inside to inspect the main room.

"Pitkin County Sheriff's Department!" she called out.

Next, she walked to the bedroom door. The room looked neat and clean, and the bed was made. She walked into the kitchen and noticed a drinking glass and a box of crackers on the kitchen counter. Not alarming. In the next room, she found several boxes of ammunition stacked next to an empty gun rack.

Hmmm. Had a weapon been stolen?[567]

◆

Another deputy had been sent up to the isolated town of Lenado. There wasn't much to be found in this dusty little town. At first, the deputy only saw a handful of dilapidated huts, weather-worn structures that looked like they might collapse in a stiff breeze. As he drove on, he could see a few more shacks clustered near the sawmill off to his right. There were no utilities here, no telephone poles. This was living off the grid at its finest. No mortgage, no rent, just shanties hanging over the steep mountainside, interspersed amid the dogwoods and aspens. Homes here had been deliberately built near the stream, as they didn't have modern plumbing. Under the blue sky and billowy clouds, the children would play outside among the sage and yellow bushes.[568]

In its heyday, Lenado had been home to around 300 residents, all actively working the local zinc and lead deposits. A colossal slump in lead prices led to the site's abandonment, except for a brief resurgence during World War I when the need for zinc necessitated its operation. Now, the area was home to around 100 people who formed a logging community. Logging roads were carved into the pristine mountainside as more and more timber was being removed.[569]

The deputy had been tasked with determining if the fugitive had been to Lenado, and he'd been instructed to find a peculiar old man who would be hard to miss. He was a miner with a mule for a sidekick, and he'd be wielding an old-fashioned gold pan and pick. The eccentric old codger was known for wearing leather pants, and his braided hair fell well past his waist. The old man hated most outsiders and loved the fact that there was still a place in America where he could hunt, fish, and essentially live off the land. Once a year or so, he'd hike down to Woody Creek for sugar, coffee, and tobacco, but he hadn't ventured past the tavern in over twenty years. If Bundy had been to Lenado, this man would know.[570]

◆

Deputy Kempfert returned to the sheriff's office to find out if the owner of the cabin was now missing a rifle. She called the caretaker, who said the owner was a man from Tucson who usually arrived in town every June or July to spend the summer at his vacation home. When Carol hung up the receiver, she informed Deputy White and the sheriff that a pump .22 caliber rifle was missing from the cabin. It had been loaded with six shells. Suddenly, both men were very interested, and Gary volunteered to go up to the cabin.[571]

Something in Carol's mind clicked. The cabin. A missing rifle. Bundy. It hadn't entered her mind when she took the call concerning a break-in, and not once did she think of Bundy while she inspected the structure without reinforcements. Seeing Deputy White's sudden interest in the burglary shed new light on the potential identity of the man calling himself Amos. *Could it be?*[572]

"Why don't you ask Leo if he'll go up there with you," the sheriff suggested. Gary extended an invite to CBI Agent Leo Konkel, and soon, the two were traveling up Castle Creek Road in an unmarked Chevy Blazer.[573]

◆

Konkel commented on the number of hidden properties they were passing once they were outside of Aspen. Deputy White chuckled and nodded in agreement.

"Yup," he said. "Deputy Flatt and I were sent out on a welfare check at one of the more remote cabins out here. Friends hadn't heard from this one guy in quite some time, so they had called and asked us to check up on him. This guy was in his thirties, and his place had no power and no running water. It was after dark, and there were no lights. So, we knocked on his door. Nothing. It was unlocked, so we went in, and Gene's lamp dies within an arm's length of the door. So, we searched the house but we only had the light of my flashlight, right? Eventually, we look up at the loft. Well, the cabin was so small that the loft was more like a built-in shelf, with a structurally suspect ladder instead of stairs.

"I tell Gene to wait where he was as it looked like there was limited room up there. I climbed up and found the owner lying peacefully in bed. I shined the flashlight on his face, checked for vitals, and told Gene to get a body bag out of the rig.

"So, I position myself against the back wall of the loft and call down for Gene to climb the ladder. We placed the guy inside the body bag, right? Gene then starts going down the ladder with the flashlight while I began sliding one end of the bag, almost vertically, over the edge of the loft. Gene, growing increasingly nervous, is standing below. When he grabs the lower section of the bag, the body starts tilting, you see? It slides suddenly inside the confines of the sack. Oh, man! Gene drops it like he's

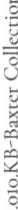

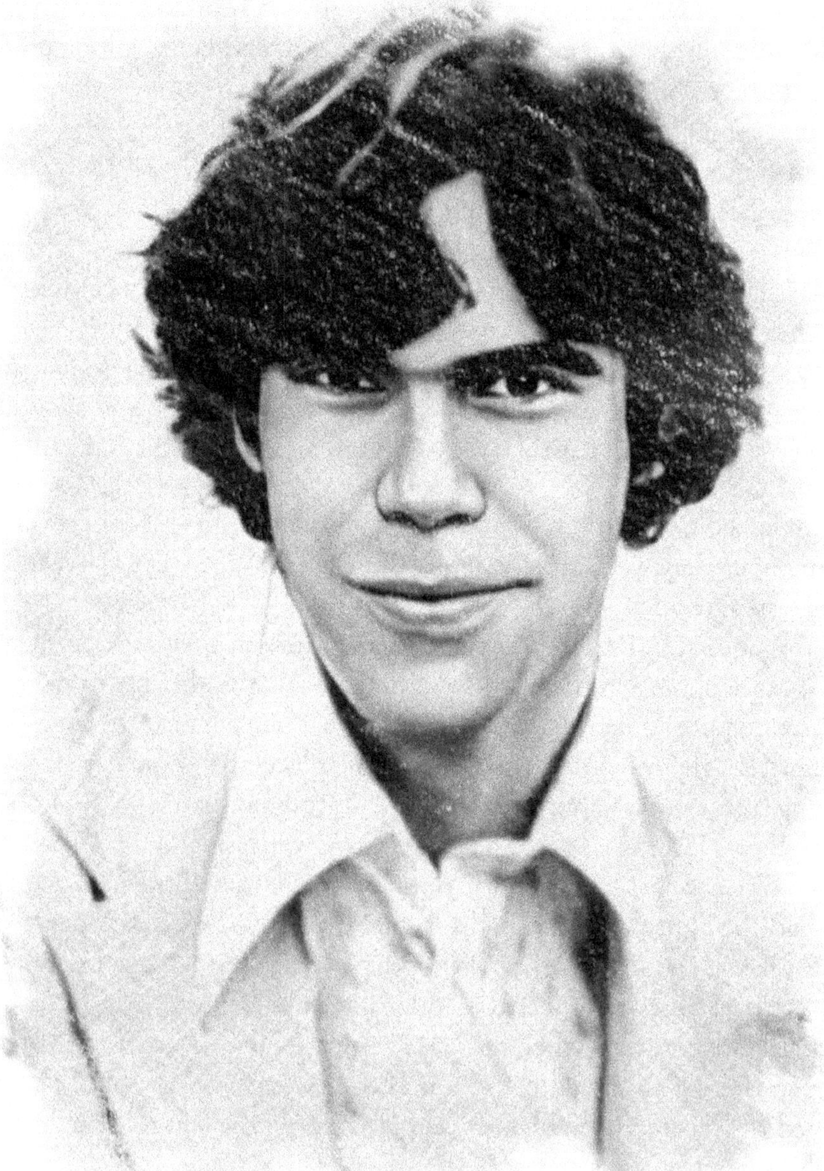

2021.010.KB-Baxter Collection

DEPUTY BOB BRAUDIS

encountered a ghost!

"He's moving!" he shouted. "He's alive! He's alive!"

Gary wiped tears from his eyes because he was laughing so hard while recalling the story. "Gene leaves me alone in the dark with a corpse in a bag. I heard him bolting out the front door and into the woods."[574]

"You get him to come back?" Konkel chuckled.

"Took me *forever* to get his butt back inside."

As they were nearing their destination, Konkel parked the Blazer off to the side of the road. The afternoon breeze was rustling through the trees. This cabin looked well-maintained and was in far better condition than most of the others they had passed driving up to the site.[575]

Together, Agent Konkel and Deputy White inspected the exterior of the structure. It looked like a quaint log cabin, complete with a chimney. Everything seemed sound, and the windows were all carefully covered with plywood. All but the one. As they approached the broken window, they could see that it was protected only by a metal screen, and someone had pulled—clawed—the corner of that screen back. *That's not as easy to do as it looks.* It was surely painful for the intruder. There was the broken window, and there was the cryptic note.

"Wonder who Amos is," Konkel asked.

"Carol said there is no Amos," Gary replied. "No one's been hired to make repairs either."

"If a man breaks into an empty cabin to steal what he can," Konkel remarked while reaching for an evidence bag, "why leave a note?"[576]

Gary's knuckles rapped against the front door, the sound echoing in the silence. No response. The only audible sound was the distant, haunting call of a killdeer plover. He tested the door, finding it unlocked. His hand instinctively moved to his holster, unsnapping the leather strap that held his revolver.

"Law enforcement!" Gary yelled as they stepped into the cabin. Leo looked to his left and noticed an entire wall of bookshelves filled with books. The owner was an avid reader. No furniture was overturned, and all drawers were closed. Nothing seemed disturbed or out of place. With the understanding that the caretaker checked the structure every Saturday, it was clear the break-in had occurred sometime during the previous week.

The men headed in opposite directions, checking every room.

"Clear!" Leo's voice echoed through the cabin as he finished his inspection of the kitchen. According to the caretaker, the intruder had raided the pantry, taking various items: stewed tomatoes, ravioli, old saltines, tins of Polish bacon, and some boxes of brown sugar. If it was Bundy, he was clearly desperate. The alpine terrain was unforgiving, and the altitude demanding. A man couldn't survive on a diet of brown sugar and saltines alone.

Everything was immaculate except for a box of crackers and a water glass on the kitchen counter. This just seemed out of place, as everything else was so clearly organized. Bending down, Leo inspected the glass closely. Nothing was readily visible, but the agent reached for an evidence bag just as Gary entered the room.[577]

◆

Leo Konkel and Deputy Gary White returned to the sheriff's department, entering through the back of the courthouse. Leo was hopeful the water glass he had collected at the cabin would yield latent fingerprints. If they did, what would be the fastest way to accurately determine whose prints had been found? He could send them to the FBI Headquarters in Washington, DC. Up until three years ago, such a request would have required thirty to forty-five days. The FBI now had a new automated system, AFIS, which could inspect 100,000 prints in a mere half-hour.[578]

"I'll dust for prints," the agent announced, beginning to conduct his orchestra. "Gary, get someone to retrieve Bundy's fingerprint card. Who's your fingerprint guy?"

"That'd be Garms," the sheriff replied. "Detective Sergeant."

"Well," Konkel continued, "have someone contact dispatch. Get this Garms fellow down here. We're also going to need samples of Ted's handwriting but nothing that was in the box of legal materials he left on Tuesday. Has to be a sample from his cell."

"I'm on it!" another deputy called out, already heading for the exit.

Gary White stepped aside and gently nudged Deputy Carol Kempfert to get her attention. The two deputies moved to another room where they could have privacy. Gary told her about their search of the cabin and the importance of the water glass. Carol's shoulders sank. She had missed it. *Good detective I'll make*, she thought.[579]

Leo gently removed the glass from the evidence bag and placed it on the counter. He opened a container of extremely fine, black powder. It would adhere to the oily residues left behind by whoever had touched the glass. He picked up a brush that held hundreds of soft bristles. The agent dipped it into the black powder, tapped it to remove any excess particles, and then began sweeping the bristles over the surface of the glass. He was careful not to apply too much pressure for fear that he would accidentally smudge the evidence. Lastly, he blew off the excess powder.[580]

The agent smiled, raising the glass for everyone to see. It was now riddled with usable prints.

"Jackpot," Kienast whispered.

◆

Detective Sergeant Dave Garms was driving when he received a radio call from dispatch.

"X-1," the dispatcher began. "Could you 10-25 the SO once you clear and meet with CBI regarding fingerprint identification?"

"10-4," Garms responded. "ETA about twenty."[581]

◆

Agent Konkel reached for a roll of transparent tape. He carefully lifted seven prints from the glass and transferred them to white card stock. Could they now be matched to Bundy? Konkel set the cards aside. They would have to wait for Garms' arrival, as he was the only one certified to make a positive identification.[582]

Konkel then turned his attention to handwriting comparison. This was not his forte, but he had a few minutes on his hands and wanted to remain productive. He examined the "Amos" note carefully, the one the burglar had left to explain away the damaged windowpane. He compared this note to a sample of Bundy's handwriting.

"I'm no expert," Leo said to the sheriff, "but it's certainly similar handwriting. Can you send both of these samples to our Denver office? Our boys in the lab can take a look."[583]

Once Detective Sergeant Garms walked into the room, he was handed Bundy's fingerprint card.

"We'll explain later," Kienast said. "Can you compare these for us?"

Eight of the fugitive's fingerprints showed ulnar loops. His right index finger had a radial loop, but his right thumb had a whorl, which was considered a tight twin loop. The detective noticed that the prints, taken from the glass, were of outstanding quality. He compared them to the prints on file.[584]

Minutes passed.

Finally, Dave nodded, and not even his mustache could conceal his debonair smile. There were enough points of identification to positively match the prints to the card on file. Theodore Robert Bundy had held this water glass. Both sets of prints would be shipped to the CBI Laboratory. There, they'd be photographed, and enlargements would be used for a more formal comparison.[585]

"Okay, boys," Kienast remarked. "We're back on track. Let's go get this guy."

"He didn't travel east after all," Garms folded his arms across his chest. "He headed south."

"Gary?" the sheriff said, louder than before, "Have Sergeant Davis call for the dogs again. I know they won't be able to be here till tomorrow morning, but make sure he gets the commitment."

"I'll update the teletypes," FBI Agent Cliff Browning said while turning toward the door. Authorities now knew Bundy was in a cabin where a rifle had been stolen. Within minutes, Browning's teletype flashed to eight different federal field offices: "Subject armed with rifle, caliber unknown. Should be considered armed and dangerous. Escape Risk."[586]

"Larry," the sheriff addressed Deputy Sergeant Spiers. "Get us a chopper at Sardy—now."

As Kienast grabbed a nearby telephone and started dialing, Agent Konkel became lost in thought. He was intrigued by the concept of small decisions having a larger impact on one's community. The caretaker didn't have to call authorities, but he did. Deputy Kempfert could have chalked the report up as nothing; cabin break-ins were, unfortunately, common in the valley. She didn't. The sheriff merely asked, almost as an afterthought, for Gary White to invite Agent Konkel to accompany him to the cabin. Given how clean the rest of the structure was, Konkel could have overlooked the presence of the water glass. He didn't. One small decision after another led to proof that Ted Bundy had managed to make his way to the Kaeser cabin.

"Nancy?" Kienast spoke into the receiver. "Listen carefully. We found Bundy's prints up at the Kaeser Cabin. I know roadblocks were scheduled to come down tonight, but I want them kept up, understand?" He slammed down the receiver just as Gary White returned to the room.

"Don says he'll take care of it," Gary offered, referring to the dogs.

"Fine," Kienast replied. "Roadblocks are to remain in place."[587]

"Perfect," Gary reached for his hat. "Let's get you to the chopper."

♦

Nancy was growing weary of all the mini-meetings, as she called them.

Searchers, dog handlers, helicopter pilots, sheriff's reserves—it seemed every group involved in the manhunt wanted a piece of her brain. Did she know anyone who lived near Hayden Peak? Should we check Cathedral Lake? Did she know if there were any Jeep trails in Maroon Creek Valley? It was her job. She understood this, but when would things finally return to normal?[588]

"You look confused," Jean said. "What's wrong?"

"Grab me a topo map, would you?" Nancy replied.

"Here you go."

"All right," Nancy began. "We know Dave identified Bundy's prints on the glass from the cabin. I ask myself...how did he get there?"

"Only two ways, really," Jean replied, using her index finger to trace two different routes on the map. "Up and over Aspen Mountain or walk up Castle Creek Road."

"Exactly. And a lot of folks believe he took the road."

"Are you thinking he took to mountain climbing?"

"Well," Nancy leaned forward, studying the map. "Castle Creek was one of the first roadblocks we set up. We've got a couple of sightings of Ted heading east toward Herron Park. If, for some reason, he turned around and headed west, jogging through town, that's what? A two-mile journey to the Prince of Peace Chapel?"

"Uh-huh."

"No way," Nancy sighed. "Are we really saying he made it that far, on city streets, undetected?"

"That's more believable than the alternative, isn't it?"

"Is it possible? He jumps out the window, somehow doesn't break an ankle, and manages to make it up the mountain?"

"Are you thinking the eyewitnesses that have him going east were mistaken?"

Nancy didn't reply right away. She leaned back in her chair while Jean drew the map closer for inspection.

"What's the elevation at the base of Aspen Mountain," Nancy asked.

"Ah...7,945 feet."

"And the summit?"

"Just over 11,000. You think he did everything he did and then hiked over 3,000 feet, up and over?"

"Sounds crazy, doesn't it?" Nancy conceded.

◆

Twenty minutes later, Gary White was sitting beside the sheriff, cramped inside a helicopter that had logged many hours during the previous five days. He was psyched and grinning like a Cheshire Cat. His hunch that Bundy may have been holed up somewhere south of town had been correct. He and Don Davis had previously flown over the very region where the cabin was located. Gary looked over at the sheriff, who was smiling as well. The men were buoyed by the fact that the instincts of the deputies appeared to be right on track. Gary was elated as the chopper wound its way up Castle Creek Valley. The breathtaking view aside, he could only think about getting Bundy into an interrogation room.

Whup whup whup!

Five days of search efforts. About 150 volunteers in the mounted posse, helicopter reconnaissance, house-to-house searches, roadblocks, and the inspection of nearly 100 remote cabins; at the end of the day, there was only one man responsible for the mammoth manhunt—Sheriff Kienast. Unfortunately, he happened to be the same man who was legally responsible for the fugitive's escape in the first place. There was talk around town of Deputy Westerlund and Sergeant Kralicek's mistakes, but the escape happened on the sheriff's watch, and he knew it. To know now that Bundy was still in the valley, a particular word reentered his vocabulary. *Hope.*

Gary looked out through the plexiglass sphere as the helicopter slowly descended into the small meadow near the cabin. The bearberry and fringed sage bowed to the high winds of the approaching rotor wash. As the aircraft set down, Gary was chomping at the bit. Interrogation had always been one of his strong suits. *I want a shot at him.*[589]

Amid the roar of the engine, Gary unbuckled his lap belt and hopped out of the chopper. He gripped his doper hat in his hand and trotted away from the aircraft. Unlike the previous few days, the plainclothes detective was now wearing a traditional uniform shirt. The sheriff followed on the deputy's heels.

Soon, the property surrounding the structure was a flurry of activity. Cars arrived, one after another. Detective Sergeant Dave Garms pulled up in his unmarked police car. He opted not to enter the cabin for the simple reason that he knew the sheriff's department had jurisdiction. Instead, he poked around outside, attempting to pick up Bundy's trail. Other officers arrived and congregated in front of the structure as the sheriff and his deputies inspected the interior of the cabin.[590]

Dave Stapleton, who had spent days searching high-altitude cabins in the wilderness near Ashcroft, was among those waiting outside when the sheriff emerged into the bright sun. Dave raked his hand through his hair before fishing mirrored sunglasses out of his pocket. He walked up to the sheriff and nodded. To all outside appearances, Dave appeared calm and serious, but on the inside, he felt like a child who had just woken up on Christmas morning.

The sheriff glanced over at Deputy Sergeant Larry Spiers, who was inspecting the ground as a cigarette dangled from his lips. Kienast drew a deep breath, put his hands on his hips, and looked around the area, contemplating the entire Castle Creek area. There must be over fifty mountain cabins in this region, many of which were unoccupied vacation homes. There was a nearby trail that, after a ten-hour hike, would bring a man to Crested Butte. From there, a fugitive could reach Gunnison and—freedom.

"Everyone, gather around!" the sheriff called out. "I want a dragnet search of the area. I want every trail from here to Taylor Lake covered."[591]

As the multitude of deputies and officers broke up, Larry Spiers slowly ambled over to the sheriff. The detective sergeant removed his cowboy hat and wiped the sweat from his brow. He stretched his back and looked around at the quaking aspens that seemed to be on the verge of enveloping the cabin.

"You know, Dick. Somewhere out there, Bundy is now armed. This is a game changer."

◆

As the sky slowly faded to a pale shade of blue, reporters, who were waiting for any tidbit of news at the courthouse, aimed their microphones in Nina Johnston's direction.

"We think we are close," she said, in reference to the activities at the cabin. "This is the only good lead we've had since he escaped." As the spokeswoman for the department, she spoke to the press without giving away too many details.[592]

The journalists and cameramen splintered and headed to their respective hotels. An eventful day had passed and the latest update was that the search would continue at daybreak. Everyone wanted to wrap things up and get some sleep.

◆

Officer Chet Zajac was back for another round on the swing shift. He was fully recharged, and the rugburn on his face was hardly noticeable tonight. Zajac hadn't been assigned to the search efforts outside of town. He was stuck with the task of conducting bar checks. The Colorado Department of Revenue Liquor Enforcement was in Grand Junction, more than a two-hour drive away, and Aspen PD had been tapped to assist in alcohol enforcement. Chet was to make sure folks weren't being overserved and ensure minors weren't being served at all. It wasn't glamorous work, but he had only been walking the beat for a few weeks.

At the corner of Main and Mill, he opened the heavy dark wood and beveled glass doors that led into Hotel Jerome, Aspen's premier social hub since 1889. He walked through the enormous lobby, seeing an elevator door open to his left. Off to his right, a man came out of the restrooms. Chet was keenly aware of each face he passed.

He could feel the tension in the lobby. Word had gotten around town about fingerprints, dirty dishes, and a cabin. It seemed clear to a lot of folks that ol' Ted was still in the area—somewhere.

"Did you find him yet?" someone asked the officer.[593]

Chet answered by shaking his head. He didn't have any details to share. His superiors weren't sharing a lot of information with him, and the sheriff's department wasn't sharing all of its knowledge with the police.

"Do you think I should buy a gun?" another person inquired. Officer Zajac didn't have an answer to that question, so he just shrugged and smiled.

Chet needed to see to his regular duties. He checked the main restrooms for potential drug use and was happy not to find anyone sniffing white powder. Sometimes, bar patrons, who understood cops were constantly checking the stalls, would opt to snort a quick line in the privacy of the elevator while it was in motion.

Chet went through a set of double glass doors into a bar full of people sitting at wooden pedestal tables. The actual bar, which spanned the length of the western wall, was packed with more patrons than barstools. In the glow of amber light from the stained-glass lamps, he scanned the faces in the crowd, looking for minors.

"What do you know?" a waiter inquired, spotting the officer. "What's going on?" Again, all Chet could offer was a shrug and a smile.[594]

The officer walked past the waiter's station toward stairs that led to the restrooms in the basement. These were primarily used by employees who worked in the building. This stairway was incredibly narrow, making it awkward to pass someone heading in the opposite direction. Upon reaching the lower landing, Chet opened the door to the men's room. The walls here were covered in deep red velvet wallpaper. As boring as these foot patrols could be at times, it was part of the department's more rigid stance against drunk driving and underage drinking.

There was one final stop for this specific bar, a courtyard with a garden and benches where you could sit and have a smoke in the fresh air. Smoking was allowed inside, but some preferred to step out for a bit of solitude.

Officers would occasionally find someone who had made their way out to this courtyard after having a bit too much to drink. During most months, hypothermia could set in if someone passed out here and was exposed for too long. The courtyard was empty tonight, but Chet was glad he was wearing his parka. It was dark and cold. Bundy was out there somewhere in that darkness. Precisely where? No one knew. But Officer Zajac was betting that Ted didn't have a nice warm parka of his own.[595]

◆

Bring on the coffee. Officer Terry Quirk decided to stop by city hall to get a fresh dose of caffeine. Terry and his wife rented a house on Mountain View Drive, with his younger brother renting the spare room. His wife operated the Hallmark store in town, and his brother had a job. It was the only way they could all afford to live in Aspen. Earlier in the day, all three had been home at the same time, comparing notes.

For part of Terry's week, his job was to hike through the brush along the banks of Hunter Creek, observing beavers feeding on willow and migratory waterbirds resting along their northern journey. It sounded so serene, but Terry pointed out that the helicopters disrupted the peace, and there was a dangerous man loose in the area. Later in the week, Terry had taken to the streets, talking to townspeople and contacting business owners. He was looking for any type of lead in the case. The helicopters had still been buzzing the town, but the number of volunteers had dropped significantly, and it seemed that the hunt had been winding down.

Terry's wife had noticed that her friends had started to let their guard down as well. But now, the fugitive's prints had been found, so it looked like Bundy was still around somewhere in the valley. Terry was surprised by this, as he figured Ted would want to put as much space between himself and the folks pursuing him. *Why stay?*[596]

Before Bundy's escape, the Quirks never locked their doors, like everyone else in the county. Now, no one could feel safe, and everyone bolted their doors. One man had been able to steal the peace of an entire community.[597]

Terry looked at the tower of Styrofoam cups beside the potluck-sized coffee urn. He preferred to drink from a mug, so he'd brought one from home. He filled his mug and added sugar. He looked at the big, round canister with a blue and white label, the powdered creamer that the department purchased.

Tonight, he wanted real cream and knew some was kept in a refrigerator behind him. It was a white Frigidaire behemoth. Terry opened the door and began searching through the contents of the wire racks inside. Officers and city employees kept their sack lunches here, along with cheerful pink cans of Tab soda. He grabbed the carton of cream sitting on the shelf above the vegetable bin. He poured a splash of cream into his coffee and returned the carton to its shelf in the fridge. He closed the door, having no idea that the mystery items in the vegetable bins and on the shelf beside the cream were dead prairie dogs wrapped in dark plastic bags.[598]

◆

Nancy was restless. She had a loaded gun, borrowed from a friend, stashed under her pillow. She was trying to get some much-needed sleep, but her mind kept replaying horrible thoughts. *Did I check the back slider? Could Ted have gotten into my place while my roommate was gone, and be hiding—just waiting to make his move?* Scenarios of him popping out of the woods and snatching some unsuspecting girl kept her on edge. With each little noise that emanated from the woods outside, Nancy endured an uneasy jumpiness. She alternated between the hopes of seeing him caught and shackled so he could never hurt another woman and the desire for a more extreme version of justice. Perhaps someone would shoot Bundy first and ask questions later.[599]

◆

Deputy Gary White was turning in for the night as well. He was at home, nine miles west of town. He put his head on his pillow and stared up at the ceiling. *Bundy...armed.* That knowledge alone made it difficult to close his eyelids, no matter how much he wanted to drift off to sleep.[600]

He thought about playing chess with the man and their discussions about everything from Africa to zoologists. It hadn't always been fun and games, though. He remembered securing Bundy's handcuffs one day and warning him not to try anything stupid. Hearing no response, Gary looked up at Bundy's face to make sure the prisoner understood the order. Ted's eyes were bright, blue, and clear, but he was looking past Gary like he was lost in his own thoughts.

"Bundy!" White watched Ted's face, making sure that he had captured the man's attention now. "If you ever try and run from me or do anything stupid, I'll kill you. Do you understand that? Straight out, I'll shoot you in the back if I have to." Gary looked his prisoner right in the eyes, raised one eyebrow ever so slightly, and waited. Bundy's face never changed, and he didn't say a word, but, finally, he gave a slight nod.[601]

Gary usually enjoyed escorting the prisoner to and from Glenwood Springs. He rarely picked up any variance in the man's tone or attitude, but Ted did seem grateful whenever he was outdoors. Gary had never heard Bundy curse or use any foul language at all, in marked contrast to his jailers. Now, the deputy knew that even *this* was an angle. Bundy had been lulling his captors into complacency for months. Hadn't the number of guards at the courthouse decreased one by one?

There were also long periods of time on the road where the men said nothing, enjoying the peace and scenery. Gary always wondered though, *what kind of secrets is this guy hiding?* Everyone has secrets. The deputy could see that clearly now.

But Deputy White had secrets of his own. One was lying right next to him in his bed. Her name was Lorrie, also known as Deputy Francis. The couple had to keep their badge-to-badge relationship as quiet as possible.[602]

"How's your back?" she asked quietly, rolling over to lay her head on his chest.

"Smarts," he sighed, "like a 2,200-pound bison kicked me in the kidneys."

Yep. Everyone has their little secrets.

◆

The Kaeser cabin held its secrets, too. At the moment, it was silent and pitch-black inside. The plywood in the windows blocked out even the tiniest beam of moonlight. The cabin had been left unlocked, which seemed to invite trouble to come walking through the front door.

The sound of a lighter was followed by a warm little flame, creating a small globe of light around Deputy Sergeant Larry Spiers, sitting in a small chair. The flame went out as Spiers took a deep drag on his Pall Mall. Now, the dark orange glow emanating from the burning tip of his cigarette was the only source of light. He sat facing the door of the cabin. There was no rush to finish his smoke, as there were plenty more sitting beside him in case the night was long. He continued to smoke with one hand. In his other hand, he slowly raised a 12-gauge shotgun till it was aimed right at the center of the door.[603]

SUNDAY

JUNE 12, 1977

CHAPTER 8
THE DOGS OF WAR

Deputy Gary White braced himself for the landing as the helicopter descended toward the meadow near the cabin. The touchdown was mild, yet the pain in his back prevented him from trusting any sudden movement, and he didn't want anyone to know that he was suffering. He checked his watch—7:45 a.m.—and saw Sergeant Don Davis approaching the aircraft. The sergeant opened the canopy door, and Gary stepped out onto the field of fringed sage.

"You all right?" Don called out over the din of the spinning overhead blades. "You look like a trainwreck!"

"This engine's not ready to pull into the station just yet!" Gary grimaced. The two men walked over toward a grove of aspens. Gary zipped his coat, blocking out the morning cold that was only amplified by the intense wind the chopper created.

The helicopter rose from the ground, creating a thunderous, juddering noise that quickly dissipated to a softer whirring as it cleared the treetops and disappeared from view.[604]

Sergeant Davis directed his friend's attention to two figures near the front door of the cabin. Sheriff Kienast was engaged in conversation with Deputy Sergeant Larry Spiers.

"Larry was here all night," Don remarked. "Long stakeout." It didn't appear that Bundy had returned, but the sergeant was commended for his efforts.[605]

"You mind if I head inside to check things out?" Gary asked.

"That's fine," Don replied, "but listen up for another chopper. It's bringing the dogs."

Everyone else stayed outside, allowing Deputy White to step inside the cabin alone. He scanned the wall of bookshelves before taking a stroll through each individual room. It was quiet, and there was that slightly musty smell that happens when a home is left empty for long stretches of time. Gary took advantage of the silence to organize his thoughts. *What was his opponent's strategy? What could his next move be?*[606]

White emerged from the cabin when he heard another helicopter approaching in the distance. He stood on the front porch and watched until this chopper landed, the door opened, and search dogs jumped to the ground. With their handlers in tow, the canines were sniffing around the vacation home. Once the dogs were put on their task, it was unmistakable when they picked up a scent, and suddenly, everyone was in motion.[607]

"That's our cue," Don jokingly said to Gary.

"Unleash the dogs of war," Gary replied.

The hounds headed west, behind the cabin, and bounded up an embankment. Deputies scrambled behind, trying to keep up with the agile canines.

From here, deputies could look down on the cabin and Castle Creek some 300 feet beyond that. Up here, they found prints on the softer ground. Deputies spread out, looking closely for any clues as they followed the dogs. Eventually, the dogs led the men back down to the creek's edge.[608]

Gary followed one of the handlers. The man's hound was focused on the task, yet, without warning, it lost the scent. Had Bundy expected search dogs and waded through the water to throw them off?

Deputy White continued searching around the trees and foliage bordering both sides of the path they were on, acutely aware that the fugitive was now armed with a pump .22 rifle. Gary owned one of these guns himself. He had inherited it and knew it well, figuring the fugitive might manage an effective shot from as much as 150 yards away.

At the academy, deputies learned to treat every incident as if a subject might be carrying a weapon. Having said that, Gary knew there was far less pressure hunting an unarmed man than an armed one. Knowing Bundy had a deadly weapon, the mental and physical stress was enormous. The deputy's danger index, if you will, was topped out, and he felt as tense as a stretched rubber band. Waiting for a shot to ring out was taking a toll on Gary. When one of the hounds barked, White flinched, his heart jumped in his chest, and a rush of adrenaline coursed right through him.[609]

◆

Less than a mile away, Sergeant Rick Kralicek and Deputy Carol Kempfert drove south along Castle Creek Road. Some gravel kicked up, pelting the underbody of the sergeant's private Jeep. The two rode in silence, scanning the road, the woods, and the open meadows. They had what they needed for this portion of the manhunt: radios, water, two shotguns, double-aught buckshot, and a body bag.[610]

◆

Nancy watched as deputies filed into the sheriff's office for another day of the hunt. They seemed weighed down as this week was taking a toll on them all. It was the sixth day of the manhunt, and Nancy felt their pain. She was running out of energy, too, and guessed that she may even have a low-grade fever. She pulled a cigarette out but didn't light it. Instead, she wiped her forehead with the back of her hand just to see if she was really running hot without giving away her secret that the demands of this week were starting to drain her as well.

Three years ago, Nancy thought she might want to become a deputy herself, so she tried it out. She donned a friend's Sam Browne leather belt and was astonished at how heavy it was, especially when riding in a patrol car or when she had to go to the restroom. Gun, radio, speed loaders—it was an extra ten pounds that had to be taken into consideration, and she had a bad habit of only visiting the ladies' room when nature's call turned into nature's scream.

That wasn't her only bad habit. She survived on Pepsi, coffee, and Parliaments, so she found that she was more suited for a career in dispatch. Working her ass off brought her a sense of purpose and fulfillment that she hadn't foreseen. She struck a match and lit her cigarette.[611]

"Nancy, could you come in here a minute?" She looked up to see Sergeant Don Davis motioning for her to come into the sheriff's private office. She grabbed a pad of paper and followed the sergeant into the room.

"I understand," the sheriff said to someone on the telephone. With his free hand, Kienast motioned his visitor to have a seat in nearby chairs. "I get it, Mike. All right. Goodbye." He hung up the receiver. "Okay," Kienast smiled while he rapped the edges of his desk. "I want a plan. If Bundy's brought back alive, what do we do next?"

Silence.

"What do you mean?" Nancy finally asked.

"Well, that was Mike Fisher on the phone. Now I'm thinking, what if Ted decides to use that rifle and gets himself killed in the process? What then?" There were plenty of people wishing for this particular outcome, but the sheriff was hoping the fugitive could be captured alive.[612]

Options and strategies were discussed. Somewhere in the conversation, Nancy realized that the sheriff and sergeant were confident Bundy hadn't made his way through the roadblocks. She could barely contain the wave of relief that flooded over her.

"What *exactly* did you promise Mike?" she asked, her pencil at the ready.

"He feels that Bundy will be hungry, dehydrated, and mentally drained, right? In that state, Ted might accidentally reveal his secrets about the Campbell case. You never know, so I said he could have first crack at him."

◆

West of the Kaeser cabin, under the noon-day sun, a young man was ambling along on an old dirt road on his family's ranch. As he rounded a corner up ahead of him, he could see a hiker walking his way. The redhead drew his .44 pistol from its holster.[613]

"Hey, you!" Bruce Sinclair called out, leveling his gun at the hiker.[614]

"Oh, hey. Hi!" the stranger replied, progressing with the assistance of a walking stick. He stopped and waved the branch at the cowboy with the bushy red beard. "How ya' doin'? What's going on?"

"Get down here!" Sinclair demanded, waving his weapon in the direction he wanted the stranger to proceed. "We're lookin' for Bundy."

"You're lookin' for who?" the hiker squinted, looking puzzled.

"Bundy. This guy's escaped, and it's dangerous for you to be up here."

"For God's sake! I didn't know that."

"Now, who are you again?"

The hiker introduced himself as a dentist from out east, but Sinclair kept his gun trained on the trespasser.

"I've got a wife and kids," the hiker remarked. "Please don't point that gun at me."

"Oh, okay. But you shouldn't be on my land. We're lookin' for this guy and he's dangerous, and you shouldn't be up here. I'm tellin' ya' to get your tail off my property."

The stranger nodded, indicating that he understood that he was trespassing and would immediately rectify the situation. He continued walking downhill past the rancher.

Still slightly suspicious, Sinclair followed to see what the man was up to. The stranger stepped off the path to pick a flower. About 300 yards down the road, the stranger stepped off the path to pick more flowers. *Is he building a bouquet? He certainly doesn't appear to be in a hurry.* The rancher kept the hiker in his sight until he disappeared in the foliage far below.

He was gone.

◆

By mid-day, at the new luxury Aspen Club Condos off Crystal Lake Road, Jill Sheeley had already given the grand tour to four potential buyers. Jill was multitasking. The owners of the lakefront complex were out of town, so she had offered to watch their Newfoundland dogs on top of her regular duties as property hostess. By 2:00 p.m., all was quiet.

She took advantage of the quiet times by sitting on the back deck in a comfy lounger. Here, she could soak up the sun, read her book, and keep an eye on the two gentle giants. This was a dream job in a magnificent location.

Suddenly, both dogs scrambled to their feet and erupted in a fit of barking. The ordinarily docile dogs had nearly caused Jill to jump out of her skin. She got up and looked out beyond the deck, trying to hush the canines. They ignored her and just kept stomping and barking. She knew the dogs were sounding an alarm, and a wave of dread washed over her. She had been reading about Charles Manson, and now her thoughts ran wild. *Bear? Human?* And just like that, she flared into a full-blown panic.[615]

The dogs continued to growl and bark. Jill ran inside, locking all the doors and windows. There was no phone to call for help, no curtains to close, and no knives in the kitchen to protect herself with—she was in a show-model condo.

Looking around for anything she could use as a weapon, she grabbed an ornamental fireplace poker, ran into the master bedroom, and shut the door. In a flash, she was under the bed. Her heart raced almost painfully. Then, the awful truth began to whirl in her mind. She was stranded here at the complex. Jill had walked to work a couple of miles from her home. She was in danger, and no one else knew it. She waited. The dogs continued to bark and snarl endlessly.

OFFICER CHET ZAJAC

Then, her mind went wild. *It's Bundy. It has to be. He'll be busting through the door at any moment, and that will be the end of me.* Covered in sweat, she prayed, thankful that the barking covered the sound of her heavy breathing and her prayers.

An agonizing amount of time passed. Eventually, the dogs relented. Jill stayed under the bed, listening intently. At some point, she found the nerve to crawl out, make her way to a window, and peek outside. She was shaking. The dogs let out a grunt now and then before they settled down. There was nothing to be seen except for the two massive Newfoundlands.

Jill and her girlfriends began locking their doors and windows earlier in the week, and they were all carrying cans of mace. She rummaged through her bag, looking for her mace. She scolded herself. *I'm so naive. If Bundy had asked me to help him load his sailboat, I wouldn't have thought twice.* Her days of trusting strangers had come to an end, and her hitchhiking days were over.[616]

♦

The afternoon passed without any excitement for law enforcement. The crews prepared for a shift change. Each deputy had been working sixteen-hour shifts or more. Deputy Bob Braudis, among others, was even asking the sheriff to pull the checkpoints. The sheriff was adamant, though—the roadblocks would remain in force until sometime on Monday.[617]

Deputy Gene Flatt overheard this conversation just after he arrived at the office. Tonight, he'd be paired with Deputy Maureen Higgins. Together, they'd man a roadblock for a few hours and then hit the streets in a patrol car.

Gene was sitting in an office chair, quietly observing his colleagues. He watched Sergeant Davis walking through the bullpen. *Ol' Don.* The sergeant always seemed to have a direct, matter-of-fact way of explaining things. Occasionally, Gene would have a moment of self-doubt and would meet with Don behind closed doors. These conversations always ended on a positive note and encouraged Gene. Don Davis was a wonderful and highly influential mentor.

Gene could hear Sergeant Rick Kralicek, who was close by, speaking to another deputy.

"I'm not going to be the sacrificial lamb here," Kralicek nearly whispered.[618]

Gene turned away as he understood it was a private moment.

He knew two men would surely be losing their jobs in the weeks ahead. Deputy Dave Westerlund couldn't possibly expect to retain his badge and gun. Rick Kralicek, the sergeant in charge on the morning of the escape, obviously understood his position was in jeopardy as well. It wasn't just because he was in a supervisory role; he was one of the two assigned guards on the Bundy detail, and yet he chose to abandon that position and head downstairs to the sheriff's office. The question that was quietly being bandied about in the halls and offices at the courthouse was—would Sheriff Kienast lose his elected position? Had he lost the confidence of the community?

While Gene was waiting for Deputy Maureen Higgins, he began thumbing through a stack of teletypes. The department was receiving all kinds of requests, mainly for interviews with Ted, if he was recaptured, and for details of evidence against him, like lab results on hair samples and copies of gas receipts. It seemed endless. It was the gas receipts that had convinced Gene that Bundy was a killer.

The case against Bundy didn't seem to be going that well. A ski brochure was circumstantial evidence. A supposed eyewitness had picked out the wrong man in open court. The deputy had kept tabs on the preliminary hearings and felt Bundy and his lawyers were scoring points every day with the judge. Gene was curious how much the gas receipt would play with a future jury. The case wasn't rock solid, and Bundy had some legal training under his belt. Gene felt that it would have been wiser for the man to stay put, beat the charges in Aspen, return to Utah to finish off his sentence there, and then he'd be a free man. Escaping made no sense. *That was a dumb move.*

Maureen Higgins walked in to begin the shift, so Gene stood up to greet her.[619]

◆

Officer Chet Zajac and his partner for the night approached the Wheeler Opera House at the west end of the Hyman Street Mall. It was a three-story structure built in 1889. Named after a prominent businessman during the silver boom, it now housed the library and other community-based offices. Chet, however, did not enter the main entrance facing Hyman. He turned and began descending a steep and narrow series of stone steps facing Mill Street.[620]

At the bottom of the stairs was a rather tall, sinewy, sunburnt bouncer who didn't bother to crack a smile. There was a cover charge to pass through the door, but the silver badges on the officers' chests were a free pass into The Pub, one of Aspen's rowdiest bars.

The door swung open, and the officers entered a lively room topped by an ever-present layer of tobacco smoke. This thick, hovering cloud was only disturbed by the passing of a waitress lifting her tray of domestic beer. The patrons were predominantly men due to the joint's reputation for spectacular bar brawls. Chet snickered. Wading through the sea of unsavory characters in The Pub, he was reminded of the cantina scene from *Star Wars*, which had just been released. *Half of these rowdy guys probably have outstanding warrants.* With too many bodies, too much smoke, and far more obscenities being exchanged than at a military enlisted man's club, The Pub presented an air of intimidation. None of this bothered Officer Zajac.[621]

There was a reason he was the department's unofficial "Use of Force" instructor. The police chief had learned that Chet was proficient in martial arts. He'd earned his blackbelt by the time he was sixteen, and he could certainly handle himself. Besides, merely passing through the crowd wearing a badge did a lot to prevent trouble.[622]

Chet and his partner split up and began meandering through the crowd, quietly scanning faces. Teens sometimes managed to work their way up—or down, depending upon one's view—the ladder of inebriation. In addition to checking for underage drinking, an officer always needed to be cognizant of what Gary White called the "Three F's—*Fat—Fifty—* from *Florida*. People often underestimated the effect of altitude on their bodies.[623]

Chet exited The Pub and walked south, past The Village Pantry. When the bars closed at 2:00 in the morning, scores of inebriated folks headed to this premier late-night breakfast joint on the Mill Street side of Wagner Park. If you had to wait in line for a place to sit, it was always worth the wait. Pancakes loaded with syrup and blueberries were the perfect ending to a night in Aspen.[624]

The officer wandered into Wagner Park, south of The Pub. There were fewer streetlamps here, larger trees, and plenty of places to remain concealed. *How many folks have we had out looking for Ted this past week? How many operational hours were expended?*[625]

Chet turned around and looked north at Red Mountain. At night, he could tell there was a lack of houselights up on the peak. There was just nobody up there in those scores of houses Chet and his colleagues had inspected. *Could Bundy be up there, living off canned goods he found in a vacation rental? Was he smart enough to leave the lights off and wait patiently?*[626]

Officer Zajac started walking along Mill Street. Although he'd only been walking the beat for a few weeks, he had made a habit of stopping by the courthouse. There was a lone deputy on duty at the county jail, and Chet had found him asleep on more than one occasion. He walked in one time and found the deputy, sans boots, with his feet up on the countertop, sound asleep.

Pay attention!" Chet had said. "You've got prisoners in here." This hadn't gone over very well with the recently roused deputy. Chet was already getting a reputation for being a conservative. He'd been hanging out too much with Gary White; that much was for certain.[627]

On a couple of nights, Chet had even walked back into the cellblock to poke his head in and see what was going on. He was surprised that Bundy would be awake, sometimes as late as 2:00 a.m.

"Hey, Ted," Zajac recalled. "How ya' doing?" The prisoner would look out the corner of his eye, recognize the officer, and smile.[628]

"How you doing?" Bundy mirrored the greeting.

"Looks like you've been exercising. Doing some pushups?"

Chet never probed the man for criminal activities. They just talked about martial arts, the weather, or other safe topics. Zajac found the bearded Bundy to be a friendly guy with a good sense of humor. He was cordial, intelligent, and an interesting conversationalist. Ted was pleasant, like a helpful next-door neighbor.

The only thing that seemed strange to Chet was how the prisoner ended their ten to fifteen-minute talks. There was no "Hey, see you later" or "Talk to you soon." They'd be talking, joking, and telling stories one minute, but when Bundy was done talking, he just shut off like an android. His facial expressions would go blank. Not cold, not aggressive—blank. He'd turn his head and walk to the back of his cell. That struck Chet as odd, and he didn't quite know what to make of it. Never in his wildest dreams did he imagine the man would leap out that courthouse window. *That should have sent the man's femur through a kidney, right?*

◆

Nancy Baxter wrapped herself up in her terry cloth bathrobe. She had just stepped out of the shower in her apartment and was getting ready for bed. *A shower and some shuteye*, she had told her relief at dispatch, *and I'll be good as new.* Lynne Unger had come to work early to assume the graveyard shift and provide her supervisor with some rest. The two women were close. They had lived together for the last half-year, and Lynne had even dated Nancy's younger brother. Nancy felt she could rest easy with her friend at the helm.

Nancy loved her new apartment. The place was quite a step up from her bachelorette pad, and it made her feel like she was finally moving on from her divorce. While drying her hair absentmindedly with a towel, she looked out her bedroom window, east toward Independence Pass. Even on this clear night, she could see the snowcapped peaks along the Continental Divide, like a purple ribbon in the sky. She typically cracked the windows when she showered to let some of the cool, bracing mountain air into the room. Not tonight. Not for the last five nights. The windows were locked, checked, and checked again. *Is he in those trees? Is he looking back at me?* She hadn't forgotten that one of the first Bundy sightings was in her neighborhood. So many homes were vacant this time of the year; their owners were probably diving off the coast of Maui or Mexico. Bundy could be anywhere...and he was armed.

Well, she wasn't taking any chances. A friend had loaned her a snub nose revolver, and she had been sleeping with it for several nights. *What the hell am I doing with a loaded gun under my pillow?* She crawled under the covers and unrolled the down comforter at the foot of the bed like she was returning the lid to a can of sardines.

Nancy looked forward to drifting off to sleep, hoping she wouldn't have a nightmare where she'd inadvertently rise in a daze, shooting herself or her roommate by mistake. She had borrowed a Motorola radio from the office and placed it on her nightstand. Lynne would contact her if anything came up. It was the graveyard shift, though.[629]

What could possibly happen?

MONDAY

JUNE 13, 1977

CHAPTER 9
CRESTAHAUS

The young woman, a high school student, realized that she never noticed the sound of her own footsteps during the day. But now, in the middle of the night, she could hear the echo of every step she took. Looking down at the asphalt road, the heels of her trendy wooden sandals were grinding a multitude of tiny granules, remnants of the constant deicing of the residential streets of Aspen.

As she strolled along West Hopkins Street, an electrical humming sound interrupted her thoughts. It grew louder as she approached a street light. *How strange*, she thought, looking up at the flickering bulb. The humming and amber glow sputtered in unison.

She heard something behind her or perhaps merely felt a presence. Glancing over her shoulder, she expected to see a stray animal poking around one of the neighbor's garbage cans. Surprised to see another person, since it was past midnight, she picked up her pace, heading for home. It was late, and her dad was probably worried about her being out at this hour, but *hey*, she was seventeen and not a child anymore. She could take care of herself. [630]

Suddenly, there were hands on her arms, and she was thrown to the ground. Before she could scramble to her feet, she heard a heavy thud and felt a sharp pain in her chest as she was knocked back to the asphalt. She had been kicked with such force that it pushed the air right out of her lungs. She struggled to inhale. Her neck was yanked so violently that she lost all ability to tell up from down.[631]

The teen winced in pain as she was dragged across the ground by her hair. It was like a nightmare where you try to scream, but the sound disappears into silent anguish. Her assailant stumbled, and the girl broke free of his grasp and rolled onto her knees. The man tried to regain his hold on her, but this time, she fought him with all her strength. Thrashing wildly, her hand smacked him right in his face, shocking him for just a moment. He stared at her as he wiped his nose and mouth. Under the streetlight, the girl could see that the blow had caused the man pain, and his pain had resulted in fury. She looked straight into his dark, evil eyes, knowing he was preparing to lunge again. She abruptly released her fear and anger at him in one primal, terrible shriek.

A light snapped on at one of the nearby homes.

Startled, the man looked confused. Then, he turned and fled into the darkness.

The girl watched him run. She stayed, frozen in place, until she heard a car start and peel off into the night. Her scalp felt like it was on fire. She breathed in—short, choppy breaths. Finally, she reached out to collect one of her sandals. She drew it close as her hands were shaking violently. She could smell the asphalt, the coal-like tar odor. She wanted to cry, but first, she screamed once more. And then…she sobbed.

◆

Officer Terry Quirk only stopped at the hospital long enough to drop off a female officer. He watched her walk through the ER doors in search of the injured teen and her father. Quirk drove back to the scene of the attack.[632]

There was nothing to be found at the crime scene, but that wasn't too surprising. A while later, Terry heard the dispatcher describing the assailant, as reported by the girl who had been assaulted.

"Suspect is reported to be around 165 pounds, clean-shaven, with collar-length, dark blonde hair. Last seen wearing a white t-shirt and blue jeans."[633]

Knowing that two deputies were on duty, Quirk responded to dispatch, seeking assistance in locating the suspect who had taken off in a vehicle.[634]

"Can we get the deputies in? I think every moving vehicle in town should be stopped, drivers should be questioned, and physical attributes should be compared to the description of the attacker. Let's get everybody." Terry turned west and began driving up and down the city streets, ready to hunt down the despicable young man who had committed the crime.

◆

The radio traffic interrupted Nancy Baxter's sleep. She rolled onto her side, opened one eye, and squinted at a digital clock next to the Motorola radio on her nightstand. Sighing, she ran her hand under her pillow to be sure that the revolver remained where it belonged. She heard Officer Quirk ask deputies to cover the east side of town. Exhausted, Nancy yawned, rolled onto her back, and permitted her eyelids to close.[635]

◆

Usually, deputies didn't double up on the graveyard shift, but Gene Flatt and Maureen Higgins had recently ended their period of duty at one of the roadblocks. They acknowledged receipt of Terry's BOLO and agreed to check out the eastern borders of town. Gene, the designated patrol officer, manned the wheel while Maureen, the junior deputy, rode shotgun. They drove quietly along Highway 82.[636]

Just east of town, headlights from a lone vehicle came down the forested, two-lane road toward the deputies. As the car neared, it briefly veered over the center line. As the two vehicles passed, the deputies sized up the driver, who appeared slumped down. Flatt continued watching the car in his rear-view mirror for a moment. The deputies agreed that the man behind the wheel was probably a drunk driver, so Flatt turned his vehicle around, flipped the gumball light on, and began his pursuit.[637]

Deputy Higgins grabbed her radio.

"Aspen, 6-6 and 6-7," she said.

"Go ahead, 6-6," Lynne Unger replied at dispatch.

"We are 10-75, with a possible 10-55, in the vicinity of Crestahaus Lodge, east of town on 82." Translated, this meant a traffic stop with a possible drunk driver.

"10-4, 6-6. 0126," Lynne replied, noting in her log the time her transmission ended. The time on the log, as well as on the tape, was for legal continuity.[638]

◆

Nancy opened her eyes. *Crestahaus? That's just down the hill. There goes Gene again, another drunk driver to add to his credit.* Nancy felt sorry for Maureen. The deputies would be tied up in the processing and report that a traffic stop incurs. *Can't he ever give it a rest and just go home and get some sleep?*[639]

◆

Seeing law enforcement lights behind him, the driver of the Cadillac stopped along the shoulder of the road. Flatt parked behind the Caddy and got out of his vehicle, noting that Crestahaus Lodge was off to his left. The gumball light was still rotating, illuminating nearby quaking aspens with harsh flashes of scarlet light.[640]

Approaching the driver's side of the blue '66 Caddy, Gene shined his flashlight inside. The driver was a thin Caucasian man wearing a plaid shirt under an old coat. This man was wearing a yellow fishing hat and wire-rimmed glasses, and there was a Band-Aid stretched across his nose.[641]

"You all right, mister?" Flatt asked the stranger.[642]

"Yeah, I'm all right," the driver said in a low voice.

"Well, *I* thought you were having a little bit of trouble driving here. Can I see your identification, please?"[643]

"Okay, just a second. I'll look for it." The driver leaned over and started rummaging through the glove compartment.

Deputy Higgins, standing outside the closed passenger-side window, aimed her flashlight at the glove compartment. Feeling that the driver was fumbling a little too long, she leaned over to get a better look at him. She didn't know this guy.[644]

The man finally found a wallet and handed Gene the registration. The Colorado driver's license had a decent photograph of a man named Paul Merihew. Gene glanced at the papers before tossing them to his partner on the opposite side of the car.[645]

Maureen examined the driver's license and vehicle registration. She had a friend who was dating Paul Merihew. Deputy Higgins took another good look at the man sitting in the Cadillac. The driver, with a Band-Aid across his nose, was *not* Paul. The deputy took a few steps away from the vehicle and contacted dispatch on her Motorola.[646]

In dispatch, Lynne was crocheting when Maureen's soft voice interrupted the quiet of the nearly empty building.

"Aspen, 6-6," Maureen said.[647]

"Go ahead, 6-6," Lynne replied.

"I need a 10-28 and 29." Maureen then whispered the digits she was reading off the vehicle's rear license plate. "Zed-George-One-Seven-Six-Five."[648]

"10-4, 6-6. 0129," Lynne replied, meaning that she understood what was being asked, was seeking the information, and to standby for the results. Maureen's request meant that she was seeking the vehicle registration information and the address of the owner of the car. Her second request had been to check if there were any warrants out for the owner or if the vehicle had been reported as stolen.[649]

Maureen's attention shot back to her partner, who had suddenly pulled his Colt Python and barked an order at the driver.

"Get out of the car," Flatt demanded. The driver did as he was told, slowly and without any fuss. Keeping the revolver fixed on the disheveled man, Gene continued directing him. "Remove your glasses and turn to face the vehicle." Again, the man complied.

Now that the driver was facing her, Maureen could see his face more clearly. She knew the driver was bluffing about his identity, so she felt it was better to let him think she and her partner were falling for the bluff rather than provide him with an opportunity to run or fight. Though this mystery man looked haggard and in no shape to fight, one never knew what a desperate man would do when cornered.[650]

"6-6, Aspen," Lynne's voice came over the radio.

"Go ahead," Maureen replied.

"Vehicle is registered to Paul Merihew at 803 Bonita Drive, Aspen, and it is clear." The use of the word *clear* meant that Merihew was not subject to any warrants, nor had the Caddy been reported stolen.[651]

Maureen then spoke quietly and calmly into her radio.

"Aspen, 6-6. We are requesting a 10-78 and will be transporting a 10-99 to the SO shortly."[652]

◆

Nancy Baxter bolted upright in bed. *10-78? Maureen's asking for backup?* It was such a seldom-used code around these parts. Nancy reached over to her nightstand and turned on the light. *Something's wrong. Maureen knows it.* Seizing the telephone, Nancy dialed her office.

"What's happening?" she asked Lynne.[653]

"Funny you should ask," Lynne replied. "Higgins and Flatt stopped a Cadillac out by the Crestahaus. Possible DUI. She's asked for backup."

"I thought that's what I heard."

Suddenly, radio communications changed. Nancy and Lynne heard Maureen nearly whisper into her radio, "Subject bears a close resemblance to Ted Bundy."[654]

"Holy Fuck, Lynnie!" Nancy yelled into the receiver. "I'll be right in."

◆

Out at the Crestahaus, the atmosphere changed drastically. Whether it was a spontaneous flare of temper or an impulsive reaction to overhearing Maureen's message to dispatch, the driver of the Caddy was suddenly riled up. In response, Flatt ordered the man to lay face-down on the road, spread-eagle. Although the driver complied, he continued to spar with the deputies verbally.[655]

"I'll have your jobs!" he threatened. "This is false arrest, and I'll have your badges, for sure."[656]

Deputy Higgins pulled her .357, providing cover for her partner. Seeing that Gene appeared to have no trouble searching the driver, she opened the passenger side door of the vehicle and shined her flashlight inside. There was a small photograph sitting on the bench seat. It was in poor shape, having been folded repeatedly. Looking closer, she could see it was a picture of a young woman with a little child. Maureen thought it looked like Liz Kloepfer—Bundy's former girlfriend. She left the photo untouched, where she had found it.[657]

Suddenly, something clicked in her head. *If* the man they had just detained was the fugitive who had been on the run all week, he was considered armed and dangerous. Where was the rifle that was missing from the Kaeser cabin? She did a rudimentary inspection under the car seats, glancing periodically to ensure that her partner was still in control of the situation with the suspect.[658]

Finding no weapon, she walked around to stand beside Deputy Flatt and the driver, who remained face down on the road. Maureen spoke professionally, even addressing the driver as *sir* so as not to tip him off that she knew his claim to be Merihew was a lie.[659]

◆

A half-mile away, Nancy was running on adrenaline. She had dressed, grabbed her helmet and jacket, and practically slid down her steep driveway to her motorcycle. Knowing the deputies would have the road blocked at the Crestahaus, Nancy opted to head downtown via the back way, up to Park Circle. She wound her way between huge boulders that blocked vehicle access at the end of the street, but the gap between was just wide enough to permit the passage of her motorcycle. When she maneuvered past the obstacles, she rolled the throttle, flying to work faster than ever before.⁶⁶⁰

◆

Officer Terry Quirk, responding to the call for backup, approached quickly from the west. He saw the Caddy, illuminated by the gumball light, just ahead. He parked in front of the Cadillac and emerged from his car, immediately feeling a sense of vulnerability. He drew his sidearm, concerned that the suspect wasn't already in handcuffs.⁶⁶¹

Sergeant Don Davis arrived next at the scene, screeching to a halt in his Chevy Blazer. The six-foot-five, imposing lawman emerged from his rig and started walking toward the Caddy. The overhead vehicle lights on all three vehicles continued rotating incessantly, illuminating the nearby trees in a hypnotic display. He stood over the suspect and smiled.

"Welcome back, Ted."⁶⁶²

Davis, as senior officer on the scene, asked Officer Quirk for his handcuffs. These were handed over, and the sergeant placed them on the fugitive.

Ted was assisted to his feet as Maureen conducted a secondary search of the vehicle for the missing rifle. It wasn't inside the passenger area or the trunk, but the vehicle would be impounded and thoroughly searched back at the sheriff's office.

◆

At city hall, Nancy burst through the door into the dispatch office. "What's the Crestahaus update?"

"It's him!" Lynne exclaimed. The two ladies just stared at one another for a moment, dumbfounded. Then, Nancy placed her helmet on a shelf. "I'm running over to the courthouse. Let me know if I should come back to help."

Is it really Bundy? Could this be it? Nancy didn't know if she should allow herself to believe it just yet.⁶⁶³

◆

At the traffic stop, Deputy Higgins took a good long look at Bundy, bathed in an eerie, spectral lightshow, the result of the ever-increasing crowd of patrol cars, each with its rotating red gumball lights. Maureen interlaced her fingers atop her head, breathed in deeply, and exhaled as if she could purge the entire foul turmoil that one narcissist had created. He was a thin, dirty man desperate for a bed, food, and attention.

Here he was, Ted Bundy. He had successfully eluded tracking dogs, search parties, helicopter patrols, and an armed posse for six days and now—apprehended less than a mile from where the whole circus had started.⁶⁶⁴

"Aspen, 6-6," Maureen radioed dispatch again. "Requesting a 10-51 to head this way." She was seeking the services of a wrecker to transport the Cadillac for processing.

Surrendering to the fact that the jig was up, Bundy morphed into the frisky, friendly prisoner Sergeant Davis had known all too well. His cocky, arrogant smile returned, yet he still refused to confirm his identity, not that anyone needed him to at this point.

Deputy Gene Flatt had brought the prisoner his breakfast numerous times. This evening's darkness, the disguise, and a massive weight loss had temporarily concealed the fugitive's identity—even from a man who had interacted with him on multiple occasions.

Sergeant Davis led the outlaw over to his Chevy Blazer, assisting him into the seat.⁶⁶⁵

"I can't think anymore," Bundy mumbled.⁶⁶⁶

The drive to the courthouse was short and sweet.

Deputy Higgins was drained, and six days of long shifts, coupled with the emotional burden of searching for someone considered a danger to her community, had taken its toll on her. From Bundy's slight *swerve* into the oncoming lane of traffic till the cuffs were placed on his wrists, the entire affair had gone down in less than ten minutes. It felt much longer to her. Throughout it all, she and Gene hadn't exchanged a single word.⁶⁶⁷

◆

Officer Chet Zajac had completed his bar checks an hour earlier. He was on foot, so he hadn't responded to the scene unfolding out near the Crestahaus. He had been monitoring the radio traffic between Maureen and dispatch and was just mentally processing the fact that Bundy was finally back in custody. He had no desire to be at the rapidly forming block party and certainly had no interest in rubbing elbows in the soon-to-be crowded halls of the courthouse. *If Ted's back behind bars,* he thought, *great. It's time to get back to work. But, what an interesting fugitive. The charming, engaging, and entertaining young man I had conversations with in the basement of the courthouse–what a strange man.*

Chet thought back to an early morning visit to the courthouse weeks earlier. He had walked out the back door of the building and spied a man standing all alone, smoking a cigarette. The stranger looked pensive, his eyes on the ground, seemingly deep in thought.

"Hey," the young officer said, beginning hopeful introductions. "Chet Zajac, Aspen PD." There was a slight upward inflection in the tone of his voice, indicating that he was also asking why the other man was behind the courthouse.[668]

"Yeah?" the stranger looked away, exhaling a plume of smoke into the brisk morning air. "I'm here with the Bundy team."

Chet continued talking, hopeful the man would reveal more about himself and why he appeared so forlorn. *Is he an attorney? A psychologist?* The stranger didn't take the bait. Chet switched tactics and told the man of his awkward midnight conversations with the prisoner.

"You know," the officer said. "It seems like, whenever I talked to him, and whenever he was done, he would just...turn off."

The other man looked off into the distance, shaking his head and chewing softly on his bottom lip like he was disturbed by whatever opinion was fighting to emerge. Then, he turned and looked the officer straight in the eye.

"I never said this," the stranger said cautiously. He looked down at the ground, taking a deep drag of his cigarette. "And, you're lying if you *say* I said it. But—" he paused. He tossed the cigarette butt to the ground, extinguishing it by crushing it with his foot while he blew the last of the smoke off to the side. "He's a mess and should be destroyed."

Zajac stood in place, watching the other man walk away. The officer didn't feel as if the pensive stranger was trying to make a bold statement. It just seemed as if he was airing his private thoughts. *He should be destroyed.* Those four words continued to ring in Chet's brain as he returned to duty.

◆

Nancy stood in the bullpen of the sheriff's department. She had been so busy for most of the week, but now she wasn't sure what to do. When the door opened, Sergeant Don Davis suddenly led Bundy into the room. There was a jubilant, celebratory vibe felt throughout as the deputies and officers witnessed his passing. Someone had created a large, handwritten banner, "Welcome Home Teddy," and taped it to a wall. Nancy watched as the prisoner was led back into the area containing the jail.[669]

Davis and Bundy were only out of sight for a few minutes. When they returned, Bundy had changed into a dark blue prison suit. Nancy thought he looked like a scruffy mechanic, but she noticed he was barefoot and walked with a slight limp. Maybe that was too strong of a word. He ap-

DEPUTY GARY WHITE

peared to be walking as if his feet were sore. She theorized that his clothes had been bagged for evidence. The prisoner had walked into the office wearing his Utah Penitentiary-issued boots, putting to rest the rumors that he had been wearing loafers out in the elements.[670]

Without thinking about it, Nancy fell right into place behind Davis as he led his prisoner toward the sheriff's private office. When the sergeant led Bundy into the small room, Nancy walked in right behind them.

She hadn't come to the courthouse to bear witness to Bundy's interrogation, and she hadn't been invited, but as she entered Kienast's office, Davis seemed mildly surprised he had been followed. Their eyes met. The sergeant raised an eyebrow as he considered her presence.[671]

"Hell," he whispered. "You've earned it." He gave an approving nod and closed the door.

The minute hand on the clock moved to 2:35 a.m.[672]

Sheriff Kienast's office was no luxury affair with modern furnishings and accessories. Although the interior partitions were drywalled, the other two walls were made of bricks, which had been set in place in 1890. No insulation had been added over the decades. The windows were high on the wall, which never helped with the poor lighting, no matter the time of day. A framed Marc Chagall exhibition poster seemed to be the only adornment in this austere setting. There were five mid-century leather chairs with wooden arms lining the walls. The desk occupied the greater portion of the northern wall, off to the left, as you entered the space. Two rounded chairs with leather seats and backs were situated in front of the desk. These chairs had been retired from a jury box and had seen better days. As the prisoner shuffled across the worn carpet toward one of these padded chairs, Nancy realized that these were probably the most luxurious surfaces he had experienced in days.

Davis, wanting a little more legroom, pulled two chairs into the center of the room. He shackled Bundy to one before taking a seat in the other, face-to-face with his prisoner. Nancy walked over to the corner of the room, rotated one of the chairs toward the men, and collapsed into its relative comfort.[673]

It was time to begin the interrogation, which would see the sergeant questioning his prisoner and hopefully eliciting incriminating responses. Before any questions were asked, Davis read Bundy his rights.[674]

Nancy observed Bundy from head to toe. He didn't resemble the handsome, confident man that had walked into the courthouse six days ago. His photograph, taken that day, was etched into Nancy's memory. Six days earlier, Ted looked healthy, determined, and well-rested. Now, he was emaciated, wild-eyed, and disheveled. He was in dire need of a shower, food, and sleep. She listened as Bundy said he understood his rights, but she wondered why he had a slight smirk on his face.[675]

Bundy seemed cooperative and more than willing to talk about his *great escape*. He informed Davis that he had been preparing himself for quite some time. He had noticed, as winter turned to spring, authorities had started opening the courtroom windows on the second floor. To his astonishment, they were left open for hours at a time, and he saw this as his opportunity. He claimed that on May 23, he had made the definitive decision to escape. It had taken him a while to overcome the natural curiosity as to what effect a failed escape attempt would have on his defense during a murder trial. After deciding to go, however, he began solidifying his plans.[676]

Ted began his preparations. He repeatedly jumped off the upper bunk of his cell and made efforts to strengthen his legs for the incredible impact they'd receive. He had walked three to five miles a day within the confines of his cell.[677]

He paid close attention to the courthouse and the men assigned to guard him. Not having to be shackled in court, he was free to quietly pace distances between known fixtures, the distance from the counselor's table to the law library, for instance. Believing that it would require a five-second window of opportunity where no lawmen were observing him, he could make his escape. Within those five seconds, he could drop from the open window and run around the corner of the building, all before the alarm could be raised. Given a ten-second window of opportunity, he could have run down the stairs and right out the front door. Having weighed the pros and cons of both scenarios, the window was the option of choice.[678]

After tracking the habits of his guards for weeks, it was apparent that Sergeant Kralicek's attention was diverted from four to six seconds each time he lit up a cigarette. On the day of the escape, however, Kralicek had departed and left Deputy Westerlund in charge. Bundy hadn't spent enough time with Westerlund to study his habits and patterns of behavior, and this had been problematic.[679]

Other preparations had been made as well. Bundy had recently been interviewed in the Garfield County Jail by reporters from Utah. At the time, he sported a beard and longer hair. His wit and sense of humor were on full display for the camera. Residents of the valley, catching the interview on TV, saw a socially unconventional personality who seemed to fit right into their community.

A day or two before the jump, Bundy shaved off his beard and had his hair cut. At this point, he resembled the Utah State law student once again. More importantly, he didn't look the same as he had in any of his recently published photos or in the televised interview.[680]

Bundy wore more clothing than was needed for a typical day in the courtroom. The prisoner's layering was part of his scheme. Under his tan corduroys, which were seen by the public, he wore a pair of jean cutoffs and, under those, a pair of white tennis shorts. In one of his pockets, he tucked a scarlet bandana. He wore a standard white t-shirt, and, over this, he wore a white long-john top, a yellow turtleneck, and then a beige turtleneck. His loose-fitting, multi-colored cardigan sweater effectively concealed the bulkiness of his layers. On his feet were wool hiking socks and the boots he had received as an inmate in Utah. Typically, he wore his brown loafers to court, but he wanted the ankle support and durability of the boots while on the run. Lastly, he tucked a picture of Liz and her daughter into his pocket.[681]

After Sergeant Kralicek and Deputy Murphy escorted him to the counselor's table in the empty courtroom, he nearly made his escape at that time. Ted noticed that the handful of people in the room were not paying him any attention. Murphy was being dismissed as he had worked the graveyard shift. Bundy was confident he could make his escape but heard traffic noise outside the window of the law library. It was the morning commute. When the judge entered the room, escape plans were instantly put on hold. There would be less traffic outside during the upcoming recess.[682]

When recess came and the courtroom began to empty, he grew agitated because Deputy Westerlund was paying him too much attention. Westerlund kept pace with the defendant as he tried on several occasions to lose the guard. Bundy then deliberately switched directions to collide with the deputy. He repeated this maneuver a couple of times, and it yielded the needed response. Westerlund took up a position by the door.[683]

Next, Ted started pacing again, just to see how long the deputy would permit him to be out of his line of sight. At first, Westerlund didn't let the man out of view for more than one or two seconds. The defendant was counting. It took him a full five minutes to *lead* the deputy up to the five seconds he needed. He watched as Westerlund was growing comfortable—complacent.[684]

It was time.

As the deputy turned his attention elsewhere, Bundy raced into the law library. The window was halfway open, so he opened it even further. At that moment, a woman entered the courtroom to retrieve her purse, and this caused an unexpected delay.[685]

Gauging the distance between the window and the ground, Ted knew it was a significant drop. If he broke his leg during the maneuver, a distinct possibility, he'd be recaptured immediately. Escape charges would follow, and years would be added to his sentence, all for nothing. Executing the jump without injury was of paramount importance.

"Didn't the height of the window concern you?" Davis inquired.[686]

"It could have been six stories," Bundy boasted. "I would have done it. I didn't want to go back to jail. It was just too pretty outside."[687]

Sheriff Kienast walked into the office at this moment.

"Welcome home, Ted," he remarked with a grin.[688]

"Thank you," Bundy replied.

◆

Sergeant Darrel Horan had been asleep at home, only a five-minute drive from the courthouse. A superior had called, waking him up, and tasked him with checking a residence on Bonita Drive adjacent to the golf course. Bundy was in custody, but he had stolen a '66 Cadillac from Paul Merihew. Horan was asked to verify that Merihew and any other occupants at his residence were alive and unharmed. There was still no sign of the rifle Bundy had stolen from the Kaeser cabin.

Horan sped north along Cemetery Lane, took a left turn on Alta Vista Street at high speed, and pulled into the first driveway on Bonita Drive. He raced up to the front door, knocked loudly, and waited—hopefully—for the lights inside to come on. He was convinced that, with the missing rifle, the stolen car, and Bundy's reputation, he was going to discover at least one body inside the residence.

A light came on. A second light came on.

Paul Merihew and his girlfriend were home, safe and secure, but were shocked to learn that the car had been stolen right out of their driveway.

Returning to his vehicle, Sergeant Horan began to process the last six days in Aspen. No lives had been lost. The town lacked equipment, and law enforcement officers had very little formalized training. It had been one big confusing mess. In no way did he want to visit the circus that was surely going on down at the courthouse. Returning home seemed like the wiser choice.[689]

◆

Back at the courthouse, Sheriff Kienast took a seat behind his desk while Sergeant Davis continued to direct the interrogation. There was an interruption by a knock, and someone came in and handed the prisoner a cup of coffee and a sandwich. Ted seemed very appreciative and greedily consumed the beverage at lightning speed, requesting a refill. Nancy continued to observe the proceedings in silence.[690]

Bundy continued telling his tale, explaining that when he jumped from the courthouse window, he landed hard, feeling an incredible jolt—and then he took off running. Knowing the judge did not permit deputies to have firearms in his courtroom didn't really factor into his decision to jump. Ted was supremely confident in his five-second plan, but *hey*, having unarmed guards was undoubtedly a bonus.[691]

Heading east, Ted said he'd raced over the front entrance steps to the building, vaulted over a thigh-high iron fence, went behind the prosecutor's office, and scaled a six-foot-high fence to gain access to a secluded roadway. He ran down the alley, parallel to Main Street, yet hidden from view by folks who were using the main thoroughfare. He passed two men who were behind a restaurant. They simply stared at him, confused. Crossing North Spring Street, he entered a grove of trees where the river coursed its way through town.[692]

During one of his trips to Aspen from Glenwood Springs, he was permitted a brief stroll to the river here for a little bit of sunshine and exercise. He had been escorted by deputies, of course, but he claimed that he had taken this opportunity to memorize streets, alleys, and even the foliage along the riverbank.[693]

Nancy felt like rolling her eyes as the man gloated, but she controlled the urge. *He thinks he's so smart.*[694]

Bundy planned to head south over Aspen Mountain, cross the Continental Divide, and emerge in the Crested Butte area. If he could get a hold of some money, he'd leave the country. If he ran into some bad luck, he could always return to Washington State to be with those he called *his people*.[695]

◆

Investigator Mike Fisher had arrived. He was leaning against the wall outside the sheriff's office, fuming mad. The investigator's best chance to break down Ted's defenses and get him to break under pressure would have been when the prisoner's mental and physical defenses were shot. Fisher could have pummeled the prisoner with questions about the disappearance, and death of Caryn Campbell. The inspector had been gathering incriminating information on Ted, and from what Fisher had learned about Bundy, he felt sure that the man was a killer. He wanted to nail Ted for every life he had stolen, and he wanted to *hear* him confess. The sheriff had promised him first crack at Bundy, but now Kienast was stealing his crucial window of opportunity.[696]

That dirtbag was being catered to as he was entertaining the sheriff with his self-accolades. Food and coffee? *Seriously*? Why had that been allowed?

His best opportunity to solve the Campbell case was evaporating as Bundy's belly and ego were getting the fuel he craved.

◆

Bundy continued to describe how he had concealed himself behind bushes on the banks of the river, never entering the water. Hidden behind the bushes, he stripped down to his white shirt and cutoffs. It was at this point that he realized he had inadvertently left two small, sharpened pencils in the front pocket of his pants. They could have punctured him had he landed wrong during his leap from the window sill, but instead, they went right through his pocket, sharp as the dickens.[697]

Stuffing all his removed clothing into a backpack created from one of his turtlenecks, he then tied the red bandana around his head. To anyone who encountered him from this point on, he would resemble an average local boy—clean-cut, handsome, and apparently on his way to go hiking.[698]

With the sound of police sirens hanging in the air, he turned south and confidently walked back through town. He passed multiple people on the streets, and scores of cars and trucks passed him. He was invisible. He belonged. He was one of them.[699]

Nancy gave him credit for thinking ahead. His escape plan was impressive, the epitome of skillful misdirection. As officers were busy erecting checkpoints on the main road leading east or west out of town, the fugitive had worked his way through Aspen in a southwesterly direction. The sheriff even acknowledged that he never imagined Bundy would have come back through town.[700]

During his authorized breaks outside the courthouse, in the weeks leading up to his jump, Ted had asked deputies all kinds of questions about Smuggler Mountain. He felt that lawmen would remember these conversations and focus their efforts in the wrong direction. The sheriff nodded, agreeing that the man's intentions resulted in the desired effect.[701]

Bundy said he had passed a condominium complex and then turned sharply west to the base of Aspen Mountain. Here, he hiked up the slopes, hugging the tree line. He did his best to remain inconspicuous, and this task was made all the easier by his revised appearance. He climbed rapidly, periodically taking a breather to look down at the resort town, thinking that he'd see red lights and all sorts of activity. There were none. Aspen, from this distance, seemed as peaceful and idyllic as the travel brochures promised.[702]

Encountering sections of terrain that were too steep for him, he began extensive zig-zag treks across the grassy ski field. This had exposed him to anyone in town with a decent set of binoculars, but he continued ascending, making use of switchbacks until he reached the peak.[703]

Nancy remained silent during the interrogation and was doing her best to maintain a poker face. Bundy was making himself out to be a grand mountaineer, but she had been up and down the face of Aspen Mountain more than once. Knowing the terrain and the altitude, she knew he was lying about how fast he had made it to the top. Perhaps it took him longer...much longer. But Ted was painting the picture the way he wanted it to be seen.[704]

With a four-mile hike and over 3,000 feet in elevation gain now under his belt, he felt a little pride in his achievement when he reached the summit. He had placed a considerable amount of distance between himself and his pursuers in a completely different direction than anyone would have guessed. Adrenaline, youth, and sheer will had gotten him this far, and descending the other side of the peak, he finally allowed himself to slow his pace. He set a reasonable new tempo and found himself enjoying the hike.[705]

Pleased with his present circumstances, he still took precautions to hide his footsteps. As he began a descent toward Castle Creek, he did his best to follow a southerly course. He hoped to discover a trail that would take him to the town of Crested Butte.[706]

As the day turned cooler, he put on more of his clothing. He was stumbling along the side of a small stream when darkness started closing in, and he didn't have a map or a flashlight. He spied the silhouette of a cabin. There was no light emanating from the home, and there were no signs of activity in or around the structure. There was the temptation to break in and seek shelter, but the desire to reach Crested Butte, the yearning to *truly escape*, caused him to press on.[707]

CHAPTER 10
CEMETERY LANE

The door to the sheriff's office opened, and one of the secretaries entered with a fresh cup of coffee for the prisoner.

"You really had us going there for a while," she remarked, smiling at him.[708]

"I thought I might have," Ted said with a coy smile. He sampled the fresh beverage, gave the woman an approving nod, and waited politely for her to depart before resuming his monologue.

Is he flirting with her? Nancy thought, trying not to show her repulsion. *He's so smug.* She'd been observing his expressions as he recalled how he had eluded authorities. When he felt that he had amused his captors with a particularly entertaining flair of storytelling, or as he indulged in a chuckle, thinking he was so clever, he was animated and energetic. Whenever the sergeant interrupted with questions, however, the captive looked down at the floor, mumbled some feeble reply, and acted like he might put an end to his storytelling. Sergeant Davis, picking up on these childish cues, would switch to questions that cast Bundy in a more favorable light. The prisoner responded to these questions with a quip or an amusing anecdote. On the rare occasion that Ted glanced over at Nancy, he appeared to register disdain. *Why are you here, woman?* Nancy was craving a cigarette, but she didn't dare move. She knew she shouldn't even be in this room, and she didn't want to do anything that could even remotely stop the prisoner from spinning his tale.[709]

Bundy continued with his narrative. As darkness fell that first night, he spent about four hours searching for a trail that would lead him out of the Conundrum Creek residential area. It was now so dark that he was unable to make out the outlines of the valley he was exploring. Believing it would be too easy to get lost, he found his way back to the babbling brook. He discovered a rocky road and was doing his best to follow it when the rain started falling, soaking him in no time.[710]

He miraculously stumbled upon a trail and followed it, but progress was incredibly slow. He figured that he only hiked two or three miles during the following four hours. Though temperatures did not dip below freezing during the night, he was cold and wet and regretting his decision to bypass the mountain cabin. Tired and confused, he knew he was confronting a very serious problem. He didn't want to travel in broad daylight and thus expose himself to possible discovery, but he was learning that it was nearly impossible to travel effectively at night.[711]

The only information he had about the area came from his memories of a map he had studied before his escape. This map had been used in court to show where Caryn Campbell's body had been discovered. Serving in his own defense, Ted had legal rights of discovery, and the document had been in his possession for a while.[712]

Early in the morning, Bundy returned to the very cabin that he'd passed hours earlier. Wanting to prove to himself that the structure was unoccupied, he observed it from several vantage points for about four hours. It was probably around eight in the morning when he decided to break into the home.[713]

Once inside, he shed all clothing, hanging everything up to dry. He toured the rooms, walked into the kitchen, and pilfered the supplies, eating whatever he could find—brown sugar and tomato sauce. He fixed himself a cup of tea.[714]

He felt as if the broken windowpane needed to be explained. He scribbled his hasty *Amos* note, posted it outside, and then closed his eyes for a nap. He planned to wait until dark, then continue his hike south toward Crested Butte.[715]

That night, he searched for anything he could use to accomplish his mission, finding a couple of shirts, a jacket, some first-aid supplies, and the most prized of his newest acquisitions, a flashlight.[716]

Having no idea how long he'd be trudging through the mountains, he contemplated a serious question. Should he take the rifle he found? There was the prospect of encountering wildlife, and a gun might provide some form of self-protection. Picking off small game could also be a bonus. There was the other side of the argument as well. Should it be discovered that he had used this specific cabin and that a rifle was now missing, would he be shot on sight? It was a very real possibility that he had to consider.[717]

He slipped on the jacket and grabbed the flashlight. Deciding that taking the rifle was worth the risk, he slung it over his shoulder and walked outside just past midnight. He closed the front door behind him. It was now Thursday.[718]

Nancy indulged in a tiny smile. She knew Ted had forgotten to wipe his fingerprints off the glass he'd used in the kitchen—*rookie mistake*.

Turning the flashlight on, he was pleased with his newfound source of illumination. He had just enough light to navigate the rocky Conundrum Trail, yet not enough to draw attention to himself. With little effort, he covered several miles, resting when he wanted to and quenching his thirst by drinking from the nearby stream.[719]

At dawn, he was still hiking south, hidden from view by trees and bushes. He had already placed several miles between himself and the cabin. During a rest break, he spied a solitary hiker off in the distance. The tiny figure was heading south along the main trail. Eventually, Bundy laid down and fell asleep amid an aspen grove high up on the west side of the valley.[720]

He awoke around mid-afternoon and reassessed his situation. For five hours, he climbed up the ridge to his right. It was challenging and steep terrain, but he reached the crest of what he believed to be Keefe Peak and started descending the other side into the Maroon Creek Valley. He was losing daylight and had to move fast to get back down to the safety of the trees.

He abandoned his rifle along the eastern slope of the ridge. Tired of lugging it around, he felt certain deputies would shoot him on sight if they caught him carrying a weapon.[721]

Around 9:30 that evening, he built a small fire and spent a cold, sleepless night in his bivouac.[722]

Several hours before sunrise, he rose and continued his descent. It was Friday now, and he had come upon a stream. Guessing that it was Maroon Creek, he hit an emotional low in his journey. Ted believed he had crossed the Continental Divide when he had surmounted the ridge the previous evening. He discovered that this was not so, a fact made all too apparent when the water was flowing in the wrong direction.[723]

Sergeant Davis nodded, prompting Ted to proceed without having to explain the blunder.

Turning north, and by the afternoon, Bundy reached the junction where two creeks merged. He took a break here as his right knee was giving him trouble. What was merely intended to be a respite, however, somehow managed to stretch into six hours of inactivity.[724]

After sunset, he set out again, proceeding along the trail bordering the east side of the creek. Later, his right knee locked up on him. Feeling like Long John Silver, Ted crossed a wooden footbridge and found Maroon Creek Road. He passed a ranch off to his left and continued walking north. It was so quiet that he could hear the approach of occasional automobiles or see their lights in enough time to step off the road and conceal himself from view. Throughout the night, he followed the winding course of the road down toward town.[725]

It was now Saturday, and one hour after another elapsed until he came to an intersection he recognized. Off to the side was the old stone Prince of Peace Chapel. He made no mention of whether he saw the deputies manning the roadblock here, but he managed to turn right, undetected, onto Castle Creek Road. He was entering the western borders of Aspen as if he were a mere homeowner out for an early walk. To all outward appearances, he looked normal. The trouble was that his knee remained locked and practically useless.[726]

He was now heading south, limping and using his flashlight only when needed. He started seeing too many signs of activity, so he hid in a forest glade just south of the official city limits.

The sun rose, and the morning turned into afternoon. It was the longest break he would encounter throughout his outdoor odyssey. Still, he opted to wait for sunset before emerging from the glade. The brutal, shifting talus fields had taken their toll on him, and, as a result, his knee was keeping him in considerable pain.[727]

Bundy's activities after dark on Saturday were quite vague. He planned to return to the cabin. He needed a night with a roof over his head and some time to come up with another means of escaping from this dreaded valley. He had five miles to cover to reach the cabin, with a steadily increasing gain in elevation, so he opted to just walk along the side of the road. He used the flashlight and hoped no one recognized him.[728]

Hours passed, and very early Sunday morning, Bundy found himself approaching the cabin. He hadn't been there since early Thursday. He was suspicious. Had anyone detected there had been a break-in? He hid behind some bushes and thought about how he could answer his own question. Then, he remembered something.[729]

Crawling to the back side of the cabin and up a bank that looked down over the creek and the structure, he inspected the dry soil. He remembered that his prison-issued boots had left prints there. He was alarmed when he discovered that now, a multitude of prints could be seen in the soil. He figured that an army of lawmen had scoured the area.[730]

He hid in the woods, demoralized. The Kaeser cabin had come to represent shelter, yet here it was, tantalizingly close but no longer safe and warm. The sound of an approaching helicopter caused him to panic. He understood that his best shot at remaining concealed was to stay put. The helicopter landed and search dogs jumped to the ground. Had he been spotted? He was confused. Exhausted from having hiked for days, there was little he could do. Deciding to remain in his hiding spot, he'd see what developed and react accordingly.[731]

The dogs, their handlers, and several deputies fanned out and began searching. They seemed interested in moving south.[732]

Ted had been on the lam for five days. The only food he'd come across was the meager rations he found at the cabin. Having hiked and climbed, mile after mile, with scant caloric intake, he had shed the pounds in rapid succession. Being hunted, truly hunted by land and from the air, had taken its toll. With his southern escape route now blocked, he would turn around and head back to town. If everyone believed he was in the Castle Creek region, he'd take advantage of that belief.

With what could only be described as a rush of adrenaline, the injured knee seemed to undergo a miraculous recovery. It suddenly felt fine. Now, had the roadblocks on Highway 82 been disbanded? At this point, the best shot at getting out of the valley was to return to the highway and procure some means of transportation.

Picking up a walking stick, he pretended to be a hiker. He encountered a redhead who drew a pistol on him, but Ted managed to convince the young man that he was merely a tourist from Pennsylvania looking for his family. When Sergeant Davis asked if his prisoner recalled the rancher's name, only the surname of Sinclair could be recalled.[733]

For the next few hours, Ted was in better spirits, believing he could blend into a crowd. This encounter with the rancher bolstered his self-confidence. Surely, if he met anyone else on his journey to town, he could talk his way out of the encounter.

By sunset, he was on the western side of town. He made his way to the highway, waiting until no cars approached from either direction and then dashed across the road. He was on the grounds of the Aspen Golf Course when his leg suddenly gave out again. Heading east, he limped over the fairways and around the bunkers and tee boxes. At the far side of the course, he stumbled and rolled down into a small ravine.[734]

He estimated that he spent an hour just lying where his body had stopped rolling. With his leg in its present condition, he knew he needed to find some means of transportation. His desire to flee superseded his need for stealth and carefully crafted plans. He was getting sloppy.[735]

Gathering up his strength, he forced himself to his feet and got moving again. There were a couple of children's bicycles on a nearby porch. He selected the larger of the two, complete with a banana seat and a sissy bar. Bundy hopped on and began pedaling north. It was a single-speed bike and would be no match for mountain passes.[736]

He passed Castle Creek Drive and then the Red Butte Cemetery. Gravestones, many from the early 1900s, were visible just off to his right, casting lengthy shadows in the waning crescent moonlight. A couple of cars passed him, illuminating this strange midnight rider in their headlights. There was Bundy, a grown man with his hodgepodge of clothing and budding beard, pedaling what could only be described as a diminutive child's bike near a graveyard. Perhaps chuckling at the site of such a comical means of transportation, neither driver called the authorities.

Then, Ted stopped. Perhaps if the stolen bike had been an adult's ten-speed, he might have had better luck, but his injured knee simply couldn't stand the punishment it was receiving. The child's bike was discarded. A car was needed.[737]

He spent quite some time checking cars in the Cemetery Lane neighborhood to see if any doors were unlocked. One driveway held three automobiles. When he came to a blue Cadillac, he found the keys in the ignition. Climbing in, he turned the car on, set it in reverse, and backed out of the driveway.[738]

Elated at this sudden turn of events, he had to decide which direction to head. Heading east would take him through town and up and over Independence Pass. Heading west would take him to Glenwood Springs.

By the time the Caddy pulled up to the intersection with Highway 82, a decision had been made. It would be east.

The Cadillac turned left onto Main Street. Cruising down the strip, Bundy felt wonderful as he passed the courthouse. Having passed through the town that he had so desperately tried to avoid for nearly a week, his spirits were high, even if he was having trouble operating the vehicle. Ted was used to handling his small Volkswagen bug, and the long Caddy was getting the better of him.

After leaving town, a blinking amber light could be seen up ahead. He slowed down, concerned that it might be a roadblock. Then, a road sign came into view with a jarring message: INDEPENDENCE PASS—CLOSED—ROCKSLIDE. Turning the car around and crouching low on the bench seat, he was now bound for Glenwood Springs. If any roadblocks were encountered downvalley, he'd try to run through them.[739]

Deputies pulled the Caddy over before he made it back into town. The jig was up.[740]

Sergeant Davis leaned back in his chair, processing everything he'd just heard. Bundy hadn't strayed farther than ten miles from the courthouse the entire time he was on the run. The prisoner refuted rumors that he had been assisted during his escape, and there was no evidence that anyone helped or hid the man.[741]

There it was. The end of his tale. The great escape. Nancy finally allowed herself to move. She brushed aside some of her hair, tucking it behind her ear. It had been hanging beside her face, almost like a protective veil, separating her from the dangerous man in the middle of the room. Vaulting over fences, running up and over Aspen Mountain like a gazelle, she felt Ted was exaggerating the physical feats he made during his time on the run. His weight loss, the injured knee, and blistered feet were not lost on her. *Too bad he didn't fall into the river*, she was thinking. *We would have found him in the sewage gate at the water plant, and that would have saved taxpayers a lot of money.*[742]

◆

In the 9News building in Denver, Ward Lucas happened to be in the office early.

"Hey, Ward!" one of his co-workers called out. "Did you hear? The fellas up in Aspen caught your guy." Ward froze momentarily. Then he looked around for his cameraman.

"We gotta get up there," Lucas whispered.[743]

As before, the entire scene between Ward and his news director played out.

"I'm telling you again, it's *not* a Denver story," the director emphasized.[744]

True to form, Lucas walked out of the office to find a flight to Aspen for himself and his cameraman.

◆

After the interview, Sheriff Kienast, Sergeant Davis, and Nancy Baxter emerged from the sheriff's office. Kienast authorized Mike Fisher to interrogate the prisoner. The investigator grabbed his crutches and entered the private office, where Bundy remained cuffed to a chair.

"Gee, Mike," Bundy remarked, taking note of the man's knee injury. "I hope *I* wasn't the cause of that."[745]

"No," Fisher grumbled. "Ted, I want to talk with you about the Caryn Campbell murder."

Bundy merely smiled.

The investigator's worst fear was now confirmed. Bundy had been fed, hydrated, and had his ego stroked with the knowledge that reporters were assembling outside, hungry for his story. The confident, charming, and defiant Ted Bundy had returned. The door to the sheriff's office quietly closed.

◆

Later, outside the interrogation room, Detective Sergeant Dave Garms ran into Officer Terry Quirk. Garms had just returned from the woods near the Kaeser cabin. Terry brought the detective up-to-speed on the details surrounding Bundy's recapture. Deputy Maureen Higgins was walking by and stopped beside the two men.[746]

Maureen watched as the door to the interview room opened, and Mike Fisher hobbled out. She looked past the investigator and spied Bundy alone in the room. The prisoner noticed her as well. He tilted his head to see past Fisher, smiled, and gave her a wink. Maureen watched as Ted's smile shifted. It went from jovial to curious, then settled into more of a smirk. Suddenly, she was acutely aware of the hairs on the back of her neck. Chilling. Though the defendant's guilt or innocence was still a matter of debate for the courts, Deputy Maureen Higgins had no doubt that the scruffy, emaciated man before her belonged behind bars. She was convinced they had recaptured a monster. She turned and walked away in disgust.[747]

Garms had been watching the entire interaction, with a clear view of the prisoner, as Ted watched Deputy Higgins walking away. No longer interacting with a woman, Bundy's face transformed. The smirk disappeared. Dave got a close look at the man. Instead of the striking blue eyes, Dave was looking into two deep, black holes. Cloaked. Unreadable.[748]

◆

At the Arapahoe County Airport, southeast of Denver, Ward Lucas and Lloyd Coleman arrived beside a small, private plane. When Ward grabbed the handle of the entry door, it fell off the aircraft. Their pilot led them to a second plane, but it had a significant puddle of oil underneath. As they looked toward a third plane, Coleman shook his head.

"The Navy teaches you that these things happen in threes," he remarked. "We've had two happen—I'm out." He took his camera and started walking back toward the hangar. Coleman refused to consider any privately owned plane. As a result, Lucas produced his credit card and purchased two commercial plane tickets to head up into the Rockies.[749]

◆

Back in Aspen, an unusual discovery was taking place over on Bonita Drive, off Cemetery Lane. Jill Sheeley opened the front door to her house. Looking over at her Porsche, she was puzzled as to why it was not sitting where it had been parked. She approached the vehicle and looked inside. The five-speed manual transmission was in the neutral position. *That's strange.* She always left it in gear because they never trusted the emergency brake. The key was in the ignition. *Okay, that's where I left it, but now it's in the "on" position.* She climbed in and tried to turn the engine over, but the battery was dead.[750]

Getting out of the car, Jill saw one of her roommates rushing out the front door on his way to work.

"Did you hear that Bundy was caught up at the Pass?" he said.[751]

Jill felt a flood of relief wash over her. She was too embarrassed to admit that she'd been scared out of her mind, hiding under the bed in a show condo less than twenty-four hours earlier.

Trotting up her driveway, back to the front door of her duplex, she noticed her neighbor approaching. It was Paul Merihew. He explained that his Cadillac had been stolen during the night by none other than Ted Bundy. Paul hadn't known his vehicle was missing until a sergeant woke him in the middle of the night. His blue Caddy had been parked next to Jill's Porsche.

DETECTIVE MICHAEL CHANDLER

She was flabbergasted. During the night, she and her boyfriend woke up when their dogs started barking. Her boyfriend had risen and performed a cursory examination of the door and window locks and returned to bed.

"Oh, my God," she said. "I think he was in my car."[752]

Jill's '72 Porsche 911 had the reverse gear clear over in the shift gate's lower right position, which is different from most cars. The injured and exhausted fugitive may have been unable to figure out how to work the gears.[753]

◆

At the courthouse, the press was ready with their cameras for the prisoner movement they had been promised by authorities. Bundy—back in custody. It was a big story.

"We're very, very relieved, to say the least," Undersheriff Ben Meyers sighed in reply to questions from reporters.[754]

It was time to bring the prisoner upstairs to face the judge and the new charges. Still cuffed, he was led down the corridor, with Deputy Flatt firmly grasping Bundy's right arm. Close behind were Deputy Higgins, still in uniform, and Sergeant Kralicek, presently off-duty and in plain clothes, with a cigarette in hand. The impromptu ensemble made its way toward multiple reporters. Flashbulbs from cameras began popping as Bundy came closer to a female journalist.[755]

"Hi, Ted!" the reporter said as she extended her microphone in the prisoner's direction.[756]

"How ya' doing?" Bundy replied, recognizing her.

"Good, how are you?"

"Uh...I'm *here*."

Bundy and his guards began ascending the stairs. A photographer, attempting to snap a picture of him, briefly stumbled.

"Don't hurt yourself trying to get a picture of *me*," Bundy remarked, enjoying the attention.[757]

As CBI Agent Leo Konkel and Deputy Sergeant Larry Spiers walked into the courthouse, they couldn't believe the circus they had entered.

"We got the rascal!" someone called out.[758]

Konkel was shocked. No one had thought to call the CBI agent at his motel.

"Where's the sheriff? he asked. "How can I interview the prisoner?" Konkel sprang into action.

Sergeant Spiers waded through the reporters, deputies, office staff, and curiosity seekers. It was quite a commotion.[759]

The prisoner was led into the courtroom upstairs and told to stand beside the oak defense table. As his handcuffs were removed, shackles were fixed securely around his ankles. Providing direct guardianship were the sheriff, the undersheriff, two sergeants, and the two deputies who had captured the man out on the highway. Another deputy stood out in the hallway. All seven law enforcement officers were armed.[760]

Judge Lohr entered the courtroom, took a seat behind the bench, and began the proceedings.

The defendant listened quietly as the deputy district attorney announced the new charges: felony escape for his leap from the courthouse window; first-degree burglary for breaking into the mountain cabin; misdemeanor theft for absconding with the $37.00 rifle; and felony theft for stealing the Cadillac.[761]

When it was Judge Lohr's turn to speak again, Ted wouldn't look up. Instead, he stared down at the table beside him, occasionally rubbing his eyes and nodding when appropriate. He shifted his weight, favoring his right leg.

"Your honor," Bundy interrupted. "May I sit down? These cuffs around my ankles are so tight." The request was granted, and Bundy slumped down onto the chair. He grabbed his right leg and turned in his seat to address Deputy Higgins.

"If they want to loosen these," he said to her, "I'll stand."[762]

Maureen said nothing—she didn't even blink. The judge was unfazed as well and continued with the proceedings.

"He looks like an animal that's been run down," someone whispered. Indeed, he did. Bundy hardly moved except for shuffling his blistered, bleeding feet or scratching at the dried blood on an injured thumb.[763]

In addition to any sentence handed down from a potential conviction in the homicide case, if convicted on all escape-related charges, Bundy could now be facing an additional ninety years behind bars. The man had truly compounded his legal problems. His week on the run hadn't changed, or even delayed, his legal proceedings. He was still scheduled to stand trial on November 14 for the murder of Caryn Campbell.[764]

The defendant propped his elbow so that his upturned palm could support the weight of his unshaven face. His eyes were red, and more than one local reporter believed he looked like a prisoner of war. He closed his eyes for brief periods. Reporters were hastily jotting down notes, as the judge had already forbidden the use of cameras or electronic recording devices in his courtroom.[765]

The judge set an arraignment date for Thursday and directed Flatt and Higgins to remove the defendant from the courtroom. The deputies rose from the spectator benches and approached the defense table. Steadying himself, Bundy finally looked directly at the judge.

"One moment, your honor," his voice sounded stronger. "It has not been addressed whether I shall be returned to the Garfield County Jail. And what about my box of legal papers?"[766]

"Your papers have been kept under lock," the judge replied. "No one has been allowed to see them. Do you still plan on conducting your own defense in the trial?"

"That hasn't been altered in any way. I still wish to be my own counsel—and I always will be."

Bundy could remain as his own counsel regarding the homicide charge, but retaining the services of public defenders Charles Leidner and James Dumont was now out of the question. Prosecutors could legally call these men to the stand as witnesses to their own client's escape. No. New attorneys would need to be assigned to Bundy's defense table, and soon.[767]

As Bundy was being led to the stairs, Deputy Lorrie Francis seemed to be lost in the shuffle. She walked directly behind the prisoner, but she was so petite that bystanders and their cameras only caught fleeting glimpses of the bespectacled deputy with the blonde hair. She kept a close eye on the prisoner despite the flashing of dozens of camera lights.[768]

Ward Lucas and Lloyd Coleman walked into the courthouse and found themselves swept up in the current of a sea of journalists, officers, and deputies at the base of the impressive staircase.[769]

Ross Dolan, from The Glenwood Post, was new to his job at the paper. Like other photographers, he leaned in and snapped a series of photographs as Bundy came down the stairs with his escorts. The prisoner looked quite weathered, but Dolan snapped photos of the man smiling broadly for the press.

Dolan looked at Bundy very closely. Could this be the guy who murdered the young nurse from Michigan in January 1975? Dolan had been a driver for the Quicksilver Cab Company at that time. One day, he drove a male passenger to the airport. As the traveler exited the vehicle, he took a moment to show the cab driver a photograph of a young woman, asking if he'd seen her. The passenger was Caryn Campbell's fiancé. Here, in the courthouse lobby, nearly two-and-a-half years later, Dolan was confronted with the man accused of murdering the pretty young nurse.[770]

"Ted!" a reporter called out. "Why did you do it?"[771]

"You just don't have enough time for me to tell you," Bundy replied.

Ward Lucas worked his way to the front of the crowd, directly to the base of the staircase, watching as the defendant was being led down toward him. Bundy, wearing a washed-out, Navy-blue jumpsuit and handcuffs, was limping. Word spread that a doctor had been called to check on the man's feet, ankles, and knee. His hair was a mess, but here he was, still smiling. His wit and charm remained at the ready, and he was obviously thrilled to be the center of attention once again. You'd think he'd just had lunch with the governor. Bundy was led past Lucas, and as this occurred, the man of the hour turned to the reporter.

"Hi, Ward!" Ted said as if they were old friends.[772]

Two or three nearby reporters immediately turned to the journalist. "Who the hell are *you*?"

Lucas was dumbfounded and didn't have an answer right away. Then, it hit him. Bundy surely knew him from broadcasts in Washington and maybe even here in Colorado. Of course, he would have been following the news about himself and the missing girls from multiple states.[773]

◆

The prisoner was escorted into the sheriff's office, where CBI Agent Leo Konkel rose to greet him. Bundy was polite and sat down in a chair.[774]

"I'd like to talk to you about how the escape happened," the agent gestured with his hand, indicating that Bundy could begin his narrative.[775]

"Well," Ted remarked. "I'll talk to you about that, but I will not talk to you about anything else. But I'll tell you how I escaped." The prisoner wasn't rude, far from it. Konkel was thinking that the man's behaviors were all consistent with the polite, charming individual he had heard about from fellow lawmen.[776]

Bundy relayed how he had managed to escape: the preparations, the jump, and his time on the run. Konkel did a lot of nodding, only asking an occasional clarifying question. When the moment was right, he threw a curve ball.

"How often have you been here to Aspen?" the agent calmly inquired. Their eyes met, and there was a moment of silence.

"I told you," Bundy replied in a cool tone. "I'm only going to talk to you about the escape."

Konkel nodded, and the conversation continued. Bundy retold stories of his adventures as a runaway. The agent let the man speak, but every few minutes, he would gently toss out another question geared toward the murder case. Even in his state of exhaustion, Ted was too sharp to give away incriminating information. Konkel concluded the meeting, disappointed that there had been no earth-shaking new developments.[777]

As Agent Konkel walked out the door, Deputy Gary White stepped in. He observed the prisoner, still sitting in his chair, cuffed, and still surviving on no sleep. Gary was known for his interrogation techniques, and he had been hoping for just such an opportunity. He simply asked Bundy if he could spare the time for a quick conversation. When he received a nod of approval, the deputy sat down in a chair a few feet away. For a moment, the former chess opponents eyed one another. Gary concluded that the Black Bishop looked defeated. But was this just part of his game?

Not far outside the door, a reporter was videotaping the two deputies who had recaptured the fugitive. Gene Flatt and Maureen Higgins had been filmed as they went about their business, filling out the required forms and paperwork that came with the job. Gene was mildly nervous, placing his left hand on his hip and trying to avoid looking toward the camera. The reporter had asked him a question, which made him feel even more awkward.

"I noted a vehicle driving erratically," Gene began, "about an eighth of a mile east of Aspen on Highway 82. We observed this vehicle for a matter of seconds. And, I turned around and pursued it, contacted it, and found Mr. Bundy driving it."[778]

"Did you recognize him right away?" the reporter asked. Gene paused, trying to figure out how to put the entire Paul Merihew affair into a single sentence.

"It took about two glances," he managed to say. "He was pretty—altered. His appearance had been altered by glasses and a minor growth of beard."

The reporter then pressed Deputy Higgins for a comment on Bundy's condition at the time of the pullover.

"Actually," she said in her soft, elegant voice. "He was pretty dopey. I think he was pretty tired. He was cooperative in that he pretended to search for his license when we asked for it. And, he wasn't aggressive toward us in any way."

"Did he say where he was heading?" the reporter asked.

"He did not," Maureen replied.

"He just stated he was going to leave the valley," Gene added, "if possible."

◆

In the Sheriff's office, Gary and Ted sat silently, simply looking at one another. Neither seemed in a hurry to speak. The sounds of multiple people conversing outside the office and down the hall were audible. Gary felt that Agent Konkel had focused on how the escape had occurred. Davis had focused on the fugitive's movements following the escape. After much thought about what he would say, Gary finally spoke.

"Ted, how did you get Deputy Westerlund to step into the hall voluntarily?"

In a quiet, measured tone, Bundy began to spill more secrets concerning the research portion of his escape plans. Gary listened, making a conscious decision not to interrupt. The deputy learned that, for months, Ted had been memorizing particular traits about the deputies he interacted with daily, both here and in Glenwood Springs. He knew who was lefthanded, who was righthanded, how they carried their guns, whether they smoked or not, which brands, and how big their strides were. Bundy had barely spent any time with Deputy Westerlund, but he was a quick learner and a keen observer of human behavior. He read Westerlund perfectly and used the deputy's smoking habit against him. Gary was impressed.[779]

It was clear that Bundy was heavy-eyed. He said he'd only received ten to twelve hours of sleep during the entire six days he was on the run. He may have covered up to fifty miles of rough terrain and lost around twenty-five pounds during his 135 hours of freedom.[780]

Finally, Bundy was led back into the jail cells. Only a couple of months earlier, Ted had been complaining of the awful conditions he had found in his cell. But now, due to sheer exhaustion, he gratefully laid down and was soon fast asleep.[781]

The reporters found Sheriff Kienast.

"Bundy said his only reason to jump was a desire to gain freedom," Dick remarked. "He had no intention, whatsoever, in harming local residents. I believe him. I don't think he represented a threat to the public."[782]

The sheriff noted that it was the mountains themselves that had beaten the fugitive. Kienast also acknowledged that the criticism of himself, as well as his department, was fully justified. Blame for the escape, according to Kienast, rested both on the individuals who left the defendant unguarded and the sheriff's office as a whole. Dick was convinced that, had they had a canine on the force at the time of the escape, the fugitive would have been apprehended quickly.[783]

Reporters asked him about potential disciplinary measures in the wake of the escape, but the sheriff merely replied that the Colorado Bureau of Investigation was already investigating the matter. Interviews with Westerlund, Kralicek, and others had already been conducted, and Kienast saw no reason to discipline anyone until he had reviewed the bureau's final report. When hearing that some members of the county were calling for his resignation, Kienast brushed off the concern, giving no indication that he'd be packing his office supplies anytime soon.

"I'm extremely proud of the deputies," he said, wrapping things up. "They have done an excellent job." He believed the whole six-day manhunt had generated a camaraderie that made the entire group a far closer organization.[784]

Sergeant Don Davis, known for not mincing words, was asked for comment.

"I believe," Davis remarked, "Ted derived a certain amount of satisfaction from the fact he pulled it off as far as he did."[785]

The party was winding down, and the crowd of rambunctious citizens and reporters slowly began to thin. Ward Lucas and his cameraman departed the courthouse, bound for their final flight from Sardy Field. Detective Sergeant Garms drove toward his cabin in Oklahoma Flats. Already pushing the whole fiasco out of his thoughts, he started making plans to sail his twenty-eight-foot, engineless boat across the Pacific Ocean. Deputies, bone-tired after the manhunt, excused themselves to go home for some much-deserved rest.[786]

◆

In the parking lot at city hall, Nancy Baxter climbed aboard her motorcycle. She tucked her hair back and secured her helmet, reflecting upon not only the last six days but the last six years. She already missed the days when you could ski right up to the bars, leave your skis and poles in a nearby snowbank, and still find them there hours later. There had been rodeos, line dancing, and a handy diet of pretzels and beer after a softball game. There was always one-heck-of-a-deal down at Little Annie's, the all-day shot and a beer for only a dollar.

She started the engine.

Hiking, fishing, and backcountry exploration had started to give way to weed, mushrooms, and now cocaine. Then came the community's first stabbing. It was an incident between a dishwasher and an inebriated cook. Then, poor Caryn Campbell went missing. A year later, Claudine Longet shot her boyfriend. Now, Ted Bundy. Aspen had lost its innocence. Bundy had put the town on the map in a way even its residents could not have foreseen.

Nancy spotted Detective Michael Chandler sitting in an unmarked car and gave him a farewell wave. He returned the gesture.

We really do have a pretty good group here, she thought. They were young, idealistic people, supporting their community every day and night, providing good coverage for a mountain town that was only beginning to feel the unrelenting encroachment of outsiders. Something echoed in her mind, however, something she'd heard at the courthouse before she left for the day. A reporter had asked a spokeswoman for the sheriff whether she felt their community was now safe from Theodore R. Bundy.[787]

"You'd better believe he's under tight security," the spokeswoman had replied. "We *won't* lose him again."[788]

Nancy tore out of the parking lot.

Detective Chandler watched the motorcycle speed away. He, too, had heard the spokeswoman's remark about not losing Bundy for a second time. The detective's first encounter with the convicted kidnapper had been in February, or maybe it was March. Hard to say. Chandler had been at the courthouse late one night, booking another prisoner into the jail. He knew Bundy was in the back, in one of the cells.

Michael's father was a television personality, recognized wherever he went in the West. His grandfather had been a legal expert known throughout the state. Michael was no stranger to celebrities in and around town: Andy Williams, Spider Sabich, Claudine Longet, and Hunter S. Thompson. John Denver was Michael's neighbor. Detective Chandler didn't gravitate to or become intrigued by the headliners, and he avoided them whenever possible.

With all the paperwork on his new prisoner concluded, Michael should have walked out the front door, but he hesitated. It was late, there was no one around, and he had no plans. Bundy was just beginning to gain some local notoriety. Michael felt a pull, a sudden desire to personally see this particular man. *Why not?*

The detective walked down a corridor, dimly illuminated by a series of flickering, amber lights in the ceiling. With the layers of stone surrounding the cells, there really wasn't much to be said for insulation. It was cold.[789]

There was a large black control box near the entry door to the cell block. Here, Chandler pulled the handle, which unlocked the gateway and permitted him to walk into the holding cell. Once inside, a guard locked the door behind him.[790]

Michael could see Bundy's cell. The door and walls were constructed of steel plates, about a quarter-inch thick, with 3x3" square holes cut in a grid pattern. It was painted a dull, raw umber. The lawman walked up to the door and peered in through the squares.[791]

On a small bench in the back of the cell sat a barefoot man dressed in his one-piece prison jumpsuit. His head was tilted down, but he locked eyes with the detective. Michael studied him. Bundy's eyes were dark, unblinking, and, for lack of a better word—sinister. There were no reporters or cameramen to pose for and no women around to impress. He appeared nearly reptilian.

The detective watched as the prisoner rose slowly and started crossing the floor of his cell toward him. Michael felt an instinctive desire to back away, even knowing Bundy would have no access to him, but he stood his ground. In a moment, the two men were less than a foot apart, on opposing sides of the prison door. The tall detective leaned down to meet the prisoner's gaze through the three-inch squares. They stared at one another in silence. Michael had never seen such cold, unfeeling eyes. Dead eyes.

"Have you ever been to Florida?" Bundy asked.[792]

APPENDIX

APPENDIX A
THE CADDY STOP
JUNE 13, 1977

Perhaps the only person who can truly understand the difficulties I faced trying to reconstruct what I call the Caddy stop is filmmaker Vince Lahey. "The real question," he notes, "lies in what happened twenty minutes after Bundy turned around and was pulled over heading back into town by Maureen Higgins and Gene Flatt." For nearly half a century, scores of questions have been raised at true crime conventions, in Ted Bundy chat rooms, and in multiple Bundy-related Facebook groups. Who ordered Bundy to the ground? Who cuffed him? Whose cuffs were used? Who drew their weapons and when? What were the words exchanged between Flatt and Higgins? Who transported the fugitive back to the courthouse?

What happened that night depends significantly upon whom you ask. "If nothing else," Lahey continues, "this only serves to convey further how fiercely competitive the Aspen Police Department and the Pitkin County Sheriff's Office were with each other. Both claimed the arrest, and both men claim they put their personal handcuffs on Bundy and never got their cuffs back."

Only five people were involved during the Caddy stop. These were Deputy Gene Flatt, Deputy Maureen Higgins, Officer Terry Quirk, Sergeant Don Davis, and Bundy himself. I managed to interview Maureen Higgins and Terry Quirk. Lahey was kind enough to provide me with a recording of his interview with Gene Flatt from November 2018. Don Davis and Bundy are deceased.

There are emotional, philosophical, and moral filters that impact how we assimilate what we are seeing, to say nothing of recalling memories nearly half a century after an event. Five people can be present at the same scene yet recall very different memories in the years that follow. These variances in memory can be so discordant that one wonders if they were involved in the same incident. Such is the case with the infamous Caddy stop. No one is being deceptive. All are being truthful according to their perceptions.[793]

DEPUTY FLATT'S VERSION

Gene Flatt states that when he spied the swerving Cadillac, he wasn't even thinking about Ted Bundy. He was convinced the fugitive had already made good his escape and was long gone. The deputy does want it to be known that it was his decision to pull the car over, and his partner—Higgins—agrees with this statement. This aligns with Flatt's reputation of aggressively pursuing folks he suspected of driving while impaired.

The first piece of controversy is evident when Flatt states that he and Deputy Higgins instantly recognized the driver. "Dick [Kienast] would not trust just everybody with Bundy," Flatt states with evident pride. "I was former military, and I was never afraid of the son of a bitch. That's why he didn't give me any trouble when we caught him that night." At least four times during the interview, the deputy made clear that he recognized Bundy on sight. "We knew who he was. I'd spent too much time around him . . . I transported him. I guarded him in the exercise yard, you know? The disguise didn't work." He went on to say, "I was managing a dangerous serial killer. I knew it, and Maureen knew it."[794]

Only hours after the Caddy stop, however, Barbara Grossman and her cameraman were in the sheriff's office. Someone pointed out to the reporter that Flatt and Higgins were the ones who recaptured Bundy. With the camera rolling, Grossman asked Flatt the direct question.

"Did you recognize him right away?" She thrust the microphone forward.

"It took about two glances," Flatt replied. "He was pretty—altered his appearance. His appearance had been altered by glasses and a minor growth of beard."[795]

In the 2018 interview, Gene Flatt stated that he asked the driver for some form of identification, and the man began fumbling around in the glove compartment. According to Flatt, he carefully drew his revolver and had it at the ready, parallel with his holster and pointing down at the ground.

"I was giving him his chance to make a move," he notes, "and I was going to shoot him. I'll never repeat that again, but I was playing him. I played him for probably ninety seconds to three minutes while I absolutely knew it was him."

"I had my gun down at my side," Flatt recalls. "Maureen had her gun on him. I looked over the top of the car, where Maureen was standing with her gun pressed up against the passenger window, and I [whispered],

Bundy. I said it low 'cause I didn't want to let Teddy know that we had figured him out. Maureen was right on the other side of the car with her gun on him. Maureen don't lie. She doesn't have any reason to, and I don't either. I'm not a liar."

"He was a cockroach. He never attacked anybody that could fight back. Listen, I'll tell you the truth. I never had a chance to shoot him that night, and neither did Maureen. It wouldn't have been right. He didn't do anything to get shot for. He needed it, but he didn't do it. But I swear to God, if he had struggled, I would have punched his ass out, and I don't know if I could have stopped because we knew he was guilty."

Flatt doesn't expressly state when he leveled his revolver at the driver. "I had my gun on him and then said, 'Hi, Ted.' It was about an inch away from the side of his head. That guy was like a porcelain statue. He didn't move a muscle, and I'll tell you why; he knew that I would pull the trigger. Okay? I'm a veteran, and that sorta thing ain't pleasant, but it can be done. If I had shot him that night, I wouldn't have been any better than he was. He never gave any cause. I would'a loved to have shot him." It was at this point that Deputy Flatt ordered the driver out of the vehicle.

With Bundy standing beside the Caddy, facing Higgins, Flatt states that he then became annoyed by Officer Terry Quirk. Apparently, the officer kept asking questions via the radio. "I had my walkie-talkie," Flatt explains, "and [Quirk] kept talking to me, and I couldn't take my attention off of Bundy. Plus, I had a gun on him. So, I finally said, I gotta get rid of this asshole, and said, 'Just come on up here!' You know? I invited him to the party."[796]

Flatt and his partner agree that as soon as he ordered the fugitive to lay on the ground, Bundy began protesting and claiming he'd have their jobs. Flatt thinks he may have even replied, "You wouldn't want our jobs."

The only reference Flatt makes regarding Sergeant Don Davis's presence at the Caddy stop is that he didn't need the sergeant to confirm whom they'd stopped. When it comes to Officer Terry Quirk, Flatt makes him out to be a passive observer at best. "While I was standing there with my gun on [Bundy]," the deputy notes, "I think [Quirk] looked around me, at Bundy, and then that was the last I saw of him."

"I got nothing against Terry Quirk," Flatt said in 2018. "He's pathetic, but he's lying. It's hurtful to me that he's bad-mouthing. He's talked really bad about Maureen. It is not true. Maureen was brave. She was a deputy, and she was doing her job, just like I was."

According to Flatt, the day after the Caddy stop, Officer Quirk began to take credit for the arrest. If that wasn't enough, he began calling into question the conduct and character of the two deputies themselves. "Apparently, he was saying that we didn't know who it was," Flatt recalls, "and that we were scared and that we were hiding in the patrol car—all kinds of horseshit. I'm going to tell you something. If you knew me personally, you'd know that was impossible. I ain't afraid of a fucking thing in this world. I never was. Maureen and I weren't running around like two idiots. We had him."

Flatt is adamant that Officer Terry Quirk played no part in arresting Ted Bundy. "[Quirk] just looked at him. I'm going to pull one witness on Quirk that he doesn't even think about," Flatt notes with a hint of disdain. "You know who that is—Ted Bundy. I'll tell you right now, Ted Bundy; I charged him with escape. Ted Bundy read me and Maureen's report thoroughly, with his lawyer . . . If he had saw any discrepancies, or lies, or anything like that, he would have cackled, and he would have had a blast running us down. And, he never [did] because he knew the truth too. He was there. And, where Quirk is getting this stuff from, I don't know, but it's really chicken shit . . . Quirk ain't even thinking about that. Bundy wasn't a fool. He would be the one that would notice. I'm sorry for Terry. I don't know what his problem is."

Flatt seems to feel that Officer Quirk had limited exposure to Bundy. "If you ask Terry Quirk if he'd ever been in the same room with him, ever, okay? He saw him one time...Terry Quirk never had any reason to be around Bundy . . . he had nothing to do with it." The main concern with this line of reasoning is that Flatt's own partner had only seen Bundy one or two times prior to the escape.

"[Quirk] wouldn't have even been up there that night if I hadn't of invited him," notes the deputy. "He wouldn't even been there if I hadn't let him come."

Flatt and Higgins had an informal agreement for many years not to engage in an argument with Quirk. "We talked about this," Flatt says calmly. "If we engage him, we're going to give him credibility. I don't care what he claims . . . It don't make no difference to me [the credit for the recapture]; I'd give it to him, except for one problem—I don't lie. Bundy's in hell. Those poor girls are in Heaven. I was not a hero. Maureen was not a hero. We just did our jobs."

OFFICER QUIRK'S VERSION

"That night is imprinted on my brain," Officer Terry Quirk recalled when I interviewed him in 2021. He felt that he and Officer Nancy Lyle were the only Aspen PD officers on duty that night. He can't remember if he personally met with Flatt and Higgins to explain the situation with the assault victim or if he merely spoke with them via the radio. He was desperate to apprehend the man who had attacked the teenager before he escaped out of town, so he sought assistance from his counterparts in the sheriff's department.[797]

He heard the radio traffic between Deputy Maureen Higgins and Lynne Unger, who was on duty in the dispatch office. When he heard the deputies were stopping someone they suspected of drunk driving, he began heading toward the Crestahaus in his Saab. While en route, he overheard Higgins' request for a 10-28 and 10-29 but also seemed to recall that something was wrong with the Cadillac's taillight.

Officer Quirk arrived on the scene several minutes before Sergeant Don Davis.

"I don't care what anybody says. This is what I recall, and this is how I saw it. When I got out of my car, Bundy was standing near the front door, driver's side, and the door was open. The door was open on the passenger's side and Officer Higgins—Maureen—was leaning over the seat, reaching under the driver's side, trying to find the alleged driver's license that he said was under the seat. Maureen's words were exactly this, 'Sir, I do not see a driver's license here under the seat.' Gene Flatt was standing by the back door [on the driver's side]. The back door of the car was closed. The trunk was closed at the time. Bundy was very fidgety. I got out of the car, looked at him, pulled my weapon. Told him to spread eagle on the ground.

"They did not recognize him. I don't think either of them had probably had him for detention duty, so I understand why they might not have. He was easily recognizable. He did have a Band-Aid over his nose. It was a regular Band-Aid. He had a blue—like a saltwater—billed cap on. Like a fishing billed cap—saltwater cap. It was light blue. Don't remember the jacket. He was fidgety as hell, and I was nervous about it. I had drawn my weapon casually. I did, and I put him on the ground and said, 'Don't move or I'll shoot you,' or words to that effect. I told him not to move. I didn't cuff him at the time."

Quirk felt that the deputies did not have control of the situation.

"Gene was saying, 'I was just thinking of going in the trunk,' and I said, 'We're not doing any of that.' One of us called back to dispatch and said, 'Send the troops.' And shortly thereafter, I remember Don Davis showing up at the scene. I don't know who else, but I know there were a number of...several people there. So, I felt very comfortable."

When asked if he could recall what type of vehicle Sergeant Don Davis drove, Quirk replied, "I don't. I think he occasionally drove a truck or something, but I don't recall it at all. I was focused on who was on the ground in front of me. I had some experiences before that, in law enforcement, and I wasn't about to make a mistake on that. So, I waited for the backup, and Davis asked for my cuffs and cuffed him, and they transported him. That's the end of the story for me."

"I did not transport him," Quirk notes. "As far as I was concerned, I was a city officer. I was doing my job. The county, I know they suffered a lot of embarrassment during that time. They needed to recover that. They needed to catch that guy. So, it didn't bother me at all that *that* was happening. I was elated that I could be there, and he had my cuffs on him. I was happy. I ducked *60 Minutes* for two weeks on that. I told them, 'I'm not talking to you. I did my job. I was just doing my job.' And you know, in retrospect, I probably should have said something at the time, but I'm not looking for any glory here."

"I looked at that guy," Quirk recalls, referencing the fugitive, "before I put him on the ground, I looked at his eyes. If there's evil in this world, that's how I would describe his eyes. They were depthless. They were terrifying. I've arrested lots of people in my time, and I can truly say they shocked me. That's all I know about him. The guy was truly evil. That's all I know about that. I feel very humbled to have even been involved in it. I feel badly. I think Maureen and Gene came out of it fine. I wasn't about to say embarrassing stuff about them. But that's the honest-to-God truth. That's what happened. That's the way it went down."

When told I would like to run my version of the Caddy stop through him, based on everyone's input, Quirk seemed pleased. "I'd love to see what you say because you're one of the two people that—other than the officers that I got the commendation from—know my side of the story. Because it's not out there otherwise. So, you take it with a grain of salt. Do with it as you see fit. It's your business, not mine. I know I'm telling the truth. And I'm not trying to cause anyone any embarrassment. After all these years, I appreciate how scared I was during that time."

Officer Terry Quirk received a merit recommendation from the Aspen Police Department on June 17, 1977, four days after the Caddy stop. Under the *reason for recommendation* heading, the reporting sergeant wrote, "Officer Terry Quirk asked for assistance from the Pitkin County Sheriff in locating a possible suspect in a sexual assault case. During that search, the sheriff's vehicle stopped a Cadillac that had been stolen and was being driven by an escaped prisoner, Theodore Bundy. The sheriff's vehicle, at this time, radioed and asked for assistance. Officer Quirk responded to the [illegible] near the Crestahaus. Upon arrival, he found two Pitkin County deputies with a party they thought looked a bit like Bundy. He also found that neither deputy was in control of the situation; although they should have known Bundy instantly, they did not know that the party they had stopped was, in fact, Bundy. Officer Quirk recognized Bundy, took control of the situation, and put Mr. Bundy into custody. Officer Quirk's actions alleviated a potentially dangerous situation due to the carelessness of the two sheriff's deputies."[798]

In the upper right corner of the form, we learn that Sergeant Darrel Horan was the superior who submitted the request for recommendation. When I interviewed him in 2020, Horan noted that he was asleep at the Silver King Apartments during Bundy's recapture and did not witness the arrest in person.

Reaching out to him in 2021 for comment on the background of this interesting document, Horan replied: "The merit award was based on what I was told the morning after the capture by Terry Quirk. I was called just after the capture and was at the police department shortly after. The other signature on the right side had to [be] someone above my rank, probably the head detective or the chief of police. There was no rule on a supervisor personally witnessing the incident on which the merit award was based. The award was based on the incident version offered by Terry Quirk."[799]

SERGEANT DAVIS'S VERSION

Sergeant Don Davis was deceased by the time I began interviews for this book. Except for one officer, everyone I interviewed had nothing but respect for the man. Everyone in the department knew the sheriff needed Davis's advice and experience, and that fact was demonstrated repeatedly throughout the manhunt.

As for the sergeant's version of events, we only have his typed report,

DEPUTY MAUREEN HIGGINS

based on his interrogation of the fugitive back in the sheriff's office. In it, the only reference to the Caddy stop is, "Bundy was headed back into town when he encountered officers Flatt and Higgins." The sergeant does mention that "Bundy was advised of his rights to silence and counsel, per Miranda." There is no reference to Officer Quirk or even Davis in the latter's report.[800]

DEPUTY HIGGINS' VERSION

For as much attention as the Caddy stop has garnered over the years, it seems that every true crime fan has missed a very small letter to the editor in the December 18, 2005 edition of The Aspen Times. In it, former Deputy Maureen Higgins made her only public comment on her footnote in history. She attempted to correct some of the mistakes she had seen in newspapers over the years. She concluded her letter by remarking, "Press accounts may not always represent events as they actually occurred. Memories can be hazy and shaded, so searching out several sides to reach an accurate account can sometimes only be an editor's dream."[801]

My correspondence with her began in December 2019, and after assuring her the book was being written from a law enforcement standpoint, she seemed pleased to finally set the record straight. She acknowledged that I was facing a monumental task and likened the entire affair to an ancient Indian parable. Several blind men encounter an elephant for the first time, and each one touches a different portion of the beast—trunk, tail, and side. Each man describes what they are encountering, yet they are limited to only one part of the elephant and cannot see the overall picture. They grow heated when their descriptions are disbelieved by their companions and, in some versions, even come to blows. Higgins understands this parable all too well and admits she can only provide one version of the recapture of Theodore Robert Bundy. Slowly, she opened up and shared her memories with me, understanding that this might be the last time all three of the surviving witnesses could provide their stories.

After receiving a call from dispatch and being briefed on the attempted sexual assault of the female student, Deputy Higgins and her partner decided to explore the eastern borders of town. She says the oncoming vehicle, the Cadillac, did not dim its headlights or run slightly off the road, as was reported in several newspaper articles. She adds that the media has exaggerated that moment. There was no fishtailing, as would be common on icy roads. The detectable movement was merely a slight swerve into the oncoming lane. She also did not shine her flashlight in the approaching driver's face, as was mentioned by several parties after the fact. Higgins notes that her partner had an affinity for pulling tourists over with the slightest provocation and loved nothing better than to cite drunk drivers. "I never would have stopped the Caddy," she adds, "as it was barely a swerve."[802]

Higgins observed her partner's interactions with the possible drunk driver. She says Flatt seemed a bit antsy from the very start, but he was alert, and they were both doing their jobs. She was unable to recall the specifics of the conversation between Bundy and Flatt but states that Bundy's recollection of that particular exchange, published in *The Only Living Witness*, seemed reasonable.[803]

Regarding the controversy over not being able to identify the fugitive on sight, she agrees that Flatt should have made the connection, as he had interacted with Bundy on multiple occasions for months. She notes that, before the traffic stop, she only saw Bundy a couple of times in the bullpen of the sheriff's office.

Higgins provided some details on the two different views she received of the man in the predawn hours of June 13, 1977. She was standing outside the passenger side of the vehicle in the dark, and there were no streetlamps on this stretch of the highway. Her partner had asked the driver for identification, and Bundy began fumbling around in the glove compartment. To assist him in this endeavor, Higgins leaned down and shined her flashlight through the window, illuminating the interior of the glove compartment as well as the right side of his face. The Band-Aid, the hat—no. "I did not think it was Ted Bundy at all."[804]

When Flatt tossed her the wallet containing the driver's license, she read the name on the identification card, spied the picture, and knew this driver was not the person listed on the card. The man was lying. That is never a good sign. It was at this point that Flatt drew his weapon and ordered the driver to get out of the car. This aligns with Bundy's statement, published in *The Only Living Witness*. Flatt had the driver remove his glasses, turn around, and face the vehicle.

This provided Higgins with a full view of the mystery man.

"Any description of Bundy that went out via radio," she notes, "news shows, or pictures presented at roadblocks, was absolutely irrelevant as he looked dramatically different when we encountered him. He could pull off a new look at a whim. Hat, Band-Aid across his nose, weak, tired, dopey and fumbling, beard—all not part of the description then, and made him unrecognizable. He could not change his height, but slumping and shuffling helped lower his impact. If you look at pictures of him at various stages throughout the years, he was quite the chameleon, even without props. His age, hair, and weight fluctuations; he looked completely different in different circumstances. He accomplished [this] with demeanor and acting skills, as well as an inherent inner evil that was fluctuating, not static in transparency. Uncanny."[805]

She says a short series of events began while she was speaking via radio with Lynne Unger in the dispatch office. She used the proper codes, requesting backup, and then whispered, "Subject bears a close resemblance to Ted Bundy." Whether Bundy overheard this statement or was simply trying to make a move, he started arguing with them. This is what prompted her partner to order Bundy to the ground. This, in turn, prompted Higgins to draw her weapon to provide cover for her partner.

As Flatt began patting down the driver, Higgins moved forward and opened the passenger side door. She shined her flashlight inside.

"There was no map," Higgins said. "He badly miscalculated distances and terrain, in my opinion. He probably thought he could make the hike to Crested Butte from the Castle Creek Valley, but he overestimated himself, and the trail is not really clear or marked (then or now). People who are not from Colorado greatly underestimate what the altitude and terrain do to you, especially without a good source of food or water."[806]

There was no newspaper as well. There is news footage depicting a newspaper on the bench seat of the stolen Caddy. The footage was shot during daylight hours, and it shows a copy of The Aspen Times, Bundy's picture plastered alongside the headlines on the front page. Higgins states that this paper was not present in the vehicle during the car stop. She surmises that it might have been placed there for a photo opportunity once the car was impounded and taken to the courthouse.[807]

Higgins knew the driver was lying about being Paul Merihew but there was still the possibility that this was an inebriated friend of Paul's who had legitimately borrowed his car.

What Higgins did find alarmed her. The small photograph of Liz and Molly. When asked whether it was in color or black-and-white, she notes: "It was so dark there, my earlier description telling you no street lighting, and even with the flashlight usage, I cannot recall. I do not even remember the daughter in the picture at all, just that there was a child. I do remember the face of the woman, which matched the face I knew to be his Washington State area girlfriend, whom he lived with before law school. She was small and had [a] baby face. The picture was tucked beside him on the car seat, had been folded repeatedly previous to being there, and was in not-so-hot shape, which drew my attention to it in the first place while sweeping the car. The picture on the seat convinced me."[808]

Higgins states that their backup arrived simultaneously. She recalls that Sergeant Don Davis and Officer Quirk, in separate vehicles, arrived at the Crestahaus at the same time. She remembers Quirk seemed concerned that the suspect wasn't already in handcuffs. She adds that she did not handcuff Bundy.

"As people gathered, it got blurred in my memory, as the relief of the physical demands [of the manhunt] were over for me, like a heavy blanket taken off."[809]

When asked about Miranda warnings, she replied, "It was not Gene, to my recall, which is dim on that particular point. I did not, so it was probably Don Davis—either in his car or at the sheriff's office. He would not have skipped it; he was a very by-the-book kind of guy." She also is adamant that she never said, "We got him," over the radio. She knows she and Flatt did not drive Ted back to the courthouse and, again, says it was probably Don Davis. Quirk also denied transporting Bundy.[810]

Higgins believes that the entire Caddy stop took only seven minutes. She wasn't looking at her watch and stated that would be a rough estimate. "Picture how fast it all went down, and it accelerated ever faster as I put my own two-plus-two together, separately than what was going on with Gene's own recognition, which dawned on him individually, in his own time. Of course, there was no discussion about it between Gene Flatt and I. It all transpired way too fast. We did not do any discussing as it all went down. Fast. No time to discuss anything, much less privately. I was on one side of the car, and he on the driver's side. In my mind, it would be more dangerous to tip Ted Bundy off that we were on to him *as* Ted Bundy and not a drunk driver. Gene continued treating him as [a drunk]. I remain convinced Gene did not know for absolute sure who we had right away, what with the surprise, the disguise, and Bundy's loud protestations after [being] told to get out of the car."[811]

Higgins has always been somewhat confused by the interest some folks have in the Caddy stop, especially in who physically snapped the cuffs on

Bundy. "There is no hero," she notes. "It's not about what law enforcement officers did right or wrong, but more about what Ted Bundy did or did not do. The arrest was a group effort, no matter what anyone claims for themselves."[812]

She wants everyone to know that it isn't really important what discrepancies exist between the officers and deputies at the Caddy stop. The importance lies in the fact that there was a whole series of incidents that had to occur for the arrest to take place when and where it did. There was the attempted sexual assault upon the teenager, which led to Officer Quirk's request for assistance from the county; Deputy Flatt's affinity for pulling over any vehicle that even remotely demonstrated the potential for an inebriated driver inside; and a community small enough for Deputy Higgins to recognize that the name and face on the driver's license didn't match the man she knew.

Unflattering portrayals in the media have contributed to the notion that Deputies Flatt and Higgins were backwoods cops who didn't understand the situation they were involved in. This is historically inaccurate. Higgins took her lead from her partner who was her senior. She performed the required inspections of the driver-provided documentation and then verified the status of the license and the vehicle with dispatch. Upon learning that the suspect was lying about his identity, she called for backup. She drew her weapon to provide cover when necessary.

As soon as her partner felt something was amiss, he drew his weapon and ordered the man out of the vehicle. He searched him and ordered him to lie prostrate on the ground. It would have been prudent to place the subject in handcuffs at this time, and Maureen concurs on this point. Flatt definitely could have done more, but he and Deputy Higgins had the situation under control.

BUNDY'S VERSION

Bundy gave his version of the Caddy stop on two occasions. The first was on February 20, 1978. In a recorded interview with Florida detectives Patchen, Bodiford, and Chapmen, Ted makes an error right out of the gate. He states that he stole a Datsun when, in fact, it was a Cadillac. He acknowledged being pulled over and even added a remark about Deputy Flatt. "He was a rookie and will always be a rookie if he was on the force for thirty years [laughter]." Bundy dismisses Deputy Higgins by merely referring to her as a *girl*.[813]

He indicates that the deputies exchanged a few sentences, essentially about being confused about his identity and needing Sergeant Davis for such an identification. He said Flatt and Higgins' patrol car was the only one on the road in the entire county that night. Shortly after that, he says there were six officers at the Caddy stop, all of whom failed to recognize him.

The second time Bundy shared his version of events was with author Stephen G. Michaud in 1980. Ted's recollections appear in the book *The Only Living Witness*, which was published three years later. In this version of the pullover, Bundy acknowledges it was the deputies who spotted the stolen Caddy. Flatt and Higgins pulled him over, and Flatt approached the driver's side window. Bundy recognized the deputy from their interactions at the county jail, and he felt the deputy should have recognized him immediately.[814]

They engaged in a brief conversation, and when asked for identification, Bundy began fishing around in the glove compartment, trying to stall in the hopes that the deputies would let him off with a warning. Bundy states that Flatt drew his weapon on him and ordered him out of the car. While he was complying with this directive, Bundy says Higgins spoke to her partner, saying, "Just wait a minute, Gene. He's looking for his I.D." This lively dialogue, according to the fugitive, continued.[815]

"Come over here," Flatt calls over to Higgins. "Who does this look like?"

"I don't know, Gene. Who does it look like?"

"Maureen. This looks like Ted Bundy."

According to Ted's account, Flatt then ordered him to remove his glasses. He complied and then the deputy shined a flashlight in his face.

"Maureen," Flatt remarked. "I don't know. But he *still* looks like Ted Bundy."

"Well," she replied. "Why don't you call Sergeant Davis and ask him to come up here? He knows what he looks like."

Sergeant Davis, according to Bundy's recollection, ". . . drove out to the scene of the arrest and quickly announced that it was indeed Ted Bundy they had arrested." By this statement, it appears evident that Bundy was under the belief that Flatt and Higgins already had him under arrest. Officer Quirk's name does not appear in Bundy's version of events. It is also noteworthy that at no time in Ted's story is he ordered to lie on the ground. Perhaps his pride required him to omit that detail.

Regarding the dialogue that Bundy says took place between Flatt and Higgins, author Stephen Michaud believes his subject turned to a mocking depiction of his captors. "Ted Bundy, raconteur, recalls the scene as a highly comic one." Bundy's former attorney, Charles Leidner, backs up this assessment, stating that after Ted had been recaptured, the defendant began insulting the intelligence of the deputies who had arrested him.[816]

What did Deputies Higgins and Flatt *really* say to one another on that memorable night? Despite Bundy's droll recollections, the record needs to show—nothing. Not a word was exchanged between them during the encounter.

The sheriff's lack of security at the courthouse contributed to the success of Bundy's escape, but Sheriff Kienast insisted the roadblocks remain in place until Monday. They would have snared the fugitive, one way or the other, in the early morning hours of June 13, 1977, as Bundy tried to drive away from Aspen. If, however, Bundy had waited in the shadows another twenty-four hours and *then* stolen a vehicle, he would not have encountered any impediments along his journey down the valley.

APPENDIX B
ROADBLOCKS, JUNE 7-13, 1977

CRESTAHAUS
The first roadblock erected was at the intersection of East Cooper Avenue and Alpine Court, adjacent to the parking lot of the Crestahaus Lodge. It was set up to prevent drivers from heading east up the valley toward Independence Pass.

CASTLE CREEK BRIDGE
A secondary checkpoint was hastily created on the west side of town. It was on Highway 82, and it was initially set up by a lone Aspen police officer on Castle Creek Bridge to quickly halt all westbound traffic. A couple of Forest Service employees helped augment this checkpoint. This roadblock was disbanded once the Maroon Creek Bridge Roadblock was up and running.

MAROON CREEK BRIDGE
The Maroon Creek Bridge Roadblock has the unique distinction of having been created solely by the citizens of Aspen, with no prodding from law enforcement. Several men, who happened to have some weapons handy, heard Detective Chandler's radio message and promptly took it upon themselves to create a checkpoint on the bridge.

SLAUGHTERHOUSE BRIDGE
A patrol unit was dispatched to the Slaughterhouse Bridge. This checkpoint was erected to prevent anyone from coming up Red Butte Drive or down Cemetery Lane, trying to access McClain Flats Road. It was considered a major checkpoint due to its proximity to the river and the Rio Grande Trail, and there was no other way to gain egress to the areas McClain Flats Road served without crossing the bridge.

CATHERINE STORE
The Catherine Store Roadblock was erected at the intersection of Highway 82 and Catherine Store Road. It was set up twenty-seven miles west of Aspen to prevent drivers from escaping to Glenwood Springs. This was

also the old turn-off to get to Carbondale. Due to its geographic location, this checkpoint was manned by Garfield County Deputies.

OLD SNOWMASS CONOCO

This checkpoint was set up fifteen miles west of Aspen, at the intersection of Highway 82 and Old Snowmass Creek Road, adjacent to a Conoco gas station. Two Pitkin County deputies initially manned it, but they were soon assisted by a Colorado State Trooper. These lawmen stopped down-valley traffic, bound for Basalt or Glenwood Springs. The roadblock also served to check vehicles headed up to, or returning from, new subdivisions like Little Elk Creek and Shield O Terraces.

NORTH MILL STREET BRIDGE

An Aspen police officer manned a roadblock on a span that crosses the Roaring Fork River just prior to the intersection with Gibson Avenue and Red Mountain Road. Placing a checkpoint here denied a fugitive access to Aspen Valley Hospital, portions of the Red Mountain region, Hunter Valley, and Smuggler Mountain. It was also close enough to the river that officers could monitor the water below.

BRUSH CREEK ROAD

A roadblock was established where Brush Creek Road meets Highway 82. This checkpoint, northwest of the airport, was manned by Pitkin County deputies. These men and women were additionally tasked with checking the nearby gravel-strewn intercept lot. Deputies routinely checked this area to see if there were any unlocked vehicles, a tempting treat for any thief.

WOODY CREEK BRIDGE

The truss-style Woody Creek Bridge was too narrow to permit vehicles to pass one another. Typically, cars waited on one side or the other and politely signaled opposing vehicles to make the crossing. Here, at a three-way intersection on the north side of the Roaring Fork River, two reserve deputies set up a checkpoint. It stopped traffic from moving farther downvalley and, once erected, gave authorities a moment's peace. They felt they had now covered every principal exit out of town.

TROOPER JIM LOYD

WATSON DIVIDE/HIGHWAY 82
A state trooper had volunteered his services for over an hour at the Old Snowmass Conoco Roadblock. He could tell there was enough manpower at the site and, understanding the overall shortage of staffing, decided to set up his own roadblock at the intersection of Highway 82 and Watson Divide Road. Within twenty minutes of standing post, the trooper was joined by two colleagues. This checkpoint was manned for only a few hours.

BRB CAMPGROUND
Along Highway 133, roughly six miles south of Carbondale, a checkpoint was set up on the two-lane highway adjacent to the KOA and BRB campgrounds. Although technically in Pitkin County, this roadblock was manned by Garfield County deputies.

WEST SOPRIS CREEK
A roadblock was established at the confluence of three separate rural roads: West Sopris Creek Road, East Sopris Creek Road, and Sopris Creek Road. It was a remote area, nestled between Basalt Mountain and Sopris Mountain. This roadblock was the brainchild of Deputy Sergeant Don Davis, who understood that blocking this intersection was one way to stop a fugitive from slipping through the back valleys and out to Carbondale.

EAST SOPRIS CREEK #1
This roadblock was manned by a lone reserve deputy and his dog. He was supposed to have manned the checkpoint where East Sopris Creek Roadblock #2 was later situated, but he had set up his position at the wrong location. This error went unnoticed for over eleven hours. This checkpoint was disbanded around 12:30 a.m. Wednesday morning.

PRINCE OF PEACE
Just shy of the Maroon Creek Bridge sits a distinctive three-way intersection. Directly south of the intersection, on a slight rise, was the Prince of Peace Chapel. As soon as this checkpoint was established, the Maroon Creek Bridge Roadblock was disbanded.

WATSON CREEK DIVIDE
This checkpoint was created just below the summit of Watson Divide, along a downhill curve, so that drivers wouldn't be able to see the roadblock until they came upon it. Manned by two reserve deputies, the site provided panoramic views of the region. The deputies could observe vehicles approaching either side of the hill.

DIFFICULT CAMPGROUND
Late Tuesday evening, a roadblock was created at the intersection of Highway 82 and Difficult Campground Lane. Two deputies from Eagle County initially manned it. Once they announced that they were set up, the Aspen PD officers near the Crestahaus disbanded their checkpoint in deference to this more easterly position.

EAST SOPRIS CREEK #2
When it was discovered that a reserve deputy was manning a roadblock in the wrong location, a fresh deputy was dispatched to create the checkpoint in its originally intended location. Where two branches of East Sopris Creek Road nearly connected, there was a little dirt road that headed uphill toward the northeast. There was a tall bluff off to the right where the deputy could tuck his patrol car out of view of approaching motorists. This checkpoint was created around 12:45 a.m. Wednesday morning.

FRYING PAN ROAD
Deputy Gary White took it upon himself to create a roadblock along the Frying Pan River, north of Aspen, on Thursday morning. White was joined by his younger brother, Gregory. White permitted his sibling to wear a deputy's shirt and ball cap and carry a shotgun. Their checkpoint was maintained for six to seven hours.

APPENDIX C
PHOTO ILLUSTRATIONS

The author provides a breakdown of the various photo illustrations that appear throughout the book:

IMAGE: "Ted Bundy's Utah Mugshot." [Front Cover].
SOURCE: 954-57-5_1- King County Archives.

IMAGE: "Ted Bundy." [Frontispiece].
SOURCE: 2013.048.0155- Aspen Historical Society, Cassatt Collection.

IMAGE: "Paul Merihew's Stolen Cadillac." [Teaser Page].
SOURCE: 2021.001.KB-Demmon Collection. This is a photograph of the infamous Caddy, taken after Bundy was recaptured.

IMAGE: "Aspen and Aspen Mountain." [Aerial photograph].
SOURCE: 1986.082.0001-Aspen Historical Society. At the top of page 11, we depict an aerial panoramic view of Aspen and Aspen Mountain, an image taken in 1978. On page 10, the author illustrated the downtown Aspen portion, to assist the reader in locating landmarks referenced in the book.

IMAGE: "Aspen Police Department—Patrolman's Badge." [Tuesday].
SOURCE: 2021.002.KB-Zajac Collection. This is the actual badge Officer Chet Zajac wore during the '77 manhunt.

IMAGE: "Ted Bundy's Latent Fingerprints." [Chapter Headings].
SOURCE(S): 251.163 P2. United States Department of Justice, Federal Bureau of Investigation (January 31, 1978). "Wanted by FBI—Theodore Robert Bundy" [Wanted poster]. Washington, D.C; United States Department of Justice, Federal Bureau of Investigation. (February 1992). Ted Bundy: Multiagency Investigative Team Report 1992. p. 1. This is routinely referred to as an FBI 10 Print Card. The top row depicts the five fingerprints from Bundy's right hand. The lower row shows those of his left hand. The individual images of these prints are identified as 1-10. The author, knowing he had a book with ten chapters, opted to depict one image at the start of each chapter: Chapter 1 (right thumb); Chapter 2 (right index); Chapter 3 (right middle); Chapter 4 (right ring); Chapter 5 (right pinky); Chapter 6 (left thumb); Chapter 7 (left index); Chapter 8 (left middle); Chapter 9 (left ring); Chapter 10 (left pinkie).

IMAGE: "Sheriff Dick Kienast." [Chapter 1].
SOURCE: 1998.034.3956- Aspen Historical Society, Aspen Times Collection.

IMAGE: "Detective Sergeant Dave Garms." [Chapter 2].
SOURCE: 1998.034.3201- Aspen Historical Society, Aspen Times Collection.

IMAGE: "Aspen Police Department—Detective's Badge." [Wednesday].
SOURCE: 2021.003.KB-White Collection. This is a badge Gary White wore later in his career when he transferred to the Aspen Police Department.

IMAGE: "Nancy Baxter." [Chapter 3].
SOURCE: 2021.004.KB-Baxter Collection.

IMAGE: "Ward Lucas." [Chapter 4].
SOURCE: 2021.005.KB-Lucas Collection. This photograph, from the Emmy award-winning journalist's private collection, depicts him interviewing Gennadi Yagodin, Chairman of the USSR State Committee on Public Education in 1988.

IMAGE: "Colorado Bureau of Investigation Badge." [Thursday].
SOURCE: 2021.006.KB-Hebrard Collection. This is actively-serving Agent Jason Hebrard's CBI badge and reflects the style that Agent Leo Konkel would have worn during the '77 manhunt.

IMAGE: "Officer Kathy Earl." [Chapter 5].
SOURCE: 2021.007.KB-Silver Collection.

IMAGE: "Colorado State Patrol—Patrolman's Badge." [Friday].
SOURCE: 2021.008.KB-Pinterest. This image reflects the style of badge that Colorado State Trooper Jim Loyd would have worn during the '77 manhunt.

IMAGE: "Deputy Gene Flatt." [Chapter 6].
SOURCE: 1998.034.3233- Aspen Historical Society, Aspen Times Collection.

IMAGE: "Federal Bureau of Investigation Badge." [Saturday].
SOURCE: 2021.009.KB-Kindpng. Former Deputy Leon Murray checked with two different departments in the Denver FBI office, and both noted that they do not permit official pictures of their badges to be taken. The image used may be credited to Kindpng and reflects the style of badge that Agents Browning and Yates would have worn during the '77 manhunt.

IMAGE: "Deputy Bob Braudis." [Chapter 7].
SOURCE: 2021.010.KB-Baxter Collection.

IMAGE: "Pitkin County Sheriff's Department—Deputy Coroner's Badge." [Sunday].
SOURCE: 2021.011.KB-White Collection.

IMAGE: "Officer Chet Zajac." [Chapter 8].
SOURCE: 2021.012.KB-Zajac Collection.

IMAGE: "Aspen Police Department—Sergeant's Badge." [Monday].
SOURCE: 2021.013.KB-White Collection. Deputy Gary White later went to work for the Aspen Police Department. This was his sergeant's badge, which reflects the style of badge that Michael Chandler would have worn during the '77 manhunt.

IMAGE: "Deputy Gary White." [Chapter 9].
SOURCE: 2021.018.KB-The Aspen Times Collection. This photograph appears on page 2-B of the June 16, 1977 edition of The Aspen Times. Publication of this rare image kindly comes from their publisher, Samantha Johnson.

IMAGE: "Detective Michael Chandler." [Chapter 10].
SOURCE: 1998.034.4065- Aspen Historical Society, Cassatt Collection.

IMAGE: "Pitkin County Sheriff's Department—Deputy Sheriff's Badge." [Appendix].
SOURCE: 2021.015.KB-Markov Collection. This is the actual badge Deputy Maureen Higgins wore during the '77 manhunt.

IMAGE: "Deputy Maureen Higgins." [Appendix A].
SOURCE: 2021.016.KB-Markov Collection.

IMAGE: "Trooper Jim Loyd." [Appendix B].
SOURCE: 2021.017.KB Loyd Collection.

IMAGE: "Civil War Statue at the Pitkin County Courthouse." [Final page].
SOURCE: 2007.022.0304-Aspen Historical Society, Aspen Illustrated News Collection.

ACKNOWLEDGMENTS

I am greatly indebted to the former members of the law enforcement community in the Roaring Fork Valley for their recollections of their departments, their procedures, personnel, and the manhunt in particular. From the Pitkin County Sheriff's Office: Gary Haynes, Keith Ikeda, Carol Kempfert, Maureen Markov, Leon Murray, Larry Spiers, and Gary White. From the Aspen Police Department: Michael Chandler, Kathy Earl, Dave Garms, Bill Grikis, Darrel Horan, Terry Quirk, Hugh Roberts, and Chet Zajac. From the Colorado State Highway Patrol: Jim Loyd. From the Colorado Bureau of Investigation: Leo Konkel. From the Aspen-Pitkin County Combined Communications Center: Nancy Baxter, Carolyn Hougland, Valarie Mathews, and JoAnne Rando-Moon.

I wanted to thank those Aspen citizens who were kind enough to share their memories with me: Marc Demmon, Sandy Detlefsen, Ross Dolan, Marnie Lucchini, Mary Meserole, Heidi Mitchell, Paul Mohn, Rick Newton, Jill Sheeley, Dave Stapleton, Marty Stouffer, David Swersky, and Tony Vagneur. Ward Lucas receives my thanks for sharing his memories of what it was like reporting about the largest manhunt Aspen had ever seen.

I also thank specific people and organizations that were helpful during the research portion of this project: John Camper, Director of the Colorado Bureau of Investigation; Steve Koch of the Pitkin County Library; Anna Scott of the Aspen Historical Society; Hannah Soukup of the King County Archives; photographer Ken Eilers; Sandy Lacock Martin, for using her detective skills to help track down elusive witnesses; and Erin Banks, for posting the footage of Barbara Grossman interviewing Detective Pete Hayward.

I owe a great debt of gratitude to two friends and colleagues. Kevin Sullivan put me in contact with Stephen G. Michaud and has always been available for my various questions. Vince Lahey was kind enough to provide me with rare primary source material: Deputy Dave Westerlund's report concerning his activities on the day of the escape, Sergeant Don Davis's report concerning the interrogation of Bundy following his recapture, the Colorado Bureau of Investigation's original report concerning not only the escape, but the break-in at the Kaeser cabin, and an MP3 audio file of his 2018 interview with Deputy Gene Flatt.

I thank Samantha Johnston, publisher of The Aspen Times, for her authorization to use material from their archives, and Stephen G. Michaud, for authorizing the use of specific material from his true crime classic, *The Only Living Witness*. Special thanks are extended to what came to be called my Three Wise Guys: Dispatch-Supervisor Nancy Baxter, Deputy Leon Murray, and Deputy Gary White. These three served as my consultants, critiquing the entire manuscript, to check for authenticity as well as to ensure the "Aspen Flavor" remained intact. I'm also grateful to Baxter, White, Jim Loyd, and Chet Zajac for providing back cover endorsements. Their time and attention to detail was greatly appreciated.

I thank Mark Myers, who laid out the book in Adobe InDesign.

I want to thank my wife for multiple reasons. Sheri led our August 2019 research trip to Glenwood Springs, Aspen, and Snowmass. Her frenetic pace of activity at the Pitkin County Courthouse, the Pitkin County Library, the Wildwood Inn, along Owl Creek Road, and during our tracing of Bundy's escape route had unforeseen benefits. We had no idea the COVID-19 pandemic was coming, which caused us to postpone future trips to Aspen. If not for her energetic, goal-achieving milestones in 2019, it would have taken considerably longer to obtain the research material needed to write this book. Not only did she edit the manuscript, but she also supported my decision to switch genres from mountaineering history to true crime. She had already recommended employing narrative non-fiction in 2015 and, four years later, suggested I take a deep dive into the case files that have fascinated law enforcement officers for over half a century.

–Ric Conrad
Lake Sammamish State Park
King County, Washington
August 28, 2024

BIBLIOGRAPHY

RECORDED INTERVIEWS

Baxter, Nancy, Interview with author, I. "Tuesday," April 5, 2020.
—Interview with author, II. "Tuesday," April 5, 2020.
—Interview with author, III. "Wednesday," April 18, 2020.
—Interview with author, IV. "Dispatch Center and Aspen PD," April 18, 2020.
Chandler, Michael, Interview with author, I. "The Bundy Manhunt," June 1, 2020.
Earl (Kennell Silver), Kathy, Interview with author, I. "The Bundy Manhunt," June 29, 2020.
Flatt, Gene, Interview with Vince Lahey, I. "The Bundy Manhunt," November 28, 2018.
—Interview with Vince Lahey, II. "The Bundy Manhunt," November 28, 2018.
Grikis, Bill, Interview with author, I. "Dogcatcher to the Stars," May 31, 2020.
Haynes, Gary, Interview with author, I. "Kienast's Department," August 18, 2019.
—Interview with author, II. "Kienast's Department," August 18, 2019.
Horan, Darrel, Interview with author, I. "The Bundy Manhunt," May 31, 2020.
Ikeda, Keith, Interview with author, I. "Kienast's Department," August 18, 2019.
—Interview with author, II. "Kienast's Department," August 18, 2019.
Kempfert, Carol, Interview with author, I. "The Deputies of Love," December 30, 2020.
Konkel, Leo, Interview with author, I. "The Fingerprints," July 4, 2020.
Loyd, Jim, Interview with author, I. "Colorado State Patrol," February 21, 2021.
Lucas, Ward, Interview with author, I. "Ted Bundy Memories," August 16, 2019.
Mitchell [Braudis], Heidi, Interview with author, I. "Smuggler Mine," February 7, 2021.
Murray, Leon, Interview with author, I. "The Bundy Manhunt," July 14, 2020.
Quirk, Terry, Interview with author, I. "Lone Wolf Memories," December 8, 2020.
Rando, JoAnne, Interview with author, I. "Six Days," April 18, 2021.
Roberts, Hugh, Interview with author, I. "The Bundy Manhunt," June 22, 2020.
Sheeley, Jill, Interview with author, I. "Bundy Memories," July 22, 2020.
Spiers, Larry, Interview with author, I. "The Bundy Manhunt," August 9, 2020.
Stapleton, Dave, Interview with author, I. "Aspen Mountain Rescue," July 17, 2020.
Stouffer, Marty, Interview with author, I. "Bundy's Cellmate," September 23, 2020.
White, Gary, Interview with author, I. "The Bundy Manhunt," August 31, 2020.
Zajac, Chet, Interview with author, I. "Red Mountain Rookie," December 13, 2020.

ORAL COMMUNICATIONS (OC)

Baxter, Nancy, Oral Communication with author, "The Dogs," May 6, 2020.
—Oral Communication with author, "Caddy Codes," February 14, 2021.
—Oral Communication with author, "Slaughterhouse Bridge Roadblock Correction," June 29, 2023.
—Oral Communication with author, "You've Earned It," June 29, 2023.
—Oral Communication with author, "Mike Fisher," June 29, 2023.
—Oral Communication with author, "The Bundy-Brunette look," June 29, 2023.
—Oral Communication with author, "Xerox Copy Machine," June 29, 2023.
—Oral Communication with author, "Brush Creek Roadblock radio dialogue," March 16, 2024.

Spiers, Larry, Oral Communication with author, "Saturday Morning with the FBI," August 9, 2020.

Stapleton, David, Oral Communication with author, "Manuscript Corrections," August 21, 2020.

Swersky, Dr. David, Oral Communication with author, "Aspen Mountain Rescue," Circa March 2020.

White, Gary, Oral Communication with author, "The Hunch," July 2, 2023.
—Oral Communication with author, "Armed and Dangerous," July 2, 2023.
—Oral Communication with author, "The Xerox Window," July 2, 2023.

WRITTEN COMMUNICATIONS (WC)

Baxter, Nancy, Correspondence with author, "Tuesday," May 13, 2020.
—Correspondence with author, "Saturday," June 23, 2020.
—Correspondence with author, "The Aspen Times," October 26, 2020.
—Correspondence with author, "Baxter & Braudis," November 9, 2020.
—Correspondence with author, "Dave Wright," November 12, 2020.
—Correspondence with author, "Art Hougland," November 12, 2020.
—Correspondence with author, "Deputy McCrocklin," November 13, 2020.
—Correspondence with author, "Marta Steinmetz," November 13, 2020.
—Correspondence with author, "Sunday," November 22, 2020.
—Correspondence with author, "City Hall," December 16, 2020.
—Correspondence with author, "Towing," December 16, 2020.
—Correspondence with author, "Dick Kreuser," December 16, 2020.
—Correspondence with author, "Bubonic Plague," December 19, 2020.
—Correspondence with author, "Top Three Bars in Aspen," January 1, 2021.
—Correspondence with author, "The Pub," January 2, 2021.
—Correspondence with author, "The Roadblocks," January 5, 2021.
—Correspondence with author, "Manuscript Feedback," January 5, 2021.
—Correspondence with author, "Lenado," January 17, 2021.
—Correspondence with author, "Old Snowmass Conoco," January 20, 2021.
—Correspondence with author, "School Evacuations," February 2, 2021.
—Correspondence with author, "Garfield County Posse," February 3, 2021.
—Correspondence with author, "The Runaways," February 7, 2021.
—Correspondence with author, "Loudspeaker Gizmo," February 9, 2021.
—Correspondence with author, "Caryn Campbell & 4-Wheel Drive Roads," February 12, 2021.
—Correspondence with author, "Codes 10-28 & 10-29," February 14, 2021.
—Correspondence with author, "The First Twenty Minutes," February 22, 2021.
—Correspondence with author, "The East Sopris Creek Nightmare," February 22, 2021.
—Correspondence with author, "The 2200 Time Check," March 1, 2021.
—Correspondence with author, "The Egg Timer," March 3, 2021.
—Correspondence with author, "The Gravel Jogging Trail," March 8, 2021.
—Correspondence with author, "Accident Prevention Teams," March 10, 2021.
—Correspondence with author, "DUIs in Aspen," March 10, 2021.
—Correspondence with author, "Worried," March 18, 2021.
—Correspondence with author, "Monday," March 28, 2021.
—Correspondence with author, "Jump vs. Drop," April 14, 2021.
—Correspondence with author, "Garms' Reply," November 9, 2022.
—Correspondence with author, "Dead or Alive," January 30, 2023.
—Correspondence with author, "The Gizmo Announcement," July 8, 2024.

Chandler, Michael, Correspondence with author, "Sidearms," December 20, 2020.

Danforth, Dave, Correspondence with author, "Dave Judy," June 28, 2020.

Demmon, Marc, Correspondence with author, "Aspen State Teacher's College," July 5, 2020.

Dolan, Ross, Correspondence with author, "Aspen Days," May 9, 2021.

Eilers, Ken, Correspondence with author, "The Lewy Photograph," May 24, 2020.

Fabien, Valarie, Correspondence with author, "Dispatch," April 27, 2021.

Garms, Dave, Correspondence with author, "The Manhunt," October 28, 2019.
—Correspondence with author, "The Manhunt Part II," October 30, 2019.

Goodwin, John, Correspondence with author, "Training in Gunnison," July 1, 2020.

Grikis, Bill, Correspondence with author, "Manuscript Corrections," June 2, 2020.
—Correspondence with author, "Prairie Dogs," December 20, 2020.

Haynes, Gary, Correspondence with author, "Maroon Creek Bridge Roadblock," December 26, 2019.
—Correspondence with author, "Lynne Unger," May 13, 2020.
—Correspondence with author, "Pitkin County Jail," June 16, 2020.

Horan, Darrel, Correspondence with author, "Manuscript Corrections," June 24, 2020.
—Correspondence with author, "Quirk Merit Recommendation," February 17, 2021.

Hougland, Carolyn, Correspondence with author, "Art Hougland," June 19, 2020.

Ice, Tom, Correspondence with author, "Garfield County Search & Rescue," February 4, 2021.

Ikeda, Keith, Correspondence with author, "Pitkin County Jail," June 16, 2020.

Kempfert, Carol, Correspondence with author, "The Notification," January 6, 2021.
—Correspondence with author, "Badge 72," March 16, 2024.

Lahey, Vince, Correspondence with Charles Leidner, "Departing Aspen," September 29, 2020.

Loyd, Jim, Correspondence with author, "Post-Jump Patrols," March 4, 2021.

Lucas, Ward, Correspondence with author, "The First Escape," July 21, 2019.

Lucchini, Marnie, Correspondence with author, "The Baseball Bats," April 22, 2021.

Markov (Higgins), Maureen, Correspondence with author, "Tuesday," December 6, 2019.
—Correspondence with author, "The Caddy Stop," December 23, 2019.
—Correspondence with author, "Bundy's Version—Feedback," December 24, 2019.
—Correspondence with author, "Caddy Stop—Manuscript Corrections," December 28, 2019.
—Correspondence with author, "West Sopris Creek Roadblock—Manuscript Corrections," December 31, 2019.
—Correspondence with author, "The Chameleon," May 20, 2020.
—Correspondence with author, "The Gredig Family," February 8, 2021.

Meserole, Mary, Correspondence with author, "Panicked Roommates," April 21, 2021.

Mohn, Paul "Stormy," Correspondence with author, "Aspen Security Patrol," May 24, 2021.

Murray, Leon, Correspondence with author, "Paperboys in Aspen," October 26, 2020.
—Correspondence with author, "Ted Bundy's FBI Fingerprint Code," November 29, 2020.
—Correspondence with author, "Legal Drinking Age in Aspen," January 2, 2021.
—Correspondence with author, "Catherine Store—Carbondale," January 17, 2021.
—Correspondence with author, "PCSO Vehicle Inventory," January 18, 2021.
—Correspondence with author, "Loudspeaker Gizmo," February 11, 2021.
—Correspondence with author, "Cross-Draw Holster," February 23, 2021.
—Correspondence with author, "DUIs in Aspen," March 10, 2021.

Newton, Rick, Correspondence with author, "The Walnut House," July 19, 2020.

Quirk, Terry, Correspondence with author, "Burned and Bitter," December 19, 2020.

Roberts, Hugh, Correspondence with author, "Bundy," June 20, 2020.
—Correspondence with author, "-39 Degrees," December 10, 2020.
—Correspondence with author, "Dick Kreuser," December 16, 2020.
—Correspondence with author, "S&W Model 49's," December 20, 2020.

——Correspondence with author, "Dick Dove," December 21, 2020.
——Correspondence with author, "DUIs in Aspen," March 5, 2021.
Spiers, Larry, Correspondence with author, "Deputized," August 10, 2020.
Stouffer, Marty, Correspondence with author, "Bundy's Cellmate," August 23—September 30, 2020.
Vagneur, Tony, Correspondence with author, "The Drunk Posse," August 1, 2020.
White, Gary, Correspondence with author, "The Roadblock," September 9, 2020.
——Correspondence with author, "The Body Bag," September 9, 2020.
——Correspondence with author, "The Pump .22 Rifle," September 14, 2020.
——Correspondence with author, "The Front Lawn," September 30, 2020.
——Correspondence with author, "The Job Interview," September 30, 2020.
——Correspondence with author, "Deputy Joel Collins," September 30, 2020.
——Correspondence with author, "South along Galena," October 11, 2020.
——Correspondence with author, "Search Dogs on Tuesday," October 12, 2020.
——Correspondence with author, "Neil Sedaka," October 23, 2020.
——Correspondence with author, "Becoming an Officer," October 25, 2020.
——Correspondence with author, "Joe Carroll White (1920—1976)," October 25, 2020.
——Correspondence with author, "Bundy's Eyes," October 27, 2020.
——Correspondence with author, "The Black Bishop," October 29 & 30, 2020.
——Correspondence with author, "Transporting Bundy," October 29, 2020.
——Correspondence with author, "Birthday Boy," October 30, 2020.
——Correspondence with author, "One More Run," November 22, 2020.
——Correspondence with author, "Claudine Longet," December 2, 2020.
——Correspondence with author, "Officer Dick Kreuser," December 15, 2020.
——Correspondence with author, "Fat – Fifty – Florida," January 1, 2021.
——Correspondence with author, "The Holiday Inn," January 1, 2021.
——Correspondence with author, "DUIs in Aspen," March 11, 2021.
——Correspondence with author, "Frying Pan Roadblock," March 29, 2021.
——Correspondence with author, "Thoughts From the Cheap Seats," April 4, 2021.
——Correspondence with author, "The Birthday Crash," April 3, 2024.
Zajac, Chet, Correspondence with author, "The .38," December 20, 2020.
——Correspondence with author, "The Pub," January 7, 2021.
——Correspondence with author, "Aspen's Volunteer Fire Department," January 7, 2021.

ADDITIONAL SOURCES IN ALPHABETICAL ORDER

9NEWS KUSA (TV)
Denver, Colorado

Lucas, Ward, "Evening News—Ted Bundy's Escape," *9NEWS/KUSA TV*, Aspen, Colorado, Utah, June 7, 1977 (2021, January 30). www.youtube.com/watch?v=p_GYD9P23h4.
Lucas, Ward, "Evening News—Ted Bundy's Escape," *9NEWS/KUSA TV*, Aspen, Colorado, Utah, June 8, 1977 (2021, January 30). www.youtube.com/watch?v=p_GYD9P23h4.

ASPEN CITY COUNCIL
Aspen, Colorado

Hauter, Kathryn, "Rodent Control," Aspen City Council, Aspen, Colorado, July 25, 1977, pp. 1-8.
Hauter, Kathryn, "Xerox Contract," Aspen City Council, Aspen, Colorado, September 12, 1977, pp. 1-12.

BOOKS

Larsen, Richard, "Bundy: The Deliberate Stranger," (New York, NY: Pocket Books, May 1986 edition). pp. 199, 207-209, 211, 220.

Michaud, Stephen G., and Hugh Aynesworth, "The Only Living Witness," (New York, NY: Signet Books, June 1989 edition). pp. 191-195.

Sheeley, Jill, "Those Were the Days: Memories of an Aspen Hippie Chick," (Aspen, CO: Courtney Press, 2019 edition). pp. 1-174.

COLORADO BUREAU OF INVESTIGATION [CBI]
Lakewood, Colorado

Konkel, Agent Leo G., Colorado Bureau of Investigation (June 16, 1977). "Burglary—Fritz Kaeser Cabin." File #77-6-006M. Denver, Colorado, 1-3.

—(June 16, 1977). "Theodore Bundy Escape." File #77-6-007M. Denver, Colorado, 1-12.

-Unknown, "Special Bulletin: Missing Person—Julie Cunningham," Colorado Bureau of Investigation, 04-11-75, Denver, Colorado, p. 1.

DEMMON COLLECTION

Demmon, Marc, "Bundy to Star in Movie." Clean Sweep (Newsletter), Aspen State Teacher's College, Vol II, No. 3, (June 1977 edition). Aspen, Colorado.

—"Ride Wanted." Clean Sweep (Newsletter/Classifieds), Aspen State Teacher's College, Vol II, No. 3, (June 1977 edition). Aspen, Colorado.

—"Escapism 234." Clean Sweep (Newsletter/New Courses), Aspen State Teacher's College, Vol II, No. 3, (June 1977 edition). Aspen, Colorado.

DOCUMENTARIES

"Conversations With a Killer: The Ted Bundy Tapes," Dir. Joe Berlinger. Radical Media, Elastic, Gigantic Studios, and Outpost Digital, 2019. Film.

FEDERAL BUREAU OF INVESTIGATION [FBI]
Washington, D.C.

United States Department of Justice, Federal Bureau of Investigation (June 9, 1977). "Ted Bundy—Fugitive" [Teletype]. Salt Lake City, Utah: FBI.

—(June 9, 1977). "Theodore Robert Bundy—Unlawful Flight" (FBI Case Status Form FD-320: File No. 88-6895). Salt Lake City, Utah: FBI.

—(June 9, 1977). "USA vs. Theodore Robert Bundy." (Arrest Warrant: Magistrate Docket No. A, Case No. 77-0075M). Salt Lake City, Utah: FBI.

—(June 11, 1977). "Ted Bundy—A.K.A. Theodore Robert Cowell" [Teletype]. Denver, Colorado, Utah: FBI.

—(June 11, 1977). "Clearing T. Bundy," [Teletype]. Denver, Colorado, Utah: FBI.

—(June 11, 1977). "Mountain Cabin—Breaking & Entering" [Teletype]. Denver, Colorado, Utah: FBI.

—(June 11, 1977). "Front and Side Views—Ted Bundy" [Teletype with Two Photographs]. Denver, Colorado, Utah: FBI.

—(June 13, 1977). "Concealing the Cabin Break-In" [Teletype]. Denver, Colorado, Utah: FBI.

—(January 31, 1978). "Wanted by FBI—Theodore Robert Bundy" [Wanted poster]. Washington, D.C.

—(February 1992). Ted Bundy: Multiagency Investigative Team Report 1992. pp. 1-49.

FLORIDA STATE ARCHIVES
Tallahassee, Florida

Patchen, Don, Steve Bodiford, and Norm Chapmen, "Statement of Theodore Robert Bundy," Recorded Interview Transcript, (February 20, 1978), Florida State Archives, Series 2084, Carton 9, Folder 25: 1-26 & 1-20.

INTERNET

-10th Mountain Division Hut Association, (2020, July 20). "The Alfred A Braun Hut System," www.huts.org.

-Ashcroft, (2020, July 21). "Ashcroft Ghost Town," Aspen Historical Society, Aspen, Colorado, www.aspenhistory.org/tours-sites/ashcroft-ghost-town/.

-Aspen Hall of Fame, (2021, April 26). "Betty Haas Pfister," Aspen Hall of Fame, Aspen, Colorado, www.steamboatlibrary.marmot.org/Archive/person:13731/Person.

-Aspen Center for Environmental Studies, (2020, December 19). "Hallam Lake," www.aspennature.org/location/hallam-lake.

-Aspen/Pitkin County (Sardy Field) Airport, (2021, January 30). "Aspen Airport: Operational, Accessible, Open to the Public since 1946," Aspen, Colorado, www.aspenairport.com/about-aspen-airport/history/.

-Avisian Staff (2014, December 2). "A History of AFIS," SecureIDNews, www.secureidnews.com/news-item/a-history-of-afis/.

-Barnett, Josh, (2020, June 15). "Manual Gearbox: A Porsche 911 History," www.total911.com/manual-gearbox-a-porsche-911-history/.

-Braudis, Bob (2019, February 15). "Former Pitkin County Sheriff Bob Braudis Discusses Interactions with Ted Bundy," YouTube, upload by Denver7—The Denver Channel, www.youtube.com/watch?v=b-NRhOw-8QI.

-Colorado State Patrol (2020, April 20). "State Patrol Ten-codes," wiki.radioreference.com/index.php/Colorado_State_Patrol_(CO)#Codes.

-DaRonch Carol (2020, May 20). "Ted Bundy first escape news clip 6/8/77," YouTube, upload by Carol DaRonch, www.youtube.com/watch?v=FPyU2ZcQ5AE.

-Dawson, Louis, (2020, July 20). "History of the Huts," www.huts.org.

-Facebook, (2021, February 12). "Jill von Flotow and the Loudspeaker Gizmo," www.facebook.com/photo?fbid=10218938125148322&set=bc.

-FBI Officer Down Memorial Page, (2020, June 20). "Special Agent Clifton Dewell Browning, Jr.," www.odmp.org/officer/2379-special-agent-clifton-dewell-browning-jr

-Field Sobriety Testing, (2021, March 27). "Brief History of Field Sobriety Testing," www.theduilawyer.com/field-sobriety-tests/.

-Hutski.com, (2020, July 21). "Summit Huts Online Guidebook," www.hutski.com/hut-routes/lind.ley/lindley-hut.html.

-JBugs, (2020, June 15). "1968 VW Shift Knob, Gear, Black," www.jbugs.com/product/79-4640.html.

-Lucas, Ward (2019, February 17). "My Interview with Netflix for the Documentary on Ted Bundy." Article retrieved from www.wardlucas.com/my-interview-with-netflix-for-the-documentary-on-ted-bundy/.
-Lucas, Ward (2019, February 8). "This Former News Anchor Flew to Aspen and Tried to Find Ted Bundy Himself." Article retrieved from www.youtube.com/watch?v=aVu4T7k1s-k.
-Morning Call, The (2021, March 1). "1967 Kaiser Jeepster Commando Convertible Deluxe," www.mcall.com/classified/autos/mc-1967-kaiser-jeepster-commando-convertible-deluxe-20170127-story.html.
-Steinmetz, Marta, (2020, November 29). "Marta Steinmetz [Profile]," www.linkedin.com/in/marta-steinmetz-9b7a3710/.
-White, Gary, (2020, September 6). "Gary White [Profile]," www.linkenin.com/in/gary-white-120556122.
-Wikipedia, (2021, March 9). "2nd Cavalry Regiment," www.wikipedia.org/wiki/2nd_Cavalry Regiment (United States).
-Wikipedia, (2021, January 30). "Aspen/Pitkin County Airport," www.wikipedia.org/wiki/Aspen/Pitkin_County_Airport.
-Wikipedia, (2020, June 15). "Basalt, Colorado," www.wikipedia.org/wiki/Basalt,_Colorado.
-Wikipedia, (2021, March 28). "Lenado, Colorado," www.wikipedia.org/wiki/Lenado,_Colorado.
-Wikipedia, (2021, February 7). "Smuggler Mine," www.en.wikipedia.org/wiki/Smuggler_Mine.
-Wikipedia, (2020, September 10). "Vortex Ring State," www.en.wikipedia.org/wiki/Vortex_ring_state.
-Wikipedia, (2021, January 3). "Wheeler Opera House," www.wikipedia.org/wiki/Wheeler_Opera_House.

KING COUNTY ARCHIVES
Seattle, Washington

954-29-4 "Calendar and Address Books," Ted Bundy Collection. Ted Bundy, "Message for the FBI—Filofax Entry," 05-23-77, p. 52. Box 29/File 4. King County Archives, Seattle, Washington.

KUTV NEWSWATCH 2
Salt Lake City, Utah

Gilmour, Sandy, and Grossman, Barbara, "Evening News—Ted Bundy's Escape," *KUTV Newswatch 2*, Salt Lake City, Utah, June 7, 1977.
Grossman, Barbara, "Bundy—Recaptured," *KUTV Newswatch 2*, Salt Lake City, Utah, June 13, 1977.

MAGAZINE ARTICLES

Boyd, Bob, "Having a Wonderful Time in Jail: Claudine & Her Young Deputy Laugh it Up," The Star magazine, May 17, 1977.
Chalmers, Robert, "Claudine Longet: Aspen's Femme Fatale," GQ Magazine [British], May 6, 2013.
Stewart, Ben, "Off-Road Time Warp: 1962 Jeep Willys Underground Concept," Popular Mechanics, September 25, 2012.

NEWSPAPER ARTICLES

Aspen Daily News

Abraham, Chad, "Ex-sheriff recalls Bundy, his escape in Aspen, manhunt," Aspen Daily News, January 31, 2019.

Wackerle, Chris, "Old Snowmass Conoco property changes hands," Aspen Daily News, December 26, 2019.

Aspen Peak

Sharpe, Oliver, "Here's How Two Aspen Natives Turned the City into a College Town," Aspen Peak, May 24, 2019.

Aspen Times, The

Anderson, Paul, "The Braun Huts: A History," The Aspen Times, March 15, 2004.

Auslander, Jason, "Explanation of Aspen's Civil War monument planned," The Aspen Times, August 24, 2017.

Chamberlain, David, "The Jaundiced Eye," The Aspen Times, June 9, 1977.

Clifford, Peggy, "Bundy's Week of Freedom," The Aspen Times, June 23, 1977.

Hanson, Georgia, "Theodore Bundy," The Aspen Times, December 18, 2005.

Harvey, Allyn, "The Shadow of a Killer," The Aspen Times, June 8, 2002.

Havlen, Naomi, "Martin Hershey, Former Top Cop and Councilman, Dies," The Aspen Times, April 12, 2002.

Hayes, Mary Eshbaugh, "Aspen History 101," The Aspen Times, December 13, 2006.

Markov, Maureen, "Bundy Redux (Letter to the Editor)," The Aspen Times, December 18, 2005.

Rollins, Bill, "Escaped Kidnapper Bundy Eludes Helicopter, Hounds, Manhunters," The Aspen Times, June 9, 1977.
—"Who is Ted Bundy?" The Aspen Times, August 4, 1977.

Sabella, John, "The Bundy Manhunt: Is a Killer Loose in Aspen?" The Aspen Times, June 9, 1977.
—"Deputies Snare Exhausted Bundy," The Aspen Times, June 16, 1977.
—"The Hub of Law and Emergency," The Aspen Times, July 14, 1977.
—"Departing Garms Sees Police Problem," The Aspen Times, August 11, 1977.

Stone, Andy, "Ben Meyers: New County Undersheriff," The Aspen Times, May 20, 1976.

Stonington, Joel, "Former Sheriff Dies in Arizona," The Aspen Times, March 28, 2006.

Travers, Andrew, "John Busch, Aspen Gay Icon and Champion of Cinema, Inducted in the Hall of Fame," The Aspen Times, January 18, 2019.

Vagneur, Tony, "Saddle Sore," The Aspen Times, October 24, 2009.

Unknown, "David Garms: Four Years Later," The Aspen Times, April 8, 1976.
—"Sheriff Announces Reorganization Plan," The Aspen Times, March 3, 1977.
—"Sheriff's Department Hires New Deputies [Higgins and McCrocklin]," The Aspen Times, circa January 1976.
—"Former Miner Now Deputy in Sheriff's Department," The Aspen Times, April 21, 1977.
—"What Do You Think of the Bundy Escape?" The Aspen Times, June 9, 1977.
—"Independence Pass to Open by Mid-June," The Aspen Times, June 9, 1977.
—"Individual Rights More Important Than Escape" [Letter to the Editor], The Aspen Times, June 16, 1977.
—"Wan and Haggard, Bundy is Arraigned on More Charges," The Aspen Times, June 16, 1977.
—"Rape Attempt Leads to Bundy's Capture," The Aspen Times, June 16, 1977.

- "Bundy Gets New Legal Help for New Charges," The Aspen Times, June 16, 1977.
- "Bundy Search Costs Put at $6,000-$10,000," The Aspen Times, June 16, 1977.
- "Bundy Determined to Escape June 7," The Aspen Times, June 30, 1977.
- "Bundy Gets Phone Credit Card Back," The Aspen Times, July 7, 1977.
- "Sheriff's Office Down Six Officers," The Aspen Times, July 14, 1977.
- "Bundy ordered Held on Escape Charge," The Aspen Times, August 4, 1977.
- "Bob Lewis leaves legacy of education, environmentalism," The Aspen Times, August 1, 2005.
- "Bruce Prior Sinclair [Obituary]," The Aspen Times, February 14, 2006.
- "Elizabeth Haas Pfister [Obituary]," The Aspen Times, November 22, 2011.
- "Richard Wall [Obituary]," The Aspen Times, December 18, 2012.
- "Marta Jean Steinmetz [Obituary]," The Aspen Times, April 17, 2018.
- "1977: City to flood golf course squirrels [prairie dogs]," The Aspen Times, July 19, 2006.

Yoder, Tom, "Letter: An Aspen Legend [Ed Golub]," The Aspen Times, September 11, 2013.

Daily Sentinel, The

Unknown, "Aspen Court Action for Bundy Opens," The Daily Sentinel, April 5, 1977.

Boland, Mary, "Bundy Recaptured at Aspen," The Daily Sentinel, June 13, 1977.

Denver Post, The

Culver, Virginia, "Longtime Channel 7 Weatherman Chandler Dies," The Denver Post, May 24, 2010.

Patrick, Pam, "Recaptured Bundy Faces New Charges," The Denver Post, June 16, 1977.

Seldner, Joseph and Pam Parker, "Bundy Escape Miffs 'Unfrightened' Aspen," The Denver Post, June 8, 1977.

Unknown, "Net Out for Bundy Hauls in Marijuana," The Denver Post, June 8, 1977.
- "Aspen Starts Door-to-Door Search," The Denver Post, June 8, 1977.

Deseret News

Unknown, "Bundy to Move from Aspen Jail," Deseret News, April 13, 1977.
- "Bundy Escapes in Colorado," Deseret News, June 7, 1977.
- "Bundy Escape: Aspen Bungled," Deseret News, June 9, 1977.
- "Aspen Lawmen Capture Bundy," Deseret News, June 13, 1977.
- "5 Coloradans Resign," Deseret News, June 30, 1977.
- "Bundy Claims Silver Lining in Predicament," Deseret News, August 1, 1977.

New York Times, The

Lichtenstein, Grace, "Aspen Jury Selection Is Started In the Longest Manslaughter Trial," The New York Times, January 4, 1977.

Post Independent, The

Burton, Lynn, "Catherine Store changes hands, but won't change ambiance," The Post Independent, April 17, 2003.

Summerlin, Ryan, "Ted Bundy Tales Come out of the Woodwork," The Post Independent, April 15, 2017.

Rocky Mountain News

Cunningham, Alan, "Slay Suspect Escapes in Leap from Window," Rocky Mountain News, June 8, 1977.
—"It's a Stirring Name," Rocky Mountain News, June 9, 1977.
—"House-to-House Hunt is On For Bundy," Rocky Mountain News, June 9, 1977.
—"Bundy Captured, Back in Court in Shackles," Rocky Mountain News, June 14, 1977.

Salt Lake Tribune, The

Lobb, Clark, "Possible Accomplice Tie Probed," The Salt Lake Tribune, June 9, 1977.
Unknown, "Bundy Left Alone in Aspen Courtroom, Leaps Out Window, Escapes into Hills," The Salt Lake Tribune, June 8, 1977.
—"Officials Hunt Aspen Area Hills for Bundy," The Salt Lake Tribune, June 9, 1977.
—"Federal Fugitive Charge is Lodged in S.L. Against Theodore Bundy," The Salt Lake Tribune, June 10, 1977.
—"Colorado Officials Claim Escapee Bundy Armed," The Salt Lake Tribune, June 12, 1977.
—"Back in Courtroom, Dead-Tired Bundy Hears New Charges," The Salt Lake Tribune, June 14, 1977.
—"Bundy Formally Charged with Four New Felonies," The Salt Lake Tribune, June 17, 1977.

Seattle Daily Times, The

Larsen, Richard W. "Ted Bundy Escapes!" The Seattle Daily Times, June 7, 1977.
—"Bundy Hunted in Mountains," The Seattle Daily Times, June 8, 1977.
—"Bundy was a Prisoner with Privileges," The Seattle Daily Times, June 10, 1977.
—"Bundy: Chatty Calmness, then a Desperate Leap," The Seattle Daily Times, June 8, 1977.
—"Bundy May Have Injured Ankle," The Seattle Daily Times, June 9, 1977.
—"FBI Joins Colorado Manhunt," The Seattle Daily Times, June 10, 1977.
—"Bundy Believed Still in Mountains," The Seattle Daily Times, June 11, 1977.
—"Bundy Traced to Mountain Cabin," The Seattle Daily Times, June 12, 1977.
—"Ted Bundy: An Interstate Enigma," The Seattle Daily Times, June 12, 1977.
—"Bundy Captured!" The Seattle Daily Times, June 13, 1977.
—"Bundy Looks Like Animal Run Down," The Seattle Daily Times, June 13, 1977.
Unknown, "Bundy's Mother: Give Up," The Seattle Daily Times, June 10, 1977.

Seattle Post-Intelligencer, The

McCarten, Larry and Fred Brack, "Colorado Escape—Manhunt for Bundy," The Seattle Post-Intelligencer, June 8, 1977.
Unknown, "Bundy Took Rifle, Ammo in Break-in," The Seattle Post-Intelligencer, June 12, 1977.

Steamboat Pilot & Today

Russell, John F., "Family, friends remember former Routt County Sheriff Gary Wall," Steamboat Pilot & Today, July 24, 2018.

Straight Creek Journal

Wolf, Ron, and Steven Winn, "Part 6: Memories of Colorado—Escape and Capture," Straight Creek Journal, October 19, 1978.

Tacoma News Tribune

Doud, Charles, "Searchers Comb Aspen for Bundy," Tacoma News Tribune, June 8, 1977.
—"Blame for Bundy's Escape Exchanged," Tacoma News Tribune, June 9, 1977.
—"Bundy May Have Joined Throng 'Escaping' in Aspen," Tacoma News Tribune, June 9, 1977.
—"Bundy's Prosecutor May Face Prosecution Himself," Tacoma News Tribune, June 10, 1977.
—"Something's Missing in Aspen Humor About Bundy," Tacoma News Tribune, June 11, 1977.
—"Bundy's Trail Grows Colder; Leads Futile," Tacoma News Tribune, June 11, 1977.
—"Search for Bundy Centers on Cabin," Tacoma News Tribune, June 12, 1977.
—"Escapees Ray, Bundy in Custody," Tacoma News Tribune, June 13, 1977.
—"Bundy Faces New Charges Stemming from his Escape," Tacoma News Tribune, June 13, 1977.
—"Bundy's Run Motive Mulled," Tacoma News Tribune, June 14, 1977.
—"Refreshed Bundy Ready to Tilt Again," Tacoma News Tribune, June 14, 1977.
Rollins, Bill, "Bundy Escapes Courtroom," Tacoma News Tribune, June 7, 1977.
Unknown, "Tip from Cellmate Redirects Search" Tacoma News Tribune, June 10, 1977.

Vail Trail, The

Lamont, Cindy, "Vail Police Chief Gary Wall—The President's Shadow," The Vail Trail, January 31, 1975.

PITKIN COUNTY SHERIFF'S OFFICE
Aspen, Colorado

Davis, Sgt. Don, "Bundy Escape Itinerary/Interrogation," (June 15, 1977), Pitkin County Sheriff's Office: 1-4.
Westerlund, David, "Statement of Deputy David Westerlund," (June 7, 1977), Pitkin County Sheriff's Office: 1-2.

QUIRK COLLECTION
South Padre Island, Texas

Horan, Sgt. Darrel, "Merit Recommendation—Officer Terry Quirk," (June 17, 1977), Aspen Police Department: 1.

END NOTES

Chapter 1, "Jackal on the Run"

1. Baxter, WC, "Tuesday," 05-13-20. Baxter's shift was supposed to end at 4:00 p.m.
2. Ibid.
3. Baxter, R/I, I "Tuesday," 04-05-20.
4. Baxter, WC, "Tuesday," 05-13-20.
5. Ibid. Baxter also notes that she used a black IBM Mag Card Typewriter.
6. Baxter, R/I, I. "Tuesday," 04-05-20.
7. There was also an overhead pipe that a prisoner could potentially use to hang himself. "Former Pitkin County Sheriff Bob Braudis Discusses Interactions with Ted Bundy," YouTube, 02-15-19. Transfer of Bundy comes from: Unk, "Bundy to Move from Aspen Jail," DN, 04-13-77.
8. That they had performed multiple escort missions comes from: Konkel, CBI, (06-16-77). #77-6-007M. p 6. Lockbox protocols come from: Haynes, R/I, I. "Kienast's Department," 08-18-19.
9. Clothing Bundy was wearing comes from two sources: Unk, "Bundy Escapes in Colorado," DN, 06-07-77; Cunningham, "Slay Suspect Escapes in Leap from Window," RMN, 06-08-77.
10. That Bundy's hands were cuffed in front comes from: Konkel, CBI (06-16-77). #77-6-007M. p 6. That he was led down the corridor comes from: Unk, "Bundy Left Alone in Aspen Courtroom, Leaps Out Window, Escapes into Hills," SLT, 06-08-77.
11. Procedures for securing the prisoner in the vehicle come from: Haynes, R/I, I. "Kienast's Department," 08-18-19. Retrieval of the weapons comes from: Sabella, "The Bundy Manhunt: Is a Killer Loose in Aspen?" AT, 06-09-77. What the deputies radioed to dispatch, prior to their departure, comes from: Baxter, WC, "Manuscript Feedback," 01-05-21.
12. Rollins, "Escaped Kidnapper Bundy Eludes Helicopter, Hounds, Manhunters," AT, 06-09-77; Unk, "Sheriff's Office Down Six Officers," AT, 07-14-77.
13. Unk, "Bundy Determined to Escape June 7," AT, 06-30-77.
14. Murphy's response to Bundy's antics comes from: Sabella, "The Bundy Manhunt: Is a Killer Loose in Aspen?" AT, 06-09-77. Bundy's response to Murphy reaching for his weapon comes from: Wolf & Winn, "Part 6: Memories of Colorado—Escape and Capture," SCJ, 10-19-78. That Bundy was a prime suspect in other homicides comes from: Sabella, "The Bundy Manhunt: Is a Killer Loose in Aspen?" AT, 06-09-77.
15. Unk, "Bundy Determined to Escape June 7," AT, 06-30-77.
16. Wikipedia, "Basalt, Colorado," 06-15-20.
17. Sabella, "The Bundy Manhunt: Is a Killer Loose in Aspen?" AT, 06-09-77.
18. Why Mark Lewy took Bundy's photograph comes from: Cunningham, "Slay Suspect Escapes in Leap from Window," RMN, 06-08-77. That Bundy smiled after hearing the camera's shutter release comes from: Wolf & Winn, "Part 6: Memories of Colorado—Escape and Capture," SCJ, 10-19-78.
19. Konkel, CBI, (06-16-77). #77-6-007M. p. 7.
20. Westerlund, "Statement of Deputy David Westerlund," (06-07-77), PCSO. Westerlund's statement is in marked contrast to Kralicek's. The sergeant stated to a CBI investigator that he was, "...aware that Deputy Westerlund was in the courtroom guarding prisoner Jimmy Walker." Konkel, CBI, (06-16-77). #77-6-007M. p. 7.
21. Konkel, CBI, (06-16-77). #77-6-007M. p. 7.
22. Ibid.
23. Ibid.
24. Bundy's court-appointed defense attorneys were Jim Dumas and Charles Leidner.
25. Unk, "Bundy Left Alone in Aspen Courtroom, Leaps Out Window, Escapes into Hills," SLT, 06-08-77.
26. Konkel, CBI, (06-16-77). #77-6-007M. p. 3.
27. Westerlund, "Statement of Deputy David Westerlund," (06-07-77), PCSO. 1.
28. That the two men switched places comes from: Westerlund, "Statement of Deputy David West-

erlund," (06-07-77), PCSO. 1. That Kralicek sent Murphy home comes from: Konkel, CBI, (06-16-77). #77-6-007M. p. 7. Court convened at 9:00 a.m.

29 Unk, "Bundy Left Alone in Aspen Courtroom, Leaps Out Window, Escapes into Hills," SLT, 06-08-77; Rollins, "Escaped Kidnapper Bundy Eludes Helicopter, Hounds, Manhunters," AT, 06-09-77. The attorney providing these arguments was Jim Dumas. Judge Lohr asked Dumas, in how many district courts had he introduced the same argument? Dumas replied that he had made the same remarks on eleven prior occasions. Each time, the presiding judge had ruled against him.

30 Konkel, CBI, (06-1677). #77-6-007M. p. 7.

31 This was a female city employee, observing the proceedings from the spectator benches. Lobb, "Possible Accomplice Tie Probed," SLT, 06-09-77.

32 Konkel, CBI, (06-16-77). #77-6-007M. p. 7. This would have been around 9:30 a.m.

33 That the room began to empty of all personnel save Bundy comes from: Westerlund, "Statement of Deputy David Westerlund," (06-07-77), PCSO. P. 1. Most of the attorneys and observers agreed to meet in the lobby on the first floor. Sabella, "The Bundy Manhunt: Is a Killer Loose in Aspen?" AT, 06-09-77.

34 Westerlund, "Statement of Deputy David Westerlund," (06-07-77), PCSO. p. 1.

35 Larsen, "Bundy: The Deliberate Stranger," pp. 207-208.

36 Westerlund, "Statement of Deputy David Westerlund," (06-07-77), PCSO. p. 1.

37 Ibid.

38 Davis, "Bundy Escape Itinerary/Interrogation," (06-15-77), PCSO. p. 2.

39 Unk, "5 Coloradans Resign," DN, 06-30-77; Unk, "Aspen Starts Door-to-Door Search," DP, 06-08-77.

40 Sabella, "The Bundy Manhunt: Is a Killer Loose in Aspen?" AT, 06-09-77.

41 Rollins, "Escaped Kidnapper Bundy Eludes Helicopter, Hounds, Manhunters," AT, 06-09-77. Why Westerlund felt Bundy may have entered the court clerk's office from the side door in the northeast corner of the courtroom remains a mystery. As Deputy Leon Murray notes, "The area inside the employee door, behind the witness stand, was considered hallowed ground. It was the back room of the court clerk's office. In the thirty-four years, six months and one day I worked there, I was never in that area." Additional source material: Rollins, "Bundy Escapes Courtroom," TNT, 06-07-77.

42 Deputy Keith Ikeda notes, "Bundy had access to the law library. There was kind of like this smokey glass. You couldn't see out of it, but you could see shadows. Bundy knew the minute [Westerlund] lit that cigarette, he had about seven to ten minutes to jump out the window." Ikeda, R/I, I. "Kienast's Department," 08-18-19.

43 In various publications over the years, this unidentified witness has been called a woman. Whitney Wulff, one of the sheriff's secretaries, stated on camera that day, that it was a man. Gilmour & Grossman, "Evening News—Ted Bundy's Escape," KUTV, 06-07-77; Unk, "Bundy Left Alone in Aspen Courtroom, Leaps Out Window, Escapes into Hills," SLT, 06-08-77.

44 Doud, "Searchers Comb Aspen for Bundy," TNT, 06-08-77. The author used this specific description of Bundy's jump as it most closely approximates what his research revealed. Colorado filmmaker, Vince Lahey, measured the distance between the windowsill and the lawn below—twenty-three feet. Lahey believes Bundy may have hung by his fingers and then dropped to the ground, which would make it a fifteen to sixteen-foot drop. Neither Lahey or the author have discovered any documentation that states Bundy hung from the windowsill and dropped. The words used throughout the various accounts, state "jump" or "jumped." Still, the possibility exists that Bundy may have used the technique mentioned by Lahey. Nancy Baxter does not agree. She writes, "[Hanging onto the sill and dropping] was never part of the narrative from those who reported it to us. It was more like he came flying out the window and hit the ground and then, re-energized when nothing broke, he took off running east." Baxter, WC, "Jump vs. Drop," 04-14-21. The witnesses' observations come from: Sabella, "The Bundy Manhunt: Is a Killer Loose in Aspen?" AT, 06-09-77.

45 Inside the raised basement, Casey Armstrong glimpsed a man running past her window at full speed. She wasn't sure what to make of it. Time passed and then she spied deputies in pursuit. Arm-

strong noticed that Bundy had a three-minute head start. Rollins, "Escaped Kidnapper Bundy Eludes Helicopter, Hounds, Manhunters," AT, 06-09-77; Unk, "Aspen Starts Door-to-Door Search," DP, 06-08-77. Undersheriff Ben Meyers believed four minutes had elapsed. Konkel, CBI, (06-16-77). #77-6-007M. p 6.

46   Westerlund, "Statement of Deputy David Westerlund," (06-07-77), PCSO. p. 2.

47   Near Westerlund, in the hallway, was a local journalist, two of his colleagues, a bystander, who happened to find the preliminary hearings of interest, and Charles Leidner. Sabella, "The Bundy Manhunt: Is a Killer Loose in Aspen?" AT, 06-09-77.

48   "Conversations with a Killer: The Ted Bundy Tapes," Berlinger, 2019. Film.

49   Marcia DeCamp, Whitney Wulff, and Colleen Curtis were the secretaries. Cunningham, "Slay Suspect Escapes in Leap from Window," RMN, 07-08-77.

50   Konkel, CBI, (06-16-77). #77-6-007M. p. 7.

51   Gilmour & Grossman, "Evening News—Ted Bundy's Escape," KUTV Newswatch 2, 06-07-77.

52   Secretary Colleen Curtis was right on Kralicek's heels as they raced upstairs. Rollins, "Escaped Kidnapper Bundy Eludes Helicopter, Hounds, Manhunters," AT, 06-09-77; Sabella, "The Bundy Manhunt: Is a Killer Loose in Aspen?" AT, 06-09-77.

53   Larsen, "Bundy: The Deliberate Stranger." p. 209.

54   Westerlund, "Statement of Deputy David Westerlund," (06-07-77), PCSO. p. 2; Abraham, "Ex-sheriff recalls Bundy, his escape in Aspen, manhunt," ADN, 01-31-19.

55   Westerlund spoke these words to Colleen Curtis as she entered the law library. Westerlund, "Statement of Deputy David Westerlund," (06-07-77), PCSO. p. 2.

56   Larsen, "Bundy: The Deliberate Stranger," P. 209.

57   Unk, "Aspen Starts Door-to-Door Search," DP, 06-08-77.

58   Leidner, as quoted in: "Conversations with a Killer: The Ted Bundy Tapes," Berlinger, 2019. Film.

59   Interviewed in 2020, Horan couldn't quite recall where he was when he learned Bundy had escaped. Nancy Baxter recalled that he was in the dispatch office with her, preparing to smoke his pipe. Horan stated, "I cannot recall if I was there, but Nancy is probably correct." Horan, WC, "Manuscript Corrections," 06-24-20.

60   Sitting in her chair in the dispatch office, Nancy Baxter was surrounded on three sides by a wide array of equipment, including four radios, a thirty-button telephone, and a CB radio monitor. Off to her left, she could flip through a nearby Rolodex organizer, to obtain the number of any state agency, from the Adams County Sheriff's Office to the Yuma Police Department. The console in front of her contained multiple alarm indicators. In addition to her regular duties, she monitored alarm systems for at least two different security companies in the city. She had direct phone lines to the chief of police and the sheriff. There was a bright red phone, mounted to the wall, which constituted the direct line to the fire department. She could sound the fire alarm, which could be heard throughout town. Sabella, "The Hub of Law and Emergency," AT, 07-14-77; Baxter, R/I, I. "Tuesday," 04-05-20; Baxter, WC, "Manuscript Feedback," 01-05-21.

61   Baxter, R/I, I. "Tuesday," 04-05-20.

62   Ibid.

63   Baxter, WC, "The First Twenty Minutes," 02-22-21.

64   Chandler, R/I, I. "The Bundy Manhunt," 06-01-20.

65   White, WC, "The Front Lawn," 09-30-20.

66   White, WC, "South along Galena," 10-11-20.

67   Chandler, R/I, I. "The Bundy Manhunt," 06-01-20.

68   Clifford, "Bundy's Week of Freedom," AT, 06-23-77; Sabella, "The Bundy Manhunt: Is a Killer Loose in Aspen?" AT, 06-09-77.

69   Sabella, "Deputies Snare Exhausted Bundy," AT, 06-16-77; Rollins, "Escaped Kidnapper Bundy Eludes Helicopter, Hounds, Manhunters," AT, 06-09-77. The secretary in question was Whitney Wulff. Gilmour & Grossman, "Evening News—Ted Bundy's Escape," KUTV Newswatch 2, SLC, 06-07-77.

70   Sabella, "The Bundy Manhunt: Is a Killer Loose in Aspen?" AT, 06-09-77. Nancy Baxter con-

firmed that several construction workers witnessed the jump. Baxter, R/I, I. "Tuesday," 04-05-20.

71   The "Freddie's" witness information comes from: Rollins, "Escaped Kidnapper Bundy Eludes Helicopter, Hounds, Manhunters," AT, 06-09-77. The "condo" witness information comes from: Cunningham, "Slay Suspect Escapes in Leap from Window," RMN, 06-08-77.

72   Sabella, "The Bundy Manhunt: Is a Killer Loose in Aspen?" AT, 06-09-77.

73   Baxter, WC, "The First Twenty Minutes," 02-22-21.

74   Baxter, R/I, I. "Tuesday," 04-05-20.

75   Westerlund, "Statement of Deputy David Westerlund," (06-07-77), PCSO. p. 2.

76   The schoolteacher was Betsy Schroeder. That officers had weapons drawn comes from: Harvey, "The Shadow of a Killer," AT, 06-08-02. Children's observations come from: Sabella, "The Bundy Manhunt: Is a Killer Loose in Aspen?" AT, 06-09-77.

77   Baxter, R/I, I. "Tuesday," 04-05-20.

78   Lucchini, WC, "The Baseball Bats," 04-22-21.

79   Meserole, WC, "Panicked Roommates," 04-21-21.

80   Lucchini, WC, "The Baseball Bats," 04-22-21.

81   Baxter, R/I, II. "Tuesday," 04-05-20.

82   Flatt, R/I with Vince Lahey, I. "The Bundy Manhunt," 11-28-18.

83   That Mark Lewy most likely brought the roll of film to be developed at The Walnut House comes from: Ikeda, R/I, I. "Kienast's Department," 08-18-19.

84   In 2020, Newton wrote, "Our lab most likely was the lab that developed the film for Mark Lewy. We generally processed all the film for the Aspen Police Department and the Pitkin County Sheriff's Office. Back in '77, we only did black and white film in-house. It was completed overnight or the same day if rush service was required. Color film, we processed off site but overnight. Our policy was to return all prints and negatives to the client after processing." Newton, WC, "The Walnut House," 07-19-20. Newton understood how important this image could be to law enforcement, so he was working as quickly as he could, given the inherent time constraints of the chemicals he would need to use. Eilers, WC, "The Lewy Photograph," 05-24-20.

85   Horan, R/I, I. "The Bundy Manhunt," 05-31-20.

86   Sabella, "Departing Garms Sees Police Problem," AT, 08-11-77; Baxter, WC, "Art Hougland," 11-12-20.

87   In correspondence with the author in 2019, Garms noted that he couldn't recall where he was when Bundy escaped. He did acknowledge that it would be normal for him to find out who was on duty, where they were located, and make his reassignment decisions based on that information. Garms, WC, "The Manhunt," 10-28-19.

88   Ibid.

89   That drivers could only make it a third of the way up Independence Pass comes from: Baxter, R/I, II. "Tuesday," 04-05-20. That the Crestahaus Roadblock would prevent anyone from existing Aspen in an easterly direction comes from: Baxter, WC, "The Roadblocks," 01-05-21.

90   Interviewed in 2021, Baxter couldn't recall whether it was Marta Steinmetz or Betty Erickson that alerted her to the roadblock's creation.

91   Baxter, WC, "The Roadblocks," 01-05-21. The Maroon Creek Bridge was a 600-foot-long, steel trestle span which was technically outside city limits and subject to Sheriff Kienast's authority.

92   Baxter, WC, "The First Twenty Minutes," 02-22-21.

93   The secretary was Colleen Curtis. The dogs were requested from Cherry Hills Village, Denver, and Summit County. Sabella, "The Bundy Manhunt: Is a Killer Loose in Aspen?" AT, 06-09-77.

94   Baxter, WC, "The Gravel Jogging Trail," 03-08-21.

95   Flatt, R/I with Vince Lahey, I. "The Bundy Manhunt," 11-28-18.

96   Baxter, WC, "The Gravel Jogging Trail," 03-08-21.

97   Flatt, R/I with Vince Lahey, I. "The Bundy Manhunt," 11-28-18.

98   Colorado filmmaker, Vince Lahey, notes, "It's named after Slaughterhouse Falls, a notorious section of the Roaring Fork River, beloved by river rafters and kayakers alike for its short but powerfully

tricky drop in the river."

99   In initial correspondence, Baxter placed the roadblock at the intersection of Cemetery Lane and Red Butte Drive. In our second research trip to Aspen, however, she provided us with a personal tour of the roadblock locations. While standing at the Slaughterhouse Bridge, Baxter acknowledged making an error in her initial email correspondence and stated that the roadblock was set up in the center of the bridge. Baxter, OC, "Slaughterhouse Bridge Correction," 06-29-23.

100 The importance of this roadblock comes from: Baxter, WC, "The Roadblocks," 01-05-21.

101 Nancy Baxter explained that 10-23 was code for "arrived at the scene," and 10-53 meant a roadblock had been established at that location. Baxter, OC, "Slaughterhouse Bridge Correction," 06-29-23.

102 Baxter, R/I, I. "Tuesday," 04-05-20.

103 "Former Pitkin County Sheriff Bob Braudis Discusses Interactions with Ted Bundy," YouTube, 02-15-19; Baxter, R/I, I. "Tuesday," 04-05-20.

104 "Former Pitkin County Sheriff Bob Braudis Discusses Interactions with Ted Bundy," YouTube, 02-15-19.

105 Baxter, WC, "The Roadblocks," 01-05-21.

106 Ibid.

107 Memories of the Catherine Store come from: Baxter, WC, "The Roadblocks," 01-05-21; Murray, WC, "Catherine Store—Carbondale," 01-17-21. The fact that it was of cinder block construction and sold day old bread comes from: Burton, "Catherine Store changes hands, but won't change ambience," PI, 04-17-03.

108 There were two types of sirens available to officers and deputies within their patrol vehicles. Which one they employed depended upon the type of terrain they were transiting through. In certain environments, the surrounding trees, buildings, and even mountainsides could absorb most of the sound. Deputies could use a pulse wail, an effective if merciless siren that wails. This was a high-low siren that everyone was familiar with, friend or foe. There was also the slow build-up of the longer howler. One alternated the sirens via a switch on a control box which was mounted on either the dashboard or between the seats of the console cubby. Murray, WC, "Catherine Store—Carbondale," 01-17-21. Information concerning the pasture near the store comes from: Baxter, WC, "The Roadblocks," 01-05-21.

109 Baxter, WC, "The First Twenty Minutes," 02-22-21. The state troopers in the lower valley had received a BOLO (be on the lookout) notice for Ted Bundy. Trooper Dan Ogan was dedicated to I-70, east of Glenwood Springs, but he was permitted to patrol up to Buffalo Valley on Highway 82. Troopers Bruce Barry and Del Sisko were in their respective patrol cars, keeping an eye out for the fugitive in Basalt and El Jebel. In Basalt, Chief Bill Thompson had Officer Jim Stryker out looking for Bundy. Portions of their town also fell within Eagle County boundary lines, so their sheriff had Deputy Danny Williams tasked to the area as well. Loyd, WC, "Post-Jump Patrols," 03-04-21.

110 Unless a driver had been given a Class 1 traffic offense, Trooper Loyd would essentially be representing the prosecution side of the counselor's table before a judge. He spent a lot of time at the courthouse. Loyd, R/I, I. "Colorado State Patrol," 02-21-21.

111 Information concerning the Conoco gas station comes from: Baxter, WC, "The Roadblocks," 01-05-21.

112 Wackerle, "Old Snowmass Conoco Property Changes Hands," ADN, 12-26-19.

113 Loyd, R/I, I. "Colorado State Patrol," 02-21-21.

114 Further information concerning the lawmen manning the Old Snowmass Conoco Roadblock may be found in: Baxter, WC, "Old Snowmass Conoco," 01-20-21.

115 Ibid. Aspenites were not used to seeing this type of cross-draw weapon as the sheriff and chief of police forbade their use. It was considered too easy for a criminal to strike an officer wearing such a holster, and then seize his revolver. Murray, WC, "Cross-Draw Holster," 02-23-21.

116 The friend in question was Sandy Detlefsen. Baxter, WC, "Tuesday," 05-13-20. Dialogue comes from: Baxter, R/I, III. "Wednesday," 04-18-20.

117 Baxter, WC, "Tuesday," 05-13-20.

118 Baxter, R/I, I. "Tuesday," 04-05-20.
119 Baxter, WC, "The First Twenty Minutes," 02-22-21; Baxter, R/I, I. "Tuesday," 04-05-20; Sabella, "The Bundy Manhunt: Is a Killer Loose in Aspen?" AT, 06-09-77; Baxter, WC, "Tuesday," 05-13-20.
120 Through correspondence with the author in 2019, Garms had little recollection of this interaction with the witness. Garms, WC, "The Manhunt Part II," 10-30-19. Details concerning this interaction comes from: Sabella, "The Bundy Manhunt: Is a Killer Loose in Aspen?" AT, 06-09-77.
121 The deputy who Baxter sent was Bill McCrocklin. Baxter, WC, "Tuesday," 05-13-20.
122 That woman was Nancy Dick, a well-respected politician, who was serving in the Colorado House of Representatives. Dialogue exchange between Dick and Baxter comes from: Baxter, R/I, I. "Tuesday," 04-05-20.
123 Ibid.
124 Dialogue exchange between Baxter and Braudis comes from three sources: "Former Pitkin County Sheriff Bob Braudis Discusses Interactions with Ted Bundy," YouTube, 02-15-19; Baxter, R/I, I. "Tuesday," 04-05-20; Baxter, WC, "Tuesday," 05-13-20.
125 Deputy Braudis knew that Nancy Dick lived alone in a secluded area, and thought it was a good idea to stop by to assure her the sheriff's department stood ready to protect the community. Trouble was, the deputy had not been directed to make such a gesture of protection. He had initially been ordered to report to the sheriff's office. Baxter brought Braudis up to speed on the concern about the rugby shirt. The deputy was filled with mixed emotions. He was upset that he'd have to report to the station, bewildered by the strange coincidence in attire, but he recognized the humor in what surely must have been an anxious few moments for Nancy Dick.
126 This was around 11:10 a.m. The location of KSPN radio station comes from: Travers, "John Busch, Aspen Gay Icon and Champion of Cinema, Inducted in the Hall of Fame," AT, 01-17-19.
127 The DJ making the announcement was Dave Judy. Danforth, WC, "Dave Judy," 06-28-20. Dialogue of the transmission comes from: DaRonch (05-20-20). "Ted Bundy first escape news clip, 06-08-77. YouTube.
128 "Me and Bobby McGee," written by Kris Kristofferson, based on a suggestion from Fred Foster. Song performed by Janis Joplin, 1971 Columbia Records. That this song was played in Aspen during the manhunt comes from: Doud, "Bundy May Have Joined Throng 'Escaping' in Aspen," TNT, 06-09-77.
129 Lucas, WC, "The First Escape," 07-21-19.
130 Lucas, R/S, I. "Ted Bundy Memories," 08-16-19.
131 This Ward Lucas-related section of the book comes from three sources: Lucas, R/I, I. "Ted Bundy Memories," 08-16-19; Lucas, WC, "The First Escape," 07-21-19; Lucas (02-17-19). "My Interview with Netflix for the Documentary on Ted Bundy."

Chapter 2, "Dragnet"
132 Haynes, WC, "Maroon Creek Bridge Roadblock," 12-26-19.
133 Ibid; Haynes & Ikeda, R/S, I. "Kienast's Department," 08-18-19. In this same recorded interview, Keith Ikeda remarked, "My friend, who was living there [in Aspen], was telling me that it was really scary, because there were all these people running around with guns. And, it wasn't just the police."
134 Haynes, R/I, I. "Kienast's Department," 08-18-19; Haynes, WC, "Maroon Creek Bridge Roadblock," 12-26-19. His friends and colleagues were John Wood and George Fridell, both of whom landed positions in the Aspen PD.
135 Ikeda, R/I, I. "Kienast's Department," 08-18-19.
136 By speaking with two colleagues, who had been hired by the Aspen PD, Gary Haynes understood Sheriff Kienast's department was undergoing a significant turnover. There was a decreasing number of carryovers and an emerging band of road warriors. Carryovers were, quite simply, men who had been hired by the sheriff's predecessor. Kienast wanted educated, more left-leaning personnel. Haynes could tell the man had a vision for his community. One could already see the transition in the personality of the department. This turnover, this dramatic shift not only in the number of personnel, but in person-

ality, was due in large part to Kienast's philosophy of what it meant to be a deputy. He believed it was hard to change a good cop into a good citizen, but it was easy to change a good citizen into a good cop. Haynes & Ikeda, R/I, I. "Kienast's Department," 08-18-19.
137   Haynes, R/I, I & II. "Kienast's Department," 08-18-19.
138   Haynes, R/I, II. "Kienast's Department," 08-18-19.
139   Ibid.
140   Eilers, WC, "The Lewy Photograph," 05-24-20.
141   Unk, "Bundy Gets New Legal Help for New Charges," AT, 06-16-77.
142   Every officer, during their first twelve months, performed on the job training. Shooting, high-speed car chases, saving lives; it was all handled on the fly, with no formalized instruction. With only three months on the job when Bundy fled, Braudis was still considered a road warrior, with nine months to go. "Former Pitkin County Sheriff Bob Braudis Discusses Interactions with Ted Bundy," YouTube, 02-15-19.
143   Unk, "Bundy Gets New Legal Help for New Charges," AT, 06-16-77.
144   Ibid.
145   This would have been around 12:20 p.m.
146   Sabella, "The Bundy Manhunt: Is a Killer Loose in Aspen?" AT, 06-09-77. Baxter, R/I & II. "Tuesday," 04-05-20; Hauter, "Xerox Contract," ACC, 09-12-77, p. 1.
147   Larsen, "Bundy: The Deliberate Stranger," p. 209.
148   White, OC, "The Xerox Window," 07-02-23. During the author's second research trip to Aspen, Nancy Baxter provided him with a personal tour of the interior of the courthouse and showed him where the Xerox copy machine used to reside. It was at the end of the hallway on the second floor. Baxter noted, "I doubt sincerely that Bundy was allowed to use the machine alone. You had to have a special key fob that allowed the number of copies to be added to your proper account, i.e. district attorney's office, sheriff's office, court clerk, etc." Baxter, OC, "Xerox Copy Machine," 06-29-23.
149   Baxter, R/I, I. "Tuesday," 04-05-20. Baxter, R/I, III. "Wednesday," 04-18-20. Baxter also recalls that there were two other pharmacies in town. Carl's was on Main Street and it had two stories. The main floor had the liquor, groceries, and pharmacy. Upstairs was the gun store. The third pharmacy, Aspen Drug, was located just up Galena Street from Aspen City Hall, on the northwest corner of East Hyman Avenue.
150   "Former Pitkin County Sheriff Bob Braudis Discusses Interactions with Ted Bundy," YouTube, 02-15-19.
151   Sabella, "The Bundy Manhunt: Is a Killer Loose in Aspen?" AT, 06-09-77. They also requested that Garfield, Eagle, and Lake County assist their endeavor by complying voluntarily with the measure. Unk, "Aspen Starts Door-to-Door Search," DP, 06-08-77.
152   Baxter, WC, "The East Sopris Creek Nightmare," 02-22-21.
153   Ibid.
154   Baxter, WC, "The Roadblocks," 01-05-21.
155   Sabella, "Departing Garms Sees Police Problem," AT, 08-11-77.
156   Through correspondence with the author in 2019, Garms had little recollection of this interaction with the witness. Details concerning this interaction come from: Sabella, "The Bundy Manhunt: Is a Killer Loose in Aspen?" AT, 06-09-77.
157   Kempfert, R/I, I. "The Deputies of Love," 12-30-20; Baxter, WC, "The Roadblocks," 01-05-21.
158   Ibid.
159   Murphy was considered overly caring by one of his fellow deputies, and there was a belief that he lacked good investigative sense. Murphy seemed to lack street skills, and this put him at odds with men like Don Davis. There was friction between them. How safe was Murphy's job? He had worked with Kienast back when both were juvenile officers with the city's police department. Rumor had it that this was why Murphy had managed to retain his position as a deputy after Kienast was elected sheriff. Ikeda, R/I, I. "Kienast's Department," 08-18-19.
160   That Kempfert smoked Marlboros comes from: Kempfert, WC, "The Notification," 01-06-21.

161 Deputy Kempfert's badge number—72—comes from: Kempfert, WC, "Badge 72," 03-16-24.
162 Radio dialogue between Kempfert and Baxter comes from: Baxter, OC, "Brush Creek Roadblock Radio Dialogue," 03-16-24.
163 Westerlund, "Statement of Deputy David Westerlund," (06-07-77), PCSO. p. 2.
164 Lahey, WC with Charles Leidner, "Departing Aspen," 09-29-20; Facebook, (02-09-21). "Charles Leidner, 06-07-77," www.facebook.com.
165 Ibid.
166 This man was fifty-year-old, Ted Pendleton. His partner was John Masterbrook. Unk, "Net Out for Bundy Hauls in Marijuana," DP, 06-08-77.
167 In Richard W. Larsen's, "Bundy: The Deliberate Stranger," Larsen notes that this incident took place on the second day of the search. Newspaper reports from The Aspen Times as well as The Denver Post, published on June 8, however, refer to the incident as having taken place the day before. Sending the sizeable haul of marijuana to the Colorado Bureau of Investigation, as per protocol, would have to wait for this manhunt business to conclude. Horan, R/I, I. "The Bundy Manhunt," 05-31-20.
168 Dialogue exchange comes from: Wolf & Winn, "Part 6: Memories of Colorado—Escape and Capture," SCJ, 10-19-78. There are also two variations of this conversation. One is attributed to Ted Pendleton and a deputy that is escorting him from his arraignment back to his cell. In conversations with law enforcement officers from the Roaring Fork Valley, however, it is evident that court was not in session every day. Arraignments took time. It does not seem probable that Pendleton would not have heard of the name Ted Bundy during that eventful week. The second source is correspondence between documentary filmmaker, Vince Lahey, and Bundy's attorney, Charles Leidner. The attorney notes this conversation took place at the jail only hours after Bundy made his leap for freedom.
169 This Ward Lucas-related section of the book comes from three sources: Lucas, R/I, I. "Ted Bundy Memories," 08-16-19; Lucas, WC, "The First Escape," 07-21-19; Lucas, (02-17-19). "My Interview with Netflix for the Documentary on Ted Bundy."
170 Dialogue comes from: Lucas, R/I, I. "Ted Bundy Memories," 08-16-19.
171 Haynes, R/I, I. "Kienast's Department," 08-18-19. Baxter confirmed that Davis and Braudis were the only two men in town who physically intimidated Bundy. Baxter, R/I, I. "Tuesday," 04-05-20. That Davis had ten years of experience comes from: Unk, "Sheriff's Office Down Six Officers," AT, 07-14-77.
172 That Davis was the legs of the department comes from: Ikeda, R/I, I. "Kienast's Department," 08-18-19. That Sheriff Kienast was smart enough to take advice from Davis comes from: Baxter, R/I, I. "Tuesday," 05-05-20; Baxter, R/I, III. "Wednesday," 05-18-20. Gary Haynes added, "Dick was more at the 10,000-foot view level and Don Davis was the sheriff, for all intents and purposes." Haynes, R/I, I. "Kienast's Department," 08-18-19.
173 Baxter, R/I, II. "Tuesday," 05-05-20; Baxter, OC, "The Dogs," 05-05-20.
174 With only three weeks on the job as a traffic control officer, many in the department believed Kathy Earl was a novice. This was simply not true. After earning a bachelor's degree at California Polytechnic State University, she worked as a correctional officer at California Rehabilitation Center—Norco. For three years, she handled what could only be described as volatile and unpredictable people. Earl (Kennell Silver), R/I, I. "The Bundy Manhunt," 06-29-20.
175 Earl [Kennell Silver], R/I, I. "The Bundy Manhunt," 06-29-20.
176 Ibid. Uniform information comes from: Baxter, WC, "Tuesday," 05-13-20.
177 Nancy Baxter writes, "...every time I think of her dumped on Owl Creek Road, I weep. It was one of the least traveled roads in the whole valley, so she [Caryn Campbell] had no hope of being found before she died. That always got me." Baxter, WC, "Caryn Campbell & 4-Wheel Drive Roads," 02-12-21.
178 Baxter, WC, "The Roadblocks," 01-05-21.
179 This Ward Lucas-related section of the book comes from three sources: Lucas, R/I, I. "Ted Bundy Memories," 08-16-19; Lucas, WC, "The First Escape," 07-21-19; Lucas, (02-17-19). "My Interview with Netflix for the Documentary on Ted Bundy."
180 Dialogue comes from: Lucas, WC, "The First Escape," 07-21-19.
181 The pilot had logged a VFR flight plan with the local Civil Aviation Authority prior to depart-

ing Denver. The Visual Flight Rules regulations were quite simple. The pilot operates his or her aircraft through weather conditions that are clear enough to permit the pilot to see where the aircraft is headed.

182   Russell, "Family, friends remember former Routt County Sheriff Gary Wall," SP&T, 07-23-18. Gary Wall had been Gerald Ford's law enforcement liaison every time the president used to come to town. Lamont, "Vail Police Chief Gary Wall—The President's Shadow," VT, 01-31-75.

183   Dialogue exchange between Wall and Loyd comes from: Loyd, R/I, I. "Colorado State Patrol," 02-21-21.

184   Dialogue exchange between Loyd and Sgt. Lacefield comes from: Loyd, R/I, I. "Colorado State Patrol," 02-21-21. An interesting historical side note here, is that Gary Wall was—at that time—investigating the Julie Cunningham Missing Person's Case, a woman Bundy would later confess to killing. Unk, "Special Bulletin: Missing Person—Julie Cunningham," Colorado Bureau of Investigation, 04-11-75, p. 1.

185   Loyd, R/I, I. "Colorado State Patrol," 02-21-21.

186   Ibid.

187   The employee from the Garfield County Jail was Lucy Moreno.

188   Deputy Leon Murray notes, "Under Colorado law, the maximum time you can be sentenced into a county jail is two years. If your sentence is longer than that, you go to a Prison." Identity of this specific fugitive comes from two sources: Larsen, "FBI Joins Colorado Manhunt," SDT, 06-10-77; Larsen, "Bundy Believed Still in Mountains," SDT, 06-11-77.

189   Folder 4, "Message for the FBI," Ted Bundy Filofax entry, 954-29-4, Box 39. KCA, Seattle, Washington, p. 52. Bundy made this entry in his planner fifteen days before he jumped. It is potential evidence that he was planning to jump even sooner.

190   Baxter, R/I, III. "Wednesday," 04-18-20.

191   Baxter had to answer to the sheriff and the chief of police, as both offices co-paid the bills for her department. Her authority, for lack of a better word, fell within clearly understood parameters. Baxter, R/S, III. "Wednesday," 04-18-20; Baxter, R/I, IV. "Dispatch Center and Aspen PD," 04-18-20.

192   Rollins, "Who is Ted Bundy?" AT, 08-04-77; Cunningham, "It's a Stirring Name," RMN, 06-09-77.

193   FBI, "Clearing T. Bundy," [Teletype]. 06-11-77.

194   Doud, "Searchers Comb Aspen for Bundy," TNT, 06-08-77; Lobb, "Possible Accomplice Tie Probed," SLT, 06-09-77. Another lead came into dispatch. A shiny, green Fiat, with no license plates, was stopped at the Crestahaus Roadblock. The occupants of this vehicle were closely scrutinized. The female driver, estimated to be around twenty-three, was considered "Indian" in appearance, with a dark complexion. When she inquired about camping areas in the region, and deputies noticed there was no camping gear within the vehicle, they leaned in closer, to observe her passenger. A Caucasian man, with blue eyes and a pale complexion was interesting enough, but the passenger bore a close resemblance to the fugitive. Deputies compared him to the flyer they had recently been handed, and concluded it wasn't Bundy. FBI, "Ted Bundy—a.k.a. Theodore Robert Cowell [teletype]." 06-11-77. That there was an unidentified passenger aboard a flight from Aspen to Denver comes from: Cunningham, "Slay Suspect Escapes in Leap from Window," RMN, 06-08-77. The pilot was Ken Roper.

195   The leader of Aspen Mountain Rescue at the time was Fred Braun. The organization's response, as well as the housekey story, come from: Swersky, OC, "Aspen Mountain Rescue," Circa 03-20. Interviewed in 2020, Dave Stapleton confirmed that his father-in-law, Fred Braun, loaned radio sets to the Aspen PD as well. Stapleton, R/I, I. "Aspen Mountain Rescue," 07-17-20.

196   Harvey, "The Shadow of a Killer," AT, 06-08-77. The psychologist who reported this sign was Dr. Ross Goldstein. Goldstein was aware of the crimes Ted Bundy was accused of committing, but somehow, the heinousness of those crimes was lost in what he called, the Robin Hood flavor of the man's escape.

197   Dialogue exchange between Baxter and Zimmerman comes from: Baxter, WC, "The East Sopris Creek Nightmare," 02-22-21.

198   This Ward Lucas-related section of the book comes from three sources: Lucas, R/I, I. "Ted Bundy

Memories," 08-16-19; Lucas, WC, "The First Escape," 07-21-19; Lucas, (02-17-19). "My Interview with Netflix for the Documentary on Ted Bundy."

199 Baxter, WC, "School Evacuations," 02-02-21.

200 Radio broadcast, asking parents to pick up their children at school comes from: Unk, "Bundy Left Alone in Aspen Courtroom, Leaps Out Window, Escapes into Hills," SLT, 06-08-77. Residents who were stuck at work, having to make calls comes from: Harvey, "The Shadow of a Killer," AT, 06-08-02.

201 Baxter, WC, "School Evacuations," 02-02-21.

202 Baxter, R/I, II. "Tuesday," 05-05-20.

203 Baxter, WC, "School Evacuations," 02-02-21.

204 Information concerning Wildwood School comes from: Unk, "Bob Lewis leaves legacy of education, environmentalism," AT, 08-01-05. Information concerning the Aspen Valley Ski Club comes from: Baxter, WC, "Tuesday," 05-13-20.

205 Mitchell [Braudis], R/I, I. "Smuggler Mine," 02-07-21.

206 Dialogue comes from: Lucas, R/S, I. "Ted Bundy Memories," 08-16-19.

207 Dialogue comes from: Lucas, (02-08-19). "This Former News Anchor Flew to Aspen and Tried to Find Ted Bundy Himself," YouTube.

208 That secretary was Whitney Wulff.

209 Unk, "Bundy Escapes in Colorado," DN, 06-07-77.

210 Dialogue comes from: McCarten & Brack, "Colorado Escape—Manhunt for Bundy," SPI, 06-08-77; Undersheriff Meyers understood that roadblocks were going up, checkpoints that were being manned by Aspen PD and his own deputies. He couldn't speak for the city police, but as far as county was concerned, they were noticeably short on marked vehicles. The county had access to a large white 4-wheel drive vehicle, a couple of different dark blue four-door sedans, a couple of white Broncos, and the undersheriff's unmarked four-door sedan. With nearly twenty deputies on staff, that wasn't going to cut it. He knew that deputies would have to use their own vehicles in the manhunt. Murray, WC, "PCSO Vehicle Inventory," 01-18-21.

211 McCarten & Brack, "Colorado Escape—Manhunt for Bundy," SPI, 06-08-77. After careful inspection of the impressions Bundy left in the grass, authorities believed he may have injured is right ankle. They surmised that he may have even waded into the icy-cold Roaring Fork River, to relieve inflammation. Larsen, "Bundy May Have Injured Ankle," SDT, 06-09-77.

212 Dialogue exchange comes from: "Conversations with a Killer: The Ted Bundy Tapes," Berlinger, 2019. Film.

213 A privately-owned helicopter service, based out of Durango, dispatched this chopper from Grand Junction, to assist in the manhunt. Cunningham, "Slay Suspect Escapes in Leap from Window," RMN, 06-08-77; Clifford, "Bundy's Week of Freedom," AT, 06-23-77.

214 Information concerning the helicopter comes from: Clifford, "Bundy's Week of Freedom," AT, 06-23-77. Information concerning the sunglasses comes from: Baxter, R/I, I. "Tuesday," 04-05-20. Maureen Markov recalls that they were Vaurnet-brand sunglasses. Markov [Higgins], WC, "Tuesday," 12-06-19.

215 Information concerning the Rocky Mountain Airways flight comes from: Sabella, "The Bundy Manhunt: Is a Killer Loose in Aspen?" AT, 06-09-77. Information concerning the misunderstanding with Aspen Airways comes from: Unk, "Bundy Left Alone in Aspen Courtroom, Leaps Out Window, Escapes into Hills," SLT, 06-08-77.

216 Horan, R/I, I. "The Bundy Manhunt," 05-31-20.

217 Cunningham, "Slay Suspect Escapes in Leap from Window," RMN, 06-08-77.

218 Spiers, R/I, I. "The Bundy Manhunt," 08-09-20.

219 Spiers, WC, "Deputized," 08-10-20; Spiers, R/I, I. "The Bundy Manhunt," 08-09-20.

220 Auslander, "Explanation of Aspen's Civil War Monument Planned," AT, 08-24-17.

221 White, WC, "Search Dogs on Tuesday," 10-12-20.

222 White, R/I, I. "The Bundy Manhunt," 08-31-20.

223 Gilmour & Grossman, "Evening News—Ted Bundy's Escape," 06-07-77.
224 White, WC, "Search Dogs on Tuesday," 10-12-20.
225 Sabella, "The Bundy Manhunt: Is a Killer Loose in Aspen?" AT, 06-09-77.
226 This Ward Lucas-related section of the book comes from three sources: Lucas, R/I, I. "Ted Bundy Memories," 08-16-19; Lucas, WC, "The First Escape," 07-21-19; Lucas, (02-17-19). "My Interview with Netflix for the Documentary on Ted Bundy." Dialogue comes from: Lucas, R/S, I. "Ted Bundy Memories," 08-16-19.
227 "Conversations with a Killer: The Ted Bundy Tapes," Berlinger, 2019. Film. The address for this specific stakeout was 4123 12th Avenue Northeast, in Seattle.
228 Markov (Higgins), WC, "Tuesday," 12-06-19.
229 Markov (Higgins), WC, "The Gredig Family," 02-08-21.
230 The secretary who called Higgins was Marcia DeCamp. Markov (Higgins), WC, "Tuesday," 12-06-19.
231 Ibid.
232 This news anchor was Sandy Gilmour of KUTV Newswatch 2, a CBS affiliate based out of Salt Lake City. Dialogue comes from: "Conversations with a Killer: The Ted Bundy Tapes," Berlinger, 2019. Film.
233 Dialogue exchange between Detective Pete Hayward and reporter, Barbara Grossman comes from: Gilmour & Grossman, "Evening News—Ted Bundy's Escape," Salt Lake City, Utah, 06-07-77.
234 Unk, "Bundy Escape: Aspen Bungled," DN, 06-09-77.
235 Dialogue comes from: Doud, "Blame for Bundy's Escape Exchanged," TNT, 06-09-77.
236 Tony Vagneur stated that this incident would have occurred around 5:30 p.m. Vagneur, WC, "The Drunk Posse," 08-01-20. Vagneur was defending the interests of the property owner, Henry Stein.
237 Dialogue comes from: Vagneur, "Saddle Sore," AT, 10-24-09; Vagneur, WC, "The Drunk Posse," 08-01-20.
238 Volunteer searchers who had focused their efforts on the Hunter Creek region, were told to cease their efforts by 10:00 p.m. Folks were thanked for their time and asked to go home, get some sleep, and report for duty again at 4:30 a.m. Information concerning roving patrols comes from: Sabella, "The Bundy Manhunt: Is a Killer Loose in Aspen?" AT, 06-09-77. Information concerning Hunter Creek comes from: Unk, "Aspen Starts Door-to-Door Search," DP, 06-08-77. The muster time for the following morning comes from: Sabella, "The Bundy Manhunt: Is a Killer Loose in Aspen?" AT, 06-09-77.
239 Sabella, "The Bundy Manhunt: Is a Killer Loose in Aspen?" AT, 06-09-77; Baxter, R/I & II. "Tuesday," 04-05-20. Vehicle specs come from: The Morning Call, (03-01-21). "1967 Kaiser Jeepster Commando Convertible Deluxe," www.mccall.com. Steinmetz preferred the reverberating whine of Ravi Shankar's sitar. She had a cassette deck installed under the dash. Having a convertible, thefts of tape decks were common, so she had it installed securely.
240 Baxter adds that, "Any time you said a letter, you had to use the Colorado law enforcement accepted words for each letter of the alphabet: Adam, Boy, Charles, David, Edward, Frank, George, Henry, Isaac, John, King, Lincoln, Mary, Ned, Oscar, Paul, Queen, Robert, Sam, Thomas, Union, Victor, William, X-ray, Young, and Zed." Baxter, WC, "The 2200 Time Check," 03-01-21.
241 Ibid.
242 Baxter, WC, "The East Sopris Creek Nightmare," 02-22-21.
243 Roberts, WC, "-39 Degrees," 12-10-20.
244 Dialogue comes from: Roberts, R/I, I. "The Bundy Manhunt," 06-22-20.
245 Dialogue comes from: Baxter, WC, "The East Sopris Creek Nightmare," 02-22-21.
246 Ibid.
247 Interviewed in 2018 by Colorado filmmaker, Vince Lahey, Gene Flatt stated, "They sent me up on top of Independence Pass. At the top, or close to it, Eagle County Sheriff and three of his deputies were there and they were loaded. They had shotguns, rifles, pistols, and they pulled down on people when they stopped them." The Pass was initially opened in late May 1977. A landslide then occurred, and drivers were only able to make it a third of the way up the pass by the time Bundy jumped. Even if

the slide had been cleared, vehicles would have been unable to proceed. The Highway Department had road barricades up and excavation equipment was parked on the scene. New guard rails and retaining walls wouldn't be completed for at least a couple of weeks. Unk, "Independence Pass to Open by Mid-June," AT, 06-09-77. The author believes that, after four decades, Flatt is misremembering the precise location of the checkpoint he manned. The Difficult Campground Roadblock meets all his principal memories: the rain on Tuesday night, darkness, and boulders coming down onto the highway. In consulting with the dispatch supervisor who directed the creation of that roadblock—Nancy Baxter—she confirmed that the Difficult Campground Roadblock was the farthest checkpoint on the east side of town, heading up toward the pass.

248 Markov (Higgins), WC, "The Caddy Stop," 12-23-19; Markov, "Bundy Redux (Letter to the Editor)," AT, 12-18-05.
249 Murray, R/I, I. "The Bundy Manhunt," 07-14-20; Ikeda, R/I, I. "Kienast's Department," 08-18-19.
250 Baxter, WC, "The Roadblocks," 01-05-21.
251 Dialogue comes from: Flatt, R/I with Vince Lahey, I. "The Bundy Manhunt," 11-28-18.
252 Dialogue exchange comes from: Baxter, WC, "The East Sopris Creek Nightmare," 02-21-21.

Chapter 3, "The Posse"

253 Dialogue comes from: Roberts, R/I, I. "The Bundy Manhunt," 06-22-20.
254 Hallam Lake is part of a twenty-five-acre nature preserve, overseen by the Aspen Center for Environmental Studies. There was a half-mile loop nature trail that was open to the public year-round, and the preserve would be a good place for a fugitive to hide and lay low until the coast was clear. Aspen Center for Environmental Studies, (12-19-20). "Hallam Lake," www.aspennature.org.
255 Quirk, R/S, I. "Lone Wolf Memories," 12-08-20.
256 Ibid.
257 Dialogue comes from: Baxter, WC, "The Egg Timer," 03-03-21.
258 Baxter, R/I, IV. "Dispatch Center and Aspen PD," 04-18-20.
259 Baxter, R/I, III. "Wednesday," 04-18-20.
260 That dispatchers had to be careful what they said over the airwaves comes from: Baxter, R/I, II. "Tuesday," 04-05-20. Ten-code information comes from: Baxter, R/I, I. "Tuesday," 04-05-20. Ten-code examples comes from: Colorado State Patrol (04-20-20). "State Patrol Ten-codes," wiki.radioreference.com.
261 Baxter, WC, "Worried," 03-18-21.
262 Baxter, R/I, III. "Wednesday," 04-18-20.
263 Ibid. Baxter believes these logs were destroyed years ago.
264 Baxter, R/I, IV. "Dispatch Center and Aspen PD," 04-18-20; Rando, R/I, I. "Six Days," 04-18-21.
265 This was Dave Wright.
266 Baxter, R/I, III. "Wednesday," 04-18-20; Baxter, WC, "Dave Wright," 11-12-20.
267 How Aspen PD officers obtained their sidearms varied from person to person. When Michael Chandler was hired, he was told to buy his own. He purchased a .357 S&W Magnum and used it until he was promoted to detective. Due to the popularity of the Dirty Harry movies, he switched to a long barreled, .44-caliber Magnum, just like the one Clint Eastwood used in the films. The weapon kicked so hard, however, that it could break someone's wrist. It didn't take long for him to hang it up and revert back to the .357. Terry Quirk carried a department-issued .357. Hugh Roberts had brought his own S&W Mod. 65 .357 when he was hired over four years ago. During Chief Marty Hershey's reign, Hougland's predecessor, all officers were required to carry the same handgun in a uniform caliber. As Hugh Roberts recalled, Hershey decided his officers should carry S&W Model 49's. These were small, lightweight, five-shot, short barreled .38 specials, designed for undercover carry only. Chet Zajac, being one of the newest members of the team, was issued one of these hand-me-down weapons. He referred to it as his peashooter and privately wished he was carrying something else. Chandler, WC, "Sidearms," 12-20-20; Roberts, WC, "S&W Model 49's," 12-20-20; Zajac, WC, "The .38," 12-20-20; Zajac, R/I, I. "Red Mountain Rookie," 12-13-20.

268 Information concerning Fast Eddie's comes from: Yoder, "Letter: An Aspen Legend [Ed Golub]," AT, 09-11-13. Information concerning what items Zajac purchased comes from: Zajac, R/I, I. "Red Mountain Rookie," 12-13-20.
269 Dialogue exchange between Steinmetz and Zajac comes from: Zajac, R/I. "Red Mountain Rookie," 12-13-20.
270 Roberts, R/I, I. "The Bundy Manhunt," 06-22-20.
271 Roberts, WC, "Bundy," 06-20-20.
272 According to the following source: Doud, "Searchers Comb Aspen for Bundy," TNT, 06-08-77, this posse formed around 12:30 p.m., yet multiple sources, interviewed independently for this book, place it in the early morning hours.
273 Dialogue comes from: White, WC, "Becoming an Officer," 10-25-20.
274 Ibid. White first went down to the police department and was given two written examinations. He then endured a rigorous psychological evaluation, which he found humorous. This was followed by two oral boards and, finally, he was accepted into the academy.
275 Information concerning the 2nd Calvary Regiment comes from: Wikipedia, "2nd Calvary Regiment," 03-09-21.
276 Whitmire's statement comes from: Flatt, R/I, Interview with Vince Lahey, I. "The Bundy Manhunt," 11-28-18.
277 Stonington, "Former Sheriff Dies in Arizona," AT, 03-27-06.
278 Flatt, R/I, Interview with Vince Lahey, I. "The Bundy Manhunt," 11-28-18.
279 Baxter, R/I, III. "Wednesday," 04-18-20.
280 Size of the posse comes from: Unk, "Officials Hunt Aspen Area Hills for Bundy," SLT, 06-09-77; Larsen, "Bundy Hunted in Mountains," SDT, 06-08-77; Larsen, "Bundy Traced to Mountain Cabin," SDT, 06-12-77.
281 Baxter, R/I, III. "Wednesday," 04-18-20. Information concerning the search dogs comes from: McCarten & Brack, "Colorado Escape—Manhunt for Bundy," SPI, 06-08-77.
282 Dialogue comes from: Baxter, R/I, III. "Wednesday," 04-18-20.
283 The airport manager was Doug McCoy. A good portion of the men he recruited were from neighboring Garfield County. Baxter, WC, "Garfield County Posse," 02-03-21.
284 Ice, WC, "Garfield County Search & Rescue," 02-04-21; Horan, R/I, I. "The Bundy Manhunt," 05-31-20; Sabella, "The Bundy Manhunt: Is a Killer Loose in Aspen?" AT, 06-09-77.
285 The various organizations that volunteered their services during the posse comes from: Sabella, "The Bundy Manhunt: Is a Killer Loose in Aspen?" AT, 06-09-77. Sunburns and five-o'clock shadows comes from: Doud, "Searchers Comb Aspen for Bundy," TNT, 06-08-77. That the mood among the posse was good comes from: Baxter, R/I, III. "Wednesday," 04-18-20. Historically, when the sheriff formed a posse, there weren't a lot of rules or regulations to follow. There was no certification needed, no document signed by Dick Kienast. These were just a handful of men with a good knowledge of the unique terrain in the valley.
286 Doud, "Blame for Bundy's Escape Exchanged," TNT, 06-09-77.
287 Captain Richard "Dick" Wall was a college graduate and a former forward observer with the 8th Army during the Korean War. A real estate mogul, he moved to Aspen where his hobby of skiing quickly morphed into a passion. Search and rescue had always interested him, so he joined the Snowmass Ski Patrol in 1964. Murray, R/I, I. "The Bundy Manhunt," 07-14-20; Unk, "Richard Wall [Obit]," AT, 12-18-12.
288 This was a tourist named David Harris. He met with a reporter prior to departing the scene, saying that several of his friends had been scared the prior night. No one got to sleep until around 4:00 a.m. Every time a dog would bark, they would jolt back to full consciousness.
289 Dialogue comes from: Doud, "Searchers Comb Aspen for Bundy," TNT, 06-08-77.
290 Unk, "Aspen Starts Door-to-Door Search," DP, 06-08-77.
291 That deputies would be required to work sixteen-hour shifts comes from: Markov, WC, "Caddy Stop—Manuscript Corrections," 12-28-19. School closure comes from: Unk, "Officials Hunt Aspen Area

Hills for Bundy," SLT, 06-09-77.
292 Dialogue from Whitney Wulff comes from: Doud, "Blame for Bundy's Escape Exchanged," TNT, 06-09-77.
293 This volunteer was Horst Bealke, a resident of Aspen. Dialogue comes from: Doud, "Searchers Comb Aspen for Bundy," TNT, 06-08-77.
294 Garms, WC, "The Manhunt Part II," 10-30-19.
295 These other three officers were: Bill Dreuding, Darrel Horan, and Robert Bennewate. Sabella, "The Bundy Manhunt: Is a Killer Loose in Aspen?" AT, 06-09-77.
296 Havlen, "Martin Hershey, Former Top Cop and Councilman, Dies," AT, 04-11-02.
297 Through correspondence with the author in 2019, Garms stated he had been observing the mixed reactions people were having to word of Bundy's escape. Since officials had initially referred to Bundy only as a convicted kidnapper, there were quite a few residents who hadn't paid too much attention to him. Garms felt the rank-and-file members of the public were going about their daily business a bit too casually. Garms, WC, "The Manhunt Part II," 10-30-19.
298 Earl [Kennell Silver], R/I, I. "The Bundy Manhunt," 06-29-20.
299 Ibid.
300 Ibid.
301 Location of city council chambers comes from: Baxter, WC, "City Hall," 12-16-20.
302 Quirk, R/I, I. "Lone Wolf Memories," 12-08-20.
303 Quirk, WC, "Burned and Bitter," 12-19-20.
304 Loafers comes from: Cunningham, "Slay Suspect Escapes in Leap from Window," RMN, 06-08-77.
305 Horan, R/I, I. "The Bundy Manhunt," 05-31-20.
306 Some of the older cars in the police department had the bullhorn attached to the roof, but the newer Saabs had them mounted inside the front grille of the car. Inside the vehicle, there were two handheld microphones. One was the standard police radio, to stay in contact with dispatch, while the other was for the external speaker. If, for any reason, this speaker failed, officers had access to handheld units that could be plugged into the cigarette lighter. Murray, WC, "Loudspeaker Gizmo," 02-11-21; Baxter, WC, "Loudspeaker Gizmo," 02-09-21; Baxter, WC, "The Gizmo Announcement," 07-08-24; Facebook, (02-12-21). "Jill von Flotow and the Loudspeaker Gizmo."
307 Unk, "Aspen Starts Door-to-Door Search," DP, 06-08-77.
308 Dialogue exchange comes from: "Former Pitkin County Sheriff Bob Braudis Discusses Interactions with Ted Bundy," YouTube, 02-15-19.
309 This secretary was Colleen Curtis.
310 Dialogue comes from: Doud, "Searchers Comb Aspen for Bundy," TNT, 06-08-77.
311 This secretary was Marcia DeCamp.
312 Baxter, R/I, III. "Wednesday," 04-18-20.
313 Unk, "Aspen Starts Door-to-Door Search," DP, 06-08-77.
314 Unk, "Bundy Gets Phone Credit Card Back," AT, 07-07-77.
315 Sabella, "The Bundy Manhunt: Is a Killer Loose in Aspen?" AT, 06-09-77.
316 Lobb, "Possible Accomplice Tie Probed," SLT, 06-09-77.
317 Telephone calls come from: Larsen, "Bundy was a Prisoner with Privileges," SDT, 06-10-77.
318 College girls bringing Bundy candy and cigarettes comes from: Summerlin, "Ted Bundy Tales Come out of the Woodwork," PI, 04-15-17. Bundy's most recent visitor had been Richard W, Larsen, a reporter for The Seattle Times. That visit had been on May 27. Larsen, "Bundy: Chatty Calmness, then a Desperate Leap," SDT, 07-08-77.
319 The Garfield County spokesman was Al Maggard. The second fugitive was Daniel Kellum. Unk, "Aspen Starts Door-to-Door Search," DP, 06-08-77; Unk, "Officials Hunt Aspen Area Hills for Bundy," SLT, 06-09-77.
320 Unk, "Bundy Escapes in Colorado," DN, 06-07-77. Further sources that state that, in 1977, Bundy was a suspect in multiple rapes and murders, across multiple states, comes from: FBI, "Ted Bundy—a.k.a. Theodore Robert Cowell [teletype]," 06-11-77; Larsen, "Ted Bundy Escapes!" SDT, 06-07-77;

McCarten & Brack, "Colorado Escape—Manhunt for Bundy," SPI, 06-08-77; Cunningham, "Slay Suspect Escapes in Leap from Window," RMN, 06-08-77; Cunningham, "House-to-House Hunt is On for Bundy," RMN, 06-09-77; Unk, "Bundy Escape: Aspen Bungled," DN, 06-09-77.

321 Dialogue of Melinda Severance comes from: Unk, "Officials Hunt Aspen Area Hills for Bundy," SLT, 06-09-77.

322 Dialogue of Deborah Pellow comes from: Unk, "Officials Hunt Aspen Area Hills for Bundy," SLT, 06-09-77.

323 In Colorado in 1977, each judicial district had an elected district attorney. This would be the top prosecutor for the region. The 9th Judicial District was comprised of Garfield, Pitkin, and Rio Blanco Counties. The main office for the D.A. was in Glenwood Springs. Tucker had a Chief Trial Deputy District Attorney just down the hall from his office. Deputy District Attorneys—subordinate to Tucker—were located in satellite offices throughout the assigned territory. In Aspen, for instance, there were two deputy D.A.s, one for felony cases while the other handled civil and misdemeanor cases. It would be Tucker's responsibility to prosecute Ted Bundy for the murder of Caryn Campbell.

324 Dialogue comes from: Unk, "Officials Hunt Aspen Area Hills for Bundy," SLT, 06-09-77.

325 Larsen, "Bundy was a Prisoner with Privileges," SDT, 06-10-77.

326 Ibid.

327 Dialogue comes from: Doud, "Bundy's Prosecutor May Face Prosecution Himself," TNT, 06-10-77.

Chapter 4, "The Black Bishop"

328 Spiers, R/I, I. "The Bundy Manhunt," 08-09-20.

329 Spiers, WC, "Deputized," 08-10-20.

330 Valerie Fabien disputes this, stating there was general fear amid the community. Fabien, WC, "Dispatch," 04-27-21.

331 Lucas, "Evening News—Ted Bundy's Escape," 06-07-77. YouTube.

332 Baxter, OC, "Mike Fisher," 06-29-23.

333 Dialogue of Candy Harper comes from: Seldner & Parker, "Bundy Escape Miffs 'Unfrightened' Aspen," DP, 06-08-77.

334 Attributed to: Harvey, "The Shadow of a Killer," AT, 06-08-02.

335 Dialogue of Stacy Standley, concerning the lack of fear in town, comes from: Seldner & Parker, "Bundy Escape Miffs 'Unfrightened' Aspen," DP, 06-08-77.

336 Dialogue of Philip Mahoney comes from: Seldner & Parker, "Bundy Escape Miffs 'Unfrightened' Aspen," DP, 06-08-77.

337 This would be the Colorado State Patrol Academy at Camp George West Minimum Security Prison in Golden.

338 Eleven months earlier, Murray passed an oral examination. Based upon a favorable recommendation, he was hired by Kienast's predecessor. This was one of the last professional acts of the sheriff before he resigned, and Dick Kienast took over the reins of the department. For eleven months, Murray had been a hardworking road warrior. Given all the duties and responsibilities of a deputy sheriff, yet scant training, Murray thrived in the chaotic work environment.

339 Dialogue exchange between Murray and Kienast comes from: Murray, R/I, I. "The Bundy Manhunt," 07-14-20. Officer John Goodwin, of the Aspen PD, states that he too was out of town, training for four days in Gunnison, Colorado. Goodwin, WC, "Training in Gunnison," 07-01-20.

340 Interviewed in 2020, Murray could not recall precisely which day he placed this call to the sheriff. The author reasons that, if Murray was the type of man willing to drop out of the academy to assist his employer, he probably telephoned Kienast as soon as he learned of the escape. Given that Murray probably learned of the escape from the evening news on Tuesday, or the newspaper on Wednesday, the author has selected to insert the telephone call at this point in the narrative. Information concerning helicopters comes from: Doud, "Blame for Bundy's Escape Exchanged," TNT, 06-09-77.

341 This Ward Lucas-related section of the book comes from three sources: Lucas, R/I, I "Ted Bundy Memories," 08-16-19; Lucas, WC, "The First Escape," 07-21-19; Lucas 02-17-19). "My Interview with

Netflix for the Documentary on Ted Bundy." At the time, Lucas was not aware that Bundy would have recognized the journalist on sight.

342   Baxter, R/I., I. "Tuesday," 04-05-20.

343   Nancy Baxter notes that these county code prefix numbers made police work so much easier back then, since they didn't have ready access to shared data banks. It was the fastest way at the time to quickly categorize vehicles as they entered an officer's field of vision.

344   Typically, stray dogs were brought to the only animal shelter in the county, LuLu's Kennel, near the airport.

345   Bill Grikis' memories come from two sources: Grikis, R/I, I. "Dogcatcher to the Stars," 05-31-20; Grikis, WC, "Manuscript Corrections," 06-02-20.

346   Information concerning the airport comes from two sources: Wikipedia, (2021, January 30). "Aspen/Pitkin County Airport," www.wikipedia.org/wiki/Aspen/Pitkin_County_Airport; Aspen/Pitkin County (Sardy Field) Airport, (2021, January 30). "Aspen Airport: Operational, Accessible, Open to the Public since 1946," Aspen, Colorado, www.aspenairport.com/about-aspen-airport/history/.

347   Lucas, "Evening News—Ted Bundy's Escape," 06-07-77. YouTube.

348   That the chopper came from Fort Carson comes from: Horan, R/I, I. "The Bundy Manhunt," 05-31-20. Information concerning the heat-detection camera comes from two sources: DaRonch, (05-20-20). "Ted Bundy first escape news clip 6/8/77," YouTube; Rollins, "Escaped Kidnapper Bundy Eludes Helicopter, Hounds, Manhunters," AT, 06-09-77. Authorities reduced the hourly rental rate of this chopper and pilot to $150.00 an hour. Kienast's budget was already constrained, but what could he do? Larsen, "FBI Joins Colorado Manhunt," SDT, 06-10-77.

349   Unk, "Sheriff Announces Reorganization Plan," AT, 03-03-77; Konkel, CBI, (06-16-77). #77-6-007M. p. 5. With Meyers sidelined to handle the staff, it was clear the position of undersheriff would be open in the months ahead. Two candidates were perceived as being the inevitable successor—Sgt. Kralicek or Sgt. Davis. Between the two men, it appeared as if the latter would eventually be setting up shop in the undersheriff's office.

350   Ibid, p. 6.

351   Interviewed in 2019, Deputy Keith Ikeda remarked, "The mentality of the police back then was that [Bundy] was an escaped felon, accused of murder. You know, just take him down." Deputy Gary Haynes added, "Yeah, that would not surprise me. I didn't know Ben Meyers, but I know that Bob would not have listened to that kind of direction." Haynes & Ikeda, R/I, II, "Kienast's Department," 08-18-19. Deputy Braudis' story concerning Ben Meyers' shoot first and ask questions later approach to the manhunt was relayed to Deputy Sergeant Larry Spiers. The sergeant also spent a great deal of time in helicopters that week and was issued a shotgun from the sheriff's department. He was additionally good friends with Meyers. When interviewed in 2020, Spiers said he received no such instruction from Meyers, but after everyone learned Bundy had stolen a rifle from the Kaeser Cabin—everything changed.

352   In addition to Deputy Bob Braudis, the other road warriors included: Clay Owen, twenty-six; Lorrie Francis, twenty-nine; Bill McCrocklin, thirty; and Maureen Higgins, twenty-seven. All five of these new deputies had completed their preliminary three months of training. Firearms qualifications, patrol duty—while paired with more seasoned deputies—and classes concerning traffic accidents, armed robbery, and civil process, were already underway. Although comfortable in their new positions, they had yet to graduate from the academy in Golden. Unk, "Sheriff's Department Hires New Deputies [Higgins & McCrocklin]," AT, circa January 1976.

353   Dialogue exchange comes from: "Former Pitkin County Sheriff Bob Braudis Discusses Interactions with Ted Bundy," YouTube, 02-15-19.

354   Ibid.

355   Ibid

356   Ibid.

357   Witness sightings and their various locations comes from: Wolf & Winn, "Part 6: Memories of Colorado—Escape and Capture," SCJ, 10-19-78. The last confirmed sighting of Bundy on the run comes

from: Sabella, "The Bundy Manhunt: Is a Killer Loose in Aspen?" AT, 06-09-77.

358   Information concerning Warren Chandler comes from: Culver, "Longtime Channel 7 Weatherman Chandler Dies," DP, 05-24-10.
359   Dialogue exchange comes from: Chandler, R/I, I. "The Bundy Manhunt," 06-01-20.
360   Ibid.
361   All Garms-related material in this section comes from: Unk, "David Garms: Four Years Later," AT, 04-08-76.
362   Chandler, R/I, I. "The Bundy Manhunt," 06-01-20.
363   Ibid.
364   Summerlin, "Ted Bundy Tales Come out of the Woodwork," PI, 04-15-17.
365   Larsen, "Bundy: The Deliberate Stranger," p. 211.
366   Doud, "Something's Missing in Aspen Humor About Bundy," TNT, 06-11-77.
367   Ibid.
368   The Bundy Burger comes from: Doud, "Something's Missing in Aspen Humor About Bundy," TNT, 06-11-77. The Bundy Cocktail comes from: Clifford, "Bundy's Week of Freedom," AT, 06-23-77. Ham-on-the-rye on the fly comes from: Doud, "Something's Missing in Aspen Humor About Bundy," TNT, 06-11-77. The dog named Bundy comes from: Wolf & Winn, "Part 6: Memories of Colorado—Escape and Capture," SCJ, 10-19-78.
369   Doud, "Something's Missing in Aspen Humor About Bundy," TNT, 06-11-77.
370   Ibid.
371   Dialogue comes from: Stapleton, R/I, I. "Aspen Mountain Rescue," 07-17-20. It was clear to Stapleton that the sheriff was out of his depth. He even joked that Kienast had to read some books to figure out, "...what the hell he wanted to do and how to go about it."
372   Ibid.
373   Sabella, "The Bundy Manhunt: Is a Killer Loose in Aspen?" AT, 06-09-77.
374   One of these pieces of evidence, considered to be circumstantial, was a head hair, discovered in Bundy's Volkswagen. It had been shown to be microscopically indistinguishable from those on the head of Caryn Campbell. The FBI had started distributing what would surely be a groundbreaking publication only five months before Bundy's bid for freedom. The book completely laid out for law enforcement officers how hair could be used as trace evidence. Historically, it took some time for average jurors to accept new developments in forensics. Would the pending jury, hearing the Campbell case, accept this new manual?
375   Ibid.
376   Stapleton, R/I, I. "Aspen Mountain Rescue," 07-17-20.
377   Unk, (07-21-20). "Ashcroft Ghost Town," www.aspenhistory.org.
378   Hutski.com, (07-21-20). "Summit Huts Online Guidebook," www.hutski.com.
379   10th Mountain Division Hut Association, (07-20-20). "The Alfred A Braun Hut System," www.huts.org.
380   Anderson, "The Braun Huts: A History," AT, 03-15-04; 10th Mountain Division Hut Association, (07-20-20). "The Alfred A Braun Hut System," www.huts.org.
381   During his 2020 recorded interview and during a subsequent telephone call, Dave Stapleton, Sr. was unable to recall the name of the deputy Kienast assigned to be his escort and bodyguard. Stapleton, OC, "Manuscript Corrections," 08-21-20.
382   Dialogue exchange between the chief and Brad White comes from: DaRonch, (05-20-20). "Ted Bundy first escape news clip 6/8/77," YouTube.
383   White, R/I, I. "The Bundy Manhunt," 08-31-20.
384   Dialogue comes from: Stapleton, R/I, I. "Aspen Mountain Rescue," 07-17-20.
385   10th Mountain Division Hut Association, (07-20-20). "The Alfred A Braun Hut System," www.huts.org.
386   Stapleton, R/I, I. "Aspen Mountain Rescue," 07-17-20; Stapleton, OC, "Manuscript Corrections," 08-21-20.

387 Sabella, "The Hub of Law and Emergency," AT, 07-14-77.
388 Ibid.
389 Nancy Baxter had four sets of radios nearby and each required various time checks to be delivered and logged. If deputies or police officers didn't reply to their own radio checks, Baxter knew something was wrong and could raise the alarm. She even held regular social functions, inviting her newest dispatchers and members of the region's law enforcement community. Through these activities, dispatchers learned the various nuances of someone's voice. As a result, if an officer's speech pattern over the airwaves seemed altered or affected in any way, this could indicate to the dispatcher that the officer was in trouble and needed assistance. Baxter, R/I, I. "Tuesday," 04-05-20.
390 That the dogs were dismissed at this point comes from: Unk, "Bundy Took Rifle, Ammo in Break-in," SPI, 06-12-77. That morale seemed low comes from: Sabella, "The Bundy Manhunt: Is a Killer Loose in Aspen?" AT, 06-09-77.
391 Wolf & Winn, "Part 6: Memories of Colorado—Escape and Capture," SCJ, 10-19-78; Horan, R/I, I. "The Bundy Manhunt," 05-31-20. That the chopper landed periodically for Braudis to check various points of interest comes from: Harvey, "The Shadow of a Killer," AT, 06-08-02.
392 Dawson, (07-20-20). "History of the Huts," www.huts.org.
393 Ibid; Stapleton, OC, "Manuscript Corrections," 08-21-20.
394 Dialogue and overall story come from: Hanson, "Theodore Bundy," AT, 12-18-05.
395 Dialogue comes from: DaRonch, (05-20-20). "Ted Bundy first escape news clip 6/8/77," YouTube.
396 Mitchell [Braudis], R/I, I. "Smuggler Mine," 02-07-21.
397 Lucas, "Evening News—Ted Bundy's Escape," 06-08-77. YouTube.
398 Spiers, R/I, I. "The Bundy Manhunt," 08-09-20.
399 Baxter, WC, "The Runaways," 02-07-21.
400 Wikipedia, "Smuggler Mine," 02-07-21.
401 Dialogue comes from: White, WC, "The Black Bishop," 10-29 & 30-20.
402 Ibid.
403 Deputy White noted in 2020, that he understands this seems easy to say, "...after the fact, that you could tell somebody was being a certain way or whatever. Hindsight's 20-20, but it was true with him." White, WC, "Bundy's Eyes," 10-27-20.
404 Dialogue exchange comes from: White, WC, "The Black Bishop," 10-29 & 30-20.
405 Ibid.
406 That baker was Cliff Little. Zajac, WC, "Aspen's Volunteer Fire Department," 01-07-21.
407 Mitchell [Braudis], R/I, I. "Smuggler Mine," 02-07-21.

Chapter 5, "Manhunters"

408 Roberts, R/I, I. "The Bundy Manhunt," 06-22-20.
409 There was some initial confusion over the rank of Aspen PD's Dick Kreuser. In December 1976, he was a patrolman. The next documented reference to his rank comes on September 12, 1977. In city council meeting minutes, he is referenced as a sergeant. The author polled the 1977-era deputies and officers, and they were divided down the line on what Kreuser's rank would have been at the time of Bundy's jump. As Kreuser has passed away, and documentation exists that the man was a sergeant three months after the manhunt, the author has chosen to list Kreuser as a sergeant in this book. Hauter, "Xerox Contract," ACC, 09-12-77, p. 11. Regarding Kreuser's feet, Deputy White notes, "All I know is, he wore clogs in uniform; never expected backup from him anytime soon if he was on foot." White, WC, "Officer Dick Kreuser," 12-15-20. Further information concerning Dick Kreuser may be found in: Baxter, WC, "Dick Kreuser," 12-16-20; Roberts, WC, "Dick Kreuser," 12-16-20.
410 Baxter, WC, "Deputy McCrocklin," 11-13-20.
411 Roberts, WC, "Dick Dove," 12-21-20.
412 Kempfert, R/I, I. "The Deputies of Love," 12-30-20.
413 Dialogue comes from: Flatt, R/I with Vince Lahey, I. "The Bundy Manhunt," 11-28-18.
414 Ibid.

415   Mitchell [Braudis], R/I, I. "Smuggler Mine," 02-07-21.
416   Departing Eagle, they had to drive westbound along the two-lane highway through Glenwood Canyon, then cross the Colorado River at Glenwood Springs, and head up valley on Highway 82. They then had to pass through four roadblocks, simply to reach the eastern side of Aspen.
417   Dialogue comes from: Flatt, R/I with Vince Lahey, I. "The Bundy Manhunt," 11-28-18.
418   Ibid.
419   Deputy Higgins was normally assigned to the Eastwood and Aspen Grove regions, just east of town. She additionally served as a liaison with human resources, focusing on consumer protection. Unk, "Former Miner Now Deputy in Sheriff's Department," AT, 04-21-77.
420   Markov [Higgins], WC, "Tuesday," 12-06-19.
421   Ibid.
422   That committee member was famed journalist, Hunter S. Thompson.
423   Deputy Higgins had earned a bachelor's degree in education from the St. Francis College in Joliet, Illinois. She joined the Peace Corps and served in Jamaica and had even worked for the Illinois Department of Children and Family Services. Markov [Higgins], WC, "Caddy Stop—Manuscript Corrections," 12-28-19.
424   Ibid. Don Davis and a couple other deputies hailed from Las Cruces, New Mexico. The police department there had gone on strike and their chief had fired everyone in the ranks as a result. When the strike concluded, he informed his former employees that they could reapply for their positions, if they were willing to jump through some new hoops. He hadn't realized, however, that Davis and the others had spied an advertisement in a newspaper for some vacant deputy positions in the resort town of Aspen. Soon, the Roaring Fork Valley had three Southwestern cowboys on the county payroll. Murray, R/I, I. "The Bundy Manhunt," 07-14-20.
425   That a Colorado sheriff was required to have an undersheriff comes from: "Former Pitkin County Sheriff Bob Braudis Discusses Interactions with Ted Bundy," YouTube, 02-15-19.
426   Dialogue and background information concerning the undersheriff comes from: Stone, "Ben Meyers: New County Undersheriff," AT, 05-20-76.
427   The department's budgeted strength comes from: Unk, "Sheriff's Office Down Six Officers," AT, 07-14-77.
428   Dialogue exchange between prosecutor and witness comes from: Larsen, "Bundy: The Deliberate Stranger," p. 199.
429   Unk, "Aspen Court Action for Bundy Opens," DS, 04-05-77; Larsen, "Ted Bundy: An Interstate Enigma," SDT, 06-12-77.
430   Dialogue exchange between prosecutor and witness comes from: Larsen, "Bundy: The Deliberate Stranger," p. 199.
431   Earl [Kennell Silver], R/I, I. "The Bundy Manhunt," 06-29-20.
432   Betty volunteered for the Women Air Service Pilots (WASPs) and, of the 25,000 who applied, she was one of 1,800 who were accepted.
433   Unk, "Elizabeth Haas Pfister [Obituary]," AT, 11-22-11.
434   Betty Pfister biographical information comes from two sources: Unk, "Elizabeth Haas Pfister [Obituary]," AT, 11-22-11; Aspen Hall of Fame, (04-26-21). "Betty Haas Pfister," www.steamboatlibrary.marmot.org.
435   Baxter, R/I, III. "Wednesday," 04-18-20.
436   Mohn, WC, "Aspen Security Patrol," 05-24-21.
437   Stapleton, R/I, I. "Aspen Mountain Rescue," 07-17-20.
438   10th Mountain Division Hut Association, (07-20-20). "The Alfred A Braun Hut System," www.huts.org.
439   Ibid.
440   White, WC, "The Roadblock," 09-09-20.
441   White, R/I, I. "The Bundy Manhunt," 08-31-20.
442   White, WC, "Frying Pan Roadblock," 03-29-21.

443 White, R/I, I. "The Bundy Manhunt," 08-31-20.
444 Interviewed in 2020, Zajac said he earned $870 a month as a rookie. Zajac, R/I, I. "Red Mountain Rookie," 12-13-20.
445 Kienast altering the pamphlet comes from: Doud, "Something's Missing in Aspen Humor About Bundy," TNT, 06-11-77. That Kienast's search sector was expanding comes from: Harvey, "The Shadow of a Killer," AT, 06-08-02.
446 Doud, Charles, "Bundy's Trail Grows Colder; Leads Futile," TNT, 06-11-77.
447 Konkel, CBI, (06-16-77). #77-6-007M. p. 1.
448 Konkel, R/I, I. "The Fingerprints," 07-04-20.
449 All quotes concerning Bundy's escape, in this section, come from: Unk, "What Do You Think of the Bundy Escape?" AT, 07-09-77.
450 Unk, "Individual Rights More Important Than Escape" [Letter to the Editor], AT, 06-09-77. In the CBI report concerning the escape, Agent Konkel writes, "Sheriff Kienast has always been concerned that Bundy was a security problem and that it was for that reason that Bundy's custody was transferred to Garfield County because the physical jail facility is more secure." Konkel, CBI, (06-16-77). #77-6-007M. p. 5. Transfer of custody, however, had more to do with the recent announcement that the conditions in the Pitkin County Jail (lack of light, ventilation, etc.) were no longer acceptable and prisoners were not allowed to be housed there for more than thirty days.
451 Konkel, CBI, (06-16-77). #77-6-007M. p. 4.
452 The elbow-nudging journalist comes from: Chamberlain, "The Jaundiced Eye," AT, 06-09-77. That Bundy requested to be free of shackles during his transport trips comes from: Konkel, CBI, (06-16-77). #77-6-007M. p. 4.
453 Unk, "Individual Rights More Important Than Escape" [Letter to the Editor], AT, 06-09-77.
454 Baxter, WC, "The Aspen Times," 10-26-20.
455 Murray, WC, "Paperboys in Aspen," 10-26-20.
456 Rollins, "Escaped Kidnapper Bundy Eludes Helicopter, Hounds, Manhunters," AT, 06-09-77. Gary White had taken a significant pay cut, switching from a career in linehaul trucking to law enforcement. When he was first hired by the Las Cruces PD four years earlier, he earned $425.00 a month and he was paid once a month. After taxes and child support, the young officer took home around $275—$285, which would need to stretch for the following four weeks.
457 White, WC, "Joe Carroll White (1920—1976)," 10-25-20.
458 JoAnne wasn't the only dispatcher who fit Ted Bundy's victim type. Jean Zimmerman's maiden name was Santoro, and she was a proud Italian American woman from Brooklyn. She wore her lengthy hair down past her shoulders, parted in the middle, and it was thick, dark hair. She had big white teeth, with a congenital space between her two front incisors. She was one of the younger women on Nancy Baxter's staff. Baxter, R/I, IV. "Dispatch Center and Aspen PD," 04-18-20.
459 The JoAnne referenced was Joanne Rando. Rando, R/I, I. "Six Days," 04-18-21.
460 The passing remark comes from: Doud, "Something's Missing in Aspen Humor About Bundy," TNT, 06-11-77.
461 Baxter, WC, "Marta Steinmetz," 11-13-20.
462 That Marta worked at the Red Onion comes from: Unk, "Marta Jean Steinmetz [Obituary]," AT, 04-16-18. Her work at the Buddhist retreat comes from: Steinmetz, (11-29-20). "Marta Steinmetz [Profile]," LinkedIn.
463 Konkel, R/I, I. "The Fingerprints," 07-04-20.
464 Konkel, CBI, (06-16-77). #77-6-007M. p. 3.
465 Ibid.
466 Sabella, "The Bundy Manhunt: Is a Killer Loose in Aspen?" AT, 06-09-77.
467 Roberts, R/I, I. "The Bundy Manhunt," 06-22-20.
468 Haynes, R/I, I. "Kienast's Department," 08-18-19.
469 Deputy Keith Ikeda noted that if there was a sighting of Bundy in Wyoming, that would mean state lines had been crossed. The FBI could generally do a UFAP [Unlawful Flight to Avoid Prosecu-

tion] warrant, and that's how they could insert themselves into an investigation. Ikeda also believed that the feds didn't even need to ask Utah or Colorado authorities. If a fugitive crossed a state line, the feds could claim jurisdiction. Ikeda, R/I, I. "Kienast's Department," 08-18-19.

470 Special Agent Melvin Jensen met with Bill Offinger. Unk, "Federal Fugitive Charge is Lodged in S.L. Against Theodore Bundy," SLT, 06-10-77. Assistant U.S. Attorney, James W. McConkie II authorized the filing and U.S. Magistrate, Daniel A. Alsup issued the warrant. "Theodore R. Bundy did move and travel in interstate commerce, to-wit, from Aspen, Colorado, to a point outside the State of Colorado, with intent to avoid confinement in the Utah State Prison under the laws of the State of Utah for the offense of aggravated kidnapping, a felony, in violation of Section 1073, Title 18. United States Code." FBI. "USA vs. Theodore Robert Bundy," [Arrest Warrant], 06-09-77.

471 FBI, "Ted Bundy—Fugitive [teletype]," 06-09-77.

472 It didn't matter that it was a detective that had approached Garms in Boulder and recruited him for the position. This selection had been approved not only by the chief of police, but by Aspen's deputy district attorney. None of this mattered; the townspeople felt betrayed.

473 Unk, "David Garms: Four Years Later," AT, 04-08-76.

474 Ibid.

475 Garms, WC, "The Manhunt Part II," 10-30-19.

476 Chandler, R/I, I. "The Bundy Manhunt," 06-01-20.

477 Ibid.

478 Horan, R/I, I. "The Bundy Manhunt," 05-31-20. Cliff Browning died in a plane crash in Laramie, WY in 1984, while on assignment with the FBI. Officer Down Memorial Page, (06-06-20). "Special Agent Clifton Dewell Browning, Jr," www.odmp.org.

479 Unk, "Bundy Left Alone in Aspen Courtroom, Leaps Out Window, Escapes into Hills," SLT, 06-08-77; Spiers, R/I, I. "The Bundy Manhunt," 08-09-20.

480 Baxter, R/I, I & II. "Tuesday," 04-05-20.

481 Ibid.

482 Unk, "Bundy's Mother: Give Up," SDT, 06-10-77.

483 Ibid.

Chapter 6, "Devil's Hour"

484 Baxter, WC, "Towing," 12-16-20.

485 Roberts, R/I, I. "The Bundy Manhunt," 06-22-20.

486 Hauter, "Rodent Control," ACC, 07-25-77.

487 Grikis, WC, "Prairie Dogs," 12-20-20. After forty-three-years, Grikis' memory is amazing. By checking the meeting minutes of the Aspen City Council, we learn they he shot 154. Hauter, "Rodent Control," ACC, 07-25-77.

488 Two months after Bundy was recaptured, the town's entire golf course was ripped up due to the extensive underground burrows created by prairie dogs. These ground squirrels were found to have the same Bubonic plague-infected fleas as those in Ashcroft. At first, the city council considered strychnine, but that idea met with too much opposition. The council approved a plan to flood the burrows, in an attempt to drive the prairie dogs out. Unk, "1977: City to flood golf course squirrels [prairie dogs]," TAT, 07-19-06.

489 That friend was Michael Kendrick.

490 Interviewed in 2020, Kempfert could not recall whether it was to check on a potential Bundy sighting or interview a potential witness in the case.

491 White, WC, "The Holiday Inn," 01-01-21.

492 Kempfert, R/I, I. "The Deputies of Love," 12-30-20.

493 This incident at The Holiday Inn comes from two sources: Kempfert, R/I, I. "The Deputies of Love," 12-30-20; White, WC, "The Holiday Inn," 01-01-21.

494 Kempfert, R/I, I. "The Deputies of Love," 12-30-20.

495 Ikeda, R/I, I. "Kienast's Department," 08-18-19.

496   Haynes, R/I, I. "Kienast's Department," 08-18-19.
497   Flatt, R/I with Vince Lahey, I. "The Bundy Manhunt," 11-28-18.
498   Baxter, WC, "DUIs in Aspen," 03-10-21.
499   Ibid.
500   Deputy Flatt paid close attention to the Accident Prevention Teams (AP-Teams) he saw working in the valley. They were created by the Colorado State Highway Patrol and dispatched to various jurisdictions, to place a heavier than normal presence on the roadways. More drivers could be cited for speeding and this would increase safety along the roads while simultaneously generating income for the state. The AP-Teams performed crackdowns on expired plates, strung traffic counters across the highway at various points between Aspen and Basalt, and arrested drunk drivers. Inclement weather, however, led to so many accidents, that the teams were soon overwhelmed. More pressure was applied to county and city law enforcement agencies. Baxter, WC, "Accident Prevention Teams," 03-10-21.
501   White, WC, "DUIs in Aspen," 03-11-21.
502   Dialogue comes from: Flatt, R/I with Vince Lahey, I. "The Bundy Manhunt," 11-28-18. Murray, WC, "DUIs in Aspen," 03-10-21; Field Sobriety Testing, (03-27-21). "Brief History of Field Sobriety Testing," www.theduilawyer.com.
503   Kienast's compliment comes from: Flatt, R/I with Vince Lahey, I. "The Bundy Manhunt," 11-28-18. Increased revenue from drunk driving arrests comes from: Roberts, WC, "DUIs in Aspen," 03-05-21. Deputy Flatt arresting two drunks a night comes from: Flatt, R/I with Vince Lahey, I. "The Bundy Manhunt," 11-28-18. That the combined agencies were pulling over ten drunk drivers a week comes from: Roberts, WC, "DUIs in Aspen," 03-05-21.
504   Sentence duration for first-time drink driving offenses comes from: White, WC, "DUIs in Aspen," 03-11-21. Drunk driving sentences compared to Longer's sentence comes from: Baxter, WC, "DUIs in Aspen," 03-10-21.
505   Flatt, R/I, I. "The Bundy Manhunt," 11-28-18.
506   White's passenger was his friend, Elias Lopez.
507   White, WC, "Neil Sedaka," 10-23-20.
508   White, WC, "The Job Interview," 09-30-20. Gary White may have been new to town, but he'd been a law enforcement officer for four years. After studying at New Mexico State University, he completed his basic law enforcement training in 1973, and was hired by the Las Cruces PD. For two and-a-half years, White investigated everything from typical property crimes to narcotics. He assisted the district attorney's office with various cases and served as the medical officer, responsible for responding to all manner of emergencies throughout the city. His superiors learned that he also had a commanding speaking voice and seemed able to work with a wide variety of personnel. The young officer found himself performing public relations duties and reporting the daily crime statistics to regional radio stations. LinkedIn, (2020, September 6). "Gary White [Profile]."
509   The officer was Joel Collins.
510   White, WC, "Deputy Joel Collins," 09-30-20.
511   Dialogue exchange and overall anecdote comes from: White, R/I, I. "The Bundy Manhunt," 08-31-20; White, OC, "The Hunch," 07-02-23.
512   This fugitive was previously reported as Sid Morley. His real name comes from: Unk, "Tip from Cellmate Redirects Search" TNT, 06-10-77.
513   Doud, "Bundy's Trail Grows Colder; Leads Futile," TNT, 06-11-77.
514   Through correspondence with the author in 2020, "Slats Cabbage" noted that this bulletin came out Friday afternoon at noon. Demmon, WC, "Aspen State Teacher's College," 07-05-20. Additional information comes from: Sharpe, "Here's How Two Aspen Natives Turned the City into a College Town," AP, 05-24-19.
515   Hayes, "Aspen History 101," AT, 12-13-06; Sharpe, "Here's How Two Aspen Natives Turned the City Into a College Town," AP, 05-24-19.
516   Ibid.
517   Demmon, *Bundy to Star in Movie.* CS, ASTC, June 1977.

518 Demmon, "Escapism 234." CS, ASTC, June 1977. Demmon, "Ride Wanted." CS, ASTC, June 1977.
519 Westerlund, thirty-seven, had spent two and-a-half years as a deputy in Red Lake County, Minnesota. He moved to Aspen in late June of 1976, to accept the same position in Pitkin County.
520 Konkel, R/I, I. "The Fingerprints," 07-04-20.
521 Dialogue distilled from Westerlund's statement to Konkel. Westerlund, "Statement of Deputy David Westerlund," (06-07-77), PCSO. p. 2.
522 Ibid.
523 This Ward Lucas-related section of the book comes from three sources: Lucas, R/I, I. "Ted Bundy Memories," 08-16-19; Lucas, WC, "The First Escape," 07-21-19; Lucas, (02-17-19). "My Interview with Netflix for the Documentary on Ted Bundy."
524 Baxter, OC, "The Bundy-Brunette Look," 06-29-23.
525 Garms, WC, "The Manhunt Part II," 10-30-19.
526 Baxter, R/I, II. "Tuesday," 04-05-20.
527 Jury selection began on Monday, January 3, 1977. Lichtenstein, "Aspen Jury Selection Is Started in the Longet Manslaughter Trial," NYT, 01-04-77.
528 The wet t-shirt contest comes from: Chalmers, "Claudine Longet: Aspen's Femme Fatale," GQ, 05-06-13.
529 Dialogue exchange between Judge Lohr and Marty Stouffer comes from: Stouffer, R/I, I. "Bundy's Cellmate," 09-23-20.
530 Stouffer, WC, "Bundy's Cellmate," 08-23-20—09-30-20.
531 Stouffer, R/I, I. "Bundy's Cellmate," 09-23-20.
532 Ibid.
533 Chalmers, "Claudine Longet: Aspen's Femme Fatale," GQ, 05-06-13.
534 Dialogue exchange between the deputy and Stouffer comes from: Stouffer, R/I, I. "Bundy's Cellmate," 09-23-20.
535 Ibid.
536 Ibid.

Chapter 7, "Amos"

537 Updated physical description of the fugitive comes from: FBI, "Ted Bundy—a.k.a. Theodore Robert Cowell [teletype]." 06-11-77.
538 General contents of this meeting, its time, and attendees, come from: Spiers, OC, "Saturday Morning with the FBI," 08-09-20.
539 Baxter, WC, "Saturday," 06-23-20.
540 Baxter, WC, "Deputy McCrocklin," 11-13-20.
541 Baxter, R/I, I. "Tuesday," 04-05-20.
542 Ibid.
543 McCrocklin had been heavily involved with the emergency medical technician educational system and the eventual formation of a statewide emergency disaster system up in Nashua, New Hampshire. Sheriff Kienast had hired him last fall because of this experience. Baxter, WC, "Deputy McCrocklin," 11-13-20.
544 Ibid.
545 Sabella, "The Hub of Law and Emergency," AT, 07-14-77.
546 Baxter, WC, "Baxter & Braudis," 11-09-20.
547 Baxter, R/I, I. "Tuesday," 04-05-20.
548 Baxter, WC, "Baxter & Braudis," 11-09-20.
549 Ibid.
550 Baxter recalls that May was a slow month, since the ski lifts had closed. It was a good time for inventory, but more importantly, annual trips to Taos and Albuquerque. She was one of thirteen women who traveled in a van caravan to the various Navajo, Hopi and Zuni outposts. Their job was to purchase quality merchandise to fill their three stores. Baxter, WC, "Baxter & Braudis," 11-09-20.

551   Baxter, WC, "Deputy McCrocklin," 11-13-20.
552   Rollins, "Escaped Kidnapper Bundy Eludes Helicopter, Hounds, Manhunters," AT, 06-09-77.
553   Dialogue exchange between Baxter and Ireland comes from: Baxter, R/I, II. "Tuesday," 04-05-20.
554   Baxter, WC, "Saturday," 06-23-20.
555   Baxter, R/I, III. "Wednesday," 04-18-20.
556   Baxter, WC, "The Roadblocks," 01-05-21.
557   That it was Deputy Kempfert that took this report comes from: Konkel, CBI, (06-16-77). #77-6-007M. p. 2. The time this call was placed comes from: Doud, "Search for Bundy Centers on Cabin," TNT, 06-12-77. The caretaker's name was Wayne Inman. That he last checked on the cabin on June 4 comes from: Konkel, CBI, (06-16-77). #77-6-007M. p. 1.
558   Dialogue comes from: Konkel, R/I, I. "The Fingerprints," 07-04-20.
559   Wikipedia, "Vortex Ring State," 09-10-20.
560   White, R/I, I. "The Bundy Manhunt," 08-31-20.
561   Ibid.
562   Ibid.
563   White notes, "The newspaper description on my injury was fake news. I didn't break my arm. I dislocated my shoulder and broke my collarbone, hence the sling. Tis the only way to secure the shoulder for healing. Trust me, a real pain." White, WC, "One More Run," 11-22-20.
564   A year later, Sabich's parents sued Longet for $1.3 million in civil court. As part of a deal, the parents agreed to drop the case if Longet signed a confidentiality agreement and agreed never to write a book.
565   Deputy Gary White's involvement with Claudine Longet come from two sources: Boyd, "Having a Wonderful Time in Jail: Claudine & Her Young Deputy Laugh it Up," SM, 05-17-77; White, WC, "Claudine Longet," 12-02-20.
566   White, WC, "Birthday Boy," 10-30-20.
567   Kempfert, R/I, I. "The Deputies of Love," 12-30-20.
568   Woody Creek Road, which climbed higher and higher as the journey progressed, was known to locals as the best place to obtain a beautiful Colorado Blue Spruce Christmas tree. This prized cargo would have to be hidden well under the tonneau cover of one's truck bed since it was illegal to cut one down. Forest Service employees rarely patrolled the area during the holidays, however, but if you were stopped, the smell of the tree limbs alone could give you away.
569   Wikipedia, "Lenado, Colorado," 03-28-21.
570   Baxter, WC, "Lenado," 01-17-21.
571   That the rifle was stolen comes from: Konkel, CBI, (06-16-77). #77-6-007M. p. 1. That it was loaded with six shells comes from: Unk, "Bundy ordered Held on Escape Charge," AT, 08-04-77.
572   Kempfert, R/I, I. "The Deputies of Love," 12-30-20.
573   Dialogue comes from: Konkel, R/I, I. "The Fingerprints," 07-04-20.
574   White, WC, "The Body Bag," 09-09-20.
575   Konkel, R/I, I. "The Fingerprints," 07-04-20.
576   Description of exterior of cabin comes from: Doud, "Search for Bundy Centers on Cabin," TNT, 06-12-77. That Konkel placed the note in an evidence bag comes from: Konkel, CBI, (06-16-77). #77-6-007M. p. 1.
577   Konkel, R/I, I. "The Fingerprints," 07-04-20.
578   AFIS stats come from: Avisian Staff (12-02-14). "A History of AFIS," www.secureidnews.com; Ikeda, R/I, I. "Kienast's Department," 08-18-19.
579   Kempfert, R/I, I. "The Deputies of Love," 12-30-20.
580   Agent Konkel was qualified to dust for fingerprints. To any readers wondering if he was a Certified Latent Print Examiner (CLPE), the answer is, no. That is only because that certification program didn't exist until August 1, 1977, some eight weeks after Bundy jumped.
581   Baxter, WC, "Garms' Reply," 11-09-22.
582   That it was Konekl that lifted the prints comes from: Konkel, CBI, (06-16-77). #77-6-007M. p. 1.

Dave Garms was qualified in the 9th Judicial District by Judge Lohr. Garms, WC, "The Manhunt Part II," 10-30-19. Additional information concerning this section comes from: Konkel, CBI, (06-16-77). #77-6-007M. p. 3.

583   Konkel, CBI, (06-16-77). #77-6-007M. p. 1.
584   Fingerprint data comes from: FBI, "Ted Bundy—a.k.a. Theodore Robert Cowell [teletype]." 06-11-77. Deputy Leon Murray eventually transferred over to the Aspen PD and was sent to fingerprint classification school. He became officially sanctioned to identify prints by Judge J.E. DeVilbiss. Murray writes, "Bundy's FBI print code: DM550813121911041313. Murray, WC, "Ted Bundy's FBI Fingerprint Code," 11-29-20.
585   Garms, WC, "The Manhunt Part II," 10-30-19; Konkel, CBI, (06-16-77). #77-6-007M. p. 3.
586   FBI, "Front and Side Views—Ted Bundy [teletype]." 06-11-77; FBI, "Mountain Cabin—Breaking & Entering" [Teletype]. 06-11-77.
587   Konkel, R/I, I. "The Fingerprints," 07-04-20.
588   Zimmerman was also taking care of walk-ins, the front counter, releasing towed vehicles, and filing and distribution once the police reports were indexed. She needed five copies of each colored report, and every copy had a specific destination: green for the police chief, pink for the detectives, blue for the officer's log, canary for the case file, and the original white for the dispatch master log. This was done so that, if anyone went on vacation, or needed to retrieve an old case, they had several ways of bringing themselves up to date or means of finding a copy of a particular incident.
589   White, R/I, I. "The Bundy Manhunt," 08-31-20.
590   Garms, WC, "The Manhunt Part II," 10-30-19.
591   Doud, "Bundy's Trail Grows Colder; Leads Futile," TNT, 06-11-77.
592   Dialogue comes from: Doud, "Search for Bundy Centers on Cabin," TNT, 06-12-77.
593   Dialogue comes from: Zajac, R/I, I. "Red Mountain Rookie," 12-13-20.
594   Ibid.
595   Source material for the bar checks and of the Hotel Jerome in particular comes from: Zajac, R/I, I. "Red Mountain Rookie," 12-13-20; Baxter, WC, "Top Three Bars in Aspen," 01-01-21.
596   Quirk, R/I, I. "Lone Wolf Memories," 12-08-20.
597   Ibid.
598   Quirk, WC, "Burned and Bitter," 12-19-020; Baxter, WC, "Bubonic Plague," 12-19-20.
599   Baxter, WC, "Sunday," 11-22-20.
600   White, OC, "Armed and Dangerous," 07-02-23. According to a newspaper article, the deputies were under orders not to shoot to kill. Larsen, "Bundy Traced to Mountain Cabin," SDT, 06-12-77.
601   White, WC, "Transporting Bundy," 10-29-20.
602   White, R/I, I. "The Bundy Manhunt," 08-31-20.
603   Spiers, R/I, I. "The Bundy Manhunt," 08-09-20.

Chapter 8, "The Dogs of War"

604   Spiers, R/I, I. "The Bundy Manhunt," 08-09-20.
605   Ibid.
606   White, R/I, I. "The Bundy Manhunt," 08-31-20.
607   That it was multiple dogs comes from: Unk, "Bundy Took Rifle, Ammo in Break-in," SPI, 06-12-77.
608   Distance between the creek and the cabin comes from: Doud, "Bundy's Trail Grows Colder; Leads Futile," TNT, 06-11-77. That they found prints in the softer ground comes from: Michaud & Aynesworth, "The Only Living Witness," p. 191.
609   White, WC, "The Pump .22 Rifle," 09-14-20. That it was multiple dogs comes from: Unk, "Colorado Officials Claim Escapee Bundy Armed," SLT, 06-12-77.
610   Kempfert, R/I, I. "The Deputies of Love," 12-30-20.
611   Baxter, WC, "Sunday," 11-22-20.
612   Baxter, WC, "Dead or Alive," 01-30-23.

613 Bundy later informed Sgt. Don Davis that the man he encountered was called Sinclair. The only red-headed Sinclair Davis knew was Bruce Sinclair, and this estimation was entered into Davis's report. Davis, "Bundy Escape Itinerary/Interrogation," 06-15-77, p. 6; Unk, "Bruce Prior Sinclair [Obituary]," AT, 02-14-06.
614 Dialogue exchange between Bundy and the rancher comes from: Michaud & Aynesworth, "The Only Living Witness," p. 192.
615 Sheeley, R/I I. "Bundy Memories," 07-22-20.
616 Sheeley, "Those Were the Days: Memories of an Aspen Hippie Chick," pp. 114-116.
617 That deputies worked twelve-hour shifts comes from: Harvey, "The Shadow of a Killer," AT, 06-08-02. Braudis pulling the sheriff aside comes from: "Former Pitkin County Sheriff Bob Braudis Discusses Interactions with Ted Bundy," YouTube, 02-15-19.
618 Dialogue comes from: Flatt, R/I with Vince Lahey, I. "The Bundy Manhunt," 11-28-18.
619 Ibid.
620 Wikipedia, "Wheeler Opera House," 01-03-21; Baxter, WC, "The Pub," 01-02-21.
621 Zajac, WC, "The Pub," 01-07-21.
622 White, WC, "Fat – Fifty – Florida," 01-01-21.
623 Ibid; Murray, WC, "Legal Drinking Age in Aspen," 01-02-21.
624 Baxter, WC, "The Pub," 01-02-21.
625 Ibid.
626 Zajac, R/I, I. "Red Mountain Rookie," 12-13-20.
627 Ibid.
628 Ibid.
629 Ibid.

Chapter 9, "Crestahaus"

630 The only information we have concerning this sexual assault comes from: Unk, "Rape Attempt Leads to Bundy's Capture," AT, 06-16-77.
631 A newspaper article notes, "...an unidentified assailant who had been following her grabbed her, knocked her down, kicked her and dragged her by the hair. She said she screamed and struggled until the assailant became frightened by the noise and ran away." Unk, "Rape Attempt Leads to Bundy's Capture," AT, 06-16-77.
632 That female police officer was Nancy Lyle. Quirk, R/I, I. "Lone Wolf Memories," 12-08-20.
633 Ibid.
634 Unk, "Rape Attempt Leads to Bundy's Capture," AT, 06-16-77.
635 Baxter, WC, "Monday," 03-28-21.
636 Markov [Higgins], WC, "The Caddy Stop," 12-23-19. Markov believes it may have been the West Sopris Creek Roadblock they manned for a few hours that night, but could not be certain. Markov (Higgins), WC, "West Sopris Creek Roadblock—Manuscript Corrections," 12-31-19.
637 Time listed comes from: Davis, "Bundy Escape Itinerary/Interrogation," 06-15-77, p. 1. This time has also been listed as 2:00 a.m. Sabella, "Deputies Snare Exhausted Bundy," AT, 06-16-77.
638 The time listed is the best educated guess of Nancy Baxter, in charge of the dispatch office in 1977.
639 Baxter, WC, "Monday," 03-28-21.
640 Location of stop comes from: Sabella, "Deputies Snare Exhausted Bundy," AT, 06-16-77. Distance from the courthouse would only have been 0.7 miles. This was verified through correspondence with Deputy Higgins. That it was fifty yards outside city limits comes from: Doud, "Escapees Ray, Bundy in Custody," TNT, 06-13-77; Deputy Flatt, as quoted on the evening news, Grossman, "Bundy—Recaptured," 06-13-77.
641 Bundy's disguise comes from: Markov [Higgins], WC, "The Caddy Stop," 12-23-19; Sabella, "Deputies Snare Exhausted Bundy," AT, 06-16-77.
642 Unless specifically cited, all dialogue between Flatt and Bundy comes from: Michaud &

Aynesworth, "The Only Living Witness," pp. 194-195.
643   That Flatt asked the driver for some ID comes from: Sabella, "Deputies Snare Exhausted Bundy," AT, 06-16-77.
644   Markov [Higgins], WC, "Caddy Stop—Manuscript Corrections," 12-28-19.
645   Unk, "Wan and Haggard, Bundy is Arraigned on More Charges," AT, 06-16-77.
646   Markov [Higgins], WC, "Caddy Stop—Manuscript Corrections," 12-28-19.
647   Dialogue exchange between Higgins and Unger comes from: Quirk, R/I, I. "Lone Wolf Memories," 12-08-20; Baxter, WC, "Codes 10-28 & 10-29," 02-14-21.
648   The license plate number—ZG-1765—comes from: FBI, "Concealing the Cabin Break-In [teletype]," 06-13-77.
649   Nancy Baxter notes, "Whenever a vehicle is stolen or a warrant is issued, it is the responsibility of the dispatcher in each jurisdiction—county or city—to enter the information into the National Crime Information Center (NCIC). This is a nationwide data base of serial numbers, identification information, and vehicle registration information from all over the country. There is a chance that the plates might not match the vehicle they are on, so it is always preferable to run a vehicle identification number (VIN) as well, so that if plates from another vehicle had been placed on the car that is stopped, it will warn the officers that that driver may be involved in more than a vehicle issue. This causes a physical print out of the information and a recording of the time and date that vehicle and driver were stopped. It is a way to keep the officers honest and informed, but it is also a built-in check that they have the person or vehicle at the scene and apprehension can take place, usually accompanied with a call for backup." Baxter, WC, "Codes 10-28 & 10-29," 02-14-21.
650   Markov [Higgins], WC, "The Caddy Stop," 12-23-19.
651   Baxter, OC, "Caddy Codes," 02-14-21; Haynes, WC, "Lynne Unger," 05-13-20; Haynes, R/I, I. "Kienast's Department," 08-18-19.
652   Dialogue comes from: Baxter, WC, "Codes 10-28 & 10-29," 02-14-21.
653   Dialogue exchange between Baxter and Unger comes from: Baxter, WC, "Monday," 03-28-21.
654   Dialogue comes from: Markov [Higgins], WC, "Bundy's Version—Feedback," 12-24-19.
655   Boland, "Bundy Recaptured at Aspen," DS, 06-13-77.
656   Markov, "Bundy Redux [Letter to the Editor]," AT, 12-18-05; Markov [Higgins], WC, "The Caddy Stop," 12-23-19.
657   Markov [Higgins], WC, "The Caddy Stop," 12-23-19.
658   Ibid.
659   Ibid.
660   Baxter, WC, "Monday," 03-28-21.
661   Markov [Higgins], WC, "The Caddy Stop," 12-23-19.
662   Dialogue comes from: Markov, "Bundy Redux [Letter to the Editor]," AT, 12-18-05.
663   Baxter, WC, "Monday," 03-28-21.
664   Doud, "Escapees Ray, Bundy in Custody," TNT, 06-13-77. Deputy Higgins' recollections of what Bundy looked like come from: Markov [Higgins], WC, "The Caddy Stop," 12-23-19.
665   Markov [Higgins], WC, "The Caddy Stop," 12-23-19.
666   That Bundy said he couldn't think anymore comes from: Doud, "Escapees Ray, Bundy in Custody," TNT, 06-13-77.
667   Markov [Higgins], WC, "Caddy Stop—Manuscript Corrections," 12-28-19.
668   Dialogue exchange between Zajac and the stranger comes from: Zajac, R/I, I. "Red Mountain Rookie," 12-13-20.
669   That law enforcement officers appeared jubilant comes from: Sabella, "Deputies Snare Exhausted Bundy," AT, 06-16-77. Inscription on the banner comes from two sources: Dolan, WC, "Aspen Days," 05-09-21; Doud, "Refreshed Bundy Ready to Tilt Again," TNT, 06-14-77.
670   Sabella, "Deputies Snare Exhausted Bundy," AT, 06-16-77. According to one article, Doud, "Escapees Ray, Bundy in Custody," TNT, 06-13-77, Bundy wore "brown, crepe-soled shoes." Nancy Baxter refutes this, saying Bundy's footwear was a hot topic of conversation the week he was on the

run. When he was discovered to be wearing his prison-issued boots, that information was immediately shared among law enforcement officers.

671 Nancy recalls that she fell in line behind Davis and only realized when she entered the office, why she was there. She wanted to be there. She turned to Davis without speaking. Their normally amicable relationship had cooled recently. There had been an incident where a maintenance truck had accidently backed off Independence Pass and Nancy had dispatched Aspen Mountain Rescue to the scene, overriding the sergeant's alternate solution to the problem. They had quarreled. Whether it was Davis's desire to have a witness to the interrogation or whether he was mending the bridge with Nancy—perhaps both—he gave an approving nod to her presence. Baxter, WC, "Monday," 03-28-21.

672 Time listed comes from: Davis, "Bundy Escape Itinerary/Interrogation," 06-15-77, p. 1. That Baxter had earned the right to witness the interrogation comes from: Baxter, OC, "You've Earned It," 06-29-23.

673 Baxter, WC, "Monday," 03-28-21.

674 Davis, "Bundy Escape Itinerary/Interrogation," 06-15-77, p. 1.

675 Baxter, WC, "Monday," 03-28-21.

676 That Bundy had been preparing for some time comes from: Unk, "Back in Courtroom, Dead-Tired Bundy Hears New Charges," SLT, 06-14-77; Unk, "Aspen Lawmen Capture Bundy," DN, 06-13-77. That Bundy saw the open windows as an opportunity comes from: Baxter, WC, "Monday," 03-28-21. After deciding to go, Bundy began solidifying his plans comes from: Davis, "Bundy Escape Itinerary/Interrogation," 06-15-77, p. 1.

677 Sabella, "Deputies Snare Exhausted Bundy," AT, 06-16-77.

678 Konkel, CBI, (06-16-77). #77-6-007M. p. 8.

679 Ibid, p. 9.

680 Baxter, WC, "Monday," 03-28-21.

681 Clothing Bundy was wearing comes from several sources: Unk, "Bundy Escapes in Colorado," DN, 06-07-77; Cunningham, "Slay Suspect Escapes in Leap from Window," RMN, 06-08-77; Wolf & Winn, "Part 6: Memories of Colorado—Escape and Capture," SCJ, 10-19-78.

682 Konkel, CBI, (06-16-77). #77-6-007M. p. 9.

683 Ibid.

684 Ibid.

685 That the window was halfway open and he opened it further comes from: Konkel, CBI, (06-16-77). #77-6-007M. p. 9. The unexpected delay comes from: Davis, "Bundy Escape Itinerary/Interrogation," 06-15-77, p. 1.

686 Dialogue exchange comes from: Davis, "Bundy Escape Itinerary/Interrogation," 06-15-77, p. 1.

687 Dialogue comes from: Unk, "Back in Courtroom, Dead-Tired Bundy Hears New Charges," SLT, 06-14-77.

688 Dialogue exchange comes from: Sabella, "Deputies Snare Exhausted Bundy," AT, 06-16-77.

689 Horan, R/I, I. "The Bundy Manhunt," 05-31-20.

690 That Sgt. Davis conducted the two-hour interrogation comes from: Konkel, CBI, (06-16-77). #77-6-007M. p. 2; Baxter observing the proceedings comes from: Baxter, WC, "Monday," 03-28-21.

691 That Bundy was confident in his five-second plan comes from: Konkel, CBI, (06-16-77). #77-6-007M. p. 9.

692 Details of Bundy's escape route come from the author's site visit to Aspen in August 2019, as well as: Sabella, "Deputies Snare Exhausted Bundy," AT, 06-16-77; Davis, "Bundy Escape Itinerary/Interrogation," 06-15-77, p. 1.

693 Baxter, WC, "Monday," 03-28-21.

694 Ibid.

695 Konkel, CBI, (06-16-77). #77-6-007M. p. 9.

696 Baxter, WC, "Monday," 03-28-21.

697 That Bundy denied entering the water comes from: Davis, "Bundy Escape Itinerary/Interrogation," 06-15-77, p. 2. A journalist reported that Bundy had crossed the river, to throw off the scent of the future search dogs he knew would be dispatched. Prior to exiting the water, Bundy walked south

for an unknown distance. He then crossed the river a second time, to emerge back along the western banks. Patrick, "Recaptured Bundy Faces New Charges," DP, 06-16-77. Anecdote concerning the pencils comes from: Patchen, Bodiford, & Chapmen, "Statement of Theodore Robert Bundy," R/I, (02-20-78), FSA, Series 2084, p. 3.

698   Baxter, WC, "Monday," 03-28-21.
699   Bundy claims to have used West End Street to travel south through Aspen. Davis, "Bundy Escape Itinerary/Interrogation," 06-15-77, p. 2. He may have used Original Street. Sabella, "Deputies Snare Exhausted Bundy," AT, 06-16-77; Doud, "Escapees Ray, Bundy in Custody," TNT, 06-13-77.
700   Wolf & Winn, "Part 6: Memories of Colorado—Escape and Capture," SCJ, 10-19-78; Sabella, "Deputies Snare Exhausted Bundy," AT, 06-16-77; Baxter, WC, "Monday," 03-28-21.
701   These memories, coupled with the man who had witnessed the jump and Bundy's subsequent departure in an easterly direction, all helped deputies deduce that their fugitive was headed towards Smuggler Mountain and Independence Pass. Baxter, WC, "Monday," 03-28-21.
702   Bundy's direction of travel at this juncture comes from: Davis, "Bundy Escape Itinerary/Interrogation," 06-15-77, p. 2; Baxter, WC, "Monday," 03-28-21.
703   Details of Bundy's route up Aspen Mountain come from the author's site visit to Aspen in August 2019.
704   Baxter, WC, "Monday," 03-28-21.
705   During his June 13, 1977 interrogation, Bundy told Sgt. Davis that he had ascended Aspen Mountain without stopping once. Davis, "Bundy Escape Itinerary/Interrogation," 06-15-77, p. 2.
706   Details of Bundy's descent come from various sources: Harvey, "The Shadow of a Killer," AT, 06-08-02; Sabella, "Deputies Snare Exhausted Bundy," AT, 06-16-77; Wolf & Winn, "Part 6: Memories of Colorado—Escape and Capture," SCJ, 10-19-78; Unk, "Back in Courtroom, Dead-Tired Bundy Hears New Charges," SLT, 06-14-77.
707   Davis, "Bundy Escape Itinerary/Interrogation," 06-15-77, p. 2. There are rumors that Bundy had a makeshift map with him during his escape. In 1978, Bundy gave a statement to several detectives in Florida, noting, "…plastic bag and a map of uh, well not a map, but what it was, was an aerial photograph of the uh, mountains around Aspen that they used in ski brochures." Patchen, Bodiford, & Chapmen, "Statement of Theodore Robert Bundy," R/I, (02-20-78), FSA, Series 2084, p. 25. Deputy Higgins is adamant that no such brochure map was found in the stolen Cadillac or on his person when he was recaptured. Nancy Baxter also notes that she did not recall Bundy saying anything about such a map during his official interrogation.

Chapter 10, "Cemetery Lane"

708   Dialogue exchange between the secretary and Bundy comes from: Doud, "Escapees Ray, Bundy in Custody," TNT, 06-13-77.
709   Baxter, WC, "Monday," 03-28-21.
710   That he was trying to get out of the Conundrum Creek residential area comes from: Davis, "Bundy Escape Itinerary/Interrogation," 06-15-77, p. 2. Rain soaking comes from: Sabella, "Deputies Snare Exhausted Bundy," AT, 06-16-77.
711   The trail Bundy happened upon was the Conundrum Trail. The estimated distance he covered comes from: Davis, "Bundy Escape Itinerary/Interrogation," 06-15-77, p. 2.
712   Wolf & Winn, "Part 6: Memories of Colorado—Escape and Capture," SCJ, 10-19-78.
713   Davis, "Bundy Escape Itinerary/Interrogation," 06-15-77, p. 2.
714   That he shed his attire in order to dry out his clothes comes from: Konkel, CBI, (06-16-77). #77-6-007M. p. 2. Fixing himself a cup of tea comes from: Davis, "Bundy Escape Itinerary/Interrogation," 06-15-77, p. 2.
715   FBI, "Concealing the Cabin Break-In [teletype]." 06-13-77. That Bundy signed the note "Amos" comes from: Unk, "Bundy ordered Held on Escape Charge," AT, 08-04-77.
716   Davis, "Bundy Escape Itinerary/Interrogation," 06-15-77, p. 2.
717   The debate over whether to take the weapon or not comes from: Sabella, "Deputies Snare Ex-

hausted Bundy," AT, 06-16-77.

718   Konkel, CBI, (06-16-77). #77-6-007M. p. 2. Time of departure comes from: Davis, "Bundy Escape Itinerary/Interrogation," 06-15-77, p. 2.

719   Davis, "Bundy Escape Itinerary/Interrogation," 06-15-77, p. 4.

720   Ibid, p. 2.

721   That Bundy grew tired of carrying the weapon comes from: Unk, "Back in Courtroom, Dead-Tired Bundy Hears New Charges," SLT, 06-14-77; That he dropped it out of fear of being shot comes from: Cunningham, "Bundy Captured, Back in Court in Shackles," RMN, 06-14-77. That he dropped it at this point comes from: Davis, "Bundy Escape Itinerary/Interrogation," 06-15-77, p. 3.

722   Davis, "Bundy Escape Itinerary/Interrogation," 06-15-77, p. 3.

723   Ibid, pp. 3-4.

724   This would have been East Maroon Creek and West Maroon Creek. Davis, "Bundy Escape Itinerary/Interrogation," 06-15-77, p. 3. It is interesting to note that, during his 1977 interrogation with Davis, Bundy said it was his right knee that was troubling him. Three years later, Bundy told author, Stephen Michaud, that it was his left.

725   Ibid, p. 3.

726   Davis, "Bundy Escape Itinerary/Interrogation," 06-15-77, p. 3; Harvey, "The Shadow of a Killer," AT, 06-08-02.

727   Wolf & Winn, "Part 6: Memories of Colorado—Escape and Capture," SCJ, 10-19-78.

728   Davis, "Bundy Escape Itinerary/Interrogation," 06-15-77, p. 3.

729   Ibid, p. 3.

730   Bundy had no idea that, at that very moment, Deputy Sergeant Larry Spiers was inside the cabin, just waiting for him to open the front door.

731   Helicopter and search dog comes from: Davis, "Bundy Escape Itinerary/Interrogation," 06-15-77, p. 3. Wait and see attitude comes from: Sabella, "Deputies Snare Exhausted Bundy," AT, 06-16-77.

732   Wolf & Winn, "Part 6: Memories of Colorado—Escape and Capture," SCJ, 10-19-78.

733   Davis, "Bundy Escape Itinerary/Interrogation," 06-15-77, pp. 3-4.

734   That Bundy crossed Highway 82 comes from: Davis, "Bundy Escape Itinerary/Interrogation," 06-15-77, p. 4. It is interesting to note that, again, Bundy does not mention seeing any officers at the intersection next to the Prince of Peace Chapel, though Nancy Baxter assures us the roadblock was still manned at that time.

735   Three years later, Bundy would tell author Stephen Michaud that he laid there for around three hours.

736   The version of stealing this child's bicycle comes from: Michaud & Aynesworth, "The Only Living Witness," p. 193.

737   The author found a section of a transcript from a recorded interview Bundy gave to Florida detectives in February 1978. In it, he clearly mentions stealing the bicycle. Bundy is giving this story to Florida authorities two years before he tells the tale to Stephen Michaud. Patchen, Bodiford, & Chapmen, "Statement of Theodore Robert Bundy," R/I, (02-20-78), FSA, Series 2084, pp. 10-11.

738   The area in which he was searching parked cars was: Cemetery Lane, the left turn onto Alta Vista Drive, and the beginning of Bonita Drive. That Bundy stole the Caddy comes from: Davis, "Bundy Escape Itinerary/Interrogation," 06-15-77, p. 4.

739   Information concerning the sign heading towards Independence Pass comes from: Sabella, "Deputies Snare Exhausted Bundy," AT, 06-16-77; Wolf & Winn, "Part 6: Memories of Colorado—Escape and Capture," SCJ, 10-19-78; In 2019, Deputy Higgins confirmed that the Pass had been "gated off, which is why he turned the car around." Markov [Higgins], WC, "Bundy's Version—Feedback," 12-24-19. Even if the slide had been cleared, Bundy would have been unable to proceed. The Highway Department had the road barricades up and excavation equipment was parked on the scene. New guard rails and retaining walls wouldn't be completed for at least a couple of weeks. Unk, "Independence Pass to Open by Mid-June," AT, 06-09-77. That Bundy would try to run through any roadblocks he encountered comes from: Davis, "Bundy Escape Itinerary/Interrogation," 06-15-77, p. 4.

740 Bundy acknowledged that the mountains were far more difficult than he had anticipated. He went so far as to say that the physical needs of his body dictated his course and actions, even while his brain told him that by following this course, he was lessening his chances of escaping successfully. Konkel, CBI, (06-16-77). #77-6-007M. p. 10.

741 Unk, "Back in Courtroom, Dead-Tired Bundy Hears New Charges," SLT, 06-14-77.

742 Baxter, WC, "Monday," 03-28-21.

743 Dialogue comes from: Lucas, R/I, I. "Ted Bundy Memories," 08-16-19.

744 Dialogue comes from: Lucas, WC, "The First Escape," 07-21-19.

745 Dialogue exchange between Bundy and Fisher comes from: Larsen, "Bundy: The Deliberate Stranger," p. 220.

746 That Garms and Quirk met at the sheriff's office comes from: Quirk, R/I, I. "Lone Wolf Memories," 12-08-20. Quirk added that he was there to try and retrieve his handcuffs. That Garms had just returned from the woods surrounding the Kaeser Cabin comes from: Garms, WC, "The Manhunt Part II," 10-30-19.

747 Markov, "Bundy Redux [Letter to the Editor]," AT, 12-18-05.

748 Garms, WC, "The Manhunt Part II," 10-30-19.

749 Coleman's dialogue comes from: Lucas, R/I, I. "Ted Bundy Memories," 08-16-19.

750 Interviewed in 2020, Sheeley added that, "The car was so funky, it had all these idiosyncrasies to it. It was always hard to get it in reverse. Hard to clutch it." Sheeley, R/I I. "Bundy Memories," 07-22-20.

751 Ibid.

752 Ibid.

753 '72 Porsche 911 reverse gear position comes from: Barnett, (06-15-20). "Manual Gearbox: A Porsche 911 History," www.total911.com; Bundy was used to having reverse in the lower-left. JBugs, (06-15-20). "1968 VW Shift Knob, Gear, Black," www.jbugs.com. Bundy, fumbling with the gears, comes from: Sheeley, "Those Were the Days: Memories of an Aspen Hippie Chick," p. 117.

754 Dialogue comes from: Larsen, "Bundy Captured!" SDT, 06-13-77.

755 This journalist was Barbara Grossman.

756 Dialogue exchange between Grossman and Bundy comes from: Grossman, "Bundy—Recaptured," 06-13-77.

757 Dialogue comes from: Sabella, "Deputies Snare Exhausted Bundy," AT, 06-16-77.

758 Dialogue comes from: Konkel, R/I, I. "The Fingerprints," 07-04-20.

759 Interviewed in 2020, Spiers noted that he learned Bundy had returned to the Kaeser cabin after all, just as the deputy had suspected he would. If Bundy had failed to see the signs that law enforcement officers had been to the scene, and had opened that front door, he would have been confronted with Spiers and his shotgun. Would Bundy have surrendered without a fight? Spiers was quick to note that if the fugitive failed to yield and opted to fight, the lawmen's reaction would have been swift and sure. Bundy would have been shot. Spiers, R/I, I. "The Bundy Manhunt," 08-09-20.

760 Patrick, "Recaptured Bundy Faces New Charges," DP, 06-16-77. Another source states there were eight armed law enforcement officers. Sabella, "Deputies Snare Exhausted Bundy," AT, 06-16-77.

761 Unk, "Back in Courtroom, Dead-Tired Bundy Hears New Charges," SLT, 06-14-77.

762 Dialogue comes from: Doud, "Bundy Faces New Charges Stemming from his Escape," TNT, 06-13-77.

763 Dialogue comes from: Larsen, "Bundy Looks Like Animal Run Down," SDT, 06-13-77.

764 Unk, "Bundy Formally Charged with Four New Felonies," SLT, 06-17-77; Cunningham, "Bundy Captured, Back in Court in Shackles," RMN, 06-14-77.

765 Unk, "Wan and Haggard, Bundy is Arraigned on More Charges," AT, 06-16-77.

766 Dialogue exchange between Bundy and Judge Lohr comes from: Doud, "Bundy Faces New Charges Stemming from his Escape," TNT, 06-13-77.

767 The dismissal of Leidner and Dumont not only occurred; attorneys, Stephen Ware and Kenneth Dresner, were appointed to replace them. Unk, "Bundy Formally Charged with Four New Felonies," SLT, 06-17-77; Unk, "Bundy Claims Silver Lining in Predicament," DN, 08-01-77.

768   "Conversations with a Killer: The Ted Bundy Tapes," Berlinger, 2019. Film.
769   Lucas, R/I, I. "Ted Bundy Memories," 08-16-19.
770   Dolan, WC, "Aspen Days," 05-09-21; Summerlin, "Ted Bundy Tales Come out of the Woodwork," PI, 04-15-17.
771   Dialogue exchange between the unidentified reporter and Bundy comes from: Doud, "Bundy's Run Motive Mulled," TNT, 06-14-77.
772   Dialogue exchanges, at the base of the stairs, comes from: Lucas, R/I, I. "Ted Bundy Memories," 08-16-19.
773   Having slipped through Colorado law enforcement officers once, some residents wanted to know whether Utah authorities would want Bundy returned to their state. Perhaps it was safer simply to have him complete his sentence in the DaRonch kidnapping affair. Utah State Prison Warden Sam Smith set the record straight. "As far as I'm concerned," he said, "there's no reason now to bring him back. We'll just let him face the Colorado charges." The warden added that he was quite relieved to have Bundy back in custody. Unk, "Aspen Lawmen Capture Bundy," DN, 06-13-77.
774   Konkel notes that his interview with Bundy took place on Monday morning, June 13, and not the day after, as listed in his own report. Konkel, R/I, I. "The Fingerprints," 07-04-20.
775   Dialogue exchange between Konkel and Bundy comes from: Konkel, R/I, I. "The Fingerprints," 07-04-20.
776   Bundy was read his Miranda warnings again but waived his rights. Konkel, CBI, (06-16-77). #77-6-007M. p. 2.
777   Konkel, R/I, I. "The Fingerprints," 07-04-20.
778   Dialogue exchanges between Grossman, Flatt and Higgins comes from: Grossman, "Bundy—Recaptured," 06-13-77.
779   White, R/I, I. "The Bundy Manhunt," 08-31-20.
780   Unk, "Back in Courtroom, Dead-Tired Bundy Hears New Charges," SLT, 06-14-77.
781   Sabella, "Deputies Snare Exhausted Bundy," AT, 06-16-77.
782   Ibid.
783   Sheriff Kienast told reporters that his deputies had amassed around sixty hours of overtime, at a cost somewhere between $6,000 and $10,000. Sgt. Darrel Horan also noted significant hours of overtime had been accrued. Confronted with a limited budget, he indicated he might have to bill the sheriff's office for expenses. Unk, "Bundy Search Costs Put at $6,000-$10,000," AT, 06-16-77.
784   Dialogue comes from: Sabella, "Deputies Snare Exhausted Bundy," AT, 06-16-77.
785   Dialogue comes from: Unk, "Back in Courtroom, Dead-Tired Bundy Hears New Charges," SLT, 06-14-77.
786   Information here concerning Det. Sgt. Garms comes from: Garms, WC, "The Manhunt," 10-28-19.
787   Baxter, WC, "Monday," 03-28-21.
788   Dialogue comes from: Unk, "Aspen Lawmen Capture Bundy," DN, 06-13-77.
789   Baxter, WC, "Saturday," 06-23-20.
790   Ikeda, WC, "Pitkin County Jail," 06-16-20; Haynes, WC, "Pitkin County Jail," 06-16-20.
791   Baxter, WC, "Saturday," 06-23-20; Ikeda, WC, "Pitkin County Jail," 06-16-20.
792   Dialogue comes from: Chandler, R/I, I. "The Bundy Manhunt," 06-01-20.

Appendix A, "The Caddy Stop"

793   Deputy Gary White noted that, during the 1970s, if a district attorney had an eyewitness to a crime, they felt as if they had a slam dunk case. It wasn't until the 1990s that law enforcement came to understand that having such a witness didn't actually mean you were receiving the complete truth. Yet, the witness wasn't lying. How was this possible? It took a while for American Justice to understand that people see things differently due to various mental filters. There's experience itself. An individual who has been a victim of domestic abuse could witness another couple's playful wrestling at a distance and completely misconstrue the meaning of the entanglement. White, WC, "Thoughts from the Cheap Seats," 04-04-21.

794   All direct quotes from Gene Flatt in this section of the appendix comes from: Flatt, R/I with Vince Lahey, I. "The Bundy Manhunt," 11-28-18. Regarding recognizing Bundy on sight, journalist Rick Larson quoted Flatt in one of his newspaper articles, "At first, I didn't recognize him." Larsen, "Bundy Captured!" SDT, 06-13-77.
795   Dialogue exchanges between Grossman, Flatt and Higgins comes from: Grossman, "Bundy—Recaptured," 06-13-77.
796   Deputy Higgins disputes this, stating that she handled radio communications while her partner interacted with the driver. Officer Chet Zajac, on foot patrol in downtown Aspen, overheard Deputy Higgins asking for the presence of Officer Quirk. Nancy Baxter, who also overheard the radio traffic, reported that it was Higgins who sought backup.
797   All quotes from Officer Terry Quirk in this appendix are from the following source unless otherwise specified. Quirk, R/I. I. "Lone Wolf Memories," 12-08-20.
798   Horan, "Merit Recommendation—Officer Terry Quirk," (06-17-77), Aspen PD: 1.
799   Horan, WC, "Quirk Merit Recommendation," 02-17-21.
800   Davis, "Bundy Escape Itinerary/Interrogation," 06-15-77, p. 1.
801   Markov, "Bundy Redux [Letter to the Editor]," AT, 12-18-05.
802   Shining of the flashlight comes from: Sabella, "Deputies Snare Exhausted Bundy," AT, 06-16-77. The Cadillac swerving comes from: Unk, "Back in Courtroom, Dead-Tired Bundy Hears New Charges," SLT, 06-14-77; Cunningham, "Bundy Captured, Back in Court in Shackles," RMN, 06-14-77.
803   Markov [Higgins], WC, "Bundy's Version—Feedback," 12-24-19.
804   Markov [Higgins], WC, "Caddy Stop—Manuscript Corrections," 12-28-19.
805   Markov [Higgins], WC, "The Chameleon," 05-20-20.
806   Markov [Higgins], WC, "Caddy Stop—Manuscript Corrections," 12-28-19. During preliminary hearings, lawyers had been using a map of the region to show where Caryn Campbell's body had been discovered. Since Bundy was serving in his own defense, he had legal rights of discovery and it was reported that he had this map in his possession at the time of his recapture. Higgins refutes this.
807   Markov [Higgins], WC, "The Caddy Stop," 12-23-19.
808   Ibid.
809   Markov [Higgins], WC, "Caddy Stop—Manuscript Corrections," 12-28-19.
810   Bundy Miranda warnings come from: Markov [Higgins], WC, "Caddy Stop—Manuscript Corrections," 12-28-19. "We got him!" controversy response comes from: Markov [Higgins], WC, "Bundy's Version—Feedback," 12-24-19.
811   Markov [Higgins], WC, "Caddy Stop—Manuscript Corrections," 12-28-19.
812   Markov [Higgins], WC, "Bundy's Version—Feedback," 12-24-19.
813   Bundy, as quoted in: Patchen, Bodiford, & Chapmen, "Statement of Theodore Robert Bundy," R/I, (02-20-78), FSA, Series 2084, p. 11.
814   In addition to bringing him breakfast back at the county jail, Flatt had escorted Bundy from the basement jail up to the courtroom and back a couple of times, guarded him in the exercise yard, and transported him to and from Glenwood Springs on at least two occasions.
815   Purported Dialogue exchange between Flatt and Higgins comes from: Michaud & Aynesworth, "The Only Living Witness," p. 194.
816   Ibid.

ABOUT THE AUTHOR

Ric Conrad is the author of *Code 1244*, an in-depth examination of the 1986 Mount Hood Tragedy. His stories were drawn from law enforcement reports, rescue workers, friends and family members of the missing climbers, and surviving members of the actual climbing party. The book is currently being made into a three-part documentary series on a major streaming platform.

In order to research the manhunt that was conducted following the first escape of Ted Bundy, the author planned for multiple trips to Aspen and the Roaring Fork Valley. In August 2019, the first of these journeys was executed without incident, wielding a wealth of documentation he was able to bring home.

In March 2020, the COVID-19 pandemic shut down further research excursions until further notice. Undaunted, Conrad began tracking down and interviewing—via telephone—the main participants in the manhunt.

In 2023, with the lifting of the Coronavirus restrictions and a first draft of the manuscript in hand, the author returned to Aspen for his second research trip. He and his wife had the privilege of meeting many of the friends he'd been writing about for years.

Left to right: Sergeant Darrel Horan, Ric Conrad, Deputy Gary White, and Deputy Leon Murray.

www.ingramcontent.com/pod-product-compliance
Lightning Source LLC
Chambersburg PA
CBHW051935290426
44110CB00015B/1992